TIMOTHY LEARY
THE HARVARD YEARS

Early Writings on LSD and Psilocybin
with Richard Alpert, Huston Smith,
Ralph Metzner, and Others

EDITED AND INTRODUCED BY
JAMES PENNER

Park Street Press
Rochester, Vermont • Toronto, Canada

Park Street Press
One Park Street
Rochester, Vermont 05767
www.ParkStPress.com

SUSTAINABLE FORESTRY INITIATIVE

Certified Sourcing

www.sfiprogram.org

SFI-00854

Text stock is SFI certified

Park Street Press is a division of Inner Traditions International

Library of Congress Cataloging-in-Publication Data
Leary, Timothy, 1920–1996.
   [Works. Selections]
   Timothy Leary, the Harvard years : early writings on LSD and psilocybin with Richard Alpert, Huston Smith, Ralph Metzner, and others / edited and introduced by James Penner.
      pages cm
   Includes bibliographical references and index.
   Summary: "The first collection of Leary's writings devoted entirely to the research phase of his career, 1960 to 1965" — Provided by publisher.
   ISBN 978-1-62055-235-3 (pbk.) — ISBN 978-1-62055-236-0 (e-book)
   1. Leary, Timothy, 1920–1996. 2. LSD (Drug)—Research. I. Penner, James, 1964–
II. Title.
   BF109.L43A25 2014
   150.92—dc23
   [B]
                                                                                2014005482

Printed and bound in the United States by Lake Book Manufacturing, Inc.
The text stock is SFI certified. The Sustainable Forestry Initiative® program promotes sustainable forest management.

10 9 8 7 6 5 4 3 2 1

Text design by Virginia Scott Bowman and layout by Priscilla Baker
This book was typeset in Garamond Premier Pro with Adobe Jensen Pro

To send correspondence to the author of this book, mail a first-class letter to the author c/o Inner Traditions • Bear & Company, One Park Street, Rochester, VT 05767, and we will forward the communication, or contact the author directly at **jameslpenner@gmail.com**.

TIMOTHY LEARY
THE HARVARD YEARS

"Timothy Leary's pivotal role in 1960s drug culture often led to his being scorned and caricatured by the mass media. James Penner's superb collection of Leary's writings from his Harvard years peels away the layers of polemic and myth that surround Leary and enable us to confront his core ideas that helped to shape the counterculture. This is an important book for everyone who wants to understand Leary and the cultural rebellion of the 1960s."

ROBERT COHEN, PROFESSOR OF HISTORY
AND SOCIAL STUDIES AT NEW YORK UNIVERSITY

"This book is a must for any serious student of psychedelics as well as those who would like to understand the full Leary, not just the media parody version that he seemed to become in his post-Harvard years. Here he comes across as a serious scientist, a committed reformer. Penner's excellent introductions place each paper in its historical context."

JAMES FADIMAN, MICRODOSE RESEARCHER AND AUTHOR OF
THE PSYCHEDELIC EXPLORER'S GUIDE:
SAFE, THERAPEUTIC, AND SACRED JOURNEYS

"James Penner's *Timothy Leary: The Harvard Years* is not only a brilliant work of scholarship but a powerful and persuasive reexamination of the foundation for some of the most important and exuberant thinking of the 1960s and '70s. Penner's own admirable introductions and thorough editorial work allow us to see Leary as a radical and vital intellectual, not just a cultural phenomenon; as a writer unafraid of risks, certainly, but also able to build humane and moving research projects built on science and on hope. This is a major, long-overdue book."

JAMES R. KINCAID, PROFESSOR OF ENGLISH AT
THE UNIVERSITY OF PITTSBURGH AND AUTHOR OF
CHILD-LOVING, ANNOYING THE VICTORIANS, AND EROTIC INNOCENCE

"The brilliantly designed experiments that Timothy Leary and his team performed with psilocybin, LSD, and DMT between 1960 and 1963 while at Harvard's Center for Research in Personality laid the foundation for the revolution we are presently witnessing in psychedelic medicine and science. James Penner has performed a valuable service by gathering and evaluating these essential, difficult-to-find research papers while providing historical context for the academic scandal that erupted in the wake of these experiments."

MICHAEL HOROWITZ, COAUTHOR OF
*MOKSHA: ALDOUS HUXLEY'S CLASSIC WRITINGS ON
PSYCHEDELICS AND THE VISIONARY EXPERIENCE*
AND *AN ANNOTATED BIBLIOGRAPHY OF TIMOTHY LEARY*

"What a fantastic service James Penner provides with his collection of writings by Timothy Leary and friends in *Timothy Leary: The Harvard Years*. Leary emerges here . . . as a writer of great relevance today, with an earnest and passionate voice."

SIDNEY HOMAN, PROFESSOR OF ENGLISH
AT THE UNIVERSITY OF FLORIDA AND
ACTOR, DIRECTOR, AND AUTHOR

"This is a great book! I've always been curious about Leary's earlier, more scholarly work, which has real substance to it. I never thought about it as a focus for a book, but it's blindingly obvious now that James Penner has done it."

MARCUS BOON, AUTHOR OF
THE ROAD OF EXCESS: A HISTORY OF WRITERS ON DRUGS
AND PROFESSOR OF ENGLISH AT YORK UNIVERSITY

For SM

But the man who comes back through the Door in the Wall will never be the same as the man who went out.

ALDOUS HUXLEY,

THE DOORS OF PERCEPTION

Contents

PART 1
The Trip in Cuernavaca
Early Utopian Writings on Psilocybin

PART 5

Historical Documents from the Harvard Drug Scandal

Acknowledgments

This book grew out of my chapter on the 1960s in *Pinks, Pansies, and Punks* (2011). As I began to collect all of Leary's scholarly work from the early 1960s, I was amazed that it was out-of-print and so hard to find. Using Michael Horowitz's *An Annotated Bibliography of Timothy Leary* (1987), I gradually acquired everything from the early 1960s that was available. I also learned that some of his work (*The Existential Transaction* [Psychological Consultation Service, 1960]) has been completely lost. *Timothy Leary: The Harvard Years* attempts to put the various fugitive texts from the early 1960s together in one volume. Assembling this book was a slow and arduous process, and I certainly could not have done it alone. I would like to thank all of my friends and colleagues who contributed to the publication of this book.

The journey begins with Michael Horowitz. Michael and Cynthia Palmer created one of my favorite books in the world: Aldous Huxley's *Moksha: Classic Writings on the Psychedelic and Visionary Experience* (Inner Traditions, 1983). *Moksha* was my model text for *Timothy Leary: The Harvard Years*. When I first conceived of the project, Michael read my book proposal and gave me valuable advice and guidance. I am very grateful for Michael's kind support.

I am also much indebted to Denis Berry of The Futique Trust and the Timothy Leary Estate. Right from the beginning, Denis was enthusiastic about my book project and the idea of creating a book that sheds light on Leary's scholarly work from the early 1960s. I am very grateful for Denis's gracious and generous support. I look forward to the day when I can send her a copy of *Timothy Leary: The Harvard Years*.

I would also like to thank all my colleagues at the University of Puerto Rico. During the early stages of the writing process, I received two TARES (research grants) that enabled me to put this book together. In particular, I would like to thank my English Department Chair, Dr. Cynthia Pittman, for supporting both of my TARE proposals and for giving me a teaching schedule that aided my writing schedule. Cynthia's enthusiasm for this project has always been refreshing. I would also like to thank our previous Department Chair, Dr. Denise Lopez Mazzeo, for supporting my research projects and for being a great friend and colleague. During my time at UPR, Denise has been a great friend and colleague. I also would like to thank the colleagues and friends who read drafts of my proposal and introduction: Madeleine Vala, Don Walicek, and Mark Wekander. Before this book was completed, Mark embarked on the greatest trip of all. Mark will always be remembered for his kindness and enthusiasm. I especially cherish my very last meetings with him.

Timothy Leary: The Harvard Years was a book that was written in two places: San Juan and Los Angeles. During my summer trips to Los Angeles, I often worked with friends and colleagues from the University of Southern California. I am grateful for the help I received from two expert librarians at USC: Claude Zachary and Ross Scimeca. Ross was always willing to track down the fugitive texts that I couldn't find on my own. Ross also took the time to mail copies to San Juan. I also want to thank my very good friend George Skarpelos for his expertise and enthusiasm. George's help was crucial in the early stages of this book. He first introduced me to Optical Character Technology (OCR). Without OCR, this project would have taken many years to complete. I also want to thank George for walking me through the maze of copyright law and for directing me to the Stanford Copyright Renewal Database. I also would like to thank an extremely important reader of my manuscript:

Jeff Solomon. Jeff read my Introduction and Afterword very closely and offered several pivotal suggestions. Jeff has been a wonderful friend and a close reader of my work for the last twelve years. His editorial advice and insight have been invaluable to me.

I am also deeply grateful for the support I have received from Inner Traditions. First, I would like to thank Jon Graham for endorsing *Timothy Leary: The Harvard Years* during the book proposal stage; Jon immediately understood the importance of this book and the need to bring Leary's early writings into print again. I am also much indebted to Jessica Wimett, who took a special interest in this book. Jessie was extremely helpful during the OCR stage of the book. Jessie also helped me navigate my way through the various copyright issues. Lastly, I would like to thank Jeanie Levitan for editorial wisdom and for keeping the book on schedule. I also would like to thank my wonderful Project Editor, Chanc VanWinkle Orzell. Chanc provided excellent advice and several important suggestions that helped shape the overall narrative trajectory of *Timothy Leary: The Harvard Years*. Chanc was particularly good at explaining the aspects of the copyediting process that mystified me. It has been a pleasure to work with her.

Lastly, I would like to thank my mother, Marilyn Penner, and all of my brothers and sisters who have always supported my work. I am not convinced that they fully understand my interest in Timothy Leary's work, but they have always supported this book and my scholarship. I also want to thank my close friends who helped me during the different stages of this book and during my many trips from San Juan to Los Angeles and back again: Fernando Jimenez, Memo Arce, David Ralicke, Oliver X., Christophe Greger, and Charlie Staveley. Lastly, I would like to express my deepest gratitude to Shirley Mori. Shirley has seen my Leary obsession grow and grow throughout the years. I will always cherish our travels together. From my cottage in Mt. Washington to the shores of Big Sur, each trip has been a source of great wonder and delight.

Which Leary Now?

James Penner

When I first began researching Timothy Leary's writings from the 1960s, I gradually realized that Leary was quite difficult to pin down. Throughout his life, Leary was keenly interested in exploring radical forms of self-transformation. It is clear that psychedelic drugs were an important part of his ongoing attempt to shape and remake his identity. I noted how multiple conflicting versions of Leary seemed to coexist within the media, the popular culture, and his biography. There was Leary, the scientist, Leary, the radical Harvard psychologist, Leary, the mystic and self-proclaimed high priest, Leary, the iconic rebel and trickster, Leary, the hippie and irresponsible advocate of LSD, and, of course, Leary, the celebrity. Leary himself was aware of all of the identities that he had cultivated and constructed throughout his life. He even referenced his own weakness for what he called "the individuality game" in an important speech he delivered for the International Congress of Applied Psychology in 1961: "[a]nd that most treacherous and tragic game of all, the individuality game. The Timothy Leary game. Ridiculous how we confuse this game, overplay it." Leary's self-critique was intended as a way of illustrating the ways in which our identity is an egotistical game that we relentlessly play throughout our lives. For Leary, psychedelic drugs were extraordinary because they offered ephemeral release from the "treacherous" identity game: a way of disentangling ourselves from the social roles that seemed to envelop our entire being.

As I began to read and sift through all of Leary's essays and articles for this book, I eventually became obsessed with the Harvard Drug Scandal of 1962 and 1963. To me, it seemed to be the quintessential prophetic event for the tumultuous 1960s; Leary's psilocybin research at Harvard was a cultural incubator for the nascent counterculture, and President Pusey's repressive actions—firing Leary and Richard Alpert without a public hearing—demonstrated how bureaucracies and cultural authorities were wont to suppress social movements that they could not control nor fully understand. As I traced Leary's trajectory during the scandal, I tried to understand how and why Leary's promising academic career was so abruptly destroyed. Was it a case of professorial self-destruction? Or was the Harvard administration overzealous in their response to a scholarly conflict over research methods that should have remained within the confines of the psychology department?

When examining the details leading up to the scandal, what surprised me the most was Leary's nonchalant attitude throughout the conflict. During the worst moments, he seemed unfazed by the prospect of being fired by America's oldest and most prestigious university. At a certain point, he even seemed to welcome being thrown out of the academy for he somehow knew that the scandal would catapult him to celebrity status and provide him with a much larger podium. Although Leary made some mistakes, his boldness—what others would deem as carelessness—seemed quite admirable to me. It was apparent that Leary's boldness was a byproduct of his Faustian experimentation with psychedelic drugs.

When I researched Leary's response to the Harvard Drug Scandal, I gathered all the articles that Leary published after he was fired in 1963. The period of 1963 to 1965 interested me the most: what would Leary say and write about when he was no longer beholden to

Harvard and the exigencies of his former profession? As I read all of Leary's post-Harvard essays, I noticed a distinct trend that emerged in the mid-1960s. At a certain point after 1965, Leary gives up writing for scholarly publications and focuses on attracting a larger audience of psychedelic followers and readers. The change can clearly be seen in the *Playboy* interview of September of 1966 and in his book *The Politics of Ecstasy* that appeared in 1968.* In some cases, *The Politics of Ecstasy* contained watered down versions of his scholarly essays. One of Leary's best articles from 1963—"The Religious Experience: Its Production and Interpretation"—was rewritten and given a new title ("The Seven Tongues of God") that was designed to appeal to hippies and the counterculture.

The new version of Leary—what might be termed the populist "hippie" version of Leary—focused on writing for the generation that was under thirty. During the course of reinventing himself in the mid-1960s, Leary's thinking and writing became, to my mind, somewhat impoverished. His writing often lacked the sophistication and complexity of his scholarly writings on LSD and psilocybin from the early 1960s.† In the context of the ongoing Viet Nam War and the 1968 election, the tone of Leary's writings on several occasions became shrill and divisive; the over 50 generation predictably became his *bête noir*: "white, menopausal, mendacious men now ruling the planet" (*The Politics of Ecstasy* 363). In his writings and interviews in the late 1960s, Leary often employed crude arguments to mock the older generation that had never experimented with psychedelic drugs: "[m]any fifty-year-olds have lost their curiosity, have lost their ability to make love, have dulled their openness

---

*Leary abandons "the science game" and begins making hyperbolic statements to the media. In the *Playboy* interview, he egregiously remarks that "[i]n a carefully prepared, loving LSD session, a woman can have several hundred orgasms" (129).

†*High Priest* (1968) is the exception to this trend. It is Leary's most impressive full-length work from the 1960s; it documents quintessential trips that transformed his life. In this highly autobiographical text, Leary explores the psychedelic experience from a wide range of vantage points. *High Priest* is vastly superior to *The Politics of Ecstasy* (1968).

to new sensations, and would use any form of new energy for power, control, and warfare" (*The Politics of Ecstasy* 123).

As the 1960s progressed, the polemical and hyperbolic version of Leary eventually overshadowed the scholarly and more introspective version of Leary. Today, the general public is most familiar with the exaggerated version of Leary that emerged in the late 1960s. In the obituaries that were written in 1996, Leary is remembered as the Johnny Appleseed of LSD and for his whacky media stunts (running for governor in California in 1970).

With the publication of *The Harvard Years,* I hope to shed light on the largely forgotten Leary of the early 1960s. The Leary of the Cambridge and the early Millbrook years is a scientist and a radical psychologist who is attempting to reform the treatment of mental illness and the clinical practices of his profession. The Leary of this era does not resort to crude polemics; he writes for skeptics as well as acolytes. He is a public intellectual with one foot in the academy and the "science game," but he is also part of a much larger social movement—the consciousness-expansion movement—that would eventually transform the *zeitgeist* of the 1960s.

As we enter the twenty-first century, Leary is relevant because psychedelic medicine is currently experiencing a revival. In the last ten years, various American universities and medical colleges (Harvard, Johns Hopkins, UCLA, NYU, and the University of Arizona) have been conducting FDA-approved studies on psilocybin and LSD. In the next five years, researchers plan to use psychedelic medicine to treat drug addiction, alcoholism, and end-of-life anxiety that stems from terminal illnesses.

When medical authorities and researchers debate the efficacy of psychedelic substances and patient-centered forms of treatment, Timothy Leary's name inevitably enters into the discussion. For some, Leary is a hero who fought for the "fifth freedom": the right to expand one's consciousness. For others, Leary is an irresponsible opportunist who recklessly promoted the recreational use of LSD. In other cases, people advocate or reject Leary without actually reading his work. *Timothy Leary: The Harvard Years* was created to promote a reexamination of Leary's early scholarly work; it contains essays and articles from the radical psychologist's most prolific period: 1960 to 1965. His writings demonstrate why he became the iconic leader of the consciousness-expansion movement of the 1960s, but, more significantly, they provide a historical context for research in the present day. Leary's early writings are fascinating because he explores the utopian potential of psychedelic drugs: their unique capacity to transform and enlarge human perception and our understanding of consciousness. From a contemporary perspective, some of Leary's research projects may appear misguided (read too utopian), but we can learn from his bold experimentation and his speculative thought process. In many cases, he was willing to ask many of the foundational questions that researchers are still grappling with today: can psychedelic drugs be used to alter self-destructive forms of behavior (i.e., alcoholism and drug addiction)? How can psychedelic drugs be used to foster the creative impulse? Can psychedelic drugs aid and facilitate mystical experiences? As research comes full circle some fifty years after the Harvard Drug Scandal, Leary—the probing scientist and radical therapist—also needs to come back into focus.

REFERENCES

Leary, Timothy. "She Comes in Colors." *The Politics of Ecstasy*. Berkeley: Ronin Publishing 1990, 118–59.

Timothy Leary and Richard Alpert (circa 1961). Leary and Alpert became close friends when Leary joined the Harvard Center for Research in Personality in the spring of 1960.

Introduction

James Penner

The year 2013 marked the fiftieth anniversary of the Harvard Drug Scandal. On May 27 of 1963, Timothy Leary and Richard Alpert (later known as Ram Dass) were fired by Harvard University. The dismissal of Leary and Alpert marked the first time a Harvard professor had been fired in over a hundred years. Nathan Pusey, the president of Harvard, personally conducted a closed-door investigation that included the interrogation of various undergraduate students who allegedly had taken psychedelic drugs with Leary and Alpert. Pusey's investigation yielded only one confession. Ronnie Winston, a male undergraduate, admitted to taking psilocybin pills with Professor Alpert during the spring semester of 1962. Winston, heir to the Harry Winston jewelry fortune, famously remarked to the President of Harvard: "It was the most profound experience of any of the courses that I have had here [at Harvard]" (Dass, Metzner, and Bravo 90). Pusey's investigation also uncovered a clandestine affair between Alpert and Winston.

In public accounts of the scandal, Harvard authorities carefully suppressed all references to the homosexual affair and fired Alpert for giving psilocybin to "one undergraduate." President Pusey's press release on May 27, 1963, states that ". . . Dr. Alpert violated an agreement which he had entered into in November, 1961, not to involve undergraduates

1

in his work with drugs."* However, Pusey's press release fails to mention the name of their informant: Andrew Weil, a twenty-one-year-old Harvard undergraduate. Weil, who would later become famous as a best-selling author and an advocate of holistic medicine, had first-hand knowledge about Leary and Alpert's drug research because he and Winston were friends and dorm mates in Claverly Hall. Weil was envious of Winston's intimate relationship with Alpert and he was angry with Leary because the Harvard psychologist had refused to let him participate in the Harvard Psilocybin Project.† Leary had made an agreement with Harvard's health authorities: no undergraduates were to participate as subjects in his psilocybin research.

As no evidence suggested that Leary had given drugs to undergraduates, he was officially fired for not completing his classes and absconding to California before the end of the spring semester.‡ While Leary was chastised for truancy in the Boston press, most people at Harvard knew the real reason for Leary's dismissal: his outspoken advocacy of hallucinogenic drugs greatly alarmed university authorities. They were especially concerned about all the sensationalist accounts that had appeared during the previous year in the tabloid newspaper, the *Boston Herald* ("Hallucination Drug Fought at Harvard—350 Take Pills").

Leary's research organization—the Harvard Psilocybin Project (HPP)—had generated a great deal of publicity, and Leary's rising popularity with graduate students created envy and discomfort in the psychology department. Leary emphasized the importance of "set" (mind-set) and "setting" (the social environment) in the psychedelic drug experience.

---

*Ram Dass (a.k.a. Richard Alpert) has criticized the official version of the Harvard Drug Scandal: "[m]y claim to fame was that I was thrown out of Harvard. They always say it was because of the drugs but it wasn't only the drugs, it was also my homosexuality" (*Birth of a Psychedelic Culture* 89).

†My account of the Harvard Drug Scandal is taken from Dan Lattin's *The Harvard Psychedelic Club* (2010) and Ram Dass, Ralph Metzner, and Gary Bravo's *Birth of Psychedelic Culture* (2010).

‡Leary's version of the story is different. He maintained that he had assigned his classes to other professors from the psychology department.

When the user is in a relaxed mind-set and the setting is highly supportive, the user typically has a positive and illuminating experience with the drug. Leary's advocacy of set and setting and the notion that researchers should take the drugs they are researching inevitably led to conflicts with his colleagues in the psychology department and with educational authorities at Harvard.

For historians of the 1960s, the Harvard Drug Scandal is a watershed event: the moment when psychedelic drugs were publically demonized and driven underground. Prior to 1963, psychedelic drugs (especially psilocybin and LSD) were "wonder drugs" that had produced, in some cases, impressive therapeutic results. Humphrey Osmond of the Weyburn Mental Hospital in Saskatchewan, Canada had successfully used LSD to treat chronic alcoholics. Osmond's LSD therapy came to be known as the psychedelic treatment model. Prior to Osmond's research, LSD had been frequently described as a "psychotomimetic drug"—a substance that produced temporary psychosis in the user. Osmond's work and several other important medical studies discredited the one-dimensional psychotomimetic thesis of the early 1950s. In 1960, Sidney Cohen, M.D., of UCLA, a leading LSD researcher in the late 1950s and early 1960s, published a landmark study on LSD and mescaline; Cohen's study, which was based on over 5,000 individual cases and over 25,000 doses, firmly established that ". . . with proper precautions [LSD and mescaline] are safe when given to a selected healthy group" (39). In the early 1960s, several leading universities and medical research centers were conducting medical and psychological research with psilocybin and LSD: Harvard, UCLA, Stanford, the University of Michigan, the Rand Corporation in Santa Monica, California, the Weyburn Hospital in Saskatchewan, Canada, Powick Hospital in England, and the Psychiatric Research Institute in Prague* (to name a few).

---

*Like Cohen and Osmond, Stanislav Grof, M.D., was a key advocate of psychedelic drugs in the the 1960s. Grof served as the Principal Investigator at the Psychedelic Research Program at the Psychiatric Research Institute in Prague. His work emphasized LSD's therapeutic efficacy.

After the Harvard Drug Scandal of 1963, it became increasingly difficult for medical researchers and psychologists to conduct research with psychedelic drugs. Anti-LSD propaganda was widespread, and in October of 1966, LSD was officially declared illegal in the United States. Although some psychologists and scientists were still completing LSD studies, funding and sponsorship for psychedelic research slowly dried up in North America and much of the world.

Today, little is known about the period when LSD and psilocybin were legal and somewhat respectable in the academy. The public understanding of LSD stems from the counterculture's misuse of the drug during the so-called "black-market" phase (post-1966).* The research period of 1943 to 1966 tends to be overshadowed by narratives of misuse and the proverbial anecdotes about LSD users walking into moving traffic or jumping out of five-story windows.

Like LSD itself, Timothy Leary remains somewhat misunderstood. For conservatives, Leary is generally associated with the worst excesses of the Summer of Love and the reckless hedonism of the late 1960s and early 1970s. For other members of the media, Leary is merely a glorified "product salesman" for LSD and the psychedelic revolution. Leary's name is inevitably linked to his six-word sales pitch—"tune in, turn on, drop out"—that became a popular mantra for the emerging counterculture.

When I began doing research for another book—a cultural history of LSD's influence on intellectuals and writers of the 1960s—I, too, had a somewhat one-dimensional view of Leary. I was primarily familiar with the long-haired Leary of the late 1960s. Leary was simply the patron saint of the hippies and the counterculture. However, when I began to research the Harvard Drug scandal of 1963 I encountered a different Timothy Leary. The Leary of the early 1960s was a Harvard professor who had short hair, wore tweed jackets, and conducted serious scientific research at the Harvard Center for Research in Personality. Prior to his appointment

---

*Black market LSD was widespread before 1966. However, the Harvard Drug Scandal marks the turning point in the public debate about psychedelic drugs. After the firing of Leary and Alpert in 1963, LSD opponents dominated the public debate.

at Harvard, Leary was a rising star in the field of behavioral psychology. His first scholarly book, *The Interpersonal Diagnosis of Personality* (1957), was described as "perhaps the most important clinical book to appear this year" (*Annual Review of Psychology*). After completing his doctorate at Berkeley, Leary was named the director of psychology research at the Kaiser Foundation Hospital in Oakland, California. In addition to his clinical research, Leary was a radical proponent of "existential transaction" psychology, which attempts to abolish the traditional hierarchy between doctor and patient. In Leary's version of transactional theory, the psychologist was a collaborative consultant who treated the patient as an equal and not as an object to be dissected, manipulated, and controlled. Leary's transactional theory has many affinities with the anti-psychiatry movement that was founded by R. D. Laing and David Cooper in England. Like Laing and Cooper, Leary wanted to reform clinical psychology and its tendency to stigmatize all forms of mental illness.*

Leary's ambitious plans to reform the treatment of mental illness and clinical practices greatly interested Harvard. Leary was hired by David McClelland, the chair of the Harvard Center for Research in Personality, in 1959, and he moved to Cambridge in January of 1960.† McClelland had high hopes for Leary's research and his existential transaction theory. Although Leary's tenure at Harvard was brief—three and a half years—he certainly left his mark. Leary's years in Cambridge were intensely productive and creative. He promoted and spearheaded three groundbreaking research projects—the Harvard Psilocybin Project, the Concord Prison Experiment, and the Good Friday Experiment—that

---

*The best account of Leary's existential transaction theory is contained in "On Existential Transaction Theory." This article was originally published as "The Diagnosis of Behavior and the Diagnosis of Experience" (1970). Leary's existentialist transaction theory is also conversant with Michel Foucault's *Madness and Civilization: A History of Insanity in the Age of Reason* (1964) and Thomas Szasz's *The Myth of Mental Illness* (1961); Leary frequently cited Szasz's groundbreaking study in his articles.

†Although Leary was hired by Harvard in the summer of 1959, he was a Visiting Professor at the University of Copenhagen during the fall semester of 1959. Leary began teaching at Harvard in January of 1960.

would, in their own way, influence the utopian Zeitgeist of the 1960s.* Although Leary was fired in May of 1963, he continued to publish in academic journals throughout the 1960s.

Leary's first experiment was the Harvard Psilocybin Project (HPP), wherein he invited creative intellectuals to Cambridge to take psychedelic drugs and document their experiences. Many important writers, musicians, and intellectuals participated in the HPP, including Aldous Huxley, Allen Ginsberg, Peter Orlovsky, William Burroughs, Jack Kerouac, Arthur Koestler, Robert Lowell, Charles Olson, Maynard Ferguson, and Alan Watts. Their *ex post facto* reports document psilocybin's ability to foster creativity. Many of Leary's findings are included in two of his earliest academic articles on creativity: "How to Change Behavior" (chapter 1 of this book) and "Psychedelic Drugs and Creativity" (chapter 4).

Leary worked extensively with Harvard graduate students. He was particularly interested in expanding the perimeters of the psychedelic experience. By taking the drug experience out of the lab and programming psychedelic trips in domestic settings, Leary discovered that an aesthetic and supportive environment could virtually eliminate bad trips (see chapter 3: "Reactions to Psilocybin Administered in a Supportive Environment").

The Harvard Psilocybin Project eventually morphed into the Concord Prison Experiment. Leary's research indicated that psychedelic drugs produced a "dramatic decrease in hostility, cynicism, depression . . . and definite increase in optimism, planfulness, flexibility, tolerance and sociability" ("How to Change Behavior"). With these impressive findings, Leary was eager to bring psychedelic therapy to an entirely new setting: the Massachusetts Correctional Institute in nearby Concord. Leary's experiment raised two important questions: could consciousness-expanding drugs help rehabilitate inmates who were trapped in a life of crime? Could highly supportive psilocybin sessions nurture moral

---

*Although Walter Pahnke was the principal investigator for the Good Friday Experiment, Leary, the faculty supervisor, was a crucial figure in the controversial research project.

transformation and bring down the rate of recidivism? Leary's controversial experiments are described in "How to Change Behavior" and documented in his three coauthored articles on the Concord Prison Experiment.

Leary's final project at Harvard—the Good Friday Experiment—attempted to explore the nature of the religious experience of ecstasy. Leary and Walter Pahnke, a medical doctor and Protestant minister, joined forces to see if psilocybin could produce an "authentic religious experience" in divinity students. The Good Friday Experiment is fascinating in that in its execution, Leary and Pahnke approach the subject of illumination with the methodology of science. Leary's article on the Good Friday Experiment ("The Religious Experience: Its Production and Interpretation") is included in this book, along with his preface, coauthored with Richard Alpert, to Alan Watts's *The Joyous Cosmology: Adventures in the Chemistry of Consciousness.* Leary and Alpert's preface was written in 1962, the same year that the Good Friday Experiment took place.

In the aftermath of the Harvard Drug Scandal of 1963, Leary and Alpert eventually settled in a majestic baroque mansion in picturesque Dutchess County, New York. Leary, Alpert, and Ralph Metzner formed the Millbrook Commune, an experimental community and research center for writers, artists, and psychedelic acolytes from all walks of life. In the coming years, both Leary and Alpert would become iconic figures for the emerging counterculture; however, Alpert's path would prove to be very different from Leary's. Alpert traveled to India where he ultimately met his spiritual guide, Maharajji (Neem Karoli Baba). Alpert's metamorphosis into Ram Dass is described in his remarkable memoir, *Be Here Now* (1971).

Today Ram Dass is a gifted synthesizer of complex and arcane spiritual concepts from the East; his eclectic embrace of various Eastern spiritual traditions (Hinduism, Karma Yoga, Tibetan Buddhism, Zen Buddhism) have inspired countless Westerners to look to the East for spiritual guidance and enlightenment. Thus, Ram Dass is perhaps best described as a "gnostic intermediary," and . . . "a bridge between ancient and modern worlds, between East and West, and between spirituality and psychology" (Walsh and Grob 208). For Ram Dass, psychedelic substances can function as a spiritual initiation to the user who is receptive and prepared for the experience: "[a]s I gained experience in the use of psychedelics, I realized that I was accessing spiritual planes of consciousness. These chemicals can get you in the door, but you don't stay in these planes like you do when you become adept at meditation. However, the psychedelics give you the faith in these new, spiritual perspectives—faith which is necessary for the later spiritual growth" (Walsh and Grob 216). Ram Dass was also keenly aware of the shortcomings of psychedelic substances: "[in some cases] the psychedelic experience is too mindblowing, it can distract from your ability to recognize the spirit in the moment. Because this moment doesn't have the pizzazz of the psychedelic moment . . . [t]he spiritual trap that psychedelics offer too much pizzazz" (216).

In one interview in 2002, Ram Dass contrasted his use of psychedelics with Leary's: "I was using psychedelics to clean myself out, Tim was using psychedelics to clean the society out."* This remark succinctly describes the different paths that Leary and Alpert took in the 1960s and early 1970s. While Leary veered toward cultural revolution and LSD evangelism, Alpert was more focused on the subjective dimension of the LSD experience; he primarily used psychedelic substances for personal growth and spiritual insights.

WHY LEARY MATTERS TODAY

When comparing Leary's early writings with his later writings from the late 1960s and early 1970s, one is struck by his willingness to seriously

---

*This quotation is taken from *Hofmann's Potion* (2002), a Canadian documentary film about LSD in the twentieth century. The film features interviews with Ram Dass, Stanislav Grof, Humphry Osmond, Albert Hofmann, Ralph Metzner, and other psychedelic visionaries from the 1960s.

consider the boundless and utopian possibilities of the drug experience. For Leary, the experience of taking psychedelic drugs was not simply "recreational." This is the chief difference between consciousness-expanding drugs in the 1960s and the general public's understanding of psychedelics today. The first-wave scholars of the research era believed that hallucinogenic drugs allow the subject and the scientist to explore new psychic terrain: higher modes of consciousness and the enigma that is the human mind. In Leary's carefully programmed trips, the subject has a profound encounter with the self and its various guises (Leary also calls this "game reality"). Leary, at his most idealistic, believed that "behavior change" was possible: "non-game visionary experiences are, I submit, the key to behavior change—drug induced *satori*. In three hours under the right circumstances, the cortex can be cleared. The games that frustrate and torment can be seen in the cosmic dimension." For Leary, the shackles of culture and social conditioning—racial intolerance, familial dysfunction, traumatic events—could be thrown off during an intense psilocybin session. Leary's bold utopianism—his devout faith in the transformative potential of psychedelic drugs—would have a powerful ripple effect on the consciousness of the 1960s. What happened in Leary's house in Newton, Massachusetts, would eventually reach a global audience of psychedelic enthusiasts.

Perhaps Leary's most powerful breakthrough is his notion of deconditioning (also called "re-imprinting" in his later articles). For him, psychedelic drugs had a demystifying effect on the user: they enabled him or her to free himself/herself from the grip of social conditioning. Leary's notion of deconditioning quickly filtered into the vernacular of the counterculture of the 1960s. For many young people taking LSD would be a profound *rite of passage*. The LSD trip would serve as a creative template for new identities and a new way of interpreting personal experience.

Between 1960 and 1965, Leary authored and co-authored thirteen scholarly articles, an IFIF manifesto, and a book review for Alan Watts's *The Joyous Cosmology: Adventures in the Chemistry of Consciousness*.

Most of this early work, representing Leary's most seminal period of writing, is included in this book.* *Timothy Leary: The Harvard Years* also includes articles from 1966 to 1970. I have included these because they are concerned with research Leary conducted while he was a Harvard psychology professor. All of the essays contained herein are reprinted as they originally appeared; none have been abridged. They are grouped into five thematic sections and each one features a preface that situates each article within the context of Leary's biography and intellectual trajectory. The first three sections contain articles from Leary's three research projects conducted at Harvard: The Harvard Psilocybin Project, The Concord Prison Experiment, and The Good Friday Experiment. The fourth section features Leary's first published articles on LSD and DMT. This section includes articles that were published after Leary was fired by Harvard in May of 1963. The final section of this book (Part 5) features articles related to the Harvard Drug Scandal of 1963. In each of these articles, Leary and his coauthors attempt to create psychedelic training centers that were not affiliated with Harvard University. It also includes Leary and Huston Smith's controversial manifesto for the International Forum for Internal Freedom (IFIF) and Leary and Alpert's somewhat bombastic response to the Harvard Drug Scandal ("The Politics of Consciousness Expansion"). This final section also includes one article from the Harvard Drug Scandal of May 1963: Noah Gordon's "The Hallucinogenic Drug Cult." This sensationalist article, which was originally published in *The Reporter,* is a fascinating historical document that illustrates the American media's reaction to the emergence of consciousness-expanding drugs in the era when LSD and psilocybin were still legal.

The essays and articles included in this book are important because

---

*I have included three articles that were published after 1965: "Programming Communication during Experiences with DMT" (1966), "The Effects of Consciousness-Expanding Drugs on Prisoner Rehabilitation," and " The Diagnosis of Behavior and the Diagnosis of Experience" ("On Existential Transaction Theory"). Each of these articles was based on research that was conducted during the Harvard Years (1960 to 1963).

they represent the most vital phase of Leary's *oeuvre*.* His later writings on drugs—*The Politics of Ecstasy* (1968), and *Changing My Mind, Among Others* (1982)—lacked the power and urgency of these early writings because Leary approaches his subject (the psychedelic experience) from a multiplicity of perspectives. The scholarly Leary of *Timothy Leary: The Harvard Years* writes for two audiences: psychedelic enthusiasts and skeptical non-users. He critiques the dominant psychological paradigms of his epoch (Skinnerian behaviorism and Freudian psychology) and boldly asserts the social and therapeutic efficacy of psychedelic drugs.

The post-academic Leary of the late 1960s, on the other hand, is not really interested in having a dialogue with skeptics and non-users. In *The Politics of Ecstasy* (1968), Leary simply makes fun of non-users and the older generation ("menopausal mendacious men") and declares them to be incurable fools: "They are bores. They hate beauty. They hate sex. They hate life" (365). The articles in this book are more compelling than Leary's later work precisely because Leary writes with the skeptics in mind. He anticipates their objections and their reservations. Leary is aware that hallucinogenic drugs are rarely viewed in a disinterested manner; that psychedelic drugs—and their extraordinary effects on the human mind— necessarily imply an ideological battle between enlightened and retrograde interpretations. Leary is at his best when he engages his skeptical opponents and makes the case for progressive research and therapy.

Leary's early writings are also remarkable because they attempt to establish a dialogue between science and religion. Although Leary employs the rhetoric of science during his psilocybin experiments, at the same time he remains deeply curious about spiritual concepts and religion's attempt to map the ineffable. Leary was often attracted to

---

*Although I have argued that Leary's scholarly work is generally more compelling than his journalistic work from the late 1960s (e.g., *The Politics of Ecstasy*), there is one notable exception: *High Priest* (1968). The latter is Leary's most impressive work from his post-academic period. Mixing journalist accounts and autobiography, *High Priest* documents all of Leary's most famous drug trips in Mexico, Cambridge, and Millbrook. *High Priest* is a bold prose experiment that successfully captures the heteroglossia of the drug experience and non-ordinary forms of consciousness.

the experiences that science and human language could not adequately describe (i.e., illumination, ecstasy, epiphany, etc.). In several articles, Leary's new found interest in religious mysticism is juxtaposed with scientific understanding of the psychedelic drug experience. The tension between these seemingly antithetical perspectives is what makes Leary's early writings so engaging some fifty years later.

When the ideological dust of the twentieth century has settled, Leary will not simply be remembered for his advocacy of psychedelic drugs, he will also be remembered as a consummate interpreter of the human psyche. His dual role—that of scientist and spiritual thinker—enabled him to interpret and elucidate the complex nature of the drug experience with perceptive clarity.

Before and after he was famous, Leary may be described as a cartographer of the unconscious. He boldly explored the *terra incognita* of the human mind and the self. When he returned from his psychic voyages, he carefully attempted to describe the strange and exquisite worlds that he had seen. The various essays and articles in this book are his glorious atlas.

REFERENCES

Cohen, Sidney. "Lysergic Acid Diethylamide: Side Effects and Complications." *The Journal of Mental and Nervous Disease* 130, no. 1 (1960): 30–40.

Dass, Ram, Ralph Metzner, and Gary Bravo. *Birth of a Psychedelic Culture: Conversations about Leary, the Harvard Experiments, and the Sixties.* Santa Fe, N.Mex.: Synergetic Press, 2010.

Devonis, David C. "Timothy Leary's Mid-Century Shift: Clean Break or Inflection Point?" *Journal of the History of the Behavioral Sciences* 48, no. 1 (2012): 16–39.

Greenfield, Robert. *Timothy Leary: A Biography.* New York: Harcourt, 2006.

Horowitz, Michael, Karen Walls, and Billy Smith. *An Annotated Bibliography of Timothy Leary.* Hamden, Conn.: Archon Books, 1988.

Lattin, Don. *The Harvard Psychedelic Club.* New York: Harper One, 2010.

Leary, Timothy. *High Priest.* New York: The World Publishing Company, 1968.

———. *Changing My Mind, Among Others.* Englewood Cliffs, N.J.: Prentice Hall, 1982.

———. *The Politics of Ecstasy.* Berkeley: Ronin, 1990.

Lee, Martin, and Bruce Shlain. *Acid Dreams: The Complete Social History of LSD: The CIA, the Sixties, and Beyond.* New York: Grove Press, 1985.

Riedlinger, Thomas J. "Existential Transactions at Harvard: Timothy Leary's Humanistic Psychotherapy." *Journal of Humanistic Psychology* 33, no. 6 (1993): 6–18.

Russin, Joseph M., and Andrew T. Weil. "Corporation Fires Richard Alpert for Giving Undergraduates Drugs." *Harvard Crimson.* May 28, 1963. (This special issue of the *Harvard Crimson* includes the full-text of President Pusey's statement to the press.)

Walsh, Roger, and Charles S. Grob. *Higher Wisdom: Eminent Elders Explore the Continuing Impact of Psychedelics.* Albany, N.Y.: State University of New York Press, 2005.

PART I

The Trip in Cuernavaca

Early Utopian Writings on Psilocybin

When Timothy Leary visited Cuernavaca in the summer of 1960, he was in the throes of a mid-life crisis. As he approached his fortieth birthday in October, Leary described himself as a "middle-aged man involved in the middle-aged process of dying. My joy in life, my sensual openness, my creativity were sliding downhill" (quoted in Greenfield, 110). Leary's first marriage had ended with his wife's suicide; his second marriage lasted less than a year. Leary was struggling to raise two children and finish his second book.

Leary had heard about magic mushrooms, but he remained somewhat skeptical about them. Frank Barron, a close friend and psychologist from Leary's days at Berkeley, had taken some the previous summer and raved about the visionary powers they inspired. When Barron told Leary about his experience, the Harvard psychologist reminded him not to babble like this in front of his colleagues because he might lose respect and academic credibility. Yet, when Leary found himself at a sunny villa in Cuernavaca he decided to try the mushrooms. After the experience, Leary struggled to contain his enthusiasm: "In four hours by the pool in Cuernavaca I learned more about the mind, the brain, and its structures than I did in the preceding fifteen as a diligent psychologist" (*Flashbacks* 33). Leary also wrote of the experience, "I discovered that beauty, revelation, sensuality, the cellular history of the past, God, the Devil—all lie inside my body, outside my mind" (*High Priest* 12). Leary's use of religious phraseology was strange even to himself because he had always been a staunch critic of Roman Catholicism.

When Leary returned to Harvard in the fall of 1960, he was convinced that psilocybin would revolutionize clinical practices and psychology's understanding of the human mind. For Leary, the trained clinical psychologist, the possibilities seemed endless. Leary contacted Sandoz Laboratories, the Swiss pharmaceutical company that had recently discovered how to chemically synthesize Mexican magic mushrooms in the form of psilocybin pills.* When Leary obtained his first shipment of pink pills in October of 1960, he officially started the Harvard Psilocybin Project (HPP).

Part 1 presents four articles that outline the foundational experiments for Leary's psilocybin inspired revolution. At the heart of the post-Cuernavaca research was the attempt to reinvent psychotherapy from the ground up. Central to Leary's project was his pre-psychedelic conception of existential transaction theory (ETT). By "existential," Leary meant that psychologists should work with people in real life situations. The hierarchies between psychologist and patients would be eliminated; the psychologist would get in the trenches with the patient, and their interactions should be described as collaborative exchanges ("transactions"). Rather than imposing theoretical models on the patient (i.e., Freudian), the psychologist becomes a "coach" who shares information with the patient. Above all, the psychologist avoids detachment (the subject-object model) and gets personally involved with the patient by sharing time and space with him or her. In the pre-psychedelic 1950s, Leary's conception

---

*Albert Hofmann, Ph.D., successfully created a synthetic version of Mexican magic mushrooms in the late 1950s. The round pink pills that Hofmann developed in the lab were labeled "psilocybin." When Leary received his first shipment, the note from Sandoz stated: "We appreciate your request and we are interested in sponsoring your work in this area. Here's a starter kit to get going and please send us a report of the results" (Greenfield 117).

of ETT was merely an unrealized theory; the goal of moving beyond the existing social roles remained too daunting in the conservative climate of the 1950s.

For Leary, psilocybin provided the radical solution that he had been grasping for in his theoretical writings. Psilocybin was revolutionary precisely because it acted as a powerful equalizing mechanism that negated the institutional roles that governed clinical practices. When the psychologist and patient tripped together, they developed strong emotional ties to one another. After the trip was over, they collaborated and shared results. In short, psilocybin provided the intense bonding experience that Leary's pre-psychedelic version of ETT had always lacked.

The four essays contained in Part 1 are utopian documents that capture the breadth and scope of Leary's therapeutic revolution. Their topics range from Leary's conception of "game theory" ("How to Change Behavior") to Leary's radical attempt to reinvent and revolutionize clinical psychology ("On Existential Transaction Theory"). "Reactions to Psilocybin Administered in a Supportive Environment" is Leary's earliest scientific article on psychedelic drugs. It demonstrates Leary's conception of "set and setting"—the science of fostering and nurturing "good trips." The last article, "The Effects of Test Score Feedback on Creative Performance and of Drugs on Creative Experience," has been out of print for many decades. It documents Leary's bold attempt to use psilocybin to stimulate creativity in the user. Leary was convinced that psilocybin could inspire and nurture creativity and what he termed "creative performance." Under the aegis of the Harvard Psilocybin Project, Leary programmed countless trips for many leading artists and musicians. "Psychedelic Drugs and Creativity" is especially important because it elucidates Leary's theory of creativity and his anti-elitist conception of the creative act.

REFERENCES

Greenfield, Robert. *Timothy Leary: A Biography*. New York: Harcourt, 2006.

Leary, Timothy. *Flashbacks: A Personal and Cultural History of an Era*. New York: Jeremy Tarcher/Perigee, 1990.

———. *High Priest*. New York: The World Publishing Company, 1968.

1

Leary's First Article on Psilocybin

How to Change Behavior

Timothy Leary

Timothy Leary's "How to Change Behavior" was presented at the International Congress of Applied Psychology in Copenhagen in August of 1961, and was also reprinted in David Solomon's *LSD: The Consciousness-Expanding Drug* (1964). Leary had organized the plenary session of the International Congress; it included several distinguished speakers, including the novelist Aldous Huxley, Frank Barron of U.C. Berkeley, Richard Alpert and Henry A. Murray of Harvard, and himself. Each speaker was also an advocate of consciousness-expanding drugs. Psilocybin—synthesized magic mushrooms—was the drug of choice in 1961.

"How to Change Behavior" was Leary's first full-length article after his famous virginal experience with Mexican mushrooms in Cuernavaca in August of 1960 and as such, this article represents his first major work on psychedelics. Leary wanted a big stage for his presentation because he had a controversial message: a symbolic break with behaviorism, the dominant paradigm in applied psychology in the early 1960s. In this article, Leary notes that behaviorism is predicated on the "subject-object model" that attempts ". . . to observe, measure, manipulate, control, and predict—the subject's overt behavior." In place of behaviorism, Leary proposes a radical new paradigm: behavior change through consciousness-expanding drugs.

Leary's new doctrine rests on the notion that all cultural behavior is simply a "game" that we play. Each game—psychology, religion, politics—has specific roles, rules, and goals. Consciousness-expanding drugs are crucial because they allow the user to see beyond the game and its rules. Leary's description of human behavior as an elaborate game anticipates postmodernism's suggestion that all forms of culture and language are simply social constructions that can be manipulated for various ideological ends ("the nationality game. It is treason not to play. The racial game. The religious game"). Leary's rejection of all social constructions is followed by a rejection of the myth of the self: "the most treacherous and tragic game of all. The game of individuality, the ego game. The Timothy Leary game. Ridiculous how we confuse it, overplay it. Our own mystics and the Eastern philosophers have been warning us about this danger for centuries."

For Leary's theory of liberation, consciousness-expanding drug are crucial because they temporarily "unplug the ego, the game machinery and the mind (that cluster of game concepts)"—a process he would later term "deconditioning." Leary notes that drugs are crucial because they allow the user to transcend this "game view" of reality. Leary's radical vision was bound to alarm and shock many of his colleagues, many of whom were card-carrying behaviorists. They resented Leary's evangelistic tone and the suggestion that their methodology was becoming obsolete.

Perhaps the most controversial idea that Leary puts forth in his paper is the need to abandon the notion that the scientist must be a detached observer. Instead, Leary advocates a hands-on approach to psychological research: the psychologist/scientist must take the drugs he/she is studying. This methodological issue would become a major point of contention in the Harvard Drug Scandal of 1963. Leary anticipates that his therapeutic approach is bound to create alarm and suspicion. Thus, Leary ends his paper with a plea for tolerance: "those of us who talk and write about the games of life are invariably misunderstood. We are seen as frivolous or cynical anarchists tearing down the social structure. This is an unfortunate misapprehension. Actually, only those who see culture as a game, only those who take an evolutionary point of view can appreciate and treasure the exquisitely complex magnificence of what human beings do and have done." Unfortunately, Leary's plea for tolerance and mutual respect fell on deaf ears. Leary would be expelled from Harvard in less than two years.

JAMES PENNER

HOW TO CHANGE BEHAVIOR

A presentation at the International Congress of Applied Psychology in Copenhagen in August of 1961, and also in *LSD: The Consciousness-Expanding Drug* by David Solomon, published in 1964 by G. P. Putnam's Sons: pages 97–113.

Timothy Leary, Ph.D.

It is my plan to talk to you tonight about methods of effecting change—change in man's behavior and change in man's consciousness.

Behavior and consciousness. Please note the paired distinction. Behavior and consciousness. Up until recently I considered myself a behavioral scientist and limited the scope of my work to overt and measurable behavior. In so doing I was quite in the *Zeitgeist* of modern psychology, studying the subject matter which our American predecessors defined some fifty years ago, behavior, routinely following the ground rules they laid down, scrupulously avoiding that which is most important to the subject—his consciousness—concentrating instead, on what is most important to we who seek to observe, measure, manipulate, control and predict—the subject's overt behavior.

This decision to turn our backs on consciousness is, of course, typically Western and very much in tune with the experimental, objective bent of Western science. Professor Huston Smith of the Massachusetts Institute of Technology has pointed out some basic differences between Western approach and the philosophies of China and India. Differences which have some importance for the applied psychologist concerned with behavior change. Professor Smith reminds us that our Western culture has stressed measurement and control of objects; whereas China has historically emphasized the rules of the social encounter; and Indian philosophy the development and expansion of human consciousness. Tonight I speak to you from a point midway between the Western and Eastern hemispheres of the cortex presenting a theory and method which is Chinese in that behavior is seen as an intricate social game; Indian in its recognition of consciousness and the need to develop a more cosmic awareness, and finally Western in its concern to do good measurably well.

I plan to present, first, some thoughts on behavior change, then some new conceptions of consciousness and its alteration, and finally some data from recent research in these areas.

BEHAVIOR AND ITS CHANGE

Except for reflexes and instinctual reactions and random muscular movements (which fall into the province of physiology) all behavior is learned.

Behavior is therefore artifactual and culturally determined. Behavior sequences might usefully be considered as game sequences.

The use of the word "game" in this sweeping context is likely to be misunderstood. The listener may think I refer to "play" as opposed to the stern, real-life, serious activities of man. But as you shall see I consider the latter as "game."

At this point you are asking for and you deserve a definition. What do I mean by game? A game is a learned cultural sequence characterized by six factors:

1. *Roles:* The game assigns roles to the human beings involved.
2. *Rules:* A game sets up a set of rules which hold only during the game sequence.
3. *Goals:* Every game has its goal or purpose. The goals of baseball are to score more runs than the opponents. The goals of the game of psychology are more complex and less explicit but they exist.
4. *Rituals:* Each game has its conventional behavior pattern not related to the goals or rules but yet quite necessary to comfort and continuance.
5. *Language:* Each game has its jargon. Unrelated to the rules and goals and yet necessary to learn and use.
6. *Values:* Each game has its standards of excellence or goodness.

Baseball and basketball have clearly definable roles, rules, rituals, goals, languages and values. Psychology, religion, politics are games, too, learned, cultural sequences with clearly definable roles, rules, rituals, goals, jargons, values. They are less explicitly formulated than the so-called sports and therein, dear friends, lies the pity. For this simple reason millions have died and we may die tomorrow.

The behavior which psychiatrists label as disease entities can be considered as games, too. Dr. Thomas Szasz, the distinguished psychoanalyst-philosopher, in his book, *The Myth of Mental Illness,* suggests that "hysteria" is the name we give to a certain doctor-patient game involving deceitful helplessness. The "bluff" in poker is a similar deceitful but perfectly legitimate game device. Psychiatry according to this model is behavior-change game.

Far from being frivolous, many so-called "play games" are superior in their behavioral science and in their behavior-change techniques to the "not-called games," such as psychiatry and psychology.

In terms of epistemology and scientific method employed, the "game" of American baseball is superior to any of the so-called behavioral sciences. Baseball officials have classified and they reliably record molecular behavior sequences (the strike, the hit, the double play, etc.). Their compiled records are converted into indices most relevant for summarizing and predicting behavior (RBI, runs batted in; ERA, earned run average, etc.). Baseball employs well-trained raters to judge those rare events which are not obviously and easily coded. Their raters are called umpires.

When we move from behavior science to behavior change we see that baseball experts have devised another remarkable set of techniques for bringing about the results which they and their subjects look for. Coaching. Baseball men understand the necessity for sharing time and space with their learners, for setting up role models, for feedback of relevant information to the learner, for endless practice of the desired behavior. And most important of all, baseball scientists understand the basic, cosmic lesson of percentage: that the greatest player gets on the average one hit in three tries, the winning team loses at least one game in three, that no team can lead the league every year, neither Rome, nor Athens, nor London, nor Moscow, nor Washington. Those who wish to measure, summarize, predict, and change human behavior could do worse than model themselves after this so-called "game."

All behavior involves learned games. But only that rare Westerner we call "mystic" or who has had a visionary experience of some sort sees clearly the game structure of behavior. Most of the rest of us spend our time struggling with roles and rules and goals and concepts of games which are implicit and confusedly not seen as games, trying to apply the roles and rules and rituals of one game to other games.

Worst of all is the not knowing that it is a game. Baseball is a clean and successful game because it is seen as a game. You can shift positions. You know the game is limited in space and in time. You know how you are doing. You sign your contract. You renew your contract. You can quit, start a new game.

Culturally, stability is maintained by keeping the members of any cultural group from seeing that the roles, rules, goals, rituals, language, and values are game structures. The family game is treated by most cultures as far more than a game, with its implicit contracts, limited in time and space. The nationality game. It is treason not to play. The racial game. The religious game. And that most treacherous and tragic game of all, the game of individuality, the ego game. The Timothy Leary game. Ridiculous how we confuse this game, overplay it. Our own mystics and the Eastern philosophers have been warning us about this danger for centuries.

Cultural institutions encourage the delusion that the games of life are inevitable givens involving natural laws of behavior. These fixed delusions tend to rigidify behavior patterns. This rigidity, as Professor Osgood pointed out in his significant opening address of the Copenhagen Congress, now threatens the very survival of the human species itself (Osgood, 1962).

So now we come to behavior change. The currently popular method of behavior change is called psychotherapy. A medical game. A curing of the psyche. Psychotherapy interprets confusion and inefficiency in game playing as illness. We call it sickness and attempt to cure it employing the medical game. Consider the football player who doesn't know the rules. Perhaps he picks up the ball and runs off the field. He is punished for not playing the game correctly. He feels badly. Shall we pronounce him sick and call the doctor?

The failure to understand the game nature of behavior leads to confusion and eventually to helplessness. Helplessness. Let's look at this word for a moment. It's a big concept in understanding science, technology, rehabilitation and, for that matter, the working of the mind itself.

The basic aim of physical science is to reduce human helplessness in the face of the physical environment. Physical science has other goals, of course: to understand, explain, control, measure, predict. But certainly these are ends rather than means. Why explain? Why predict? To lessen fearful ignorance. The technologies which have grown up around the physical sciences, engineering, medicine, also take as their goal the reducing of human helplessness.

Do they not stem from the same survival motive? And the social technologies—psychiatry, social work, applied psychology—is not their goal the reduction of confusion and the increase in human freedom?

Judged by these criteria the game of Western science has not been a glorious success. Our helplessness in the face of physical disease has certainly diminished. Our control over natural forces has given us a sense of mastery. We live longer and healthier lives. Good.

We have created a game model—the subject-object model—which allows us on the one hand to dominate "object" but which has created a world full of human objects. Most of what we do in the name of science results in more and greater human helplessness.

The science game creates wonder drugs whose action is not understood by the user. And worse yet we turn over these drugs to those who play the doctor game, the medical game—whose roles, rules, rituals, language, goals and values place the patient into a passive object status.

The science game, the healing game, the knowledge game are magnificent human structures. They are our proudest game accomplishments. But they are great only as long as they are seen as game. When they go beyond this point the trouble begins—claims to a nongame reality status: the emergence of experts, professionals, priests, status-favored authorities; claims to power and control and priority. Look at the A.E.C. Look at the A.M.A. And watch out! At this point you will find that games which began with the goal of decreasing human helplessness end up increasing it.

Human beings inhabiting those areas of the globe which the geographic game calls East are, for the most part, well aware of the foregoing issues. It's hard for Westerners to back away, and see the artifactual game structures. We are so close to our games. We have been born into them. And we are born into a philosophic system which glorifies hierarchical expertise on the one hand and helplessness on the other: monotheism, the Judaic-Christian tradition. Monotheism, that game started by a few persecuted outcasts (game losers) in the Mid-Eastern desert: the subject-object game; the false duality game; the manipulating, predicting, controlling game. Monotheism breeding helplessness.

Now, let's apply this general discussion of helplessness and the behavior game to the issue of behavior change. In spite of our apparent executive control over nature we have had small success in developing behavior change games. Indeed most of our attempts to change behavior increase human helplessness, lessen human freedom and thereby exaggerate the problem we set out to solve. Our behavior change games invariably set up structures which give more power to the few and less power to the many, invidious role models: doctor-patient; professor-student; inequitable rules involving secrecy and control; the one-upmanship language we call jargon.

When people come to us and ask us to change their behavior, why can't we do it? Why can't we teach them to see the game structure of human society? The problem seems simple enough. Why can't we find out what games they are caught up in? Find out what games they want to commit themselves to? Make them explicit? Help them discover the rules of the game, the role, the rituals, the goals, the concepts? Expose them to models of successful game playing; encourage them to practice; feed back objective appraisals of their performance; care for them and their game struggles? How do you care for them? You share time and space with them. Nothing else can substitute. We have little else to offer. If we don't, they'll learn the games of those who do share time and space. If they're prisoners, then who will teach them behavior games? Who shares the most time and space with prisoners? That's right, the other prisoners, older criminals and younger criminals. So who influences behavior in what direction? And who shares the most amount of time and space with prisoners? That's right, the prison guards who, in most American prisons, teach them how to play the role of robber in the game of "cops and robbers." And we professional middle-class experts? How much time and space do we share with the prisoners? An hour a week on the medical ward?

O.K. It sounds simple enough, doesn't it? Just show people that their social identity and their entire cultural commitment is a game. They aren't aware of it. Sure, just tell them.

Yes, you smile when I say this. It's not quite that easy, is it? Here's the rub. Few people, a very few people (and we Westerners call them mystics) are willing and able to admit that the game is a game. Most of our people become upset and even angry when the game is identified—the game of "I-and-all-I-stand-for."

At this point when you hear the word "mystic" you may be uneasily wondering if you are going to be subjected to a vague metaphysical discourse on general principles. Perhaps you will be surprised to hear me suggest the hypothesis that the most effective approach to the "practical" games of life is that of applied mysticism. Identify the game structure of the event. Make sure that you do not apply the rules and concepts of other games to this situation. Move directly to solve the problem avoiding abstractions and irrelevant rituals. A mystic Martian or a person from a different culture might be an excellent consultant for a behavioral problem. They might be able to cut through irrelevant games rules to what is most relevant to survival and peace of mind.

How can we make the point? How can we learn the lesson? How can we Westerners come to see that our own consciousness is infinitely greater than our little egos and the ego games into which we are so blindly caught up? That the universe within our skulls is infinitely more than the flimsy game world which our words and minds create?

Put in a sentence—the task is to see that the mind is a tiny fragment of the brain-body complex. It is the game-playing fragment—a useful and entertaining tool but quite irrelevant to survival, and indeed usually antagonistic to well-being.

The process of getting beyond the game structure, beyond the subject-object commitments, the dualities—this process is called the mystic experience. The visionary experience is the nongame, metagame experience. Change in behavior can occur with dramatic spontaneity once the game structure of behavior is seen. The visionary experience is the key to behavior change.

CONSCIOUSNESS AND ITS CHANGE

How do we obtain the visionary state?

There are many methods for expanding consciousness beyond the game limits. Mr. Aldous Huxley this afternoon presented a scholarly history of the same classic and modern methods. Margaret Mead, the American anthropologist, has suggested several cross-cultural methods. Have a psychotic episode. (This is to say, just stop playing the social game for a while and they'll call you insane, but you may learn the great lesson.) Or expose yourself to some great trauma that shatters the gamesmanship out of you. Birth by ordeal is a well-documented phenomenon. The concentration camp experience has done this for some of our wisest men. Physical traumas can do it. Electric shock. Extreme fatigue. Live in another and very different culture for a year where your roles and rituals and language just don't mean a thing. Or separate yourself from the game pressure by institutional withdrawal. Live for a while in a monastic cell. Or marry a Russian. Sensory deprivation does it. Sensory deprivation cuts through the game.

Certain forms of sensory stimulation alter consciousness beyond games. The sexual orgasm is certainly the most frequent and natural, although so brief and so built into interpersonal courtship games that it has lost much of its mystical meaning in the West. We have recently learned from W. Grey Walter and William Burroughs about photostimulation as a means of consciousness alteration. Concentrated attention to a stroboscope or flicker apparatus can produce visionary experiences.

The most efficient way to cut through the game structure of Western life is the use of drugs, consciousness-expanding drugs. From here on I shall use the abbreviation CE to refer to consciousness-expanding substances, such as LSD, mescaline, psilocybin.

Now the reaction of the Western world to consciousness-expanding drugs is extremely interesting. We tend to apply our familiar game roles, rituals, goals, rules, concepts to the non-game experience produced by these substances. Those of you who have not had the shattering exposure to such old and worshipped plants as peyote and the sacred mush-room and cannabis or such startling newcomers as psilocybin* and lysergic acid will wonder at this point about the nature of these experi-ences. What do these substances do? The neuro-physiological answer—the answer from outside—to this question is not yet ready. The answer from the inside (from the awareness of the subject) can be cast in count-less metaphors. Let's try a physiological analogy. Let's assume that the cortex, the seat of consciousness, is a millionfold network of neurons, a fantastic computing machine. Cultural learning has imposed a few, pitifully small programs on the cortex. These programs may activate perhaps one-tenth or one one-hundredth of the potential neural con-nections. All the learned games of life can be seen as programs which select, censor, alert and thus drastically limit the available cortical response (Mr. Aldous Huxley's reducing valves).

The CE (i.e., consciousness-expanding) drugs unplug these narrow programs. They unplug the ego, the game machinery, and the mind (that cluster of game concepts). And with the ego and mind unplugged, what is left? Not the "id"; no dark, evil impulses. These alleged negative "forces" are, of course, part of the game, being simply anti-rules. What is left is something that Western culture knows little about: the open brain, the uncensored cortex—alert and open to a broad sweep. Huxley and Dr. Barron have told you in their own words what is left, and there is no need to add my lumbering prose.

There is need, however, to ask another question. Why is this ecstatic, brain-opening experience so strange and horrid to Western culture? Why have our ancestors and our colleagues tended to ignore and even to oppose the visionary experience? Mr. R. Gordon Wasson,

---

*Psilocybin is a synthetic of the active ingredients of the sacred mushroom of Mexico. The divinatory mushroom was introduced to the Western culture by Professor Roger Heim of Paris and R. Gordon Wasson of New York and synthesized by Dr. A. Hofmann of the Sandoz Laboratory in Basel, Switzerland, who is also known through his work on lysergic acid. We are grateful to Sandoz, Inc., for providing the research materials used in these studies.

banker, mycologist, anthropologist, gentleman-scholar turned mystic, has traced the persecution of the divine and divinatory mushroom back through the millennia. Why the irrational fear so often aroused by research on CE drugs even to this day? Perhaps because our Western world is committed to overplaying the objective, external behavior game.

In particular we overvalue the mind—that flimsy collection of learned words and verbal connections; the mind, that system of paranoid delusions with the learned self as center. And we eschew the non-mind, non-game intuitive insight outlook which is the key to the religious experience, to the love experience.

We seem to oppose any process which puts the game of here and now onto the long evolutionary timetable. This is a natural opposition and a healthy one. It is the greatest game of "the game" versus the "non-game." Behavior versus consciousness. The universal brain-body versus the cultural mind. The ego versus the species. A dialogue old and holy, like the dialogue of sea against land.

But this old game should be made explicit if it is to be fun. Unfortunately, the West has no concepts for thinking and talking about this basic dialogue. There is no ritual for mystical experience, for the mindless vision. What should provoke intense and cheerful competition too often evokes suspicion, anger, and impatience. What can be holy and intensely educational in the action of CE drugs on the cortex finds no ritual for application. This is to me one of the greatest challenges of our times.

The nongame visionary experiences are, I submit, the key to behavior change—drug-induced *satori*. In three hours under the right circumstances the cortex can be cleared. The games that frustrate and torment can be seen in the cosmic dimension. But the West has no ritual, no game to handle the CE drug experience. In the absence of relevant rituals we can only impose our familiar games, the politics of the nervous system, the mind controlling the brain. Physicians seek to impose their game of control and prescription. The bohemians naturally strive to impose their games of back-alley secrecy. The police, the third member of the happy, symbiotic drug triangle, naturally move in to control and prosecute.

Clearly we need new rituals, new goals, new rules, new concepts to apply and use these precious substances for man's welfare, to give the brain back to the species.

A group of investigators in the United States and Europe are now at work building up new games for the visionary experience, trying to develop new roles, rules, rituals, concepts and values. While these will, of course, vary from group to group the goal remains constant: expansion of consciousness, freedom of brain from the mind, freedom of the cortex from those centers—reticular (?), diencephalic (?), prefrontal (?)—which control, alert, censor and select what the cortex attends to. The work has hardly begun. This much is clear. The theory of the new game will be simple and basic. Space and time will be among the few variables required. Human equality will be a central principle, for the mystic experience tells us that the game differences between men are infinitely small compared with the age-old species similarities.

In our research endeavors we have developed eleven egalitarian principles based on the game nature of the human contract: equality in determining role, rule, ritual, goal, language, commitment; equality in the explicit contractual definition of the real, the good, the true, the logical; equality of the right to speak and to have access to relevant information. Any contract between men should be explicit about any temporary suspension of these equalities.

This past year at the Center for Research in Personality, Harvard University, two research projects [the Harvard Psilocybin Project and the Concord Prison Experiment] have attempted to put these egalitarian principles into operation. The first of these is a naturalistic study of drug-induced visions and the games which Americans impose on these new experiences. The second is a systematic study of the effects of consciousness-expanding drugs in a rehabilitation program. I hope that a description of these two projects will illustrate and clarify the preceding discussion.*

A NATURALISTIC STUDY OF PSILOCYBIN

The purpose of this study was to determine the effects of psilocybin when administered in a naturalistic, supportive setting, to observe the rituals and language imposed by Americans on an experience quite alien to their culture. One hundred and sixty-seven subjects were given the mushrooms, 43 female and 124 male. Of these, 26 were internationally distinguished intellectuals, scholars, artists; 10 were medical doctors, 73 were professional intellectuals, 21 nonprofessional normals, 27 were drug addicts (psychological or physical), and 10 were inmates in a state prison.

The eleven principles for the human contract led to the following operations:

1. Participants alternated roles of observer and subject, i.e., the researchers took the drug with the subjects. The humanizing effect of this procedure cannot be overestimated. Among other things the subject-object issue is clearly settled.
2. Participants were given all available information about the drug.

---

*The Director of the Center for Research in Personality, Prof. David C. McClelland, has provided these two projects with advice, support, and has labored to interpret our work to the nonvisionary world. All American psychologists are indebted to Professor Henry A. Murray for his pioneer explorations into the human condition. From his neighborly presence, friendly interest and deep understanding of man's potentialities we have benefited. Dr. Frank Barron and Dr. Richard Alpert have been coinvestigators in the mushroom research. Dr. W. Madison Presnell has lent psychiatric experience, administrative enthusiasm and clinical wisdom. George Litwin, James Ciarlo, Gunther Weil, Ralph Metzner, Ralph Schwitzgebel and Jonathan Shay have played important roles in charting the new realms of consciousness. Edward Travers, John Molinski, James Maloney, Frank Rafferty, Rodney Harrington, Henry Kinney, and Donald Levine have made significant contributions to the Concord project. Mr. George Litwin and his staff have taken responsibility for the computer analysis of the questionnaire data. Mrs. Pearl Chan, research administrator, has made things run.

An atmosphere of mystery and secret experimentation was avoided.

3. Participants were given control of their own dosage. A maximum dosage was determined by the research team and this maximum number of tablets was given to the subject and he was free to dose himself at the rate and amount desired.

4. A comfortable, homelike environment was employed. The sterile impersonality of the laboratory was avoided.

5. Subjects were allowed to bring a relative or friend. No subject took the drug in a group where he was a stranger.

Three sets of data were obtained: questionnaires covering the reactions; written reports and tape recordings; observations by the research team.

While the results of this study are too extensive to summarize at this point, a few major conclusions can be stated: The psilocybin experience is pleasant and educational; seventy-three percent of our subjects reported the experience as "very pleasant" or ecstatic; ninety-five percent thought the experience had changed their lives for the better.

Three out of four subjects reported happy and insightful reactions. When we recall that the drug was given only once under informal circumstances, with no attempt to be therapeutic or problem-oriented, these data stimulate thoughts about the healing-educational possibilities of psilocybin. But how do these changes come about?

The most common reaction reported is the sudden perception of the effect of abstractions, rituals, learned-game routines—ecstatic pleasure at being temporarily freed from these limitations, a game-free honesty. Set and suggestive contexts account for ninety-nine percent of the specific response to the drug. Thus, you cannot sensibly talk about the effects of psilocybin. It's always the set and suggestive context triggered off by the drug. A fascinating tension between these two factors—set and context—inevitably develops. If both are positive and holy then a shatteringly sacred experience results. If both are negative then a hellish encounter ensues. There is, of course, the tendency for people to impose their familiar games on to the psilocybin experience. The more rigidly committed to the game, the stronger this tendency. If the drug-giving person is secure, flexible, supportive, then the experience is almost guaranteed to be pleasant and therapeutic. Intensely deep communication occurs. Deep insights of a personal, social, and philosophic nature take place.

THE USE OF PSILOCYBIN IN A REHABILITATION PROGRAM

For many people one or two psilocybin experiences can accomplish the goals of a long and successful psychotherapy, a deep understanding and game-free collaboration between participants plus insight. But what then? People vary tremendously in their readiness to move forward from this point. Many of the 167 subjects in our naturalistic study were able to exploit the close, honest relationship and the insight. They were already involved in rewarding games to which they could return with renewed vision and energy.

But many of our subjects came through the psilocybin experience with the knowledge that they were involved in nonrewarding games, caught in routines which they disliked. Some realized that they had no games they wanted to play. The "therapeutic" effect of the experience did not last for these subjects. Expanded consciousness narrowed back. They were left with pleasant memories of their visionary journey and nothing more.

After insight comes the deeper question as to the meaning of life: What games to play? Behavior change must follow change in consciousness.

Our research group is now committed to a series of investigations which seek to develop methods for perpetuating the positive effects of the psilocybin experience, methods for helping the subject select and learn new games which give meaning to life.

The first of these projects concerned itself with the rehabilitation of inmates in a state prison. In helping prisoners we have of course found that the prisoners have rehabilitated us—changed our notions about crime, punishment, taught us about their games, made us see the limitations of our middle-class conceptions, expanded our consciousness and given deeper meaning to our lives.

Ten volunteer prisoners. A maximum security prison. The recidivism rate is eighty percent. Eight of the ten would be expected back in prison a year after release. In baseball terms, eighty percent is the error percentage our team attempted to lower.

After three orientation meetings with the prisoners, the drug was given. I was the first one to take the drug in that bare hospital room behind barred windows. Three inmates joined me. Two psychologists and the other inmates served as observers—taking the drug three hours later. The psilocybin session was followed by three discussions, then another drug session, then more discussions. At this point the inmates had taken the drug an average of four times. There had been not one moment of friction or tension in some forty hours of egoless interaction. Pre-post testing has demonstrated marked changes on both objective and projective instruments: dramatic decreases in hostility, cynicism, depression, schizoid ideation; definite increases in optimism, planfulness, flexibility, tolerance, sociability.

The group has become a workshop for planning future games. Some prisoners are being trained to take over the functions of research assistants. They are performing the tasks of a vocational guidance clinic—preparing occupational brochures for inmates about to be released, making plans to act as rehabilitation workers after their release, for organizing a halfway house for ex-convicts. Other prisoners are using their time to prepare for the games to which they will return—the family game, their old job.

The psilocybin experience made these men aware of the stereotyped games in which they had been involved, the game of "cops and robbers," the game of being a tough guy, the game of outwitting the law, the game of resentful cynicism. "My whole life came tumbling down and I was sitting happily in the rubble." But insight is the beginning, and the more demanding task is to help these men choose new games, help them learn the rules, the roles, the concepts, the rituals of the new game—practical, collaborative reality education. Of course, this phase of our work requires help from others. But the helpers get helped. The businessmen who help our inmates get jobs are invited into a new and exciting game which gives more meaning to their lives.

Our work progresses slowly and against strong opposition. Our new game of allowing criminals to take over responsibility and authority and prestige as experts on "crime and rehabilitation" brings us into game competition with the professional middle class. Anger and anxiety is aroused. Society has always produced and needed a criminal class. When criminals drop their roles and begin to play a different game, incredulous panic can ensue. Can society play its game without some men acting the part of criminals? If criminals are no longer criminals, where do the rest of us stand? The game of rehabilitator and client (i.e., a professional and a criminal) is being threatened. People are upset when their games are changed.

But our new game has begun. The game statistic for measuring success is clearcut. Eighty percent of convicts return to prison. Next season will reveal how well we have played our game.

SUMMARY

Let me summarize. We have been concerned with change in behavior and change in consciousness. It is considerably easier to change behavior if you understand the learned-game nature of behavior. This sort of insight can be brought about by the administration of consciousness-expanding drugs, of which psilocybin is the most effective. But insight must be followed by behavior change. In the "rehabilitation game" we have been developing, the role of the helper is threefold. He provides a serious, supportive context for the CE experience, sets up an atmosphere in which insight can quickly occur. He then joins with the subject in an all-out collaborative process of selecting and mastering new games. He keeps accurate records of his activities and those of his subjects so that the success of his game performance can be objectively appraised by his fellow men.

A final word of clarification: Those of us who talk and write about the games of life are invariably misunderstood. We are seen as frivolous, or cynical anarchists tearing down the social structure. This is an unfortunate misapprehension. Actually, only those who see culture as a game, only those who take this evolutionary point of view can appreciate and treasure the exquisitely complex magnificence of what human beings do and have done. To see it all as "serious, taken-for-granted reality" is to miss the point, is to derogate with bland passivity the greatness of the games we learn.

Those of us who play the game of "applied mysticism" respect and support good gamesmanship. You pick out your game. You learn the rules, rituals, concepts. You play fairly and cleanly. You don't confuse your games with other games. You do not impose your game rituals on others' games. You win today's game with humility. You lose tomorrow's game with dignity. Anger and anxiety are irrelevant because you see your small game in the context of the great evolutionary game which no one can win and no one can lose.

REFERENCES

Osgood, Ch. E. "Towards international behavior appropriate to a nuclear age." *Psychology and International Affairs,* Proceed. XIV Int. Congr. Appl. Psychol., vol. 1, 109–132. Copenhagen: Munksgaard, 1962.*

---

*[Charles E. Osgood was a distinguished American psychologist and noted communication theorist. In his keynote address for the Copenhagen Conference, he referenced the possibility of nuclear annihilation. Osgood was an articulate proponent of dialogue and reciprocal steps, such as nuclear disarmament, that would build trust and reduce tension between the superpowers. —James Penner]

2

On Existential Transaction Theory

The Diagnosis of Behavior and the Diagnosis of Experience

Timothy Leary

In 1958, while on sabbatical from the Kaiser Foundation Hospital in Oakland, California, where he had been appointed director of psychiatric research in 1955, Leary traveled to Torremolinos, a small Spanish town on the Costa Del Sol. He was planning to write a new book that would revolutionize the practice of psychotherapy. In this unpublished manuscript, Leary boldly proclaimed that our "current theories of personality, our methods of assessment, and our techniques of treatment have not succeeded in helping man and his society to solve the pressing problems which he faces." In place of the status quo, Leary proposed a dynamic new approach to psychology and psychotherapy: existential transaction theory.

Leary's conception of existential transaction deeply impressed David McClelland, the new Director of the Harvard Center for Research in Personality, when they met in Florence during the summer of 1959. According to Leary's autobiography, McClelland remarked of Leary's theory and manuscript, "There is no question that what you're advocating is going to be the future of American psychology . . . You're spelling out the frontline tactics. You're just what we need to shake things up at Harvard" (*Flashbacks* 18).

Existential Transaction—the manuscript that so impressed McClelland and helped Leary get a position at Harvard—does not exist today. Although Leary mentions it in his book *Flashbacks: A Personal and Cultural History of an Era,* there is no existing manuscript in the Timothy Leary collection at the New York Public Library, nor at any library anywhere else. Since *Existential Transaction* has completely disappeared, this original article is a valuable document because it is the only existing account of Leary's existential transaction theory.

Although "The Diagnosis of Behavior and the Diagnosis of Experience" was published in Alvin Mahrer's *New Approaches to Personality Classification* in 1970, it really reflects Leary's work from the late 1950s and his work at Harvard during the early 1960s. In the article, Leary offers a definition of his terminology: "[b]y *existential* I mean a concentration on flexible concepts and methods which grow out of the unique changing situation. By *transactional* I refer to an open collaborative attitude between the psychologist and the person studied." The key idea in Leary's radical theory of psychotherapy is the attempt to break down and deconstruct the relationship between the psychologist and the patient. Leary's phrase "transactional" implies "an open collaborative attitude between the psychologist and the person studied" (212). Leary notes "when we study our fellowman we must treat him as what he is, a human being, and not an object to be dissected, manipulated, controlled, predicted by scientists and or clinicians" (213). Leary's humanistic desire to liberate the patient from the existing paradigms of psychotherapy would eventually be embodied in affective forms of therapy that emphasized the subjective experience—consciousness rather than behavior—of the patient and the need to spend valuable "space-time" with the patients in nonprofessional settings (avoiding the sterile environment of hospitals and mental health facilities). Leary argues that the doctor should act in more of a consulting capacity, rather than functioning as an authority figure. Leary even suggested that the psychologists should avoid the code of objective detachment from the subject/patient; instead, they should "get involved, engaged in the events they're studying. They should enter each experiment prepared to change as much or more than the subjects being studied" (*Flashbacks* 17).

By emphasizing the subjective experience of the patient and the notion of active participation of the psychologist, Leary was making a clean break from Skinnerian behaviorism and Freudian psychoanalysis, the dominant theoretical paradigms in psychology departments in the late 1950s. While behaviorism demanded that psychologists remain detached and objective, Leary attempted to create a new form of psychotherapy that featured empathy, and collaboration with the patient.*

Although Leary had no experience with psychedelic drugs when he first conceived his existential transaction theory in the late 1950s, it is clear that LSD and psilocybin were exactly what Leary was looking for. When taken by the patient and the psychologist, psychedelic drugs offer an immediate and radical form of praxis in the sense that they destabilize hierarchical relationships and—in the right setting and circumstances—foster a more equal and honest relationship between doctor and

---

*Leary's notion of "active participation" with the patient aligned him with the so-called anti-psychiatry movement of the early 1960s. Leary's existential transaction theory is conversant with Thomas Szasz's *The Myth of Mental Illness* (1961), R. D. Laing's *The Divided Self* (1960), and Michel Foucault's *Madness and Civilization* (1961).

patient. Leary's willingness to take psilocybin with inmates at the Concord State Prison in 1961 and 1962 is proof of his radical commitment to the tenets of existential transaction theory. Although Leary's terminology changes in the mid-1960s, his notion of existential transaction remains at the heart of his humanist conception of psychology and his radical attempt to reform clinical practices in the 1960s.

JAMES PENNER

REFERENCES

Leary, Timothy. *Flashbacks: A Personal and Cultural History of an Era.* New York: Jeremy Tarcher/Perigee, 1990.

THE DIAGNOSIS OF BEHAVIOR AND THE DIAGNOSIS OF EXPERIENCE

From *New Approaches to Personality Classification* by Alvin Mahrer, published in 1970 by Columbia University Press: pages 211–36.

Timothy Leary

EXISTENTIAL-TRANSACTIONAL DIAGNOSIS

Modern dynamic psychology claims to study the internal and external aspects of human nature—the indirect and the direct, the covert and the overt, the said and the unsaid, the done and the undone, the experienced and the expressed. This relatively new intellectual position has made a flashy contribution to our conceptions of human nature. The impact of dynamic theory upon every aspect of intellectual life (and I want to stress *intellectual* as opposed to practical) is currently so evident that I need not pause to elaborate or demonstrate.

And now this said, I shall proceed to a critical examination of the practical applications of this broad field, in particular, psychodiagnosis.

Current theories of personality, our methods of assessment, and our techniques of treatment have not yet succeeded in helping man and his society to solve the pressing problems which he faces. I would suggest that the reasons for this disappointing performance are philosophic. Dynamic psychology is based on scientific philosophies which are outdated, ineffective, one-sided, and in terms of human values—dangerous. The outmoded philosophies to which I refer are the impersonal, abstract, static, externalized, control-oriented conceptions of nineteenth-century physics which led men to classify the elements and processes of a depersonalized subject matter and to determine the general laws which governed these elements and processes.

I am convinced of the need for a science of psychology which is existential and transactional. By *existential* I mean a concentration on flexible concepts and methods which grow out of the unique changing situation. By *transactional* I refer to an open collaborative attitude between the psychologist and the person studied.

Now at this point you have every right to ask about the meaning of these two terms—existential and transactional. Certainly any reasonable contract between author and reader would call for specifications of these terms, would call for operational definitions spelling out exactly how human ingenuity can be applied to human problems. How can we use our brains to do good and to do good well and to do good measurably well? May I summarize some of the specific ways in which we might make our endeavors more existential, i.e., more in tune with the specific reality:

1. Why not study natural data, events as they occur, rather than artificial situations which *we* arrange in our offices (e.g., tests, experiments)?

2. Why not use a conceptual language which arises from the data rather than imposing our own favorite, prefabricated variables upon the situation? Here I suggest we should be more flexible and eclectic in selecting concepts, recognizing the semantic flimsiness of verbal abstractions.

3. Since behavioral transactions are not static but continually

changing why not continue to collect natural records throughout the term of the transaction being studied? Why not expect
our techniques and our concepts to change throughout the term
of inquiry, as our subject matter changes?

4. Since behavioral transactions are not standardized, but always
   unique and then repeatable, why do we routinely rely on our
   own SLANT (Standardized Language for the Analysis of Transactions, e.g., tests)? Why not let the natural transaction produce
   its own records which we can SCORE* and measure and inter-
   relate? If and when the need for standardized tests grows collaboratively out of this natural situation, why not construct, revise,
   or design a measuring instrument for this unique situation?

5. Why do personality and clinical psychologists ignore or blur
   the difference between consciousness and behavior? Why not
   develop maps, models, and measures for describing inner events
   and relate these with separate models and measures for describing external behavior?

You will see that I am suggesting in these five points that we *not*
impose our favorite standard variables, tests, experiments, concepts, symbols on the situation. I see this as a form of intellectual narcissism which
Western science has held up as the ideal, and I am implying rather a collaborative surrender to the unique data, a yielding to the data, a calculated
and sensitive passivity to the idiosyncratic facts of the unique reality we
are studying. I suggest that we attempt to select from the enormous store-
house of verbal abstractions available to us those which seem to fit the
human situation we deal with. Let the situation determine the variables.

Next let me list some specific ways in which we can make our
endeavor transactional, i.e., emotionally realistic. Here I refer to methods by means of which we can accept and adjust to this following reality: that when we study our fellowman we must treat him as what he

---

*SCORE is shorthand for Schema for the Classification of Recorded Events.

is, a *human being,* and not as an object to be dissected, manipulated, controlled, predicted by scientists or clinicians.

1. The problem we study should not grow out of our intellectual needs or our practical concerns, or out of our professional inertia or our personal preoccupations, but should rather be a collaborative decision on the part of the subject and ourselves. The patient helps define the variables.
2. When feasible and relevant, the subject or patient should help design and construct the record-collecting devices or test forms.
3. The patient or subject should be seen and treated not as a passive thing to be done to but as the equal of the psychologist in the collaborative research. The patient, after all, is the world's leading authority on the issue at hand—his own life and the transactions in which he is involved. Here I am urging *phenomenological equality.* Always get the viewpoint of the patient on every issue, question, and decision, and treat this viewpoint as equal to your own.
4. I now come to the inevitable and unmistakable criterion of unreality and depersonalization on the part of the psychologist: *secrecy.* Although psychologists regularly claim to hold no secrets, although we are committed to the open society, although we say that the patient must help himself and work out his own solutions—in reality, we act as though there are secrets. Most of our psychometric, clinical, and institutional machinery is set up on the basis of secrecy. Our professional identity is tied to the mysterious, based on the practice of keeping information from the subject. But let us look at this secrecy in the cold light of the following reality. We are, after all, dealing with human beings. We cannot treat human beings objectively, i.e., as objects, without eliciting exactly the same reactions. If we depersonalize patients, rest assured they will depersonalize us back. If we keep secrets from them, rest assured they will keep secrets from us.

5. Next, I want to speak directly to the topic of this book: psycho-diagnosis. The notion of one person observing, measuring, and then forecasting the behavior of another grows out of the philosophy and methodology of nineteenth-century physics. I hold it to be dehumanizing and insulting, and, what is worse, ineffective. Note how diagnosis is based on secrecy. If we collaborate with the subject, plan and think with him then diagnosis in the classic sense is impossible. The design is corrupted. Note too that diagnosis is based on highly subjective symbol selection on the part of the scientist who decides what to measure. The collaborative sort of research which I am endorsing accepts a different notion of diagnosis and prediction. The subject and the therapist (i.e., the collaborators in the joint research) agree as to which natural records they wish to change. They set up criteria as goals and then they both work to meet the forecasted standards.

Clinical psychology, psychiatry, and psychotherapy are involved to a much greater degree than our professional pride would like us to admit in a complex, fascinating game of secrets with our clients. This game is entertaining. It is much more complex than chess, demanding knowledge of a broad set of vague concepts and repertoire of gamesmanship techniques. It is more important than chess, being played for the highest prizes known to man—profitable fees, life adjustments, and the most prized token of all, man's pride in his inviolacy and individuality.

But what does philosophy have to do with diagnosis? I think it has a lot to do with the topic of our book, for I believe that our philosophic assumptions underlie what men do. What we assume and think and what we do not think clearly underlie the behavior which follows. If we wish to appraise or improve the efficacy of our behavior as diagnostician, we must inquire into our assumptions about the reality which we confront.

In place of or in addition to the complex conceptions of modern dynamic psychology, I should like to suggest a very commonsense notion of human behavior. Men live two lives: an inner life of consciousness and an outer life of behavior. All the behavioral sciences, and all of their applications—education, social welfare, politics and political science— all these disciplines concern themselves with nothing more than how men experience and how men act. A realistic psychology is one which takes into account the uniqueness of human awareness, the incredible multilevel nature of consciousness—learned, sensory, somatic, cellular— and the relation of inner experience to behavior.

Underlying almost all theories of consciousness, whether they are dynamic, psychedelic, or nondynamic, is the basic premise: what a person does is determined by how he experiences, and what a person experiences is related to what he does. There are many qualifications to this axiom. Certainly we would want to distinguish between consciousness and talking. What a person says is often not what he experiences. Then, too, there are many awarenesses which do not lead to action directly and indeed may inhibit action. Included here would be fear fantasies, consummatory (as opposed to blueprint) fantasies, fantasies about the past, fantasies about supernatural events. All of these are, of course, related indirectly to future action and these relationships hinted at by dynamic psychology can, I believe, be studied quite simply and profitably by a realistic point of view. Let me illustrate. If an underdeveloped community states that it wants economic growth, but we discover that the consciousness of villagers is concerned with sexual imagery, then we can expect increases in the birth rate and a low economic rate of growth. There are, I recognize, many complications involved in these issues, which space prevents us from discussing.

Consciousness may well be the most misunderstood and overlooked aspect of human psychology. Our dynamic theories have consistently tended to mystify the topic of consciousness, forcing the content of man's awareness onto the procrustean bed of favorite concepts. Our social and moral norms often drive experience underground. Just as the dictator finds it difficult to penetrate the conforming behavioral facade of his subjects and can never tell what they really think, so do we psychologists run into walls (which we may call resistance and denial) when we seek to extract, for our own purposes, the inner content of our subjects.

Consciousness is the blueprint for action. Action is an expression of consciousness. What we rarely are aware of, we rarely do. People will share their inner blueprints with you when it is reasonable, feasible, and relevant *to their interests to* do so. They are eager to collaborate but reluctant to yield.

THE PHILOSOPHY OF THE INTERNAL AND EXTERNAL

Psychological diagnosis must take into account the difference between internal and external phenomena. Western psychology has never satisfactorily resolved the tension between internal-subjective and external-objective. We have consistently imposed the method, language, and goals of the external upon the internal continuum. *The two can be related only if their logical separation is kept clear.*

Art and Science

First, we must distinguish between two different approaches to reality—the scientific and the artistic.

Science is the study of behavior, events external to the experiencing nervous system. Science is the study of recorded movements and the communications of these movements to others for the purpose of changing their symbol systems.

Art is the study of experience, events registered *by* the molecular, cellular, somatic, and sensory communication systems within the body—and the communicating of these experiences to others, for the purpose of sharing, i.e., of "turning others on." Art can be just as precise, disciplined, systematic as the symbol systems of external science.

Existential-transactional diagnosis requires that the psychologist teach the patient how to be a scientist in observing his behavior and an artist in describing his experience.

Failure to make the distinction between external-internal, between the mechanically recorded external and the neurally registered internal, leads to a variety of confusions. It is necessary, first of all, to realize that a different ontology, epistemology, logic, ethic, and politics is required for internal and external events. Our notions about objectivity then become clarified. Only external events (recorded behavior) can become part of a scientific (game) contract. Internal events (sensory, somatic, cellular, molecular experience) require an artistic contract, i.e., an explicit contract between the "one-who-turns-others-on" and the "one-who-is-to-be-turned-on." The patient must become an artist who cares enough about the psychologist to turn-him-on to his experience.

Reality Is Experiential, Subject Matter Is Observable

Internal ontology concerns *reality,* which is always subjective-experiential. Reality is what is registered by your neurons, your cells, and your recognition molecules. External ontology concerns *subject matter,* which can be contractually defined within the scope of inquiry.

Truth Is Experiential, Fact Is Observable

Internal epistemology concerns *truth,* which is always subjective-experiential. *Truth* is what is registered by your neurons and cells and molecules. Thus in the internal, nongame world of direct experience there is no difference between truth and reality. External epistemology concerns *fact* which can be contractually legislated within the scope of inquiry. Words always define a subjective or experiential epistemology unless operationally defined.

Internal Logic Is Association, External Logic Is Symbol Relating

Internal logic concerns associations, which are always subjective-experiential, the connections made by your neurons and your molecular receptors. External logic deals with formal systems of *relating* external symbols.

Good Is Experiential, Right Is Observable

Internal ethics concerns the good, which is always subjective-experiential. Good is what feels good to your sensory, somatic, cellular, and molecular receptors. External ethics concerns rules governing behavior, which can be defined only within the scope of contract—the right and wrong of the game.

Internal Freedom and External Freedom

Internal politics concerns the freedom to move along the static-ecstatic continuum, freedom and control of consciousness. External politics concerns the freedom and control of behavior.

The philosophy presented above is summarized in Table 1.

TABLE I. THE PHILOSOPHY OF INTERNAL AND EXTERNAL

Philosophic Issues	Internal	External
which governs your experiencing and your behavior whether you know it or not.	i.e., within the sensory, somatic, cellular and molecular recognition systems—always private and unique to me—but communicable to other by means of art.	outside the nervous system—movements in space-time which can be made part of social contracts with others.
ONTOLOGY What is reality?	REALITY is always "my reality," what is registered by my cellular, neural, and molecular recognition sytems.	SUBJECT MATTER There can be no external or consensual reality, only subject matter agreed upon (or confusedly not-agreed-upon) with others.
EPISTEMOLOGY What is truth?	TRUTH is always "my truth," always unique. What I "know," i.e., what my cellular, neural, and molecular systems register, what I sense, experience.	FACT There can be no external truth, only facts consensually agreed upon in explicit game contracts with others (or disastrously implicit and different).

TABLE I (continued)

LOGIC	ASSOCIATIONS	RELATIONSHIPS
What is related to what and how?	The network of connections in my cellular, neural, and molecular systems that links units of "my reality." Always unique to me.	The connections of symbols and sequences of subject matters. Formal systems (grammatical, mathematical, or game) which should be consensually agreed upon explicitly with others.
ETHICS	GOOD AND BAD	RIGHT AND WRONG
What is good?	The attraction-repulsion network of "my unique imprint structure" What moves toward or away from the goals of "my games," biological or personal social.	in terms of external game rules, which should be consensually agreed upon with others, but which, disastrously, are usually implicit.
POLITICS	FREEDOM AND CONTROL	FREEDOM AND CONTROL
Freedom	of my own consciousness, or my own systems, cellular, neural, and molecular, my brain vs. my symbolic mind. Power or slavery of consciousness	of behavior, the familiar politics of social and personal behavior. Where you place your body and the movements you can make in space-time. External power or slavery.
CREATIVITY	NOVEL EXPERIENCE	NOVEL BEHAVIOR
	beyond symbols. Can be produced by ecstatic or psychedelic experience by molecular intervention.	can be taught or coached.
SYSTEMATIC STUDY AND COMMUNICATION	ART	SCIENCE
	Everyone is an artist (creative or robot) when they communicate about experience.	Everyone is a scientist (accurate or inaccurate) every time they study or communicate about events in space-time.

The Application of the Philosophy of Internal and External to Psychological Research

When we set out to study consciousness and such elusive states of consciousness as ecstasy, we must be specially sensitive to the delicate ontological web which we approach. Psychodiagnosis provides excellent illustrations of the effects of confusing these issues.

There is the observer's "subject matter" and there is the subject's "reality," and usually these have no relation. The psychiatrist sees hebephrenic psychosis while the subject may be experiencing molecular ecstasy. The outside observer has an entirely different view from the experiencing person.

There is the observer's "fact" and the subject's "truth." The psychiatrist asserts it is a fact that the subject sat in a catatonic state for two hours, refusing to talk; the subject knows the truth to be that he was spinning far out of space-time into an ecstatic dance of molecules which made words inadequate and irrelevant. Notice, of course, that both are "right." But the conflict in perspective leads the patient to feel misunderstood, makes the patient feel bad, and makes the psychologist feel frustrated. The aim of psychodiagnosis should be to make the patient feel wiser and feel good.

There is the logic which relates external symbols such as words and ritual sequences and there is the internal neurological association network—each cell in the brain connected on the average with 25,000 other cells and the number of associations per second greater than "the number of atoms in the universe." Observer logic and neurologic cannot communicate; so the patient is committed to the mental hospital.

There is the ethic of game rules and there is the molecular, cellular, somatic, sensory "feel-good."

There is the politics of external freedom and control and there is internal freedom, freedom from your own mind, freedom to feel good, freedom to let the cerebral network flash in associations without being limited to game perceptions, freedom to find "truth" within, freedom to contact a cellular or molecular reality beyond game dimensions.

From the standpoint of *science* there is the need for languages and measurement methodologies for external behavior, i.e., movements in space-time. From the standpoint of *art* there is the need for languages and methodologies capable of paying respect to the flowing complexity of the internal, the countless levels of neurological decoding, the countless levels of consciousness. Table 1 summarizes these distinctions and the different perspectives to which they give rise.

THE DIAGNOSIS OF BEHAVIOR

Once the philosophic distinctions between internal and external are clear the definition and the operations of behavioral psychology become straightforward. Indeed they become simplistic to the state of boredom. Pure behaviorism (excluding consciousness) is the measurement and control of robot action. The challenge of psychology is the systematic correlation of behavior and consciousness.

Behavioral science is human engineering. The empty and dull nature of this enterprise is concealed by the tendency to confuse behavior and consciousness. The terms used by psychologists and behavioral scientists tell us how the mind of the scientist works. Psychoanalytic theory, for example, tells us how analysts experience the world.

The languages used by psychologists to describe interpersonal events actually are removed from and unreliable projections onto behavior. Aggression, dominance, dependence do not refer to acts of people. They refer to states of mind. They are terms for describing consciousness.

Let me illustrate from my own studies of interpersonal behavior. In a lengthy series of investigations starting in 1948, I found that almost all the concepts in the English language which refer to interpersonal motives could be arranged in a two-dimensional grid. This circumplex model has been tested out in several subsequent studies by other psychologists (Leary, 1956; Lorr, 1962; Foa, 1961). Minor variations exist in placement around the circular continuum, but the interpersonal circle works. But why does it work? Did an omnipotent psychologist deity decide that interpersonal behavior is circular? To answer these questions you must make the external-internal distinction. The terms used by layman and psychologist to describe interpersonal events (and for that matter almost all events) have to do with implied motivation; they have nothing to do with movements in space-time. These terms refer to states of consciousness. We *experience* the world in terms of mythic images. The terms for our experience fall into a circumplex model because our Western consciousness is egocentric. Copernicus to the contrary, most of us really experience a geocentric universe and an egocentric world.

We naïvely experience the world in terms of radii extending out from us. Power is above us. Submission is south. We are compelled to and away from others in horizontal vectors. Our magnificent cortex is capable of experiencing complexity a thousandfold greater than our verbal language. But our simple conceptual minds cannot grasp more than two or three dimensions. In 1948 my own mind boggled at more than two dimensions for experienced interaction. Thus the circle of experience.

Behavior is movements in space-time, that is all. The ontological issue is single: movements in space-time.

Interpersonal behavior refers to the movements of two or more persons who share the same space-time.

Measurement of behavior is the recording and indexing of movements in space time. The decision as to which behavior to record and which indices to use is based on subjective choice on the part of the measurer. Transactional theory holds that the movements of any structure in space-time will be better understood if the experiential perspective from within the structure is known. The atomic physicist must "experience" like an atom. In psychodiagnosis the collaboration of the subject should be sought in the selection of what to record and what labels to use.

Psychotherapy is a complex and ontologically confusing game. It combines changes in consciousness (psyche) with a medical abstraction (therapy). Our Harvard research project (Leary, Metzner, and Alpert, 1965) did not use the term psychotherapy. We attempted collaboratively to alter or expand consciousness. We also tried collaboratively to change behavior. We tried to reduce helplessness—internal or external.

In order to develop a science of behavior we require new schemata and new languages for measuring and classifying movements in space-time. Our present schemata are inefficient because they confuse internal-external. They jumble together the observations, interpretations, evaluations of the experiencing scientist, with narrow measurements of the subject's behavior. Another source of inefficiency is the application of cumbersome global terms to broad-ranging sequences of changing movements.

These two confusions are illustrated by the case of the three Parisian Behavioral Diagnosticians. André, age 6, Marcel, age 8, and Pierre, age 10, walking through the Bois de Boulogne ran across an undressed couple making lively movements on the grass. André, age 6, exclaims, "Look, they are fighting." Marcel, a sophisticated 8, replies, "Oh, no, André, they are making love." Pierre, a true Parisian at 10, adds, "Yes, and very badly too."

The empirical studies of the reliability of psychiatric diagnosis suggest a similar difficulty in labeling and evaluating behavior in terms of global experiential terms.

There are two types of schemata for measuring behavior which correspond to the two aspects of my definition—(1) movements, (2) space-time. I should like to present first a model for classifying space-time factors and then proceed to schemata for measuring movements.

Classification of Space-Time Elements of Behavior

The first step in diagnosing behavior is to determine where the subject spends his time, how long, how frequently, and with whom. Location in space-time is a relatively straightforward task. Recording, measurement, and cartographical representation present certain economic and technical problems involving use of electronic devices, but philosophically the issues seem clear-cut.

The most direct measures of interpersonal behavior would be based on continuous recordings of movements, but for practical diagnostic purposes it is useful to collect samples locating the subject in space-time and clarifying the movements made. Let me illustrate. For a two-week period in 1962, I carried a kitchen timer bell with me throughout the day. At the moment of waking in the morning I would set it to ring in ten minutes and continued to reset it for ten-minute intervals until retiring in the evening. The bell set up an internal discipline of "waking-me-up," in the sense of G. I. Gurdjieff, and allowed a time-sample of my behavior (movements in space-time) during the day. As each shrill jangle interrupted my inner train of consciousness and my outer game sequence I would enter on a sheet: (1) the time, (2) the place, (3) a description of my behavior, (4) my posture, (5) number of others present, (6) behavior of others, (7) a classification of my behavior according to a game-classification. (See Table 2 on page 56.)

I also entered on the sheet a summary of my consciousness (where my head was at) in terms of a complex system of internal diagnosis (see last section, below).

A tabulation of these seven behavioral categories made it possible to construct summary indices on a daily and weekly basis (see Table 2). Such summary sheets reveal with amazing clarity my ecological and behavioral characteristics during this period. I note that five times more units were spent with daughter than son (oedipal factors?).
I note that 60 percent of my posture involved the barbarous instrument we call a chair (chairman behavior? power motives?). I note that 41 percent of the time was spent alone (introversion? alienation?).

A very powerful diagnostic and therapeutic tool is thus available to the psychologist. Diagnosis involves the subject himself studying his own behavior. This leads directly to the functional corollary: if you want to change your behavior, start by changing your space-time locations. My interpersonal relations could easily be changed by spending more time with my son, more time sitting on the floor looking up at others, and so on. (Changes in consciousness must go along with alterations of behavior to avoid robotization.)

TABLE 2. SHEET FOR RECORDING TEN-MINUTE SAMPLES OF SPACE-TIME LOCATIONS AND THE CONTENTS OF CONSCIOUSNESS

Time	Place	Movements	Posture	Others Present	Other's Movements	Other's Posture	Movements Indexed According to Game
9:30	Bed	Sleeping	Lying	0			Body maintenance
9:40	Bathroom	Washing	Standing	0			Body maintenance
9:50	Bedroom	Dressing	Standing	0			Body maintenance
10:00	Kitchen	Cooking	Standing	4	Eating	Sitting	Body maintenance
10:10	Kitchen	Cooking	Standing	4	Eating	Sitting	Body maintenance
10:20	Bedroom	Dressing	Standing	0			Body maintenance
10:30	Car	En route to church	Sitting	3	En route to church	Sitting	Religion
10:40	Church	Listening	Sitting	35	Listening	Sitting	Religion
4:00	Son's room	Watching TV	Sitting	1	Watching TV	Sitting	Recreation
4:10	Son's room	Watching TV	Sitting	1	Watching TV	Standing	Recreation
4:20	Daughter's room	Helping with homework	Standing	1	Homework	Sitting	Intellectual

The diagnosis of interpersonal behavior in noncircular form is also facilitated by the space-time location system. Here again we ignore such tempting variables as dominance-submission, hostility-affiliation (which reflect only our Western states of consciousness), and we focus simply on the basic interpersonal question: what space do they share? what time do they share? We thus define a powerful entity (in psychological jargon, a variable) which we might call intimacy, commitment, involvement. We might hazard a behavioral operational definition of *love as the amount of space-time shared.*

Here is the basic interpersonal issue—how much space-time will you share? Your office? Your home? Your bedroom? Your body? What kind of time will you share? Day or night? By appointment only?

The shared-space-time definition of love uplevels the emotional definition. The fact that the husband and wife spend thirty years together day and night is considered much more important than the kind of emotional game they play (fighting, submitting, cooing, dominating).

Table 3 on page 58 illustrates a matrix for diagnosing interpersonal behavior according to this behavioral scheme. Time is plotted along the horizontal axis—the more formal and briefer duration on the left and the more intensive, informal on the right. The space continuum runs from the most mutual public location (bottom) up to the most intimate (internal body space shared).

My hypothesis is this: all other factors (i.e., kinds of movements) being held constant—the more space-time shared the greater the influence in changing behavior. If you want to change someone's behavior—share space-time with him. Your space-time is the most valuable and potent instrument you have. Following this hypothesis we should expect that the upper right corner of the grid defines the most potent behavior-change relationships and the lower left the least. Thus we see that mother-child relationships (nine months of internal body sharing) and marital relationships (extended duration of internal body sharing) are the most potent situations. The college lecture and the doctor-patient interviews are the least potent. This hypothesis suggests that if you can't "mother them" or

TABLE 3. ILLUSTRATION OF A SIMPLIFIED SCHEMA
FOR CLASSIFYING SPACE-TIME ASPECTS
OF INTERPERSONAL BEHAVIOR

Space Sharing	Time Sharing		
	Low duration scheduled time— usually occupational	*Medium duration nonscheduled time—usually friendship*	*Extended duration—usually familial or tribal*
Sharing internal body space	Prostitution, transient sexual contacts	Lovers	Mother-child, husband-wife
Reciprocal home sharing	Mutual entertainment with colleagues, friends	Entertaining friends	Family or tribe
Neutral nonwork locations	Dining and recreational contacts	Dining, drinking, and recreational contacts	Family or tribal outings
His home only	Professor's tea for students		
Reciprocal office	Visits between colleagues		
His office only	Doctor-patient		
Public rooms	College lectures		

marry them, the best way to influence behavior is to engage in reciprocal home visits or meet regularly in extra-work locations (bars, restaurants, beaches). The most successful programs for dealing with our most difficult social "problems," Alcoholics Anonymous (Co-Founder, 1957), the Slack-Schwitzgebel street-corner project (Slack, 1960; Schwitzgebel, 1962), Synanon, Halfway Houses, and the student volunteer work with mental patients (Kantor and Greenblatt, 1962), utilize this principle and scrupulously avoid the power-loaded environment of the scheduled interview in the expert's office.

Other space-time grids can be constructed which specify other factors relevant to the inquiry at hand—free vs. paid time, free vs. paid space, day vs. night space, time sharing, and so on. Such schemata spotlight the most basic behavorial issues—where, when, and with whom.

There are many practical applications of such schemata. Often we get so involved with dynamic theories and diagnostic impressions that we forget that the first functional issue in behavior change is presence. Clinicians seem to prefer subjective internal language, so they talk about "motivation for treatment." Will the patient come? Will he continue to come? How can we change him if he won't share space-time with us?

During 1962–1963 our Harvard Psychedelic Project tested these theories in the rehabilitation of prisoners in a Concord, Massachusetts, reformatory. In the prison these space-time factors became dramatically and logically obvious. Consider a young "delinquent." He is sentenced to prison at age 19. Now who is going to shape his behavior? Those with whom he shares most space-time. And who are they? Other prisoners. The older convicts with whom he shares cell, meal table, shop bench, yard time (and very often body space). Old pros in the cops and robbers game. Next to other convicts he will share most time with guards. Many prison officers, like prisoners, share the same belief about the unchangeability of personality. "Cons are all alike, they don't want to change." "Cops are all alike. They'll never give you a fair shake." Onto this scene comes the middle-class professional. He calls the convict into his room in the prison clinic and spends from thirty to forty minutes a week. His well-intentioned interventions according to the space-time formula are pitifully limited. The same situation exists in mental hospitals. Fellow patients, attendants, nurses, and doctors—a descending order of behavior-change potency. A recent book by Kesey (1962) has presented this issue in beautiful detail.

What are the implications of the space-time formula? First—don't send the kid to prison. Keep the disturbed person out of the hospital. Keep them outside, sharing time and space with persons whom you want them to emulate. If incarceration or commitment is necessary then do everything you can to change the movements (talk and action) of the persons with whom the subject shares space-time. In our prison project we spent most of our time with older convicts discussing rehabilitation programs and coaching them to lead groups for other convicts. Convicts act as research technicians, test interpreters, tutors for university graduate students (Leary et al., 1965a). The more responsibility for behavior change assigned to convicts, guards, fellow patients, attendants, the more behavior will change. The role of the professional changes too in the light of the space-time formula. The number of patients or clients with whom we can share even formal occupational office space-time is limited. The professional should share his space-time with those who share intimate space-time with the subjects. They are the effective change agents. The professional becomes collaborative consultant rather than doctor or therapist.

Measuring Movements

Behavior is movements in space-time. The preceding section has discussed a schema, a formula, and some applications of the space-time issue. We shall now consider the measurement of the second part of the definition—*movements.*

Remember our three youthful French diagnosticians? When they leave the Bois de Boulogne and report to the folks back home, what is the epistemological status of their observations? No records exist of the movements they observed. Their report is subjective. What exists is their memory. This points up a basic issue about behavior which is often overlooked. From the scientific point of view we never study behavior—a jumble of observed movements in the grass—we can only study records of behavior. We observe movements. But we measure and index records.

The ontology and epistemology of the behavioral sciences is quite simple. There are only four kinds of records of behavior:

1. Records of muscle movements, physiological or cinematographic.
2. Records of vocal movements (tape recordings).
3. Nonverbal artifactual records of behavior (Greek vases, drawings, things made).
4. Records of verbal behavior (written or spoken).

Since 1955 I have been developing schemata for counting and measuring records of natural behavior (Leary, 1964a; Leary and Gill, 1959): process analysis of the freely expressed. Behavior can be described in terms of indices based on objective counts. A tape recording of verbal behavior during a ten-minute period yields up one hundred indices (counts not ratings) which can be charted as they vary over time. The molecular units are simple counts of movements. How many words spoken? How many references to self? How many references to mother? Interpersonal behavior is described in terms of comparisons of the patterns of indices of the participants sharing the same space-time.

The comparisons of the participants in terms of the simplest counted indices provide exciting and revealing evidence of the interchange. Figure 1 presents an illustrative profile of one type of verbal movements made by a patient and therapist during twelve hours of psychotherapy. The

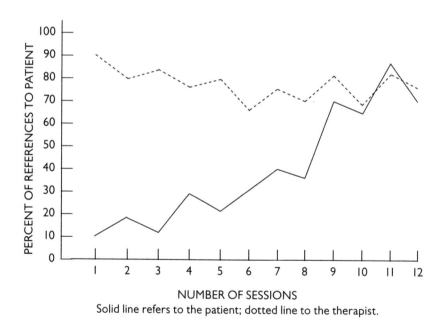

NUMBER OF SESSIONS
Solid line refers to the patient; dotted line to the therapist.

Figure 1. Percentage of Verbal Movements by Patient and Therapist Referring to Patient as Subject during Twelve Hours of Psychoanalytically Oriented Psychotherapy

therapy sessions were taped and transcribed. Nonprofessional technicians counted the number of references to the patient by the patient and by the therapist. The index percent of references to patient (Pt%) is obtained by dividing the number of references to patient by the total number of statements in the interview.

First, we notice that the patient refers to herself only 10 percent of the time during the first session and continues to avoid herself as subject until the ninth session. From this time on, her verbal noises can be scored as referring to herself at least 50 percent of the time. Profiles of indices of behavior varying over time can be irrelevant or vitally useful depending upon the task-goal. In this illustration the reluctance to talk about self in the early sessions could be experienced by and labeled by a clinician as externalization. This one profile tells us some little thing of importance—she starts off not talking about herself.

But when we consider the therapist's profile a more meaningful pattern emerges. We notice the extreme discrepancy. In the first session the therapist is concentrating on little else than the patient (87 percent). Her low indices now take on greater significance. The patient and therapist are clearly not together. She refuses to discuss *his* topic—her. And the therapist is not following her conversational lead.

Indices of the free natural movements of persons sharing space and time are invariably dynamic and revealing. This type of measure is obvious, molecular, simple to convert and index, and loaded with philosophic and social dynamite.

First there is the linguistic reform. A new language develops; a language of objective indices based on molecular events. Pt% means percent of references to the patient. The term $(Pt^1—Pt^2)$ defines a discrepancy—the references of speaker 1 compared with those of speaker 2. In another publication (Leary et al., 1965a) I have presented a language of over seventy indices which can be combined into thousands of discrepancy terms (comparing the same speaker at different times or different speakers at the same time). This reduces and can even eliminate the need for a verbal, conceptual language. The index language of behavior becomes like that of chemistry: a list of basic indices and an endless list of possible combinations. Chemistry would be slow to advance if it depended on verbal vocabulary—salt, sugar; the situation is no different for a psychology of behavior.*

There is a second philosophic implication underlying profiles of natural records. Notice that we score and index the therapist's behavior as well as that of the patient. A strict behavioral approach is also existential in that the subject-object, doctor-patient relationship is undercut. Figure 1 ruthlessly profiles the movements of both participants without distinction of role or status. The approach is automatically transactional—forcing us to the recognition that all our contexts are interpersonal and that we never study a patient but always the patient-in-his-interpersonal-field.

In a preceding section I have mentioned Schema for the Classification Of Recorded Events (SCORE). The SCORE technique of recording and indexing movements has two implications of which we must be aware. SCORE does not rely on the verbal concepts and theoretical abstractions upon which we psychologists rely. Perhaps even more radically, it puts the doctor-scientist-expert into the field of inquiry alongside the patient.

The same two issues reappear when we study the interpersonal implications of psychological tests. Psychological tests are paradoxical procedures. They are based on a philosophy which postulates essences or enduring internal traits and which encourages the notion that one group of people (professionals) can study another group (patients or subjects) in terms of the phenomenological abstractions held by the professionals. Most psychologists are democratic by temperament and intellectually committed to field, cultural, and interpersonal assumptions. Yet they routinely rely upon tests and experiments which are manipulative and one-sided, which measure the movements of only one member of the transaction. This is not very democratic.

---

*Psychology, unlike chemistry, has also to deal with internal events—experience, consciousness. A different set of terms and methods are required for the internal.

We have found it more profitable to stick to an interpersonal point of view in our scientific posture as well as our concepts. Whenever it is feasible and reasonable we collect records from all participants—not just in free, natural recordings, but also where tests or standardized structural instruments are used, and even in the doctor-patient situation in diagnosis.

When we use the interpersonal checklist (a standardized form) we ask the patient to rate himself and his therapist. We also ask the therapist to rate himself as well as the patient. Patients, clients, subjects are diagnosing professionals all the time. It is only good sense to include within the scope of inquiry the patient's diagnoses and therapist's responses to tests.

The conventional one-sided, patient-only test does not of course lend itself to interpersonal measures, because these tests are designed to measure internal traits. For interpersonal* measurement, a different type of assessment instrument is required—one which is designed for the specific situation, often constructed by all participants, filled out by all participants, and interpreted by all. The standardized language of the test holds only for the interpersonal group (i.e., the group who share space-time). Such an instrument would have to be modified to fit a different interpersonal context. Thus we have the Smith Family Mood Questionnaire, the Ace Company Creativity Scale.

THE DIAGNOSIS OF CONSCIOUSNESS

Consciousness is energy received by structure. Structure is energy in transitional state. There are as many levels of consciousness in the universe as there are forms of energy. Each form of energy creates structures which receive, store, and transform it.

There are as many levels of consciousness available to the human

---

Interpersonal is used here as movement of two or more persons sharing the same space-time.

being as there are neurological, sensory, anatomical, cellular, molecular, atomic structures within the human body. The human body is a galaxy of communication systems, i.e., energy patterns being sent and received by structure. When a psychologist sets outs to define the levels of consciousness he usually comes up with mental abstractions which tell us only about his own trip. The classic levels of consciousness are varieties of "game symbols." Thus, Freud defines the conscious as routine, conventional, normal game awareness; the unconscious as unthinkable, naughty (repressed) games, and the superego as consciousness of highly valued good games. Freud is not defining different levels of awareness, he is simply listing symbols of differing social meaning. Such listings differ among psychologists and from culture to culture.

An empirical, existential psychology of consciousness recognizes the energy-structure nature of consciousness, defines the levels of consciousness in terms of observable physical structures, and specifies the chemical-electrical processes which produce the predicted level of consciousness. The topic of human consciousness has vexed psychologists and philosophers for thousands of years. Why? Because of the lack of scientific instrumentation and empirical knowledge about the physiology and biochemistry of the human body and the life process.

The body is the seat and center of consciousness. Our theory of consciousness must come to its senses and resurrect the body. Consciousness is a biochemical process. Our knowledge of consciousness must be based on our understanding of psychochemical process. An empirical science of consciousness had to await the development of instruments for changing consciousness. Before the discovery of the microscope, physiology and medicine were crude sciences based on macroscopic observation. Before the discovery of psychedelic chemicals, psychology and psychiatry were in the same state as physiology and medicine before the microscope. We are now able to define the different levels of consciousness, to produce them, to study them systematically, and to make our observations of consciousness replicable.

At our present level of neurological and biochemical understanding (crude and primitive) it is appropriate to consider seven levels of consciousness:*

1. Sleep
2. Stupor
3. Symbolic
4. Sensory
5. Somatic
6. Cellular
7. Molecular

The order in which these levels of consciousness are listed is based on the age, speed, power, complexity, expansiveness, and planful wisdom of the energy-structure.

Molecular energy, for example, is older, faster, more complex, more pervasive, and "wiser" than the cellular. Molecules plan, design, and manufacture grosser forms of energy structure. Cellular structure is older, more enduring, more complex, more pervasive, and wiser than bodies and somatic organs, etc. The DNA code plays its game in terms of species, classes, and Linnaean kingdoms—animal versus botanical.

Psychological diagnosis (except in the most administrative sense) cannot be carried out unless the diagnostician is aware of the level of consciousness (or combination of levels) of the other. In the words of those born after 1945, the diagnostic question is: "Where is your head at?" The seven levels just listed help you locate your head.

Notice that each of these levels of awareness can be produced or turned off by chemicals—naturally produced by or introduced into the body:

---

*These levels of consciousness are described in greater detail in other publications: Leary, 1962, 1964a, 1964b, 1965a, 1965b, 1965c, 1966a, 1966b, 1967; Leary, Metzner, and Alpert, 1965; Metzner, 1963; Weil, Metzner, and Leary, 1965. The applications of this theory of consciousness to issues of diagnosis, measurement, and psychotherapy are presented in the following publications: Fisher, 1963; Leary, 1965d, 1966b; Leary et al., 1965a.

1. *Sleep* is produced by fatigue by-products or opiates, barbiturates, tranquilizers. These chemicals "turn-off" emotions, symbol discrimination, sensory awareness, etc.

2. *Stupor,* including emotional awareness (emotional states are a form of stuporous consciousness contraction), is produced by endocrine processes and by alcohol. These chemicals turn-off symbol discrimination, sensory awareness, somatic sensitivity, etc.

3. *Symbolic awareness* is facilitated by undefined psychoactive humors (serotonin?) and by energizers such as caffeine, coca, pep pills. These chemicals turn-off sensory awareness, somatic sensitivity, cellular memory, etc.

4. *Sensory awareness* is produced naturally by biochemical-electrical stimulation of the nerve endings of the external sense organs and facilitated by marijuana and mild doses of more powerful psychedelic chemicals (hashish, mescaline, LSD). Powerful sensory stimuli and chemicals like marijuana can focus consciousness away from (i.e., turn off) emotional, symbolic, somatic, cellular, and molecular awareness or can entangle these latter in hallucinatory combinations.

5. *Somatic awareness* is produced naturally by energy exchanges at the sympathetic and parasympathetic nerve endings of the internal somatic organs and by exercises or chemicals which specifically stimulate somatic organs. Autonomous nervous system activity turns-off emotional, symbolic, sensory, cellular, and molecular consciousness or entangles these latter in hallucinatory combinations.

6. *Cellular awareness* is produced naturally at the intersection points between the neurological and the cellular and can be induced by the more powerful psychedelics—psilocybin, mescaline, LSD. Here we deal with "out-of-the-body" experiences, racial and phylogenetic memories which have been reported throughout human history and which have been substantiated by leading philosophers (some Western, mainly

Eastern) and psychologists (including Fechner, Jung, Freud, William James).

7. *Molecular consciousness* is produced by strong doses of LSD, and such newer psychedelics as STP.

The state of consciousness known by that vague, catch-all term *hallucinatory* is explained, in this system, as a double or multiple exposure of two or more levels of consciousness. Hallucinations are real. They are combinations of two or more levels of reality. Imagine looking at your doctor's face—one eye normal, the other eye attached to a microscope. The resulting sensory collage is analogous to a hallucination. From the standpoint of psychiatric diagnosis, it is crucial that the diagnostician understand the various levels of consciousness and be alert to the level of the patient. Logical, symbolic communication is distorted or vitiated when the other-one's consciousness is at a nonsymbolic level. This is often confusing and frustrating to the diagnostician who operates exclusively at the logical-symbolic level.

Imagine the diagnostic or psychometric interaction between a "straight" doctor and a patient at these different levels of awareness:

1. Patient sleeps; he does not respond. He is diagnosed as comatose. He cannot play the symbol game with the doctor.

2. Patient is in a stuporous or intoxicated state. He reacts to the doctor's symbols only in emotional behavior: cries, laughs, snarls, boasts. Patient is diagnosed as psychotic or delirious or drunk. The doctor must change the patient's level of consciousness before he engages in symbolic communication.

3. Patient is at symbolic level of consciousness. Conventional communication results: "How are you?" "I am depressed."

4. Patient is at the sensory level. Doctor talks symbolically. Patient centers on fact that doctor has bad breath (olfactory) or that the light shines eerily off the yellow stain on the doctor's teeth. Communication is impossible but the patient gets blamed for

being psychotic. A sensitive diagnostician attempts to "tune-in" on the patient's level of consciousness.

If the patient is caught at the level of sensory awareness you can reach him only through the senses. A good diagnostician, therapist, priest, husband, etc. can "turn-on" to the level of consciousness of the other-one.

5. Patient's consciousness is trapped at somatic level—let us say in the circulatory system. Doctor suggests patient go to the dance tonight. Patient is aware of blood pumping up his arteries, squeezing into the capillary network in his skull. He feels blood dripping in his head. His head feels marshy and soggy. How can he consider going to the dance? The sensitive clinician determines that the patient's consciousness is trapped in his body and knows how to contact and free the patient.

6. The patient's consciousness is flipped out beyond the body into cellular memories. His protein file cards are spinning racial recollections. He sees the doctor as a furry wolf, a thin, long-legged heron, an ominous dark spider. He cringes. The doctor labels the patient psychotic. He could say: "You see me as many things. I am friendly and want to help you."

7. The patient is spun into the molecular level of consciousness. Everything—his body, the outside world—is seen as a shimmering mosaic of vibrations. The psychiatrist is seen as a shuttling pattern on the retinal TV screen. The patient is transfixed in wonder and confusion.

Each of these levels of personality has many sublevels, defined in terms of observable structure. At the symbolic level the game must be defined in terms of the criteria of social games. At the sensory level consciousness can be trapped in the eye, ear, nose, etc. An enormously complex but operationally obvious system for the diagnosis of consciousness is available.

Space-time-game classifications diagnose behavior. Where is the patient's body at? The seven levels of consciousness diagnose where the patient's head is at. Accurate localization of behavior and consciousness is the task of diagnosis. Accurate diagnosis, collaboratively worked out with the patient, is effective therapy for both patient and doctor.

REFERENCES

Co-Founder. *Alcoholics Anonymous comes of age.* New York: Harper, 1957.

Fisher, G. Dosage levels of psychedelic compounds for psychotherapeutic experiences. *Psychedelic Rev.,* 1963, No. 1.

Foa, U. Convergences in the analysis of the structure of interpersonal behavior. *Psychol. Rev.,* 1961, **68** (No. 5), 341–55.

Kantor, D., and Greenblatt, M. Wellmet: a house where students lead mental patients to rehabilitation. *Ment. Hosp.,* March 1962.

Kesey, K. *One flew over the cuckoo's nest.* New York: Viking Press, 1962.

Leary, T. *Interpersonal diagnosis of personality.* New York: Ronald Press, 1956.

———. How to change behavior. *Proceedings of Fourteenth Congress of Applied Psychology.* Copenhagen: Munksgaard Press, 1962.

———. The effects of test score feedback on creative performance and of drugs on creative experience. Paper read at 1962 Utah Conference on Creativity. In C. W. Taylor (Ed.), *Widening horizons in creativity.* New York: Wiley, 1964a.

———. Introduction. In D. Solomon (Ed.), *LSD—the consciousness expanding drug.* New York: Putnam, 1964b.

———. *Measuring verbal interaction in Freudian and Rogerian psychotherapy.* Millbrook, N.Y.: Unitas Press, 1964c.

———. The experiential typewriter. *Psychedelic Rev.,* 1965a, No. 7.

———. Neo-symbolic communication of experience. *Psychedelic Rev.,* 1965b, No. 8.

———. Programmed communication during the psychedelic session. *Psychedelic Rev.,* 1965c, No. 8.

———. The religious experience: its production and its interpretation. In G. Weil, R. Metzner, and T. Leary (Eds.), *The Psychedelic Reader,* New Hyde Park, N.Y.: University Books, 1965d.

———. Politics and ethics of ecstasy. *Cavalier,* July 1966a.

———. *Psychedelic Prayers after the Tao te Ching.* New Hyde Park, N.Y.: University Books, 1966b.

———. The politics, ethics and meaning of marijuana. In D. Solomon (Ed.), *Marihuana papers,* New York: Bobbs-Merrill, 1967.

Leary, T., and Clark, W. H. The religious implications of consciousness-expanding drugs. *Religious Educ.,* 1963.

Leary, T., and Gill, M. The dimensions and a measure of the process of psychotherapy: a system for the analysis of content of clinical evaluations and patient-therapist interactions. In E. A. Rubenstein and M. B. Parloff (Eds.), *Research in psychotherapy.* Washington, D.C.: American Psychological Association, 1959. Pp. 62–95.

Leary, T., Metzner, R., Presnell, M., Weil, G., Schwitzgebel, R., and Kinne, S. A change program for adult offenders using psilocybin. *Psychother.,* 1965a, **2,** 61–72.

Leary, T., Metzner, R., and Alpert, R. *The Psychedelic Experience.* New Hyde Park, N.Y.: University Books, 1965b.

Lorr, M. Approaches to interpersonal behavior schema. Paper read at Seventh Annual Research Conference on Chemotherapy Studies in Psychiatry and Broad Research Approaches to Mental Illness. Veterans Administration, Cincinnati, Ohio, March 27, 1962.

Metzner, R. The pharmacology of psychedelic drugs. *Psychedelic Rev.,* 1963, No. 1.

Schwitzgebel, R. Critical analysis and evaluation of the experimenter-subject role relationship in the reduction of known male adolescent crime. Unpublished doctoral dissertation. Harvard University, 1962.

Slack, C. Experimenter-subject psychotherapy: a new method introducing intensive office treatment for unreachable cases. *Ment. Hyg.,* 1960, **44** (No. 2), 238–56.

Weil, G., Metzner, R., and Leary, T. *The psychedelic reader.* New Hyde Park, N.Y.: University Books, 1965.

3

On Set and Setting Theory

Reactions to Psilocybin Administered in a Supportive Environment

Timothy Leary, George H. Litwin, and Ralph Metzner

This article represents the early phase of Leary's scientific work with psilocybin. Leary had begun lecturing at Harvard in the spring of 1960 and, after his initial life-changing experience with magic mushrooms in Cuernavaca in the summer of that year, the Harvard psychologist opted to completely change the focus of his research when he returned to Cambridge that fall. Given his rebirth experience in Mexico, Leary was convinced that psychedelic drugs were the new frontier of psychology and therapy. Leary ordered a large supply of psilocybin (synthesized magic mushrooms) from Sandoz* and began experimenting with the drug and devising a research agenda that eventually became the Harvard Psilocybin Project.

---

*Sandoz was the Swiss pharmaceutical company that pioneered the development of various hallucinogenic drugs (LSD and psilocybin) in the 1950s and early 1960s. Albert Hofmann, the chemist who discovered LSD in 1943, worked for Sandoz; Hofmann was also the first chemist to synthesize Mexican magic mushrooms (psilocybin).

"Reactions to Psilocybin Administered in a Supportive Environment" is significant because it represents one of the first attempts to move psychedelic research out of the medical environment (hospitals and mental illness facilities) and into comfortable domestic settings. Leary and his researchers attempted to administer the drug in an informal environment (Leary's living room). The emphasis on "set" (mind-set of the user) and "setting" (providing pleasant social environment) was crucial to the Harvard Psilocybin Project. Leary and his research team—Metzner and Litwin—pushed the boundaries of what constitutes a psychedelic drug experience; they provided "easy chairs, rugs, and cushions" as well as "a wide range of recorded music, books, paintings and prints." In many cases, food and drink were also offered to make the participants feel at ease. As mentioned previously but bears repeating again, Leary and his co-authors stressed the importance of a comfortable and relaxed set and setting because they discovered that bad trips could be virtually eliminated if a warm and supportive social environment was provided for the subjects.

This article also contains a critical overview of the research literature on hallucinogenic drugs in the early 1960s; it references "psychotomimetic theory" (the notion that hallucinogenic drugs induce model forms of psychosis), as well as studies that suggest that psychedelic drugs produce mystical and religious experiences. The psychotomimetic theory, which was popular in the 1950s, was becoming obsolete in the early 1960s. Its reductive premise—that psychedelic drugs were dangerous drugs that produce temporary psychosis—was too one-dimensional for most LSD researchers. As mentioned in the Introduction, Sidney Cohen's salient study, "LSD and Side Effects" (1960), proved that "with proper precautions . . . [hallucinogenic drugs] are safe when given to a selected healthy group" (39). Cohen's study also indicated that "occasional complications" (i.e., bad trips) could be avoided if "certain safeguards" are applied. Cohen's article disproved the psychotomimetic theory because it was based on extensive research (5,000 individuals who had taken LSD and mescaline on over 25,000 occasions). Leary, Metzner, and Litwin's article builds on Cohen's work and offers research that disproves the basic tenets of the psychotomimetic thesis. A key discovery for Leary was the notion that psilocybin greatly "heightens suggestibility" in the subject. Thus, if the researchers present aesthetic stimuli to the participant during the trip the user will, in most cases, have a positive experience with psilocybin.

In the early 1960s, the recognized importance of set and setting enlarged the medical and therapeutic parameters of the psychedelic experience. For Leary and other progressive researchers, the science of programming "good trips" was the new paradigm for therapy and "behavior change" advocates in the field of psychology.

JAMES PENNER

REFERENCES

Cohen, Sidney. "Lysergic Acid Diethylamide: Side Effects and Complications." *The Journal of Nervous and Mental Disease* 130, no. 1 (1960): 30–40.

REACTIONS TO PSILOCYBIN ADMINISTERED IN A SUPPORTIVE ENVIRONMENT

From the *Journal of Nervous and Mental Disease* 137, no. 6 (1963): 561–73.

Timothy Leary, Ph.D., George H. Litwin, A.B., and Ralph Metzner, Ph.D.

Center for Research in Personality, Harvard University, Cambridge, Massachusetts.

The authors wish to express their gratitude to Dr. Carl Henze and Mr. Sidney Gimpel of Sandoz Laboratories, which supplied psilocybin, and to Richard Alpert, Gunther Weil, Sheila Sostek, and Mrs. Pearl Chan for their cooperation and help. This project was supported in part by grants from the Uris Brothers Foundation and from the Laboratory of Social Relations, Harvard University.

◆ ◆ ◆

In recent decades Western civilization has discovered that the inges-tion of certain plants can produce astonishing effects upon human consciousness. This information has been held for centuries by certain non-literate tribes who have used the plants in religious and medical procedures. Interest in these substances has been stimulated by the achievement of chemists, most notably Dr. Albert Hofmann, of the Sandoz Laboratories in Basel, Switzerland, who have succeeded in syn-thesizing the active agents in these plants. Among these the best known are the peyote cactus, from which mescaline is derived, the mushroom *psilocybe mexicana,* the South American vine *yage* or *caapi,* and the seed of *ololiuqui,* also from Mexico. LSD-25, an ergot derivative, is an artifi-cially synthesized substance with properties and effects similar to these others. The substance used in a recent study is *psilocybin,* a synthetic of the Mexican "sacred mushroom" introduced to Americans by the mycologist R. Gordon Wasson. The active ingredient, psilocybin, was synthesized by Dr. Hofmann.[6, 11]

The physiological action of these drugs is not well understood, although some investigators have suggested that the common biochemi-cal denominator may be the indole nucleus, which is found in most of these drugs and is also in serotonin. Elkes[5] provided an excellent review of the relevant literature.

Both from our own observations and from a survey of the litera-ture one may conclude: 1) that these substances are not "addictive,"[2] i.e., although tolerance develops, no case of addiction has ever been reported; 2) they are neither sedatives nor tranquilizers—subjects often report heightened sensitivity to stimuli and excitability and there is no evidence that the drugs have anxiety-reducing effects; 3) they cannot be classed with energizers or stimulants, since although there is increased sensitivity there is usually a reduction in task-oriented energy, and sub-jects often sit very quietly. Although some investigators[1] have classified these drugs as "psychotomimetic" (i.e., as inducing "model psychoses"), others have reported that "mystical" or "religious" experiences are produced.[11] It is clear from these disagreements that attempts at strict categorization of the effects of these materials are premature. It is the present hypothesis that the attitude of the experimenter toward the subject matter is an important variable. It influences the expectation or set which he communicates to his subjects, and it determines what kind of setting he provides for the ingestion of the drug; these in turn have marked effects on the nature of the experience.

Most investigators would, however, agree to the statement that these drugs alter consciousness. The purpose of the present research was to investigate some of the ways in which consciousness may be altered. The two major practical difficulties in carrying out such an inquiry are 1) the role of set and suggestion, mentioned above, and 2) the fact that both everyday and scientific language are extremely inadequate for describing altered states of consciousness.

METHOD

There are several ways of handling the problem of variability in expectation. This study is a preliminary investigation of unusual states which have little or no place in existing social situations. The writers have attempted to impose few preconceptions or rituals of their own on the experience, in order to obtain as wide a variety of reactions as possible. In other words, subjects (Ss) have been allowed to bring their own rules, roles and games to the experience. In practice this led to a broadly conceived "naturalistic" setting.

To create a relaxed and natural atmosphere, the drug was given in comfortable home surroundings. Because the desired facilities were not available, the living rooms of the homes of the senior investigators were used. It was possible to close off these rooms from the rest of the house and prevent interruptions. All of the rooms were moderate or large in size. Easy chairs, rugs and cushions formed the basic furniture. A wide range of recorded music, books and paintings or prints was made available. Food and drink were offered. Lighting and other such matters were left to the choice of the experimental group members. The only exceptions are the experimental sessions conducted for prison inmates, which were run in a large separate room in the prison hospital, furnished as comfortably as possible with beds, mattresses, table and chairs. Recorded music and some books were also available there.

No psychological or medical test procedures were introduced during the session. *Ss* were requested to fill out a questionnaire and write a detailed free report about their experiences after the session was terminated. A psychiatrist was present or on call in the majority of sessions, although comprehensive psychiatric examinations were not performed. Psychological fitness of *Ss* was determined by a panel of clinical psychologists on the basis of interviews and informal talks. No *Ss* were rejected outright on psychological grounds, although several persons who volunteered were dissuaded from participating as a result of discussions about the experience with the writers.

Although no formal preparation took place, informal discussions were held with every *S* and with each experimental group prior to the experimental session. These were question-and-answer discussions for the most part, in which the group leader tried to do the following: 1) give some sense of the range of possible experiences, from religious, through therapeutic or "insight" experiences, to psychotic-like states that could include terror and loss of reality contact; 2) advise individuals who were very hesitant not to participate; 3) describe the typical experiences that were occurring in the writers' research, which were mostly very pleasant, and to create the feeling that a pleasant or even ecstatic experience was possible; 4) give some information on the effects of dosage. *Ss* were allowed to regulate their own dosage within a safe maximum set by the experimenter (*E*). *Ss* participated in determining the composition of the group in which they were to take the drug, and wherever possible it was arranged that each *S* have at least one friend present.

All experimental sessions were conducted by an experienced

group leader, usually one of the senior investigators. One or more experienced members of the research project served as assistant group leaders. To create a sense of equality and shared experience, and to dispel the fear that often accompanies relationships between *E*s and *S*s, at least one of the research team took the drug with *S*s.

In the present study the three sources of data were 1) a questionnaire filled out by *S*s after the experience; 2) a free subjective description of their reactions,* and 3) behavioral observations by *E*. The present report concentrates on the questionnaire responses.

SUBJECTS

During the course of this first naturalistic study psilocybin was administered to 175 *S*s, of which 127 were men and 48 were women. The median age was 29.5 years, with 70 per cent of *S*s falling in the range 22 to 35 years.

All *S*s were volunteers and unpaid. The selection factor constitutes an important limitation. During the past 18 months the writers have been engaged in lecturing and talking to many people about psilocybin. Of those who hear about this work, it was estimated that roughly one-third are immediately interested, one-third neutral, and one-third have strong reservations about participating in such a project. *S*s used in this study do not sample this wide range of initial reactions: most naturally come from the first group. This has strong implications for the "set" or "expectation" of *S*s. Although no data on "set" were collected prior to the drug experiences, the content of the informal discussions coupled with the volunteers' bias would suggest a fairly strong positive "set," that is, for a pleasant and insightful experience.

As to occupation, *S*s included graduate students, professional writers and artists, academic psychologists, musicians, housewives and inmates of a correctional institution.

---

*Coding schemes for analyzing the content of free response descriptions of altered state of consciousness are being developed and these data will appear in later papers. Following this study a much more extensive questionnaire was developed and is being used.

DOSAGE

Most previous research with psilocybin used dosages around five to ten milligrams. The writers have, however, found it useful to allow a much wider range of dosage. A reasonable and safe limit was established, and *S*s were allowed to determine their own dosage under this limit. The writers' position has been that 0.5 mg. per kg. of body weight is a reasonable limit to set for a six- to eight-hour period.

The actual median dosage in the present study was 16 mg. of psilocybin. The total range was from four mg. to 100 mg. and the interquartile range was from 12 mg. to 20 mg. Large doses (over 50 mg.) were a result of second ingestions after a considerable time lapse (eight to twelve hours). The distribution of dosages is very modal, the most frequent dosages being 12 mg. and 20 mg. This is undoubtedly a result of *E*s' suggestion that 12 mg. would be a "moderate" dose and 20 mg. a "full" dose for a person of normal size. When body weight is controlled for, the median dosage is 0.23 mg. per kg. and the interquartile range from 0.16 to 0.30 mg. per kg.

RESULTS

1. All *S*s are presently alive and healthy. No lasting physical effects were reported or observed. The sample included a woman who volunteered to take psilocybin at an average of two-week intervals during pregnancy with the knowledge and approval of her obstetrician. For a period of one year after delivery, both mother and child have showed no detrimental effects whatsoever. The mother reported that her own mental status and her reaction to the baby were much improved over those in four earlier pregnancies.

2. No psychological casualties were reported. No *S*s were hospitalized or developed enduring psychotic or neurotic symptoms within a six-month period after the ingestion of psilocybin during which follow-up data were obtained.

3. With respect to dosage, 20 to 30 mg. seems to have provided an optimal initial experience in a group setting.

4. There was no tendency towards addiction. While approximately ninety per cent of *S*s stated that they want to repeat the experience some time, there is no evidence for physical or psychological dependence. There were no withdrawal symptoms or serious hangovers. Indeed, after one or two very profound or "shattering" insight experiences, *S*s typically tended to regard further ingestions with some ambivalence.

5. Psilocybin appears to be somewhat different in effects from both mescaline and LSD. These differences are relatively minor compared to the similarities in the effects of expectation and setting. Characteristically, the psilocybin experiences seemed to last four to six hours, while both mescaline and LSD produce experiences lasting eight to twelve hours. In the dosages used in the present study (12–30 mg.) psilocybin produced a milder reaction than the standard dosages of mescaline (500 mg.) or LSD (100–200 μg.) reported in the literature. A few experiences with very high doses of psilocybin (60–80 mg.) have suggested that it is also capable of producing the deeper and more radical type of experience usually reported with LSD.

Before presenting the results of the questionnaire some observations on *controls* and *placebos* might be in order. It is customary in evaluating the effect of a new drug to compare it with the effects of an inert substance, under "double-blind" conditions. This technique has not been adopted here because the writers' primary interest lies not so much in the particular pharmacologic substance involved (as opposed to other substances) but in the psychological processes produced by some radically new and unusual experiences (which happen to be chemically induced). It is true that, as far as the main descriptive statements are concerned, it is not known whether similar statements could not also be made after the "blind" ingestion of an inert substance, or after sensory isolation, hypnosis or sleep deprivation. Furthermore, the present generalizations are restricted by the fact that all experiments were carried out in the same supportive, naturalistic setting by one group of investigators. Thus the conclusions are of the form: "when psilocybin (or a similar substance) is given in the kind of naturalistic environment described above, with a permissive, non-structured set, the following types of experiences tend to occur . . ." Given that framework, the writers have attempted to delineate the range of experiences, to describe the effects of background situation and repeated ingestion.

QUESTIONNAIRE RESULTS

A total of 157 *S*s were asked to complete questionnaires after their initial sessions; 98, or 62 per cent, returned them. The following results are based on the *initial psilocybin experience* of 98 *S*s (73 men, 25 women). The analysis of the questionnaire results is presented and discussed in the following sections: basic effects, effect of background variables, effect of the situation, effects of dosage, intercorrelations of the first and second experiences.

Main effects: In this sample of 98 first experiences the mean dosage was 18.1 mg. with a standard deviation of 11.6. With body weight controlled the mean is 0.26 mg./kg. and the SD 0.15. The mean time for major effects was 6.5 hours (SD = 9.8); mean time for minor effects was 16.8 hours (SD = 25.9). *S*s were asked for how many hours they thought someone should have been with them to be a help and companion: the mean time reported was 2.9 hours with a SD of 3.5.

The percentages of *S*s answering the various questions descriptive of the main effects are shown in Table 1 on page 82. To summarize these figures it may be said that in the kind of setting provided, which was seen as "supportive" by 78 per cent of *S*s, the majority of the initial mushroom experiences are reported to be positive and useful. Seventy per cent reported pleasant or ecstatic experiences; 88 per cent learned something or had insights; 62 per cent reported that the experience changed their

TABLE I. PERCENTAGE OF SUBJECTS GIVING VARIOUS RESPONSES TO QUESTIONS ABOUT SOME MAIN EFFECTS (*N* = 98)

I. How supportive (relaxing, warm, accepting) was the total situation?

Very Supportive	Mildly Supportive	Neutral	Mildly Rejecting	Very Rejecting
56%	22%	10%	9%	2%

2. Was the experience pleasant?

Very Unpleasant	Unpleasant	O.K.	Very Pleasant	Wonderful or Ecstatic
3%	4%	23%	38%	32%

3. Did you learn a lot about yourself and the world?

More Confused	Learned Nothing	Learned Something of Value	Learned a Lot	Tremendous Insights
2%	9%	43%	22%	23%

4. Has the mushroom experience changed you and your life?

Much Worse	Worse	No Change	Changed for Better	Dramatically Better
0%	1%	37%	50%	12%

5. To what extent were the important aspects of your experience *interpersonal* (sharing something with others)?

Mostly Interpersonal	Many Aspects Interpersonal	Some Aspects Interpersonal	Few Aspects Interpersonal	Entirely Personal
11%	32%	29%	13%	15%

6. To what extent was your experience perceptual (with some actual images or forms) as opposed to abstract?

Mostly Perceptual	Many Images	Some Images	Mostly Abstract	Entirely Abstract
18%	18%	33%	20%	10%

7. How about taking the mushrooms again under trustful, secure circumstances?

No!	Rather Not	Don't Care	Like To	Very Eager
0%	4%	6%	34%	56%

lives for the better; 90 per cent stated that they wished to repeat the experience. The two questions concerned with the *content* of the experience are the fifth and sixth; 72 per cent of Ss reported primarily interpersonal as opposed to personal experiences. This can probably be attributed to the fact that all experiences took place in groups, and the interpersonal aspects have been stressed by the writers in published papers and informal descriptions. Asked to estimate relative proportions of abstract and perceptual experiences, most Ss reported some images; the distribution was approximately normal, with a slight bias towards perceptual experience.

Effect of background variables: In this section the relationship of certain background factors to the main effects is considered. These relationships were measured by means of Pearson product-moment correlations. There were no significant relationships of main effects with age, sex or body weight. The limited assessment of main effects should be taken into account in evaluating these results.

Subjects were asked to indicate the extent of their previous experience with drugs such as "mescaline, LSD, marijuana, etc." on a scale from one to five, with scale-points identified as "none," "tried once," "2–10 times," "use fairly regularly," "very dependent or addicted." This scale correlated significantly* with dosage ($r = .25$), with time for consumption ($r = .25$), with length of major effects ($r = .26$), with rated familiarity to previous experiences ($r = .21$) and with the pleasantness of the experience ($r = .26$). In other words, the more experienced Ss tended to take higher dosages, spaced out over a period of time, to be aware of drug effects longer and to have felt the experience as less alien and more pleasant than did less experienced Ss. The experienced Ss also tended to rate themselves as more flexible.

Subjects were asked to state how often they drank alcohol and how easily they became intoxicated. Neither of these two variables correlated significantly with main drug effects, although drinking Ss tended to take larger drug doses ($r = .19$) and to take longer to consume the drug ($r = .27$).

---

*$r = .20$ at the .05 level of significance and .26 at the .01 level.

Finally, *S*s were asked to rate themselves on flexibility and on the degree to which they normally experienced real joy in living. *S*s who rated themselves as flexible were more likely to be previous drug users and drinkers, to have longer-lasting major effects ($r = .22$), and to rate the experience as familiar to ordinary life experiences ($r = .19$). In evaluating these findings it should be kept in mind that the whole questionnaire was filled out by *S* after the experience, so that it is possible that his ratings on these personal characteristics were influenced by his experience.

Effect of the situation: One set of situational factors arises out of the composition of the group in which *S* took psilocybin. Groups varied in size, in number of people taking the drug as opposed to number serving as nonparticipant observers and in number of people present "known at least fairly well" to *S*. Other factors are 1) the amount of apprehension *S* reported feeling before the experience and 2) how supportive he perceived the situation as being. Again, it must be cautioned that these two ratings might well be influenced by the experience itself; a suggestion which is born out by the clustering of pleasantness, insight and supportiveness which appeared, to be reported below.

Since it was thought that the effects of *group size* might be curvilinear and therefore not be apparent in product-moment correlations, the distribution of groups was broken into thirds and the results analyzed by chi-square. Table 2 shows the effects of group size on pleasantness, amount of learning and perceived supportiveness.

It can be seen in Table 2 that there was a slight non-significant tendency for small group experiences to be more pleasant; and there is suggestive evidence that most learning took place in moderate-sized groups (six to eight people). "Amount of learning" was tapped by Question 3 (Table 1) rated on a five-point scale. Small groups were also seen as more supportive, which in turn was related to pleasantness.

The number of people taking the drug was related positively to group size ($r = .55$) and negatively to supportiveness ($r = -.28$). It was also related negatively to pleasantness ($r = -.24$) and amount of learning

TABLE 2. SOME EFFECTS OF GROUP SIZE*

A

Group Size	Pleasantness	
	Low	*High*
Small (2–5)	7	23
Moderate (6–8)	12	20
Large (9–21)	11	15
$x^2 = 2.2$; *df* = 2; nsd.		

B

Group Size	Learning	
	Little	*Much*
Small (2–5)	18	12
Moderate (6–8)	15	17
Large (9–21)	17	9
$x^2 = 1.9$; *df* = 2; nsd.		

C

Group Size	Supportiveness	
	Low	*High*
Small (2–5)	8	22
Moderate (6–8)	14	18
Large (9–11)	19	7
$x^2 = 13.6$; *df* = 2; *p*<.005.		

*N = 88; certain ambiguous cases were eliminated.

($r = -.25$); in other words, the larger the group of people who actually took the drug, the less supportive and pleasant the experience tended to be. One of the questions on the post-session questionnaire was: "Of all those present, how many did you feel you knew at least fairly well?" The answers to this question did not correlate with any of the drug-effect variables. In the present setting, then, neither the presence of former observers taking drugs nor the presence of friends made the experience more positive.

Answers to the question, "How apprehensive were you about taking psilocybin?" were assigned scores from one to five, with scale points as follows: "very apprehensive," "some apprehension," "mild apprehension," "no fear," "eager to try." This scale correlated significantly positively with pleasantness of the experience ($r = .33$), with the degree to which the experience was interpersonal as opposed to personal ($r = .23$) and with the stated desire to repeat the experience. It was correlated negatively with supportiveness ($r = -.22$); i.e., supportive settings made for less anxiety.

Supportiveness, scored on a five-point scale ranging from "very supportive"—5, to "very rejecting"—1, as perceived by *S*, was related to pleasantness ($r = .43$), to amount of learning ($r = .28$), to positive life-changes and to degree of interpersonal aspects ($r = .32$).

Both group size *per se* and size of group which took the drug were related to expressed desire for a medically-trained psychiatrist, ($r = .23$ and .39, respectively) which may be taken as an index of anxiety.

To summarize this section, small supportive groups were seen as providing the most pleasant experience and also the most learning and effect on life. Large groups tended to be seen as rejecting and anxiety-provoking. This effect of group size was particularly marked if one counts the number of people actually taking the drug—the larger this was, the more unpleasant the experience tended to become. Finally, a positive expectation, as indicated by the "apprehensiveness" and "supportiveness" scales, tended to be followed by a positive, interpersonal experience.

Effects of dosage: Dosage was correlated very highly ($r = .71$) with reported duration of major effects;* this correlation may be artificially high due to the fact that some of the very high dosages were taken with long periods interspaced. (This is supported by the correlation of .80 of dosage with time for consumption.) The correlation of dosage with length of minor effects was .24. Dosage was also correlated with the amount of learning ($r = .30$); higher dosages were

---

*All correlations involving dosage here are computed controlling for body-weight, i.e., in mg. per kg.

more apt to produce perceptual as opposed to abstract experiences ($r = .21$). *S*s who took higher dosages were also more likely to oppose the presence of a medically-trained psychiatrist, which have stemmed in part from the background of the more experienced *S*s who took higher dosages.

Intercorrelations of main effects: Pleasantness was related both to amount of knowledge gained (.41) and to positive effects on life (.24). It was also related to the stated desire to repeat the experience ($r = .39$). Correlations with antecedents have already been reported: pleasantness was related to supportiveness of the situation, to previous drug experience and to absence of apprehension. The more pleasant experiences were more often interpersonal rather than personal ($r = .26$).

The amount of knowledge gained was related very strongly to the reported change in life ($r = .58$); it was also related to dosage ($r = .25$), as well as pleasantness and supportiveness. The more learning felt to have taken place, the less likely a person was to feel that a psychiatrist should have been present ($r = -.28$). The amount of change in life reported was correlated with amount of learning and was related to about the same variables.

The only significant determinant of whether the experience was perceptual or abstract appeared to be dosage, with higher dosages having produced more perceptual experiences ($r = .21$).

What determines whether an experience will be primarily interpersonal or primarily personal? There was a tendency ($r = .18$) for larger groups to make for more personal experiences and also for groups perceived as rejecting ($r = .32$). Perhaps this represents some kind of withdrawal from contact in threatening situations; pre-drug apprehensiveness correlated with personal as opposed to interpersonal experiences ($r = .23$); pleasantness and the desire to repeat were related negatively ($r = -.26$ and $-.23$, respectively), to a personal experience. In summary, the large-group, unpleasant, anxious experiences were more often personal; the small-group, pleasant, supportive experiences were mostly interpersonal.

TABLE 3. UNROTATED CENTROID FACTORS LOADING FROM THE FACTOR ANALYSIS OF INITIAL EXPERIENCE QUESTIONS (*N* = 98)

Factor	Variable	Loading
I	Dosage	.66
	Time of major effects	.60
	Amount of learning	.56
	Pleasantness	.51
	Positive effect on life	.44
	Previous drug experiences	.38
	Supportiveness of situation	.35
	Desire to repeat experience	.35
	Male vs. female	.35
	Interpersonal vs. personal	−.30
II	Number taking drug	.60
	Group size	.53
	Number of friends present	.41
	Dosage	.37
	Age	.36
	Frequency of drinking	.33
	Time of major effects	.31
	Pleasantness	−.39
	Desire to repeat experience	−.43
III	Dosage	.61
	Time of major effects	.41
	Male vs. female	−.41
	Desire for psychiatrist	−.39
	Group size	−.44
	Number of people taking drug	−.39
	Supportiveness	−.19
	Pleasantness	−.13
	Amount of learning	.11

Psychiatric setting: Ss were asked whether they thought a medically-trained psychiatrist should be present. Of the 98 Ss, 12 per cent were strongly or mildly opposed, 65 per cent said they didn't care and 23 per cent were in favor. They were also asked if they would have been happier if an antidote had been available, and 18 per cent answered they would have been happier, 82 per cent said they would not. Ss who were in favor of the presence of a psychiatrist were more likely to have come from groups with many people taking the drug ($r = .39$); they were likely to have taken smaller dosages ($r = -.26$) and to have reported little learning ($r = -.28$).

Factor analysis: In order to summarize the matrix of correlations reported above, a centroid factor analysis was performed and four factors extracted. Unrotated loadings for the first three significant factors are shown in Table 3. Factor I apparently represents a cluster of intense, positive educational experiences; much of the common variance is probably attributable to "halo effects" of subjective ratings. Factor II seems to be the unpleasant, large-group experience cluster; and Factor III an intense, small-group experience, unrelated to pleasantness, found more often in women.

Comparison of first and second experiences: A subsample of 35 *S*s took the drug and the questionnaire a second time. Table 4 shows the means and standard deviations of the major variables on the first and second experience. Only one of the differences between means attained the .05 level of significance (using the *t*-test for correlated means). The one significant difference is that group size tended to be smaller the second time; this was in part due to the writers' negative experiences with

TABLE 4. MEANS AND STANDARD DEVIATIONS OF VARIABLES FOR FIRST AND SECOND EXPERIENCES (*N* = 35)

Variable	First Time		Second Time	
	Mean	*(SD)*	*Mean*	*(SD)*
Group size	8.6	(7.8)	6.1	(2.5)*
Number taking drug	5.4	(2.5)	5.0	(2.3)
Supportiveness of situation	1.7	(1.1)	2.0	(1.2)
Dosage (mg.)	17.5	(7.1)	16.8	(7.3)
Pleasantness	4.0	(1.1)	3.7	(1.1)
Amount of learning	3.8	(1.0)	3.6	(1.0)
Positive effect on life	3.9	(0.6)	3.9	(0.6)
Interpersonal aspects	2.9	(1.3)	2.4	(1.3)
Perceptual aspects	3.0	(1.1)	3.3	(1.1)
Desire to repeat	4.5	(0.7)	4.5	(0.7)

*Significant at the .05 level.

large groups initially. Thus, it would seem that there were no systematic overall differences between first and second experiences.

We may ask further whether experiences tended to be *consistent*, e.g., whether an *S* who had had a pleasant experience the first time was also likely to do so the second time. In order to answer this question, correlations were computed between scores on a given variable the first time and scores on the same variable the second time; high correlations would have indicated high consistency from first to second experience. Table 5 shows these correlations for the major variables. It can be seen that there was no consistency in the major dimension of pleasantness, learning and effect on life. The perceptual vs. abstract and interpersonal vs. personal dimensions of the experience approached consistency, especially the interpersonal aspect. Group size was not significant, i.e., *S*s were equally likely to have been in smaller or larger groups the second time; however, they did tend to be in groups where the number of people taking the drug was the same as the first time.

A third type of sequence analysis was also attempted: namely, to predict what aspects of the first experience could be used to predict the second experience. Again, correlations between different variables for the first and second times were computed.

Amount of learning and pleasantness were again correlated with each other the second time ($r = .39$). The three variables found to be the best predictors of pleasantness and learning the second time were 1) conceptual vs. perceptual, 2) amount of learning and 3) length of time any aid needed. The correlations are shown in Table 6. Only correlations of .33 or above were statistically significant (at the .05 level), but the trend is consistent: the more the first experience was conceptual or abstract as opposed to perceptual, the better the second experience tended to be; the negative correlation with "time aid needed" presumably reflected some residual anxiety connected with the drug experience, which would have made the second time less valuable. Finally, the less was learned the first time, the more beneficial the second time was reported to be.

TABLE 5. CORRELATIONS INDICATING CONSISTENCY OF FIRST AND SECOND EXPERIENCES (*N* = 35)

Variable	Pearson r	p
Group size	.08	ns
Number taking drug	.54	.01
Supportiveness of situation	.17	ns
Dosage	.55	.01
Pleasantness	−.02	ns
Amount of learning	−.25	ns
Positive effect on life	.29	ns
Interpersonal aspects	.32	*
Perceptual aspects	.27	ns
Desire to repeat	.63	.01
Desire for trained psychiatrist	.75	.01

*Approaches significance at the .05 level (*r* = .33 is .05 level).

TABLE 6. FIRST EXPERIENCE VARIABLES PREDICTING PLEASANTNESS AND LEARNING IN THE SECOND EXPERIENCE

First Time Variable	Second Time Pleasantness	Second Time Learning
Conceptual aspects	.32	.28
Amount of learning	−.37	−.25
Time aid needed	−.32	−.34

The three variables which best predicted whether the experience would be personal or interpersonal the second time were 1) the felt effect on life, 2) the amount of learning and 3) the desire for a trained psychiatrist. The correlations were −.34, −.30 and .42, respectively; the more learning and effect the first time, the more interpersonal the second experience became; but the more a person wanted a psychiatrist the first time, the more personal the second experience became. One possible interpretation of these findings is that two divergent outlooks on the use of these experiences developed; they were used either for increased communication between people, or for analytic self-exploration.

DISCUSSION

It is clear that these results must be regarded as tentative and preliminary. Their generality is limited by the fact that they are based solely on conscious self-evaluation, *after* the experience and the fact that all *S*s were interested volunteers. Further studies are now under way in which other forms of records (e.g., fantasy material, behavioral observations) are made both before and after the drug experience and in which *S*s' expectations are measured. With these limitations in mind, the data presented suggest the following conclusions:

In a supportive setting, with a positive set, experiences with psilocybin tended to be reported by *S*s as pleasant, educational and life-changing.

Group size and atmosphere were important determinants of drug response: large groups (more than eight) tended to be seen as rejecting and reactions were less pleasant; smaller groups (less than six) were seen as more supportive and reactions were more positive. Larger groups also tended to make for more personal as opposed to interpersonal experiences.

Dosage was related to duration of effect and to amount of learning or insight.

Although the present data reveal little individual consistency between first and second experience, it does seem possible to make some predictions about the second experience from the responses to the first. For example, amount of learning the first time correlated negatively with pleasantness the second time. Also, wanting the presence of a psychiatrist the first time correlated with having a personal as opposed to interpersonal experience the second time. This last finding was tentatively interpreted as indicating that two uses of the drug experience may have developed—one for increased interpersonal communication, the other for analytic self-exploration.

The present data are in no sense adequately descriptive of the content of the experience; a separate, more detailed content study is in preparation. A few extracts from the accounts written by *S*s after their experience are given here to illustrate some of the conclusions given above.

1. A graduate student in psychology, who took 30 mg. of psilocybin in a group of five other graduate students and two observers or guides, wrote: "Then, I began a series of growth or learning experiences. I felt that understanding about oneself and about all human beings was part of the secret. The ability to communicate (on a deep level) was very important, as was the growth of competence and control over oneself and one's world . . . One of the most disturbing insights was the fact that science was just a small game with its own set of rules . . . It was even more circumscribed than the game of life in the Euro-American tradition . . . Part of my successive growth and learning experience included the sensation of trying to incorporate everybody within myself. This I saw very strongly as one of the main causes of human suffering—how alone we all were . . . Another part was that of accepting one's own defects, the parts of oneself one usually keeps hidden— physical desires, areas of incompetency, anti-social desires."

2. A female graduate student, who took psilocybin with three long-standing friends and fellow graduate students, reported that as she looked in the mirror she "was delighted to see that my skin was dissolving in tiny particles and floating away. I felt as though my outer shell was disintegrating, and the 'essence' of me being liberated to join the 'essence' of everything else about me. All of this time I was drifting about in a wonderously beautiful heaven of visual imagery and music."

3. Another female graduate student, who participated in a group session with five others, had an unpleasant experience marked by nausea and loneliness. She wrote afterwards: "I'd say I realize now how very committed I am to the 'game of self,' with intellectual 'dealing with myself' as the major feature of the game; I see how helpless I am without the intellectual crutch, and how unfree, as a result. I think I was using the drug situation in the service

of another game I had going with some of the people present—coercive, being helpless so as to elicit help, and that when this failed, the despair began."

4. A theology student, who participated in a five-person group session, illustrates the positive interpersonal experience: "During the whole experience the fact that I was sharing this with others was exceedingly significant. . . . The atmosphere could hardly have been made more pleasant and congenial. The freedom, spontaneity, and personal warmth within the group and between members of the group became very meaningful. . . . In these moments the psychology vs. theology business dropped off, the faculty-student barrier just did not matter, even the friend-stranger game was minimized. For these moments we interacted not as role players or as status seekers but as human beings—men who share common sorrows and common joys."

5. A female graduate student, who took 30 mg. of psilocybin with seven other participants, illustrates a negative interpersonal experience, in writing: "I felt very keenly the hostility and separateness of those present, one from another, though I didn't feel hostility myself and I didn't sense hostility against me, except at one point where A. was coming on very hostile toward everyone. The wandering from room to room and the tremendous activity of everyone bothered me somewhat. I somehow felt I should be able to calm everyone . . . The sense of helplessness in the face of the arguments they were having continued. The noise level of the session was a contributing problem which fed into the tension I felt at this point . . ."

It can be seen that although the accounts usually did not refer directly to group size as a factor in determining the nature of the experience, the tone and atmosphere of the group were clearly recognized as important. It may be that the effect of group size was indirect—that it was harder in large groups to establish and maintain a quiet positive "set."

6. Finally, a report from a graduate student who took 40 mg. in a four-person group: this illustrates the effects of higher dosages. He had taken 30 mg. initially and after one hour requested another 10 mg. "The extra pill made the experience even more intense and prolonged the major effect to five hours. Soon after the pill, the parts of my body seemed to have been dismembered and put back on without my realization. . . . Tears were coming out of my right eye and the left side of my face was smiling. My legs were weightless, hollow and dead. It was quite intriguing, but I began to feel that I was losing my mind. There was a candle on the floor which I held my hand over. I felt no pain for about ten seconds. Then a sharp pain began to slowly ooze into the palm. After removing my hand, inspection showed that it was black with the soot of the flame and ordinarily I'm positive I would have been badly burned. I decided that pain was something that kept us in contact with the physical world which I had left. . . . The most significant thought during the period was the sense of being randomly knocked about like a molecule in the universe. The others were in the same universe with me, but exactly where, I had no idea. Although I did not suffer emotionally, I felt cosmically alone and separate. I realized that the implicit faith that we understand one another (which I also realized was most of the time incorrect) connected us through the belief in some sort of consensus of understanding. . . . I also felt that the only reasonable way to live in the same world was to love and to realize that no one else will ever fully share or understand this basis of our actions, nor will we understand theirs. But the faith, which is completely sustained of and by itself within ourselves alone, is the basis of others' actions and provides the necessary consensus to achieve some sort of simultaneity of time and place in the universe. Love, and the faith in love keeps us from being cosmically alone."

This last description illustrates the kind of "mystical" or "transcendent" experience that has been reported as occurring with LSD by other investigators.[9, 10] Although this is not the place to enter into a detailed discussion of the significance of such experiences, it may be pointed out that some of the psilocybin and LSD descriptions are remarkably similar to classical descriptions of mystical experiences and religious conversions.

The results reported here were congruent with the findings of other investigators, who have studied the subjects' claims following one experience with LSD. Thus, Ditman et al.,[4] reported that 72 per cent of 76 subjects look back on their LSD experiment as "a very pleasant experience." Sixty per cent of patients and 32 per cent of normals claimed improvement and greater understanding of self.

How may one account for these findings, which are somewhat at variance with reports by the majority of psychiatric investigators, who regard psilocybin, LSD and similar drugs as "psychotomimetic" and potentially dangerous? Several factors presumably affect the total response to these agents. 1) *Selection:* As already pointed out, Ss in this study had volunteered after hearing about the work; their initial set was positive and interested. 2) *Preparation:* Through discussion and reading, Ss were prepared to expect insight and expanded awareness, as well as pleasantness. The importance of preparation has also been stressed by Sherwood et al.[10] 3) *Setting:* The naturalistic, non-structured environment of the present experiments differed considerably from the usual controlled experimental setting. Malitz et al.[8] also indicated the importance of expectation and setting in accounting for the difference between their results with psilocybin and the accounts by Wasson. 4) *Suggestibility:* It seems likely that one of the effects of psilocybin and related drugs is to heighten suggestibility.[2] This would increase the response of the individual to stimuli in the environment and to interpersonal interactions. It would also in part account for the sensitivity to group tone and atmosphere. Hyde[7] has also reported that group experiences with LSD are more pleasant than individual experiences, and that supportive, non-structured situations make for more pleasant experience than task-oriented structured situations. 5) *Attitudes of the experimenter:* The expectation of the investigator may have a profound effect on Ss, both through the kind of preparation he provides and through the kind of setting and interpersonal interaction he arranges for Ss. 6) *Personality:* In the present study, personality variables were not measured. A self-rating on flexibility was shown to predict some aspects of the psilocybin reactions. Many other investigators have stressed the importance of personality variables in determining the drug-response.[3, 7]

Although the exact mechanisms of action of psilocybin are not known, many theories exist as to the nature of the changes brought about by it and similar drugs. The present data, which merely indicate the kinds of subjective responses one may obtain when psilocybin is given in a supportive environment, do not enable one to decide between these theories. Tentatively, however, it may be proposed that one of the psychological mechanisms involved is a diminution or suspension of the normal processes of perceptual selection and inhibition. This would be consistent with the reports of "insight," with increased suggestibility to external and internal stimuli and with the varying influence of personality. The difference in the results obtained by different investigators may be accounted for by the fact that the expectation of E will influence Ss in their state of heightened sensitivity and suggestibility.

SUMMARY

A study has been described in which psilocybin was given to 175 Ss from various backgrounds in a naturalistic environment. Ninety-eight initial experiences were assessed by means of questionnaire, both in terms of major dimensions of the experience and in terms of the contribution of background and situational factors. A comparison of first and second experiences was made for a subsample of 35 Ss. The results were discussed with reference to extracts from subjective accounts written by Ss. The role of various set and setting variables was described and a tentative psychological mechanism proposed to account for the effects of these variables.

REFERENCES

1. Beecher, H. K. Psychotomimetic drugs. *J. Chron. Dis.*, **8**: 253–285, 1958.
2. Cohen, S. The therapeutic potential of LSD-25. In Featherstone, R. M., ed. *A Pharmacologic Approach to the Study of the Mind,* pp. 251–257. Thomas, Springfield, Illinois, 1959.
3. DiMascio, A., Rinkel, M. and Leiberman, J. Personality and psychotomimetic drugs. Psychopharmacology Research Laboratory, MMHC, Boston, Research Report, 1961.
4. Ditman, K. S., Hayman, M. and Whittlesey, J. R. B. Nature and frequency of claims following LSD. J. Nerv. Ment. Dis., **134**: 346–352, 1962.
5. Elkes, J. Psychotropic drugs: Observations on current views and future problems. In *Lectures on Experimental Psychiatry,* pp. 65–114. Univ. of Pittsburgh Press, 1961.
6. Hofmann, A. Chemical aspects of psilocybin, the psychotropic principle from the Mexican fungus, *Psilocybe mexicana* Heim. Paper presented at the First International Meeting of Neuropsychopharmacology, Rome, 1958.
7. Hyde, R. W. Psychological and social determinants of drug action. In Sarwer-Foner, G. J., ed. *Dynamics of Psychiatric Drug Therapy,* pp. 297–312. Thomas, Springfield, Illinois, 1960.
8. Malitz, S., Esecover, H., Wilkens, B. and Hoch, P. H. Some observations on psilocybin, a new hallucinogen, in volunteer subjects. Compr. Psychiat., **1**: 8–17, 1960.
9. Savage, C., Terrill, J. and Jackson, D. D. LSD, transcendence and the new beginning. J. Nerv. Ment. Dis., **135**: 425–439, 1962.
10. Sherwood, J. N., Stolaroff, M. J. and Harman, W. W. The psychedelic experience—a new concept in psychotherapy. *J. Neuropsychiat.,* **3**: 370–375, 1962.
11. Wasson, R. G. The hallucinogenic fungi of Mexico: An inquiry into the origins of the religious idea among primitive peoples. Botan. Museum Leaflets, Harvard University, **19**, 1961.

4

Psychedelic Drugs and Creativity

The Effects of Test Score Feedback on Creative Performance and of Drugs on Creative Experience

Timothy Leary

Despite the rather pedestrian nature of this article's original title ("The Effects of Test Score . . ."), this piece of writing is actually a crucial one in Leary's scholarly trajectory of the early 1960s. It is important because it elucidates Leary's philosophical understanding of the drug experience ("altering consciousness") and its widespread cultural importance with regard to creativity and creative performance. In 1962, Leary participated in the Utah Creativity Research Conference that was held at the Mount Majestic Lodge and Manor in the Wasatch Mountains of northern Utah. This interdisciplinary conference featured scholars from a wide range of academic fields. Leary's article contains findings from three of his research projects at Harvard in the early 1960s: the Harvard Psilocybin Project, the Concord Prison Experiment, and the Good Friday Experiment. Each of these research projects contributes to Leary's understanding of creativity and highlights how programmed psychedelic sessions can foster greater creativity in the subject.

This 1962 article ("The Effects . . .") is specifically concerned with the nature of creativity and the question of how to nurture the creative impulse. It is also concerned with the various attempts to objectively measure creativity using questionnaires. Leary posits that any discussion of creativity must in some way address the dichotomy between the internal and the external. If the behaviorists believe that external behavior is the only form of empirical truth that we can know, Leary, a staunch critic of behaviorism, identifies with Eastern religious traditions that value the internal experience (what Leary terms "consciousness"). Leary notes that Eastern religions "place greater emphasis on consciousness," they see "matter and behavior as forms of consciousness," and they stress "the mystical rather than the mental." Leary's belief in the primacy of consciousness ("cortical receptivity") is central to his theory of creativity and the creative impulse.

For Leary, creativity is inevitably related to the process of social conditioning. Leary argues that learned behavior (also called "game consciousness") is negative in the sense that it blocks and inhibits the development of creativity: "Too often learned sequences, the perceptual, verbal, and sociological, tend to clutter up this magnificent instrument ('the human brain')." For Leary, the brain "has incredible perfection. It is an absolutely accurate instrument, just like the heart, the liver, perfectly designed to perform its function. Far from being a *tabula rasa*, the human brain in terms of its natural function is capable of a wide range of awareness which has nothing to do with anything that has been learned or anything that is verbal." For Leary, the freeing of the mind—what Leary terms "cortical receptivity"—can occur when one takes psychedelic drugs in a supportive and creative environment. Thus, for Leary psychedelic drugs can expand consciousness and stimulate creativity by making the subject aware of "non-game realities."

Leary's research with psychedelic drugs informs his anti-elitist view of creativity. He believes creativity can be taught and nurtured. However, Leary's most radical claim is his utopian view of creativity and cerebral cortex: "creativity is not a function of lucky heritage or elite training. There are more visions in the cortex of each of us than in all the museums and libraries of the world. There is a limitless possibility of new combinations of the old symbols. A true democracy of creativity—experienced and performed—is possible and is, indeed, close at hand." Leary's article also contains a Question and Answer session. In this dialogue, Leary responds to questions from Frank Barron and other scholars who attended the Utah Creativity Research conference.

JAMES PENNER

THE EFFECTS OF TEST SCORE FEEDBACK ON CREATIVE PERFORMANCE AND OF DRUGS ON CREATIVE EXPERIENCE

From *Widening Horizons in Creativity* by Calvin Taylor and Frank Barron, published in 1964 by John Wiley and Sons: pages 87–111.

Timothy Leary, Harvard University*

Of all the artificial, dualistic abstractions imposed by language upon the unfolding unity of life, one of the most useful is the distinction between internal and external. Although our mental processes and our cultures are based upon this differentiation, American behaviorism tends to ignore it and prefers to pretend that only movements "out there" are real and that events registered "in there" are inaccessible to systematic inquiry.

The purpose of this paper is to call attention to the internal, to the neglected issue of consciousness, and to suggest its relevance for the interpretation, measurement, and development of creativity. The emphasis which we Westerners place upon external behavior and material

---

*Now with the International Federation for Internal Freedom.

phenomena is basically a religious decision, betraying our assumptions about the nature of man, the meaning of life, and the goals of existence.

As I have listened to the words exchanged around this table during the past two days, I have been impressed by the underlying unanimity as to the basic religious assumptions. Such a conference could only be held in a materialistic (and in America, Protestant) context. From what other religious background could come the emphasis upon action, the external, the material; from what other religious background could come the confident optimism about doing things to nature? Protestantism is of course one of the more recent expressions of monotheism,* and from this monotheistic background comes the familiar anthropocentric and manipulative definition of creativity. "In the beginning," says the Bible, "God created the heavens and the earth." "I believe," says the Christian, "in one God, Creator of Heaven and Earth." The basis of Muslim science which kept the intellectual flame going for so many centuries is the similar belief in a single, unified Will, Allah, the "almighty, omnipotent, Lord of the Worlds, the Author of Heaven and Earth, the Creator of life and death in whose hand is dominion—and inexhaustible power."

When we assemble here in this magnificently architectured mountain scene to talk about creators and creativity, we might profit by keeping explicit the fundamental tenets upon which our conceptions are based, by being aware of other conceptions, and by keeping alert to the practical as well as spiritual implications of "nonmonotheistic" approaches to man and his nature.†

The other conception of man (historically the older, and numerically the greater) places greater emphasis upon consciousness, sees mat-

---

*Among other active expressions of a monotheistic approach to life are Catholicism, Islam, Judaism, Marxism, and psychoanalysis.

†The most influential nonmonotheistic religions include Hinduism, Taoism, and Southern, Northern, and Zen varieties of Buddhism. Among Western philosophers expressing a mystical, pantheistic point of view we can include most of the early Christians, Gnostics, Plato, Herodotus, Pindar, Pythagoras, Socrates, the later Christian mystics, Blake, Swedenborg, a high percentage of our poets, and, more recently, our own American psychologist William James and the late Swiss psychoanalyst, Carl Jung.

ter and behavior as forms of consciousness, stresses the mystical rather than the mental, and centers divinity and creativity within the realm of human awareness. According to the monotheist, God and heaven and earth are all "out there," and man relying on his spiritual or creative capacity must do something about it. According to the nonmonotheist, what does or does not exist out there is irrelevant; what counts is what is inside. Everything relevant is psychological, is in consciousness. All the universes exist (discovered or undiscovered, created or uncreated) within the human skull. "The psychic self," says Jung (1960), "and the giver of all data are one and the same. The world of gods and spirits is truly nothing but the collective unconscious within me."

Now our basic religious beliefs are of tremendous importance not just morally-theologically, but practically as well, because they determine our philosophy and our psychology. If we are committed to an external, monotheistic belief, our conceptions of what is real, what is true, how things are related, and what to do become defined in external terms. Our psychology similarly takes on a behavioristic and materialistic coloring involving adjustment, normality, socialization, achievement, performance, manipulation of symbols, and deification and reification of words. Creativity is defined as innovation, original production.

For the past two years I have been occupied with research on consciousness—its experimental alteration and expansion. Such research is not new. Even in the West (via introspection and via inferences from so-called dynamic techniques) psychologists have been inquiring into consciousness. What is most eccentric about our studies at Harvard is the combination of methods which are very Western—drugs—with a research philosophy which is currently out of vogue in American administrative psychology. Our data have taught us that the criteria, methods, language, and goals of behavioral psychology do not always apply when we set out to study the internal events of consciousness. We have found ourselves becoming increasingly passive and collaborative, increasingly convinced that the study of consciousness demands an ontology, an epistemology, a logic, and an ethic which is frankly subjective. We have found it increasingly necessary to involve ourselves in the scope of inquiry, to expand our own awareness in order to keep in any sort of touch with our subjects.

We follow here a form of experimentation which is somewhat new and suspect in the West but which is actually the oldest and most traditional form of psychological investigation—the disciplined, systematic expansion of one's own consciousness. The experimental search for inner creativity is, we recall, over three thousand years old and possesses a literature of method and finding which dwarfs our own. Our civilization, our culture, our psychology, and our conception of creativity cannot afford to ignore these achievements and these methods.

But in attempting a productive synthesis, the difference between the two approaches must be respected. Western psychology has never satisfactorily resolved the tension between internal-subjective and external-objective. We have consistently imposed the methods, language, and goals of the external upon the internal. *The two can be related only if their logical separation is kept clear.*

During the past few years I have worked out some philosophical and methodological solutions to this problem. It is my plan today to present a conceptual model for dealing with behavior, on the one hand, and consciousness, on the other, and then to apply the model to problems of diagnosis and change in two kinds of creativity.

BEHAVIOR—ITS MEASUREMENT, DESCRIPTION, AND CHANGE

Behavior is movement in time/space. The first step in measuring behavior is to locate it reliably in space/time.*

A method for diagnosing space/time aspects of behavior has been devised and applied to behavior-change projects (Leary, 1962b).

The measurement of movements is more complex. Indeed we can

_____

*Any attempts to "measure" behavior directly via observation, labeling, or naming brings us into the mind of the observer and repeats the old confusion of internal/external.

directly measure not movements but only the records of movements—artifacts, recorded sounds, films, records of verbalization. We measure records of movements by reliably determining their extension and duration and then by counting frequency.

Such units of extension-duration provide objective indices of behavior. These molecular indices define the vocabulary of behavioral science. Hundreds of such indices now exist—EEG, GSR, MAT score, the scales of the MMPI, verbal content counts, etc. Until recently such terms were scattered, with no logical relationships. Psychology is in the position of chemistry before Mendeleev. The language of the behavioral sciences will eventually develop, as did that of chemistry, with index terms related systematically into formulae. A crude attempt to develop a systematic grammar and measures for the vocabulary of behavioral indices (with particular reference to verbalizations) has been described in other papers (Leary, 1962b, 1962c) and will be referred to in the section of this article concerned with the training of creative behavior.

Behavior units exist in infinite numbers and endlessly combine and interact, providing a confusing jumble of events. For descriptive purposes it is useful to classify behavior sequences in terms of the cultural games of which they are expressions (Leary, 1962a). A game is a behavior sequence characterized by:

Goals	Values
Rules	Space/Time locals
Roles	Strategies
Rituals	Language

All learned behavior is considered part of cultural game systems. Instinctual behavior, physical and biological processes, random movements are called play.* Many people object to the word "game" because it is seen as derogating the seriousness of life's actions. This, of course, brings us to religious issues—the meaning of life. To avoid this debate

---

*This definition of natural processes as play follows the Hindu conception of Lila.

one can substitute the term ACTS for game behavior. (ACTS refers to Artificial, Culturally learned, Temporary Sequences.)

For the past several years I have been engaged in the application of these theories and methods to behavior change, for instance, the therapeutic implications of the space/time issue—who goes to whom, when, for how long. Another example is the explicit contract involved in the helping game, the effect of the expert role as opposed to collaborative determination of roles, rules, languages, goals, rituals, and values of the behavior-change sequence. A further illustration is the effect of the coaching model and feedback of results in bringing about and maintaining change (Leary, 1960, 1961b; Leary, Metzner, Presnell, Weil, Schwitzgebel, and Kinne, 1963).

Some extensions of these principles and methods to changing creative performance will be suggested later.

CONSCIOUSNESS—ITS DESCRIPTION AND CHANGE

The description of subjective states of awareness has always presented philosophical problems—ontological (what is real?), epistemological (what is fact?), and logical (how are images related?).

One cause for the problem is that we tend to impose upon the inner world the same terms we use to describe external events, movements, and things. Now the young child, we are told, does not do this. He experiences directly. The process of education and learning is designed to teach the child not to experience directly. He is trained to impose game structure upon his perceptions of the world. He learns to interpret everything around him (and indeed everything inside of him e.g., the sickness game, the toilet-training game) in terms of its game meaning.

The recent evidence from experimental and developmental psychology suggests that learning is a process of elimination, screening out. We discriminate, select, censor, and distort to fit what we see within the limits of what we expect to see. I refer here to the work of Piaget, Brunswik, and the Gestalt school, the Ames illusions, and the visual experiments of Land.

The well-trained, self-confident adult (and, in particular, the intellectual) finally arrives at that point where he possesses mental machinery to interpret, discriminate, and label everything he perceives and to relate these percepts to others.

I am convinced that the brain, as a body organ, has incredible perfection. It is an absolutely accurate instrument, just like the heart or the liver, perfectly designed to perform its function. Far from being a *tabula rasa,* the human brain in terms of its natural function is capable of an extraordinary range of awareness that has nothing to do with anything that has been learned or anything that is verbal. As a matter of fact, you might argue that the cortex, without external behavioral or verbal impositions upon it, is a perfect organ for survival. Too often, the learned sequences, the perceptual, verbal, and sociological, tend to clutter up this magnificent instrument. It is as though our knowledge of hydraulics led us to feel that we could improve cardiac function so that we built springs about the heart to help it contract or imposed our plumbing knowledge upon that magnificent instrument.

While the cultural process greatly simplifies socialization and reduces anxiety (we end up with a name and explanation for everything we perceive), a heavy price is paid for these advantages. Direct experience is lost. We live in a plastic world of labeled abstractions.

Game consciousness is obviously very limited. Non-game awareness of the continuously changing panorama of inner and outer events is infinite. We socialized adults give away about 99% of our available cortical receptivity.

We deal here with the Faustian bargain. For the handful of concepts in Webster's dictionary and for the power of ego control we exchange the timeless infinity of direct game-free awareness.

But not all men make this bargain. There are some to whom we attach such labels as mystic, visionary, artist, esoteric, orientalist—who have warned us for centuries about the Faustian bargain. Such people have stubbornly insisted that it is possible to avoid a complete commitment to the word game, the ego game, and the social game. They tell us that it is possible to transcend (temporarily) the limits of the "I," the limits of the conceptual and the social, and that it is possible to make direct contact with an infinitely expanded universe. Most of us find these warnings disturbing. We have worked so hard to maintain ego control. We'd be lost without *our* egos. And then we have the dread example of those who are unable to (or refuse to) play a consistent ego, word, or social game. Those pariahs we call psychotic.

Even if we were to wish to transcend ego and word—what good would it do? Does a language exist to describe these experiences? How can we apply these ultra-mundane visions to our on-going ACTS?

But there is, of course, a language. It is the oldest language in the world—the nonverbal language of spontaneous dance, painting, sculpture, weaving, ceramic; the verbal language of religion, poetry, song, myth, esoterica; and the abstract language of mysticism. We are surrounded by clues (manmade and natural) constantly reminding us that there's more— look, there's more. The clues even extend into the academic. The oldest psychological literature in the world is devoted to exactly these issues— the description of ego-transcendent experience and the application of the experience to personal happiness and social harmony. The greatest psychotherapist in world history possibly was the Buddha. "The goal is not to explain the world to those who are thirsty for knowledge. The goal of my teaching is salvation from suffering." Possibly the greatest sociologist and behavior-change coach in world history was Confucius (Jen, Chun Tsu, Li, Te, Wen). Who has expressed the social contract more clearly? Can we afford to leave these concepts out of our behavioral science textbooks?

But even if we accept the psychological and social potentialities of the ego-transcendent state, there come the final questions: How can we attain it? How can awareness be expanded? How can consciousness be changed?

Here again we have a wealth of technical information. Three thousand years before Freud or Wundt, detailed methods were devised for the systematic expansion of consciousness. There are five major forms of Yoga, all designed to provide non-game control of consciousness. One of these, the Raga Yoga, is a disciplined system of psychological experimentation for consciousness expansion. Also threading back to the origins of history, shrouded in myth and deliberate secrecy, are the mystery cults and fraternities—ancient mental health societies, using spontaneity, ritual, and hallucinogenic plants to expand consciousness, to break out of the game for purposes of ecstasy, mental rehabilitation, creative education, and spiritual initiation. These sacred mystic bands were the originators and earliest preservers of every major religion and practically every major philosophic and intellectual movement the world has known. That is where it always starts—in the expanded cortex.

Psychologists and physiologists are currently experimenting with the same methods—limited environment, sensory deprivation, physical shock, prolonged starvation, and sleeplessness. The ego-transcendent state (today in this time of great emphasis upon ego identity) is called by different labels—primary process thinking, psychotomimetic states— but the experience seems to be the same.

The safest and simplest method for consciousness expansion is, of course, the pharmacological. Drugs such as LSD, mescaline, and psilocybin (chemical synthetics of ergot, peyote, and mushrooms, respectively) produce brief and dramatically intense alternations in consciousness.

For the past two years I have been associated with a research project which has studied the effects of psilocybin upon more than 400 volunteer subjects. The therapeutic and theoretical implications of these studies have been reported elsewhere (Leary and Metzner, 1964; Leary, 1962a; Leary, Metzner, Presnell, Weil, Schwitzgebel, and Kinne, 1963; Leary, Litwin, and Metzner, 1963), and results relating to creativity have been described by Barron (1962b). Here let it suffice for me to say that the drugs are physically safe, are psychologically harmless (unless in irresponsible hands and even their residuals are negligible and debatable), bring about extravagant claims of improvement and insight (Ditman, Hayman, Whittlesey, 1962; Leary, 1962a; Leary, Litwin and Metzer 1963; McGlothlin, 1962), usually produce dramatic ego transcendence, and in many cases stimulate creative awareness.

Our project has followed up on these promising leads in two directions: (1) the application of the consciousness-expansion experience to rehabilitation of prisoners, education of graduate students, and inspiration of the clergy; and (2) the development of new linguistic forms for communicating nongame experiences. Just as our studies of molecular units of behavior led to the development of new index vocabularies (Leary and Gill, 1959; Leary, 1962c), so has our study of consciousness led to the development of a new vocabulary for ego-transcendent awareness utilizing charts and crude inner-space cartography (Leary, Metzner, and Alpert, 1964).

This paper began with the statement that different languages, philosophies, and methods of change were required to deal with behavior, on the one hand, and consciousness, on the other. In the preceding two sections of this paper I have discussed, first, behavior—its measurement and change—and then, consciousness—its description and methods for change.

In the sections to follow I propose to apply these notions to the diagnosis and change of creativity, that is, of creative behavior and of creative awareness.

THE MULTIDIMENSIONAL DIAGNOSIS OF CREATIVITY

There is experience and there is performance. *Awareness* can be creative—our experience can be direct, fresh, outside of game connotations; or it can be reproductive, that is, within the interpretative framework of the already learned, in which case we see only what we have been taught to see.

Performance can be creative—we can produce new combinations (whatever the game medium); or it can be reproductive—a repeating of old combinations.

When we oppose these two dichotomous continua of experience and performance in orthogonal axes, a diagnostic circle is obtained. Four "types" of creativity are defined by the four quadrants of the diagnostic circle shown in Figure 1.

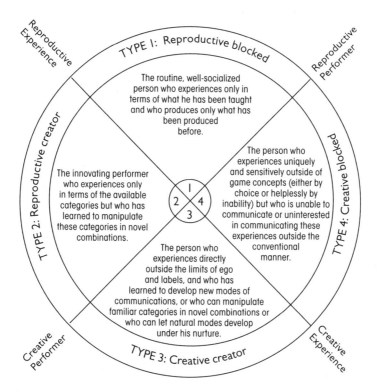

Figure 1. Categories for diagnosing creativity in terms of performance and experience. The diagnostic grid is defined by the two axes: experience and performance. Each axis runs as a continuum from creative to reproductive.

Type 1.*The reproductive blocked* (no novel combinations, no direct experience), which I estimate to comprise about 75% of our American population.

Type 2. *The reproductive creator* (no direct experience, but crafty skill in producing new combinations of old symbols), comprising, let us say, the most visible, successful 12% of our population.

Type 3. *The creative creator* (new experience presented in novel performances), of which we can hope for 1% in any Golden Age.

Type 4. *The creative blocked* (new direct experience expressed in conventional modes), a somewhat cryptic 12%.

These four "types" of creativity are obvious by definition and seem to require no elaboration. What does deserve amplification is the social perception of these four types. A person in any of these four quadrants can be seen as effective or as incompetent by his culture—and, for that matter, by cultural subgroups.

If we divide each type into those labeled by their contemporaries as (A) effective and (B) ineffective, we obtain the eight categories presented in Figure 2. These two-dimensional circular grids can be used to plot test scores or content-analysis indices along the two coordinates in order to diagnose the individual. Thus we can work not just in terms of eight types, but in terms of two continua which define a wide expanse of diag-

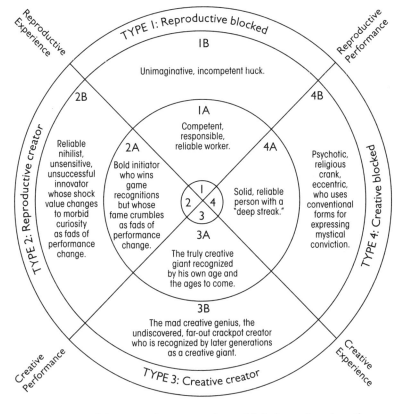

Figure 2. Schematic diagrams of social labels used to describe types of creativity. Inner circle illustrates positive social labels, and outer circle negative labels.

nostic space. This system, of course, leads itself to multilevel diagnosis and to the same variety of applications as the interpersonal circle (Leary, 1957). The same mathematical and psychometric methods apply. We can plot the location of scores on check lists of creative experience and creative behavior executed by the subject or by appraisers of this performance. Multilevel discrepancy indices can thus be calculated (Leary, 1956).

THE DEVELOPMENT OF CREATIVE BEHAVIOR

In a previous section I have reviewed some of the methods of behavior change suggested by measurement in space/time theory and the game model. Now let me illustrate a pilot-study which tested some of these methods in a creativity-change program.

The general procedure is as follows. The subject picks out a goal and practices the game sequences which lead to success. The goal must be behavioral and capable of measurement. Much confusion is caused because people engage in games for which there is no way of scorekeeping. Is the game over when the New York Yankees "feel" they have won? Suppose that the Detroit Tigers "feel" they have won, too. Suppose that the scoreboard shows that the Tigers won, but they or their supporters "feel" they lost. The movements in space/time (men crossing home plate) have to be the criterion.

Thus *feedback* on performance is a key issue. In most of life's crucial games we stumble in the dark, not knowing how we are doing. The first step, then, in behavior change is *explicit* definition of the game, learning the rules, roles, rituals, language, values, and strategies. You need some way of scorekeeping and you have to study the *space-time locale* and be at the proper ball park. You aren't going to be a creative artist if you share your space/time with salesmen. You must be sure that you have an explicit contract with your colleagues. It is disappointing to come thundering over the goal line for a touchdown only to be greeted with yawns because the gang is playing tennis. We tend to do this all the time. I spend a good part of my professional life doing this. I've done it at this conference and am probably doing it right now.

You should get a good coach. Behavior, being movement in space/time, is not changed by words and is not changed by repeating mistakes. And practice is needed. "Happiness he who seeks may win," says the Buddha, "if he practices."

In 1961 Frank Barron, William Meyers (at that time a Harvard graduate student), and I initiated a creativity-change project at the Rhode Island School of Design which allowed for a preliminary and crude check on some of these hypotheses (Barron and Leary, 1961). By matching pairs of students on faculty ratings of creativity forty volunteer subjects of the junior class at the Rhode Island School of Design were divided into two groups (A and C) whose creativity ratings had equal means and equal standard deviations. Also, IQ scores were available on all subjects.

First both groups were tested, under identical conditions, with the Barron Originality, Independence of Judgment, and Preference for Complexity Questionnaires, and the Levinson Revision of the Adorno F Scale, the Bales Balanced F, the Keniston-Couch Agreement Response Scale, the Meyers College Attitude Test, the Barron-Welsh Art Scale, and the Guilford Plot Titles Test.

Then, after an intermission, the groups were separated. Group C was asked to "play the role of an extraordinarily original and creative person"; group A, to play the role of a highly intelligent (authoritarian) person. Both groups were then given the Guilford Unusual Uses Test and the Barron Originality, Independence of Judgment, and Preference for Complexity Questionnaires, in that order.

The results indicated that group C (creative set) improved in performance relative to group A, on these tests of ability to think up ideas. This indicates that the creative set increases creative performance, and the authoritarian set decreases creative performance. We may conclude that creativity is not a static quality present in a fixed amount in a given person, but rather that it is susceptible to considerable increase given conditions of high personal motivation and social support. It is also susceptible to considerable decrease, given conditions of interfering motivations and alien social climate. It also suggests that role-playing, or set taking, is a specific mechanism for increasing creativity.

The related finding that creativity has a social as well as a personal motivational aspect was shown by the results at the Rhode Island School of Design study on the three Barron questionnaires.

With the creative set, group C increased their scores over their earlier scores with standard instructions. Group A, with the authoritarian set, decreased their scores on the Barron questionnaires. Since these tests are measures of interpersonal and social attitudes, we may conclude that mind sets which affect creative performance also affect interpersonal and social orientation, and vice versa. Creative performance is thus to be viewed in an interpersonal and social context (Meyers, 1963).

Stated in the language of the game model, the results suggest that (1) creative behavior is a game sequence; (2) people have considerable voluntary control over their creative behavior (and, we suspect, other "deep" variables, such as depression, dependence, ego strength, etc.) within stated space/time game lines; and (3) if the game contract is made explicit, behavior will change drastically in the direction that the game role and goal demand. The experiment also suggests that people automatically shift rituals, adjust new rules, and employ the appropriate language once the commitment to goal and role is made—and within explicit space/time limits.

A second test of the game-model approach was then executed. A sample of fifty juniors was selected (at random) for a feedback study. Barron and I met with each subject, opened up the test folder, and explained his creativity test results. We centered on the creativity test scores and attempted to relate them to the student's stated game goals. In every case we found that the student's creativity scores and ratings of originality by faculty members checked closely with his game ambitions.

For instance, one student of commercial design with low scores on originality was rated as solid, responsible, but unimaginative by teachers. She produced a California Personality Inventory profile high in socialization, conformity, stability, and social participation. She consistently checked items which indicated close identification with middle-class family values. We went over this student's creativity questionnaire item by item, indicating where she checked in the "noncreative" direction. Emerging from the subsequent discussion was this message. "I'm a normal, conventional person looking forward to a steady, interesting job in advertising, a good income, and a happy family life. I've no desire to be a tortured genius, sacrificing home and income for the risky Bohemian independence of the artist."

While the student body at the Rhode Island School of Design was significantly above average on indices of aesthetic performance and interpretation, there seemed to be little discrepancy between the level of creativity and the professional goals selected. Painters and sculptors had higher scores on independence of judgment, spontaneous flexibility, and social deviance than did architects or industrial designers.

One conclusion that I draw from these Rhode Island studies is that creativity cannot be judged outside its game context. If we could automatically double the creativity scores (and the personality correlates) of the entire student body, we would probably be causing endless game mixups and conflicts.

Instead of the global term "creativity" it seems more useful to think about (1) the "creativity game" (I want to act like a creative person) and (2) the innovating or original performance in any game sequence. The former is a "personal game" and can be coached *à la* psychotherapy. The teaching of innovating behavior seems to be a simpler behavior-change proposition. You simply use feedback and coach your subjects.

First the game goal must be defined in objective terms. Let us define creative behavior as the production of new combinations of responses which meet a stated criterion of acceptability.

This sort of behavior can be coached. The production of innovating combinations can be made a systematic routine by employing the game model. The procedure is as follows. List all the known roles, rules, rituals, language terms, and strategies of the game being performed. Then systematically permute these into new combinations. Select the most promising of the new combinations and try them out.

Another method for producing novel intergame combinations is to list as many different games as possible along the two axes of an orthogonal grid. Each box defines an intergame or interdisciplinary matrix. We then simply combine terms (role, ritual, strategies, etc.) from each of the two paired games. Among the many combinations most will be eccentric, some poetic, and some useful enough to label the "originator" as a creative performer.

Table 1 [on pages 118–19] presents a general illustration of this technique. I have employed the grammatical structure of the behavioral index language mentioned in an earlier section of this paper. Index numbers are omitted and category names employed for the sake of simplicity. Three major categories of games are listed: self games, social games, and chemical-physical measures. Self and cultural categories are subdivided. The double-lined boxes running diagonally from lower left to upper right define intracategory combinations. Within each category there are hundreds of games—for example, under occupational-financial, we would list all jobs, economic processes, etc. These can be combined into new combinations.

Above the intradisciplinary diagonal we have listed sample interdisciplinary combinations which define new intellectual and scientific games. The terms listed are only a small fraction of those possible. Fame in the behavioral sciences usually comes to the shrewd innovator who places old terms in new combinations and applies these to an observed situation. This sort of fame is, it seems to me, an indication of the primitive philosophic and methodological status of the behavioral sciences. Each box in Table 1 contains the seed for dozens of Ph.D. theses and books, and even for new disciplines.

Below the diagonal we find sample combinations of terms, illustrating intergame combinations. Some are traditional; others, new. The list of such terms is endless, and such combinations are best made by systematic machine methods.

TABLE I. THE COACHING OF CREATIVE PERFORMANCE: SAMPLE MATRIX

Biological-Chemical-Physical Play	Chemical-physical	Physico-dynamics	Sexual-physical	Affective physical	Interpersonal physical	Psycho-physical	Physical-economical
	Bio-chemical	Bio-dynamics	Bio-sexual	Bio-affective	Interpersonal biology	Psycho-somatic	Bio-economic
Cultural Games	Intellectual-scientific	Intellectual dynamics	Sexual intellection	Affective intellection	Intellectual interpersonistics	Intellectual cognitive	Intellectual economics
	Social-political	Socio-dynamics	Sexual politics	Political affective	Political interpersonal	Political intellectual	Political economics
	Aesthetic	Aesthetical dynamics	Sexual aesthetics	Affective aesthetics	Interpersonal aesthetics	Cognitive aesthetics	Economic aesthetics
	Philosophical religious	Religious dynamics	Sexual religious	Affective religious	Interpersonal religious	Cognitive religious	Religious economics
	Recreational	Recreational dynamics	Sexual recreational	Affective recreation	Interpersonal recreation	Cognitive recreation	Television, stage, radio
	Occupational-financial	Economical dynamics	Sexual economics	Affective economics	Interpersonal economics	Cognitive economics	Intragame combinations
	Cognitive	Cognitive dynamics	Sexual cognition	Affective cognitive	Interpersonal cognitive	Intragame combinations	IBM
Ego Games	Interpersonal	Interpersonal dynamics	Sexual interpersonalistics	Interpersonal	Intragame combinations	Competitive thinking	Aggressive marketing
	Affective	Affective dynamics	Sexual affective	Intragame combinations	Dependent anxiety	Anxious thinking	Secure job
	Sexual	Sexual dynamics	Intragame combinations	Sexual bliss	Oral nurturance	Phallic mind	Oldest profession
	Psycho-dynamic	Intragame combinations	Repressed orality	Inhibited anxiety	Acted-out rage	Projected intelligence	Introjected wealth
		Psycho-dynamic	Sexual	Affective	Interpersonal	Cognitive	Occupational

Ego Games

USED FOR PRODUCTION OF NOVEL INTERGAME COMBINATIONS

Recreational-physical	Chemical religion	Aesthetical physical	Physical politics	Intellectual-physical	Bio-physical	Intragame combinations	Chemical physical
Recreational biology	Religious biology	Aesthetic biology	Biology politics	Intellectual biology	Intragame combinations	Electron microscope	Bio-chemical
Intellectual recreation	Theology	Intellectual aesthetics	Intellectual politics	Intragame combinations	Biological theory, well exploited	Physical theory	Intellectual-scientific
Political recreation	Religious politics	Political art	Intragame combinations	Brain trust	Politics of the nervous system	A.E.C	Social, political
Aesthetic recreation	Religious art	Intragame combinations	Picasso's Dove	The beautiful theory	Tranart	Electronic music	Aesthetics
Religious recreation	Intragame combinations	Gothic art	Religious crusade	Barron Art Scale	Wallace theory of evolution	Leibnitz	Philosophical-religious
Intragame combinations	Notre Dame football	Home art kits	Olympic games	Crossword puzzles	Zoological hobbies	The chemistry set	Recreational
O'Mally's Dodgers	Church bond drive	The art gallery	Oil politics	Academic politics	Drug industry	Chemical plants	Occupational-financial
Chess	Talmudic thinking	Cerebral art	Communist art	Cognitive theory	Neurological experiments	Magic mushrooms	Cognitive
Cooperative play	Christian love	Beautiful relationship	Massive rehabilitation	Leary's circle	Sheldon's types	Marital thermo-dynamics	Interpersonal
Happy games	Buddhist serenity	Serene painting	Spanish anguish	Research on moods	Psycho-somatics	The unstable nuclei	Affective
Already exploited	Dionysian rites	Folies Bergeres	Latin lovers	Kinsey	The oldest game	Hormones	Sexual
Repressed play	Projected sin	Introjected beauty	Dulles' foreign policy	Rorschach theory	Libido	Freudian thermo-dynamics	Psycho-dynamic
Recreational	Religious philosophic	Aesthetic	Social-political	Intellectual-scientific	Biochemical	Chemical-physical	

Cultural Games	*Biological-Chemical-Physical Play*

The most efficient use of this method for creating new performance combinations would involve coding the terms from every cultural game on computer cards. The list of game symbols (usually words) and artifacts (also represented by words) is finite and indeed relatively small. Computers could run through all possible game combinations which would then be evaluated for pilot-study trial. I cannot think of any creative performance which could not be facilitated (and, indeed, most performances entirely produced) by machine. Behavior is movement in time/space, and almost all movements in time/space are better performed by machine. Personal game behaviors are, of course, excepted from this generalization.

This statement will be considered a derogation or enhancement of human status, depending on your religious point of view. If your values are material, external, game-oriented, then you will be shocked at the statement that creative performance is best done by machines. If your values are spiritual and if you emphasize consciousness, then you will be delighted. Turn over creative performance and game innovation to machines, by all means, and this will provide more time and energy for man to develop new games from the untapped treasure of his internal life! Remember that a machine can create new combinations of old game units, but only a living organism possesses consciousness from which spring new games.

There are trends in modern literature and art, which suggest that this same point is occurring to some "creative experiencers." Certainly after James Joyce's lexicographical experiments (Huxley, 1959), the function of literature must be seen as conventional or innovating manipulations of a rather impoverished set of verbal symbols. This point of view has been advanced by the work of Burroughs and Gysin (1960), whose cut-up technique makes possible intensely effective communications. Burroughs and Gysin take scissors, cut up their own discursive productions, and put the pieces in a hat along with cut-up phrases from other relevant works. They then pull out phrases one by one, and the fortuitous combinations get the message across in powerful strokes.

Examples of the first rough draft of this cut up-and-combine technique are presented below without any polishing whatsoever.

> Cut the Word Lines with scissors or switchblade as preferred. The Word Line: keep in Time . . . cut the in lines . . . Make out lines to Space. Take a page of your own writing or a letter or a newspaper article of a page or less or more of any writer living and or dead. . . . Cut into sections. Down the middle. And cross the sides. . . . Rearrange the sections. . . . Write the results message. Who wrote the original words is still there in any rearrangement of his or her whatever words. . . . Can recognize Rimbaud cut up as Rimbaud. . . . A Melville cut up as Melville. . . Shakespear moves with Shakespear words. . . . So forth anybody can be Rimbaud if he will cut up Rimbaud's words and learn Rimbaud language talk think Rimbaud. . . . And supply reasonably appropriate meat. All dead poets and writers can be reincarnate in different hosts. (Burroughs and Gysin, 1960)

This cut-up method is, of course, a semiautomatic way of doing what poets have done for centuries—arrange shocking new combinations of phrases from unexpected game contexts. Burroughs and Gysin are telling us that the great poets when "cut up" remain themselves. Baudelaire "cut up" remains Baudelaire. The next step in this logical development of the word game is developing the poetry-writing machine.

Again, one's emotional reaction to these suggestions betrays his religious basis. If you evaluate words in the values of the monotheistic orthodoxies—Talmudic, scholastic, fundamentalist—then you are disturbed by the poetry machine. If you see the human spirit as far transcending (and indeed shackled by) words, then you are pleased at this spirit-freeing development.

In the past few paragraphs I have attempted to summarize too much—a theory and method of behavior-change, the application of this theory and method to creative performance, illustrations from empirical studies and *avant garde* literature, and, finally, some speculations about the future spiritual implications of man's intelligence reliance on machines.

THE EXPANSION OF CREATIVE AWARENESS

The only remaining task is to speak briefly about the final issue: the expansion of creative awareness, the constructive alteration of consciousness. This can be done, simply and directly, by the use of hallucinogenic drugs. The research with which I am associated has administered psilocybin to more than four hundred persons, many of whom are emotionally and financially dependent on being creative. I interpret our findings to confirm those presented by Frank Barron (1962b) and Aldous Huxley (1954, 1956, 1959). Artistic and literary folks respond ecstatically and wisely to drug experience. They tell us that this is what they have been looking for. They revel in the new and intense and direct confrontation with the world about them. Poets and painters have always tortured themselves to transcend ego-space/time boundaries. They do this by every means possible (including psychosis) and have been doing it with and without chemical stimulation for centuries. They are doing it today. I would estimate that well over half of the non-academic poets, writers, and composers in America today have experimented profitably with consciousness-altering vegetables or synthetics. I exclude our approved national narcotic—alcohol—from this estimate.

Our work with psilocybin has raised some interesting issues with respect to creative vision and creative performance. We have run more than one hundred psilocybin sessions in a maximum security prison. In addition to bringing about significant test changes in the direction of greater socialization and apparently lowering the crime rate (Leary, Metzner, Presnell, Schwitzgebel, and Kinne, 1963), these sessions have convinced me that the creative vision, the mystical illumination, is not the prerogative of the intellectual or the theologian. It is a function of the cortex when the cortex is temporarily relieved of word and ego games. More than half of our semi-literate prisoners reported in blunt, nonabstract words what have to be interpreted as mystical experiences (Leary and Clark, 1963). In other words we can take a lower-class, uneducated criminal, whose creativity diagnosis would be type 1-A, reproductive blocked (and socially inefficient) and, via psilocybin, he can experience what Blake saw in his visions. It's all there in the cortex after all.

This is to say, we can help him move from type 1 to type 4—creative blocked. But he does not have the language or the literary skills to communicate his vision. He tells us: "Yeah, doc. I saw all these flames of fire, and, wow, I was scared 'cause l knew it meant the end of me, but then, when I realized it can't really hurt because we're all part of the same thing anyway, so I relaxed and went into it and wham, it was like being in heaven or something, out beyond all those little things we're hung up on and then it was like being reborn and . . . ." Reports like this come from the most verbal of our prisoner group. The majority just look us in the eye, shake their heads in awe, and say simply, "Gee, Doc, those mushrooms are really something out of this world."

In terms of the diagnostic schema, the problem is to help the prisoner move from type 4 (creative blocked) to type 3 (creative creator). Here is where the game model helps. We obviously cannot wait fifteen years while the prisoner finishes graduate work in English Literature, that is, learns the literary game. The status and caste distinctions of the intellectual middle class have successfully shut out the lower-class kid from training in verbal felicity. But what we can do is coach him in the creative production of new combinations. We ask him for the major themes of his vision—fire, death, rebirth, the blind ruthlessness of cops, the ineffectiveness of his mother's religious lectures. Not having an IBM storage system, we go to the next best thing—books and articles which contain phrases about these topics, encyclopedia articles on fire, death, and rebirth, and criminology. We have passages typed out. We cut them up, and a group of convicts sit around a table pulling phrases out of a hat to construct a mystical poem in blank verse.

Creativity is not a function of lucky heritage or elite training. There are more visions in the cortex of each of us than in all the museums and libraries of the world. There is a limitless possibility of new combinations of the old symbols. A true democracy of creativity—experienced and performed—is possible and is, indeed, close at hand.

C　**(Barron) [Commentator]:** In describing the feedback study with art students, I think you should add what we did exactly. We took the scales that measure originality, and with every student we went over item by item the direction of response which he gave and compared it with the scored direction of response. In other words, what the students learned was how the actual measures indicated creative people behaved, item by item. In a sense, what we were doing was educating them to behave in a way that would enable them to answer those questions or take those tests in the same way as the persons who had demonstrated creativity in what they did. And then we had them take the tests again.

In a sense we were "teaching the tests," after they had taken the tests once. The realistic self-appraisal is extremely impressive because very frequently, when you tell a person how a creative individual answers an item, he will say, "Yes, I know that." I might add, right at this point, that I don't think in terms of the game business, but the same process is involved.

Brown has been doing some very interesting work along the same line. He has his subjects take the Barron-Welsh Art Scale. Then he takes a little child's book in which the two main characters are William Elephant and somebody Owl. They come upon a bunch of clothing lying on the beach. They have never seen human clothes before, and the book tells how William Elephant puts this clothing to some very unusual uses. (It is like an unusual test.) Mr. Owl keeps telling the elephant he can't do that, but he does, anyway. Brown has his subjects read this little story.

Then he says, "Now let that part of you which is William Elephant take over and take this art test again." And people know how to respond. That's the whole point.

C [**Commentator**]: To what degree is there a spread effect, or is this something specific to this test on which you taught them how to perform?

S [**Leary**]: I am convinced that the effect will spread to behavior in general. I think that you can take almost anyone if he is motivated and if he is willing to inquire into the matter carefully enough to make the changes which seem indicated. You can specify the ways in which you can produce greater creativity. You can change your behavior within game limits.

C: I thought that in terms of creativity the subjects did not change, that they said, "No, I don't want to change, that is the way I am."

S: Most of them were doing about what they wanted to do. Suppose that you have a person who says, "Yes, I want to be more creative than I am." I think that you can work with that person in these ways.

C: Maybe we need to form a society like Alcoholics Anonymous just to work with those people who want the treatment, who want to be more creative.

C: Why try to get somebody to do something when he doesn't want to?

C: Can't you develop the desire to be creative by changing goals, establishing goals?

C: Yes, that's what is involved in all this.

S: That is exactly the sort of program we developed in our psilocybin therapy program in the state prison. After the prisoners had psilocybin sessions, presumably they had some distance from their own role situation. We faced the problem of how to help those who wanted to change their life patterns. It's no easy matter. We used the game model which was very successful in the prison. Game language makes a good deal of sense to prisoners. A group of prisoners set up a club, a game which was called "Stay Out." They interviewed other prisoners and said in a blunt way, "if you want to join this club, you have to go along with the game goals. The goal of baseball is to make runs; the goal of football is to score touchdowns. But in this particular situation our goal is to *stay out*. And if anyone plays on our team who doesn't want to make touchdowns, who doesn't want to stay out, then he should quit." Positions are set up; strategies are planned. Principles such as cooperation are in effect.

C: It isn't all quite that simple. You could probably persuade people to change their responses on personality tests if they really wanted to appear creative and testified that they did. If you instructed them how to do this, they would then remember what you said and would turn around and indeed change their test responses. But if you ask them then to design a dam which will hold back so much water, or present another sort of problem with more of an ability-type measure, perhaps they couldn't solve this.

S: Right. You have to distinguish between motivation and technical performance. It's impossible for me to hit 61 home runs in Yankee Stadium in one year, even though I want to play that game.

C: I just wanted to make what was an obvious point.

C: What is the subject's perception of time during the drug state? Does he feel as if it has taken four to five or more hours or as if he may have been under for half an hour? Does he have any concept of this?

S: The time sense is dramatically altered. Several thousand things can occur in seconds. At other times it may seem like centuries between two events. Space/time is, of course, a learned, artifactual aspect of our psychological life.

C: Could you trace the connection of the drugs to the desire to make a change?

S: There are several ways in which psilocybin is useful in bringing about change in prisoners. The first has to do with getting the prisoner to give up his own professional role, which is just as important to him as our role is to us. These roles have been carefully and conscientiously developed. We want to get the prisoners as well as ourselves to flatten out the association curves, to use Mednick's phrase.

Now prisoners are notoriously the most difficult members of society to persuade to do this. A psilocybin experience, if it is run in a supportive non-manipulatory way, is almost guaranteed to undercut these role commitments. As the subject in Frank Barrow's movie said, "Who is _____ ?" This is a classic identity reaction of our subjects. It's as though the ego is seen as one little dot on a huge expanse of other possibilities.

Intensely close relationships develop among most people who had this experience together. In the past, when these visionary experiences were accidental, the social aspects, the group mystic experience, was never understood. A Dominican father in southern Spain had this experience in one century, and a Hindu on the bank of the Ganges in another century. The possibility of communication did not exist. And because the disciplined mystic experience involves a withdrawal from games and social interaction, your monastic or hermit doesn't have people around. The group drug experience allows this to happen.

C: You speak of social experience. Do you give these drugs to several prisoners simultaneously in the same room?

S: Yes.

C: The fact that they can see other possibilities—does this mean that anything different is going to happen, just because they see other possibilities?

S: Not necessarily.

C: Are these other possibilities other types of games, or are they non-game things?

S: When we began this work we knew very little about the contents of mystic experience. It was difficult to put into words, and we couldn't map these experiences or diagram them in three-dimensional space/time. Currently, our main project has to do with a mapping and diagramming of these experiences. The prisoner, ahead of time, can plot on a map his associative hierarchies. He can decide to stay away from some things, and he can attempt to plan which areas of consciousness he wants to go into. Set and setting account for 99% of what happens. We don't talk about "drug effects." We talk instead about "set-setting-plus-drug effects." In the prison we attempted to arrange the setting in such a way that it would stimulate awareness of the issues the prisoner wanted to study.

Here is an example of "game learning" by means of a nongame experience. In the past three months we have given psilocybin to 33 Christian ministers, priests, and some officials of Eastern religions. Twenty-seven of these 33 subjects (who came with a set which was religious and who took the drug in a setting which was aimed at generating these experiences) reported the most intense religious experiences of their life. I cite this as an example of how a disciplined, collaborative preparation determines the setting, and how a serious preparation of set and expectations can alter consciousness in the direction you want to go. This, we recall, is the goal of Eastern philosophy. I see a natural combination here of Eastern and Western points of view. I think that it is possible to get deep creative insights into whatever behavior sequence or professional occupation you are involved in, as, for example, our ministers.

C: You didn't turn any Protestants into Buddhists, did you?

S: Most of the religious subjects reported the most intensive religious experience of their lives, but there was some question as to whether this experience was Christian. The cortex in its nongame traction contact with the life process moves beyond sectarian ritual. Aldous Huxley tells us that every religious ritual and mythology was originally designed to bring about these experiences. I agree.

We are experimenting with different kinds of religious denominations. Some divinity sent floating down our stream a man who was ideally suited to help us. He was an M.D., taking a Ph.D. in a divinity school. A stubborn, idealistic, Midwestern experimentalist who had nothing to do with the drug himself, he determined to test the hypothesis that the drug experience was religious. He did something that none of us would ever have done, a most reckless, audacious scientific performance.

On Good Friday, in the chapel at one of the universities in the Boston area, he had 20 divinity students and 10 experienced project members participating in a double blind study. There was a very experimental manipulation of setting. The subjects were moved from one room to another according to schedule. This was quite contrary to almost all our principles that you shouldn't impose too much marching up and down on subjects, interfering with their own experience. Half of the subjects, including half of the researchers, ingested psilocybin while the rest of the group had nicotinic acid, a placebo which gives mild somatic affects. There was no question as to who was "control" and who was not. If you ever consider running a double blind study with these drugs, you must not have controls around experimental subjects because no one will be fooled. I knew at once that I had placebo. I knew immediately that two subjects in my group had placebo. I could tell by their red faces and their restless "game" activity that they had nicotinic acid. But they thought that they were on the verge of a mystic experience. They were winking, "We're the lucky ones." They started the "drug game," saying, "Isn't this great. The poor fellows in the other room are being left out of it." Later, after we had been in the chapel and saw other subjects reclining on the floor, obviously completely out of this world, the two called me and said, "Let's go back into the other room." They started playing the drug game again: "How long has it been?" "Gee, I thought I had it." "Now what did you feel exactly?"

C: They were still Christians, in other words.

S: A door banged open, and a man walked in, looked out the window, and said, "Magnificent." And he turned without looking at us as he walked out—it was clear that he was not "playing" social games. We all knew who was placebo and who was mystical.

C: Has anyone ever rejected the experience, or indicated that it was not as euphoric as you have described it?

S: Nine per cent of our subjects have reported unpleasant experience.

C: Anxiety arousing or just unpleasant?

S: Most of these subjects fought the experience. For example, in the Good Friday experience there were ten divinity students who had the real thing. One of them fought it all the way. He kept repeating: "Now when is it going to get over? I'm just not in control of myself. Now, didn't you say it would last four hours? When do I start losing the effects? I'm just not in control of myself."

C: Did this person have to work to fight it?

S: Oh, yes, very hard.

C: He didn't go nongame?

S: No.

C: Are the people who fight it also nonhypnotizable by an appropriate scale? Is there any relationship with this need for control?

S: We have not investigated that. I am confident that there would be a correlation. There is a magnificent selectivity operating here because the cortex is a rather accurate instrument. Some people are committed to control themselves in such a way that the notion of ego transcendence or ego loss is threatening. They sense this ahead of time, and they don't volunteer: if they do volunteer, they don't show up or they postpone it. This was the case of the one resistant divinity student. He didn't show up at the first orientation meeting and came late to the second. If it had not been for the social pressure of the divinity school, which was whipped up to a great fervor, he never would have gone through with it.

C: I got from Barron's report the impression that the subject, even though agreeing beforehand that she would dance or paint when the drug came, didn't want to do it and the effects didn't materialize. However, you give the impression that the prisoners could in a sense set themselves a task for the next session and that at this time they were going to determine what the life goal might be. Is this something that happens often? On this point the two reports seem to be in conflict.

S: It is possible that if I had pressed them that they would. But I didn't feel like asking them to do it.

The first session is a very important one. You can't plan for your first session. No matter how much you talk about transcending the ego, giving up the ego game, surrendering to the greater power, when it happens there are always moments of fright. Of course, courage is the key to creativity or to any relinquishing of the structure of the ego and the ego game. So I would never suggest planning a first session except to keep it free from external stimuli. It is obvious to us that almost as much courage and discipline is needed to explore and control the fantastically rapid space flights through consciousness as in planetary space voyage. It is only after one, two, or three sessions that a person can move with some foresight or planning to the point where he wants to be.

C: Since food habits are often associated with religion, have any religions started to include some of these mushrooms and such as part of their habits so that they can then have this kind or religious experience—either Eastern or Western religions?

S: These drugs have always been used for religious purposes, not as part of the diet but as part of the ceremony. Now pharmacologists are starting to use tryptomines, which provide a one-hour experience. This gets us down to the Sunday morning church service possibility.

C: Almost all the behavior that you have described has been essentially pleasant, positive, exploratory, a wonderful kind or experience. Hasn't there been any violent destructiveness, or hasn't anyone flown off the handle? You mentioned one prisoner who showed a lot of anger and so forth for the first session, but behavior doesn't seem to go amuck.

S: Some hellish experiences do occur in every session, but in general we have found activity of any sort to be considerably subdued.

C: Has there been any study of autonomic behavior during a session? Are physiological changes correlated with this? Generally physiologically, is the drug a depressant except for the cortical activity?

C: There are some physiological side effects, such as a drop in blood pressure and some muscle tonus changes toward more flaccidity. With LSD physiological results have been very close to nothing, even when the subject was reporting a wave of some kind of feeling. This happened in the only case that I have observed. The polygraph went along as though nothing had happened.

C: It makes a difference when the experimenter is able to establish rapport with the subject in repeated administrations, as Jarvik did, for example. For his sixty cases with LSD, he showed there is no decrement in functions such as arithmetic reasoning and various others.

A person can, if he makes the effort while under the influence of the drug, return himself to ordinary ego functioning. In certain motor performances, there was a slight decrement.

REFERENCES

Barron, Frank. "The Creative Writer." *California Monthly*. 1962a, 72 (5), 11–14, 38–39.

———. "Psychotherapy and Creativity." In G. S. Nielsen Ed. Proceedings of the XIV *International Congress of Applied Psychology, Copenhagen, 1961*. Copenhagen: Munksgaard, 1962b Vol IV pp. 36–49.

———. "The Relationship of Ego Diffusion to Creative Perception." Ed. Calvin Taylor. *Widening Horizons in Creativity*. New York: John Wiley & Sons, 1964.

Barron and Timothy Leary. "To Find and Foster Creativity." A Report of the Rhode Island School of Design. Providence, R.I. 1961.

Burroughs, William and B. Gysin. *The Exterminator*. San Francisco: Auerhahan Press, 1960.

Ditman, K. S., M. Hayman, and J. R. B. Whittlesey. "Nature and Frequency of Claims following LSD." *Journal of Nervous Disorders*. 134 (1962): 346–352.

Huxley, Aldous. *The Doors of Perception*. New York: Harper, 1954.

———. *Heaven and Hell*. New York: Harper, 1956.

———. The Island. New York: Harper, 1959.

Joyce, James. *Finnegan's Wake*. New York: Viking Press, 1959.

Jung, Carl. *Psychological Types*. New York: Harcourt Brace, 1923.

———. "Psychological Commentary." In W. Y. Evans-Wentz Ed. *The Tibetan Book of the Dead*. London: Oxford University Press, 1960.

Leary, Timothy. "How To Change Behavior." In G. S. Neilson Ed. *Clinical Psychology*. Copenhagen: Munksgaard, 1962a.

———. "Interpersonal Behavior and Behaviorism." Harvard University, 1962b (dittoed).

———. "Measuring Verbal Interaction in Freudian and Rogerian Psychotherapy." Harvard University, 1962c (dittoed).

Leary, T., & W. Clark. "Religious Implications of Consciousness-Expanding Drugs." *Religious Education*, 1963.

Leary, T., & M. Gill. "The Dimensions and a Measure of the Profess of Psychotherapy." In E. Rubenstein Ed. *Research in Psychotherapy*. American Psychology Association, 1959.

Leary, T., G. H. Litwin, and R. Metzner. "Reactions to Psilocybin Administered in a Supportive Environment." *Journal of Nervous and Mental Diseases.* 137:6 (1963).

Leary, T., R. Metzner, and R. Alpert. *The Psychedelic Experience.* New Hyde Park: University Books, 1964.

Leary, T., R. Metzner, M. Presnell, Gunther Weil, R. Schwitzgebel, and S. Kinne. "A Change Program for Adult Offenders Using Psilocybin." Cambridge: Psychedelic Review Service.

McGlothlin, William. "Long-Lasting Effects on Certain Attitudes in Normals: An Experimental Proposal." California: Rand Corp., 1962 (mimeographed).

Meyers, W. "Creativity as a Set or Role." Unpublished doctoral dissertation. Harvard University, 1963.

PART 2

Altering Human Nature

Psychedelic Drugs and the Concord
Prison Experiment

The Concord Prison Experiment (CPE) was undoubtedly Leary's boldest research project. It proposed that his psilocybin therapy could foster behavior change in hardened criminals. The CPE was also revolutionary because it put the core principals of Leary's existential transaction theory (ETT) into practice. Leary's team of psychologists—mainly idealistic Harvard graduate students—would get in the trenches and take psilocybin with inmates at the Massachusetts Correctional Center in Concord. The goal was prisoner rehabilitation through group therapy and a psilocybin-induced transformative experience. In 1968, Leary described his pitch to the prisoners as a combination of game theory and his mantra of "tune in, turn on, drop out": "The solution was obvious. The prisoners had to turn-on, see the game the way it was, then drop out. Just stop playing the bad-boy game. See it, laugh at it, and drop out" (*High Priest* 200).

The CPE can also be viewed as an extension of Leary's initial psilocybin research. The Harvard Psilocybin Project (HPP) had indicated that psychedelic drugs could enhance the creative process and, in many cases, stimulate greater creativity in the user. Most of the writers and musicians who participated in the HPP described how psilocybin was an amazing psychological lubricant for all facets of the creative process. While Leary's findings were interesting to many scholars, some psychologists were skeptical about Leary's results because his *ex post facto* reports were too subjective (i.e., unreliable because they were written by people who had taken psychedelic drugs). Thus, Leary began to search for a more rigorous way to prove psilocybin's therapeutic usefulness. His solution to the problem of providing "hard" empirical evidence was the CPE. Leary would run psilocybin sessions with prisoners to stimulate behavior change. The long-term goal was prisoner rehabilitation. Leary describes his initial enthusiasm for the Concord Prison Experiment in *Flashbacks:* "I had two purposes in mind: first, if we could change the behavior of violent criminals with our drugs, we'd demonstrate that our methods and theories worked where nothing else did. Second, prison rehabilitation would provide us with the behavior scientist's dream, an iron-clad objective index of improvement—the recidivism rate" (79). Leary's project was ambitious because "fifty to seventy per cent of offenders paroled or released return within a five-year period, with a nationwide average of 67%."

Part 2 contains two of Leary's three articles that were published on the Concord Prison Experiment.* Although Leary's methods and findings have been criticized in recent decades, these articles are important historical documents that capture the ambitious attempt to reform the clinical practices of psychotherapy and prisoner rehabilitation.† Leary's articles illustrate the powerful bonding experience that psychedelic drugs engender. The utopianism of the Concord Prison Experiment—

---

*"The Use of Psychedelic Drugs in Prisoner Rehabilitation" was too lengthy to include in this volume. It was published in *The British Journal of Social Psychiatry* 2 (1967–1968): 27–51.

†See my prefaces for "A New Behavior Change Program Using Psilocybin" and "The Effects of Consciousness-Expanding Drugs on Prisoner Rehabilitation." For an extensive critique of Leary's Concord Prison Experiment, see Rick Doblin's "Dr. Leary's Concord Prison Experiment: 34-Year Follow Up Study," *Journal of Psychoactive Drugs* 30, no. 4 (1998): 419–26.

especially the notion of radical empathy—would have significant influence on the Zeitgeist of the 1960s.

REFERENCES

Leary, Timothy. *Flashbacks: A Personal and Cultural History of an Era*. New York: Jeremy Tarcher/Perigee, 1990.

———. *High Priest*. New York: The World Publishing Company, 1968.

5

Reforming Aggression: The Concord Prison Experiment

A New Behavior Change Program Using Psilocybin

Timothy Leary, Ralph Metzner,
Madison Presnell, Gunther Weil,
Ralph Schwitzgebel, and Sara Kinne

"A New Behavior Change Program Using Psilocybin" is the first of three articles that were based on the Concord Prison Experiment. It features six authors who participated in the research: four Harvard graduate students, the prison psychiatrist at the Massachusetts Correctional Institution (Dr. Madison Presnell), and Leary himself. Many other Harvard graduate students participated in the project, but they were not listed as co-authors. Although the Concord Prison Experiment was conducted in 1961 and 1962, this article, the first of three on the experiment, was published in 1965. The second article—"The Use of Psychedelic Drugs in Prisoner Rehabilitation"—appeared in the *British Journal of Social Psychiatry* in 1968 as an expanded version of "A New Behavior Change Program Using Psilocybin."

The third article, "The Effects of Consciousness-Expanding

Drugs on Prisoner Rehabilitation," originally appeared in *Psychedelic Review*, volume 10, 1969, and also in Leary's book *High Priest*; it is also the next article of this book.

The rationale of the project was based on Leary's existential transaction analysis and game theory. The prisoner is taught to recognize how "self-defeating games [i.e., returning to a life of crime] are maintained largely through inability to recognize the features and rules of the game one is involved in, and through inability to detach the self from its actions." In Leary's project, psilocybin allows one to unplug from everyday roles and rituals. Moreover, the state of detachment that psilocybin may provide can offer insights into how to constructively change problematic repetitive behavioral patterns.

Both articles document the utopian optimism of the early 1960s. Leary believed that psychedelic drugs and existential transaction therapy could produce behavior change even in hardened criminals. As we know, transactional theory implied that participants must share time and space with the prisoners, and that Leary and his graduate students should treat the inmates as equals rather than as patients. Leary's emphasis on taking drugs with the inmates was an attempt to refute the doctor-patient model of treatment.

The results of the Concord Prison Experiment appeared to be promising at first. "A New Behavior Change Program Using Psilocybin" reports that "after termination of the program the rate of new crimes has been reduced from 28% to 7%." However, the authors also noted "[that] if parole violations are counted the overall return rate has not changed." In the 1990s, the findings reported in both articles were challenged by Rick Doblin in his article, "Dr. Leary's Concord Prison Experiment: A 34-Year Follow Up Study" (1998). Doblin argues that "Leary's report of a dramatic treatment effect was the result of a misleading use of base rate data." The main problem was that the Concord Prison Experiment was based on a recidivism rate derived from a ten-month release period. For most researchers, a ten-month release period was simply too brief to be conclusive. Moreover, Leary and his co-authors failed to mention that the base rate study figure used for comparison was actually thirty months. Leary's critics argue that he published their results too quickly and that he should have waited for the thirty-month results. However, Leary was not in a position to do a follow-up study because he had been fired by Harvard in May of 1963.

Doblin also questions Leary's notion of psilocybin-induced behavior change. In his follow-up study, Doblin presents a foundational critique of Leary's prisoner rehabilitation program: "[the Concord Prison Experiment indicates] [t]he myth of psychedelic drugs as magic bullets, the ingestion of which will automatically confer wisdom and create lasting change after just one or even a few experiences. Personality change may be made more likely after a cathartic and insightful experience, but only sustained hard work after the drug has worn off will serve to anchor and solidify any movement toward healing and behavior change" (425).

In an interview shortly before his death in 1996, Leary acknowledged Doblin's criticisms and commented on the lessons of the Concord Prison Experiment: "The key to a long-term reduction in overall recidivism rates might be the combination of the pre-release administration of psilocybin-assisted group psychotherapy with a comprehensive post-release follow up program modeled on the Alcoholics Anonymous groups to offer support to the released prisoners" (Doblin 424). The psychologists working on the Concord Prison Experiment made some attempts to stay in touch with prisoners post-release, but they did not have resources to establish a halfway house with regular meetings. The lack of a strong post-release support system can also be considered a major flaw in the Concord Prison Project's intervention strategy.

JAMES PENNER

REFERENCES

Conn Darling, Diane, Rick Doblin, and Ralph Metzner. "Prison Behavior Change and Experimental Mysticism: Two Classic Studies from the Harvard Psilocybin Project." *Sacred Mushroom of Vision: Teonanácatl.* Rochester, Vt.: Park Street Press, 2004.

Doblin, Rick. "Dr. Leary's Concord Prison Experiment: A 34-Year Follow Up Study." *Journal of Psychoactive Drugs* 30, no. 4 (1998): 419–26.

Leary, Timothy. *Flashbacks: A Personal and Cultural History of an Era.* New York: Jeremy P. Tarcher/Perigee, 1983.

Leary, Timothy, Ralph Metzner, Madison Presnell, Gunther Weil, Ralph Schwitzgebel, and Sara Kinne. "A New Behavior Change Program Using Psilocybin." *Psychotherapy: Theory, Research and Practice* 2 (July 1965): 61–72.

Leary, Timothy, and Ralph Metzner. "Use of Psychedelic Drugs in Prisoner Rehabilitation." *British Journal of Sociology* 2 (1967–68): 27–51.

A NEW BEHAVIOR CHANGE PROGRAM USING PSILOCYBIN

From *Psychotherapy: Theory, Research and Practice* volume 2, July 1965, pages 61–72.

Timothy Leary, Ralph Metzner, Madison Presnell, Gunther Weil, Ralph Schwitzgebel, and Sara Kinne

The help, advice and encouragement of the following persons are gratefully acknowledged: Edward W. Grennan, Superintendent of Massachusetts Correctional Institution, Concord; David C. McClelland, Ph.D., Director of the Center for Research in Personality, Harvard University; Norman A. Neiberg, Ph.D., Director of Psychological Research in the Division of Legal Medicine; and David Houghey, Ph.D., Director of Psychological Research in the Department of Correction; Bernard Dee, Institutional Parole Officer; William P. Ryan, head Correctional Social Worker; Cornelius Twomey, Chairman of the Parole Board and Martin Davis, Chief of Parole Division. The following graduate students contributed actively to this program: Stephen Berger, Jonathan Clark, Don Fowles, Rudolf Kalin, David Kolb, George Litwin, Jonathan Shay, James Uleman, and Michael Hollingshead.

◆ ◆ ◆

This paper describes the procedure and results of a new kind of behavior change or rehabilitation program. The methods used here may have applications to a wide range of settings in the field of rehabilitation or behavior change.

The program aims to produce such changes in prisoners' ways of thinking and living as will enable them to stay out of prison once they are released. It is well known that our contemporary prison systems do not perform this function (usually called "reforming" the criminal). Fifty to seventy percent of offenders paroled or released return within a 5-year period, with a nationwide average of 67% (Mattick, 1960).

Many attempts have been made to develop treatment programs which would better serve the purpose of "reform" or "rehabilitation."

Our program may be summarized as follows:

(1) It is a collaborative group program; we avoid as much as possible the traditional doctor-patient, researcher-subject, or professional-client roles.

(2) The program is relatively short and emphasizes the crucial importance of certain far-reaching "insight" experiences (produced by consciousness-altering drugs).

(3) The program has a built in evaluation procedure. Records of changes serve as feedback for the group members and to communicate the activities of the group to other research workers.

The program does not require expensive professional personnel. It does require persons (usually non-professionals possessing a certain egalitarian wisdom) who are experienced in the procedures we have developed.

Although the particular combination of methods used in this program is new, some of the methods have been used successfully by others within institutional settings. Stürup (1957) has developed a group "total treatment" program for criminals, involving insight experience, self-help in changing patterns of interaction and the concept of the "chain-reaction" by which groups are encouraged to further their own learning and progress. The Highfields project, which uses "guided group interaction" to provide insight and assumes that increased responsibility makes for change, is also similar in many respects (McCorkle et al., 1958). Feedback and self-evaluation by the group has been discussed by Jenkins (1948). Most writers on group treatment have agreed that the learning and change takes place through observation and understanding of "here-and-now" experience and behavior. The group behavior which serves as the focus around which the learning takes place may be role-playing (Levit and Jennings, 1960) or psychodrama (Moreno, 1959); or it may be some set of stimuli brought in from the outside, such as a problem or a case-history (Slater, 1961). In our case, this group experience around which the therapeutic process is constructed is the shared insight experienced by psilocybin.*

Although psilocybin per se has only rarely been used in therapy (e.g. Duché and Laut, 1961) other drugs from the same group such as LSD-25 have of course been widely used as adjuncts to therapy (e.g. Abrahamson, 1955; Cutner, 1959; Sandison, 1954). More recently Tenenbaum (1961) also reports the use of LSD with criminal offenders in a prison setting.

The halfway house for parolees is also an integral part of our program. There have been many attempts to establish such transitional institutions, based on the principle of support coming from others who have shared similar experiences. The St. Dismas Home in St. Louis for ex-convicts, the Synanon, Inc. group in California for ex-addicts, and especially Alcoholics Anonymous are some of the better known examples.

PROCEDURES

This program was carried out in the Massachusetts Correctional Institution, Concord, a maximum security prison for younger offenders, between February, 1961, and January, 1963. Concord's daily average population in 1959 was 395, the average age is around 21 or 22. During 1959, 67% of the 247 men committed were recidivists, i.e., had served former commitments, mostly in county jails or juvenile institutions.

---

*Grateful acknowledgement is also made to Sandoz Pharmaceuticals, and its director, Carl Henze, M.D., for supplying us with psilocybin and for his continued interest and cooperation in our program.

The program as now developed through pilot studies, and continual revision and improvement over the period of a year may be divided into five stages: selection, testing, change program, pre-parole period and parole. In describing the stages we will distinguish between what we actually did and what we would now do, having learned from our mistakes.

Stage 1: Selection. Candidates for the program were selected by the prison parole officer according to the following criteria: (1) they were eligible for parole in three to five months' time; (2) they had not had more than one previous parole violation.

We now add a third criterion: we do not accept inmates who will be paroled out of state because of the difficulty of keeping adequate follow-up records. The group thus selected is interviewed by a clinical psychologist and a psychiatrist jointly, the program is explained and volunteers are accepted. Of the 40 men interviewed 2 refused and 6 did not complete the program for technical reasons. Thus only 32 men are involved in the final evaluation.

During our pilot studies we also accepted inmates from sources other than the parole officer. Three were referred by the prison psychiatrist. One was accepted because of his interest in the project. These were older men with longer records and longer sentences.

We now feel that it is wiser to adhere strictly to the criteria developed because otherwise the project becomes involved with power struggles in the institution which may cause tension in the groups. Also, older inmates serving long sentences pursue somewhat different objectives in the group than men who are about to be paroled. These different goals need not conflict but they are distinct: a young offender at Concord is most likely to concern himself with post-release adjustment to life outside. An older offender serving a 15–20 year sentence is more likely to be trying to find ways of adjusting to prison life.

It should be noted that the participants are not necessarily men who have sought help for "psychological" problems. Simultaneous individual therapy for participants in the group program may be a valuable complement. However, the group program, with its emphasis on collaborative ways of self-help, provides a behavior change setting for many men who would refuse to seek help within the traditional psychiatric framework.

We have experimented with different sizes of groups, five to ten inmates with three psychologists. Large groups are too unwieldy. For the major experiment the groups consisted of three new inmates, one psychologist and one additional inmate who had already participated in the program once.

Stage 2: Testing and feedback. After an initial discussion meeting the inmates take a battery of personality tests consisting of the MMPI (Minnesota Multiphasic Personality Inventory), the CPI (California Psychological Inventory), the Maher Sentence Completion Test (Watt & Maher, 1958), designed especially to measure cynicism in prisoners, and a TAT (Thematic Apperception Test) constructed especially to measure a variety of motives.

Then follow three to four discussion meetings (twice a week). Test results are "fed-back" and personal situations are reviewed. The group is told about the possible experiences with psilocybin and encouraged, on the basis of their test results and the information on psilocybin, to plan and initiate their own individual personality change programs. This may take the form of statements such as "I want to understand what drinking means to me" or "I want to try and reduce my paranoid suspicions." We have found, however, that the *first* time a person takes psilocybin most can be learned by not imposing any plans or pre-conceived interpretation on the experience. Thus, goal-setting becomes more important for second or third experiences. Group leaders carefully avoid imposing *their* expectation. They emphasize the wide variety of different individual experiences that can be had. Any planning must come from the subject himself.

Stage 3: Change program. The group meets for an all-day session in a room in the prison hospital and takes psilocybin. The main effects of the drug usually last about 3–4 hours but the group stays together all day for support and discussion.

During the session, the atmosphere is relaxed and permissive. Beds are provided for subjects to lie down if they wish, music is also available, the session is not interrupted by visitors or guards. No interpretations are made, although the more experienced group members are always ready to handle panic or paranoia by providing a warm, supportive "reality" orientation. To do this, it is necessary that the group leaders have experienced the effects at some time, since they would otherwise be incapable of understanding the reactions the members of the group are having. We have experimented with different dosages and now usually start with 20 or 30 mg., and in subsequent sessions increase up to 50 or 70 mg. Large dosages should only be taken by an experienced subject in a very secure situation, since they can be quite shattering. The prison psychiatrist is always in attendance during the session to handle any adverse physical reactions, although we have never had any except transient minor nausea and headache. In order to minimize suspicion on the part of the inmates and to increase the sense of collaborative trust, we have found it advisable for one of the group leaders to take a small amount of the drug (5–10 mg.) in initial sessions.

After the session, a series of three to four discussion meetings is held, during which subjects work through their experiences, compare, analyze and try to integrate into everyday life what they have learned. Then follows a second all-day session with psilocybin and further discussion meetings.

Our program in the major study consisted of 6 weeks of bi-weekly meetings, with two psilocybin sessions.* However, there is some evidence that a longer (perhaps 8-week) program with at least three psilocybin sessions would be better. Partly this is because the first session tends to be minimal in terms of learning, since subjects often spend a major portion of the day fighting the experience off. Only when con-

---

*The pilot group usually had three sessions; some of the later group members also participated as assistant group leaders, hence the number of psilocybin sessions is not constant. The actual distribution is as follows: 15 had two sessions, 9 had three, 4 men had four, and 5 had five. One man, a chronic alcoholic and multiple parole violator, was given the drug once outside of the regular program; he is not included in the main sample. We feel that alcoholics present a special problem and have not attempted to cope with it here. Other investigators, however, (Chwelos, et al., 1959) have reported considerable success using LSD-25 with alcoholics.

fidence in the experience and in the group is established, through this first experience, does real learning begin.

After the final discussion meetings the men are re-tested with the same battery of tests and the results again fed back.

Stage 4: Pre-parole period. Around this time most of the men come up before the parole board and will either be given a date or deferred. If they are paroled, they move into a special *pre-parole group.* In this group they discuss the nature of parole, employment opportunities, difficulties and legal problems they may have. We provide whatever help we realistically can. We have been aided in this by graduate students from Harvard University who work in Concord as part of their training in clinical psychology. Psychologists may meet individually with inmates to work out anticipated special problems. The rationale underlying these procedures is to minimize abruptness, shock and difficulty in adjusting to non-prison life.

Those men who are not paroled but have been through the program participate as assistant group leaders in one of the next groups. This serves both to increase inmate collaboration and responsibility and to maintain contact with all our participants.

Stage 5: Parole. This phase of our program was never fully developed. We now realize that it is necessary to set up a halfway house where members of the project can meet regularly and discuss mutual problems along Alcoholic Anonymous lines. For practical and material reasons we were limited to irregular individual contacts with group members. In making such contacts we have found it necessary to "set the limits" of our contract rather widely. Thus most ex-convicts will not come to a middle-class institution like a university unless highly motivated. The only alternative is for the group leader to seek out the men in the community, e.g., in bars or homes, sometimes at unusual hours, as the need arises.

RATIONALE OF THIS PROGRAM

The guiding principles underlying this program are that the problem of changing behavior is not one of "curing" and "illness." Our approach is outside of a medical framework *(cf.* Leary, 1961), and more in line with an existential approach. We assume that self-defeating behavior patterns (such as recidivism) can be overcome by recognizing the *game-quality* of conduct (Szasz, 1960). A "game" is any learned behavior sequence with roles, rules, rituals, values, specialized languages and limited goals. Self-defeating games are maintained largely through inability to recognize the features and rules of the game one is involved in, and through inability to detach the self from its actions; they are maintained further through lack of instrumental capacity (power, knowledge) to carry out one's preferred games successfully. Helplessness is the key obstacle to efficient game performance.

Thus many of our procedures are designed to reduce helplessness. Relationships which imply or emphasize power differences are avoided as much as possible. Decisions are made collaboratively by all group members whenever possible. Any knowledge or resources the group leaders have are shared with the group members. This is the rationale for feedback of the test results and interpretations. Maximum responsibility for his own change processes is given to each prisoner. He is encouraged to practice new games and given the help of whatever resources we have.

New interpersonal or behavioral games can only be acquired in shared time and space. In the field of criminology this principle was formulated in the "differential association theory" of Sutherland (1955). Prisoners learn their games from the two groups that share most time and space with them, *viz.* other prisoners and guards. No middle-class role-relationship could possibly compete with or counteract that influence. Goffman (1957) has made a similar point with reference to the role of attendants in mental hospitals. Therefore we have stressed the importance of mutual collaborative problem-solving at all stages of the program.

The role of the drug experience. The drug used in this project, psilocybin, is a synthetic derivative of *psilocybe Mexicana,* the "Sacred Mushroom" of Mexico. It was discovered by R. Gordon Wasson in 1954, synthesized by A. Hofmann of the Sandoz Laboratories in Basel, Switzerland, and is classified with the group of drugs variously known

as "hallucinogenic," "psychotomimetic" or "consciousness-expanding"—
a group that also includes mescaline and LSD-25.

We have found that in a benign, supportive setting and with a favorable set, psilocybin can produce a state of dissociation or detachment
from the roles and games of everyday interaction (*cf.* Leary, Litwin, and
Metzner, 1963). This detachment, or temporary suspension of defenses,
can provide insight and perspective about repetitive behavior or thought
patterns and open up the way for the construction of alternatives. If
the defenses are abandoned in a non-anxiety provoking situation, the
experience also serves to establish a quite profound level of trust and
communication between members of the group.

If the situation is such that suspicion or fear are aroused then the
drug experience will only lead to an intensification of defensive maneuvers. This often happens the first time the group takes the drug and
hence it is important to prepare each group member intensively for what
he may experience. Subjects who are caught by surprise and become
afraid of the effects will attempt to fight the experience, e.g., by becoming hypochondriacal about physiological changes, or by obsessive talking, writing or moving around, or by paranoid accusations against the
group leaders or against people present who have not taken the drug.

This is why previous experience with [the] drug is important. An
inexperienced person is likely to communicate his own anxiety about
the reaction. The group should be, to quote Gerald Heard (1959),
". . . concerned but not anxious, interested but not engrossed, diagnostic
but not critical, aware of the seriousness and confidential value of what
is being conveyed and all the more incapable of coldness or shock, aloofness or dismay . . . Any sense of fear or alienness means that the root
danger and origin of all breakdown, i.e., separation is present."

During the main effects of the drug, which start about half an hour
after ingestion and last 3–4 hours, a minimum of interpretation or analysis is done; participants are best left free to explore whatever material
comes up, whether it be entirely personal or involve interpersonal issues
with other group members. Afterwards, when ordinary reality relations

have been re-established, there is generally a very fruitful period for discussion and review. (See *Handbook on the Therapeutic Use of LSD* by Blewett and Chwelos, 1959.)

Psilocybin has the advantages over LSD and mescaline of (a) being relatively short-lasting and (b) involving minimal somatic side effects.

Two special problems: (1) the two or three days after an intense insight-producing drug experience can be quite painful and depressing as the subject attempts, usually with some difficulty, to integrate the enormous quantity of material into his habitual life-patterns. Hence group support, exchange of experience and discussion, is particularly important at this time. (2) The *second* problem is that with group psilocybin experiences that are repeated there is a danger for certain persons to attempt to use the experience to maintain or improve their "games" rather than to see through them. This can express itself in narcissistic preoccupation with one's own "profound" experiences and a certain superior aloofness towards other less experienced group members. This is exemplified in the case of S., described below, who in one session repeatedly demanded more of the drug and when it was refused became irritated and withdrawn. It should be the role of one of the other group members or of the leader to point out in a calm, non-critical way whenever a person gets caught in an ego-enhancing pattern for its own sake. Such selfishness tends to obstruct the progress of a really therapeutic and enlightening experience.

TWO EXAMPLES

The Case of J. J. is a 28-year old Negro who was serving a 5-year sentence for robbery. (6 prior arrests of which 5 were for drunkenness.) He attended a school for retarded children until the age of 17.

The group leader reported that from the start "J's behavior in the group was cooperative and interested. Although he did not talk a lot he followed the group program very closely." During the first psilocybin session he experienced feelings of confusion and isolation.

In his report he wrote: "I kept saying to myself in thought—where do you belong?" Through discussions afterwards he gained some insight into his experience, and his relationship. The second experience, in the same group of 4 men as before, was much more intense and emotional, with hallucinations of colors, of positive and frightening scenes; it apparently stimulated him to do some thinking about his life.

A few weeks later J. was released on parole. His employer was quite satisfied with his work. At the time of the follow-up evaluation there had been no arrests of J. since his release from prison two years earlier and no indications of criminal involvements.

The Case of S. S. was a 48-year-old white man who was serving time on charges of being a common and notorious thief, forgery, larceny and escape. He had a prior history of 30 arrests, the first one being at the age of 12. The offenses were mostly drunkenness (9) and thefts of small amounts of money by the use of bad checks. He had served eleven prior commitments with a total time of fourteen years in prison.

On the initial tests S. presented the classic picture of a "hardened inmate." The Pd and Ma scales on the MMPI were both elevated—the well-known profile of acting-out criminals.

During the first psilocybin session, S. was suspicious and attempted to control and suppress the changes that were occurring, partly due to a competitive situation with another inmate.

For the second session, in the same group, he was given a larger dose (40 mg.) since he was a very heavily-built individual. Out of the shell of the hardened criminal emerged a sensitive, lonely, child-like human being. "At the time of the peak of the drug's effect I had a terrific feeling of sadness and loneliness, and a feeling of great remorse of the wasted years. . . . It seemed to me that I was crying inside of me and a feeling as if tears were washing everything away. And I was hollow inside, with just an outer shell standing there watching time stand still."

He continued in a second group as assistant group leader. With a group of three younger inmates it was possible for him to assume a role of responsible and encouraging leadership. In the two sessions with this group he was able to experience and explore certain more alien and unacceptable aspects of his personality. In one it was the fear of death which he envisioned in the form of a summoning figure; in the other it was his own selfishness (in demanding drugs). After both experiences he reported feeling very detached from prison life, uninterested in gambling or even talking to anyone except those in his group.

In describing the influence of the project experience on his life, S. wrote: ". . . before taking this drug my thinking always seemed to travel in the same circles, drinking, gambling, money and women and sex as easy and I guess a fast life . . . Now my thoughts are troubled and at times quite confusing, but they are all of an honest nature, and of wondering. I know what I want to be and I am sincere in my mind when I say I will try very hard to make it so. I also know that the mushroom drug, in group discussions, and tests, the group therapy is most important. Because there is then also an opening of the mind, and you also get a better understanding of yourself and also the people who are in your group. You feel more free to say and discuss things, which you generally do not do."

He was discharged some weeks later, unexpectedly released from several outstanding warrants and was rather disoriented by the sudden change. However, he obtained a job with a construction company, he worked ten to thirteen hours a day and one month later was promoted to assistant foreman of a small crew. He and two friends subsequently started an auto body paint shop. A few months later he became assistant cook in a large restaurant. Two years later he was still out of prison and working successfully.

Evaluation: Our evaluation research was designed as follows. After a series of pilot group experiences involving a total of nine inmates, the main treatment group of 12 men was run through the program from September to October, 1961. The men met in 4 groups of 3 inmates each, with one psychologist and one inmate from the pilot groups serving as group leaders. A control group of ten men was given the pre- and post-tests at the same time as the treatment group, but did not have any other contact with the program. After the first six-week program they then became the second experimental group, with members of the first group serving as assistant leaders.

THE DESIGN DIAGRAMMATICALLY

	Tests	Six Weeks	Tests	Six Weeks	Tests
Experimental Group	I	Treatment	II	–	–
Control Group	I	Nothing	II	Treatment	III

The actual results will be presented separately for the three sets for data—personality tests, behavior ratings and return rates.

A. Personality Tests. Table I [on page 154] shows the MMPI scores from pre- and post-tests for the pilot and experimental groups. It should be remembered that the schedule and time-period intervening between pre- and post-tests for the pilot subjects was somewhat longer and more variable than for the experimental subjects. The number of subjects involved in the analysis is less than the total sample owing to incomplete test-protocols or subject dropout. All means are based on T-scores, except for the ego-strength scale, which is based on raw scores. It will be seen that although on several of the scales (D, Pd, Sc, Ma) there are changes in the expected direction, these are not significant. The drop in the psychopathic deviate scale is almost significant at the .05 level. The significant decreases in the two validity scales (L and F) indicate that subjects are less likely to put on a good front or answering at random after the treatment program.

Table II shows the MMPI scores for the Control group before the control period (I), at the end of the control period and before treatment (II), and after treatment (III). Three comparisons were made, all using Wilcoxon signed-rank tests and 2-tailed probability levels. Comparing I and II no difference was predicted and none was found. Comparing the

TABLE I. MEAN MINNESOTA MULTIPHASIC PERSONALITY INVENTORY SCORES OF PILOT AND EXPERIMENTAL GROUPS

Scale	Pilot Group (N = 8)		Experimental Group (N = 11)		Significance*	
	pre	post	I—pre	II—post	A	B
L	50.1	50.1	54.9	49.6	p<.01	NS
F	64.7	50.2	60.5	53.1	p<.05	p<.01
K	57.1	51.1	52.4	51.0	NS	NS
Hs	51.0	45.5	47.5	46.6	NS	NS
D	61.1	50.1	58.8	52.7	NS	NS
Hy	58.0	56.1	53.0	54.7	NS	NS
Pd	77.8	73.6	71.1	60.0	NS	near
Mf	50.9	50.7	62.3	62.7	NS	sig.<.05
Pa	50.1	50.5	56.1	56.6	NS	NS
Pt	50.6	50.4	56.9	51.5	NS	NS
Sc	62.1	50.6	58.2	52.7	NS	NS
Ma	65.0	65.6	66.8	64.2	NS	NS
Si	50.2	46.1	47.4	49.2	NS	NS
Es	—	50.0	47.2	46.9	NS	NS

Col. A: Significance of difference from pre- to post-test for Experimental Group.
Col. B: Significance of difference from pre- to post-test for Pilot and Experimental Groups combined.
*All significance estimates made with Wilcoxon signed-rank test. Probability levels are two-tailed.

changes from I to II with the changes from II to III it was predicted the latter would be greater. However, the differences were not significant on any of the scales. It will be noted that on several of the scales (Hy, Pd, Pt, Sc) there is a U-shaped trend, with a tendency for scale scores to rise on the third testing after the treatment. This might reflect some peculiar effects due to repeated testing. The fact that the mean F-score did not change also indicates that the validity of these post-treatment scale scores is somewhat doubtful. When I and III, i.e., first and last tests are compared, only the D-scale shows a significant decrease (p < .02).

Table III shows the mean scale scores from the CPI (California Psychological Inventory) for the pilot and experimental groups. Again, significance of change was estimated for the experimental group alone and for pilot and experimental groups combined. Significant increases

TABLE II. MEAN MINNESOTA MULTIPHASIC PERSONALITY INVENTORY SCORES OF CONTROL GROUP

Scale	Controls (N = 9)		
	I	II	III
L	44.3	34.8	43.1
F	65.1	64.9	63.9
K	45.7	48.3	48.7
Hs	49.4	47.8	48.7
D	62.2	59.7	57.1
Hy	53.0	49.7	53.9
Pd	76.8	68.8	79.7
Mf	56.4	52.7	55.4
Pa	54.7	56.8	59.9
Pt	61.8	58.9	62.1
Sc	66.3	61.9	65.7
Ma	67.8	67.8	72.3
Si	57.3	55.9	53.1
Es	44.4	46.1	46.4

TABLE III. MEAN CALIFORNIA PERSONALITY INVENTORY SCORES OF PILOT AND EXPERIMENTAL GROUPS

Scale	Pilot Group (N = 8)		Experimental Group (N = 12)		Signif.*	Signif.
	pre	post	I—pre	II—post	Exp. Grp.	Pilot & Exp. (N = 20)
Do	49.1	56.4	50.4	51.0	NS	NS
Cs	54.3	61.0	49.1	54.6	NS	p<.01
Sy	53.4	58.5	47.3	56.0	p<.02	p<.01
Sp	57.5	62.4	52.4	59.5	p<.02	p<.01
Sa	63.0	61.0	56.3	56.3	NS	NS
Wb	46.1	54.5	43.0	52.5	p<.01	p<.01
Re	34.4	47.0	33.2	41.0	p<.05	p<.01
So	32.6	41.8	31.9	40.4	p<.02	p<.01
Sc	42.8	48.9	38.9	46.3	p<.05	p<.01
To	42.2	52.1	41.8	49.5	p<.02	p<.01
Gi	45.5	53.4	40.2	48.5	p<.01	p<.01
Cm	53.8	56.4	52.6	54.6	NS	NS
Ac	45.6	54.6	39.9	47.2	NS	p<.01
Ai	48.0	53.6	44.0	49.0	NS	p<.02
Ie	48.1	57.4	43.5	52.3	p<.05	p<.01
Py	44.0	51.2	46.8	47.1	NS	NS
Fx	50.8	52.0	51.4	48.3	NS	NS
Fe	50.0	48.3	52.2	51.6	NS	NS

*Wilcoxon signed rank test two-tailed.

are shown on 12 out of 18 scales, the most marked being on Sociability, Sense of Well-Being, Socialization, Tolerance and Intellectual Efficiency. The socialization-maturity scales (Re, So, Sc) and the achievement scales (Ac, Ai, Ie) as a group all show significant increases. Table IV shows pre-, middle- and post-tests for the control group. None of the changes from I to II are significant except an increase in Good Impression (p < .01), which occurs also in the experimental group. Except for this scale then, the treatment group changed significantly more than the control group. For the final testing (III) only 7 subjects were available, hence the comparison of changes from I to II with changes from II to III, as well as on the overall change from I to III becomes very unreliable. In fact, none of the differences are found to be significant, although they are in the predicted direction. There is however a significant increase from I to III on the Dominance scale for the control group (p < .05).

A different method of analysis is to compute change-scores for each

TABLE IV. MEAN CALIFORNIA PERSONALITY INVENTORY SCORES OF CONTROL GROUP

Scale	Controls (N = 12)		III (N = 7)
	I	II	
Do	34.1	34.7	40.7
Cs	38.9	40.2	46.0
Sy	37.9	41.9	46.6
Sp	49.8	52.2	51.6
Sa	55.0	52.7	53.3
Wb	32.7	38.1	43.6
Re	25.8	26.4	32.0
So	22.6	27.8	26.3
Sc	31.5	38.5	41.0
To	32.7	33.3	42.7
Gi	33.3	40.6	42.1
Cm	46.7	48.1	50.4
Ac	27.5	31.7	34.0
Ai	38.5	40.2	45.6
Ie	28.4	32.3	39.7
Py	37.2	42.3	44.6
Fx	58.3	56.4	52.9
Fe	48.0	50.8	54.3

subject and compare mean change-scores in the experimental and control groups, using the Mann-Whitney U-Test. This is a direct estimation of the significance of difference in change, rather than the indirect method of comparing pre- and post-test scores in the two groups. On the MMPI only the decreases on the F and K scales are significantly greater in the experimental than the control group (p. 10). On the CPI the increase in Tolerance (To) for experimental subjects ($N = 20$) is significantly greater than for control subjects ($N = 12$); the two-tailed p-value is < .05. The increase in Achievement via Conformity (Ac) is significantly greater for experimental subjects ($N = 12$) than for the control subjects ($N = 12$); the two-tailed p-value is <.10.

Interpretation. There are two problems which make the interpretation of these data difficult. One is artificial, one is substantive. The *artificial* problem is that the final test scores (III) of the control group are not apparently very reliable, and hence the with-in-group comparison cannot be made adequately. The *substantive* problem is that given the existence of significant changes after the treatment program on the CPI it is not known which features of the program are responsible for the changes. Firstly, the fact that most participants are about two to three months removed from parole introduces some ambiguity. Wheeler (1961) has shown that there is increasing conformity to staff and community norms in prisoners' attitudes just prior to release. However, two facts make this explanation of the data implausible: (1) the changes observed by Wheeler occurred in the last six months prior to parole—there is no evidence to suggest that this trend is continued linearly over such short periods as 6 weeks; (2) this general norm-shifting effect should apply to the control group also, which, as we have seen, does not change. A second factor is the possibility that the feedback of results has simply made the subjects "test-wise" and this can account for all the variance. Although the tests were taken honestly, i.e., there was no possibility of memorizing all the items of a scale and their direction, it is true that we do not know whether the feedback alone could have produced these results. We can only say now that this requires further analysis. For example, eventually, it will be possible to correlate success on parole with changes in personality tests. Ferdinand (1962) reports similar CPI changes in a group of juvenile offenders treated by "milieu therapy."

The *Sentence Completion Test* used here (*cf.* Watt and Maher, 1958) consists of the responses to 41 sentence stems, coded according to a five-point scale from "extreme disapproval, non-conformity, very negative" (1) to "praise, approval, conformity, extremely positive" (5). The content of the stems covered a variety of social institutions, e.g., law, family, sports, arts, business, etc. Three scores were computed for each person: (1) mean across all items, (2) frequency of very positive responses—4's and 5's, and (3) frequency of very negative responses—1's and 2's. Table V shows the means for two groups—the pilot plus experimental and the control group. On the mean "positive attitude" score the experimental and the controls increase, but the experimental group more. When only the extreme positive or negative responses are counted the experimental group changes (positively), the control group does not. Again the results from the third test are bedeviled by sample shrinkage. Since this test was not used in the feedback program, it is not subject to the same confounding variables as the MMPI and CPI. It would seem that a concomitant of the program is a decrease in cynical and hostile attitudes towards a variety of social institutions.

B. *Behavior Ratings.* Two types of behavior ratings by independent observers were collected, but both are subject to many sources of unreliability. (1) The regular quarterly *institutional work reports,* by the inmate's work-instructor are six rating scales covering work competence,

TABLE V. SENTENCE COMPLETION TEST DATA

Measure	Pilot & Experiment Groups (N = 19)			Control Group (N = 11)				
	Pre	Post	Signif.*	I	II	III (N = 6)	I vs II	II vs III
Mean	2.99	3.15	$p < .01$*	3.05	3.13	3.20	$p < .05$*	NS
Freq. Pos.	10.7	13.6	$p < .01$†	12.8	13.3	14.5	NS	NS
Freq. Neg.	10.9	9.5	$p < .01$†	7.8	7.4	8.7	NS	NS

*t-test, 2-tailed
†Wilcoxon sign rank test, 2-tailed

industry, cooperativeness, etc. When July, September and December work reports were examined there were not consistent trends on any of the scales over the period of the program; nor were there any significant differences between experimental and control groups. However, the samples in this analysis are very small (4 to 9) and the ratings are made by *different* observers. Thus the absence of discernible trend is not really surprising. (2) A *special rating sheet* for officers was constructed on eleven areas of interaction and behavior. The "experimental group" here consists of 13 men still in the prison who had gone through the program; the "control group" are a matched sample, selected according to the same criteria, but never having had any contact with the project at all. Again, there is the problem of the effects of different raters, and their possible bias about the project affecting their judgments. With these reservations in mind, Table VI provides some suggestive evidence. The results are given in mean ratings (the scales were either four- or five-point) and the significance of differences was computed by means of chi-square. None of the differences between the groups are significant, but 4, 5, 6, (which approach significance) very tentatively suggest that participants are seen as less excitable and as getting along better with officers and with other inmates.

TABLE VI. MEANS OF OFFICERS' RATINGS

Question	Exp. $\bar{X}$ (N = 12)	Control $\bar{X}$ (N = 12)
1. Cooperative	3.5	3.5
2. Hardworking	2.8	3.2
3. Responsible	3.0	2.8
4. Not excitable	2.8	2.4
5. Get along with officers	3.0	2.7
6. Get along with inmates	3.1	2.5
7. Influence	.75	1.0
8. Talk with officers	1.5	1.8
9. Friends	1.6	1.7
10. Parole success	2.5	2.6
11. Estimate of project	2.0	1.8

C. *Return Rates.* One and a half years after termination of the project (18–26 months after release from prison). The recidivism rate in this project does not differ from the expected rate derived from base-rates for the Concord Reformatory as a whole (Metzner & Weil, 1963). In that study 56% of the 311 men released from Concord during 1959 had returned two and a half years later. Out of the 32 men involved in the project, four are still in prison and one escaped. These must therefore be omitted. Of the 27 men released, 11 are still on the street and 16 have returned, a return rate of 59%.

Expected Rate of Return by Type of Return

In the base-rate study half of the recidivists were returned for parole violations and half for new offenses. These two types were then combined for further calculation of predictive categories. In other words we would expect 28% of the released men to be returned as parole violators and 28% as new offenders. When we look at the figures actually obtained, we see that only two out of the 27 men (7%) were returned for new offenses, while 14 out of 27 (52%) were returned as parole violators. This discrepancy has a probability of less than .01 of occurring by chance, using the binomial distribution. In other words, there is a significant reduction in the rate of new crimes and a significant increase in the rate of parole violations. This dual effect accounts for the lack of difference when the overall rate of return is considered.

One may speculate about the reasons for the rise in parole violation. Perhaps the men on the psilocybin project received an extra careful degree of parole supervision. The project had aroused a lot of interest in the Department of Correction, and it was impossible to prevent the parole officers from knowing which of their charges had been involved in it.

Expected Rate of Return by Prognostic Categories

In the base-rate study referred to above, expectancies were computed for six different sub-classes of offenders. The categories were obtained empirically on the basis of their predictive efficiency. Thus for example, men with no prior arrests and no prior commitments have an expected return rate of 22%. Men with prior commitments, who committed offenses against a person (but not sex offenders) or against property and who are non-white, have an expected return rate of 86%. Thus, these categories enable one to obtain a more precise expectancy for any particular sample than simply the overall rate.

Table VII compares for each category the percentage returning in the experimental and base-rate samples.

Although the experimental subsamples are too small to make statistically valid comparisons, the figures indicate a reduced return rate in groups 1 and 6 and an increased rate in group 2. It should be remembered that these figures for new offenses are parole violations are combined and therefore do not enable one to specify in what category a significant reduction of new crimes occurred.

TABLE VII. RATES OF RETURN BY PROGNOSTIC CATEGORIES

Description	Base-Rate Sample		Psilocybin Sample	
	N	% Return	N	% Return
1. No prior commitments; no prior arrests	23	22	2	0
2. Some prior commitments; sex offender or parole violator whose age at last commitment was more than 24	27	30	3	100
3. No prior commitments but some prior arrests.	59	37	3	33
4. Sex offenders or parole violators with prior commitments aged 24 or less at last commitment.	44	61	3	67
5. Some prior commitments; offense against person (except sex) against property or combination; whites	137	69	13	62
6. Some prior commitments; offense against person (except sex) against property or combination; other ethnic group.	21	86	3	67
Combined	311	56	27	59

Conclusion. Of the three types of evaluation, the most important is the rate of return. It is a completely objective behavioral index, not subject to any of the distortions of personality tests and clinical impressions. The main conclusion can be stated as follows: One and one half years after termination of the program the rate of new crimes has been reduced from 28% to 7%, although if parole violations are counted the overall return rate has not changed. It is proposed that these results warrant further research into the potentials of the methods used, especially since no other method of reducing the crime rate exists.

FUTURE DEVELOPMENTS

From our experience in this project we would offer the following suggestions for an improved rehabilitation program designed to decrease the recidivism rate of offenders with relatively short sentences.

If the core of the rehabilitation or change process is some form of intense group experience designed to bring about insight then it is essential that the environment in which this insight takes place is supportive of applying such insights to behavior. The ideal solution to this problem is to involve the entire institution, officers, psychologists, as well as inmates, in a joint change process, as in the Herstedvester Center in Denmark (Stürup, 1959). We have attempted to tackle this problem by placing some responsibility for stimulating behavioral change on older, more experienced inmates.

It is highly undesirable to have an inmate return to the same frustrating environment after experiencing an internal liberation. An alternative would be to have the group experience (whether it involves drugs or not) occur outside of the prison, immediately after release, in a special transitional center. This would serve both as a sort of retreat for internal change and as a halfway house to prepare the convict for regular life on the streets.

The second suggestion concerns the importance of the follow-up period. Many convicts are reluctant to get involved in middle-class activities. The doctor-patient model, in which a client regularly visits the office of a professional, is simply not applicable. In practical terms,

Officer's Name _____ Inmate's Name_____

Date_____

Please rate this inmate on your own observations *during the past two weeks*. As far as possible, rate the inmate on the way he *acts*, rather than your interpretation of the meaning of his behavior.

1. How cooperative is this inmate?

☐ always cooperative   ☐ usually cooperative   ☐ sometimes cooperative   ☐ seldom cooperative   ☐ never cooperative

2. Is he hard-working or lazy?

☐ very hard-working   ☐ fairly hard-working   ☐ average   ☐ fairly lazy   ☐ very lazy

3. Is he responsible or irresponsible?

☐ very responsible   ☐ fairly responsible   ☐ average   ☐ fairly irresponsible   ☐ very irresponsible

4. How excitable is this inmate?

☐ gets excited very easily   ☐ gets excited quite often   ☐ average   ☐ usually calm   ☐ always calm

5. How does he get along with officers?

☐ gets along very badly   ☐ gets along badly   ☐ normal   ☐ gets along well   ☐ gets along very well

6. How does he get along with other inmates?

☐ gets along very badly   ☐ gets along badly   ☐ normal   ☐ gets along well   ☐ gets along very well

7. Does he have power and influence among other inmates?

☐ has a lot of influence   ☐ has some influence   ☐ has a little influence   ☐ has no influence at all

8. How often does he talk with officers about things other than work?

☐ very often   ☐ sometimes   ☐ seldom   ☐ never

9. How many friends does he have among inmates?

☐ very many   ☐ a fair number   ☐ a few   ☐ none

10. What is your estimate of his chances of staying out on parole?

☐ no chance at all   ☐ poor chance   ☐ some chance   ☐ good chance   ☐ excellent chance the "therapist" must be prepared to visit his clients at all times of the day or night in bars or homes, to help find employment, to lend money, etc., because these are the accepted "tests" of a trusting relationship. This is not to say that there should be no structure at all to the relationship, but the structure should come from a definite contractual agreement about the purposes of contacts—and not from arbitrarily imposed space-time limits. For further elaboration of these two ideas see the discussions by Leary (1961), Schwitzgebel (1961) and Eissler (1950).

REFERENCES

Abrahamson, H. A. "Lysergic acid diethylamide (LSD-25): III. As an adjunct of psychotherapy with elimination of fear of homosexuality," *J. Psychol.,* **39,** 127, 1955.

Blewett, D. B., & Chwelos, N. *Handbook for the therapeutic use of lysergic acid diethylamide-25: Individual and group procedures,* 1959.

Campbell, D. T. "Factors relevant to the validity of experiments in social settings." *Psychol. Bull.,* **54,** 297–312, 1957.

Cartwright, D. Achieving change in people. *Hum. Rel.,* **14,** 381–392, 1951.

Chwelos, N., Blewett, D. B., Smith, C., & Hoffer, A. "Use of LSD-25 in the treatment of chronic alcoholism." *Quart. J. Stud. Alcohol.,* **20,** 577, 1959.

Cutner, M. Analytic work with LSD-25. *Psychiat. Quart.,* **33,** 715–757, 1959.

Duché, D. J., & Laut, J. "Effets de la psilocybine dans un cas d'hysterie." *Annales Médico-Psychologiques,* **119** (3), 590, 1961.

Eissler, K. Ego-psychological implications of the psychoanalytic treatment of delinquents. *Psychoanal. Study of the Child,* **5,** 97–121, 1950.

Eysenck, H. J. The effects of psychotherapy. In *Handbook of Abnormal Psychology,* ed. H. Eysenck, New York: Basic Books, 1961.

Frank, L. K. Change through group experience. *Social Welfare Forum,* Proc. Nat. Conf. Soc. Welfare, Chicago, New York: Columbia, 1958. Pp. 225–268.

Ferdinand, T. N. An evaluation of milieu therapy and vocational training as methods for the rehabilitation of youthful offenders. *J. Crim. Law, Criminol., Police Sci.,* **53,** 49–54, 1962.

Fox, V. Group methods in criminology. *Group Psychother.,* **15,** 40–45, 1962.

Goffman, E. Characteristics of total institutions. In: *Symposium on Preventive and Social Psychiatry,* 43–84. Washington, D.C.: Walter Reed Army Institute of Research, 1957.

Heard, G. *Training for a Life of Growth.* Santa Monica: Wayfarer Press, 1959.

Jenkins, D. H. Feedback and group self-evaluation. *J. Soc. Issues,* **4,** 50–60, 1948.

Konopka, G. *Group Work in the Institution.* New York: Morrow, 1954.

Konopka, G. The generic and the specific in group work practice in the psychiatric setting. H. B. Trecker, (ed.). New York: Whiteside, 1956.

Leary, T. How to change behavior. In: G. Nielsen (ed.) *Intern. Congr. of Appl. Psychol.,* Copenhagen, 1961. (Vol. IV)

Leary, T., Litwin, G., & Metzner, R. Reactions to psilocybin in a supportive environment. *J. nerv. ment. Dis.,* 1963 (in press), **137,** 567–573.

Levit, G., & Jennings, H. H. Learning through role playing. In: *Planning of Change,* Bennis, W. G., Benne, K. D. & Chin, R. (eds.), New York: Holt, 1961. Pp. 706–710.

Massachusetts Commissioner of Correction. *Statistical Reports,* 1959.

McCorkle, L. W., Elias, A., & Bixby, F. L. *The Highfields Story: An Experimental Treatment Project for Youthful Offenders.* New York: Holt, 1958.

Metzner, R., & Weil, G. Predicting Recidivism: Base Rates for Massachusetts Correctional Institution Concord. *J. Crim. Law, Criminal., Police Sci.,* 1963, **54,** 307–316.

Moreno, J. L. Psychodrama. In: S. Arieti, (ed.), *American Handbook of Psychiatry.* New York: Basic Books, 1959. Pp. 1375–1396.

O'Halloran, W. Group psychotherapy and the criminal—an introduction to reality. *Am. J. Correction,* 1961.

Rosow, H. M. Some observation on group therapy with prison inmates. *Arch. Crim. Psychodyn.,* 1955.

Sandison, R. A. Psychological aspects of the LSD treatment of the neuroses. *J. Ment. Sci.,* **100,** 508, 1954.

Schwitzgebel, R. Critical analysis and evaluation of the experimenter-subject role relationship in the reduction of known male adolescent crime. Ed.D. Dissertation, Harvard University, 1962.

Slater, P. E. Displacement in groups. In: *Planning of Change,* Bennis, W. G., Benne, K. D., & Chin, R. (eds.), New York: Holt, 1961. Pp. 725–736.

Stürup, G. Group therapy with chronic criminals. *Acta Psychother.,* **7,** (Suppl.), 377–385, 1959.

Sutherland, E. H. *Principles of Criminology,* Philadelphia: Lippincott, 1955.

Szasz, T. *The Myth of Mental Illness.* New York: Hoeber-Harper, 1961.

Tennenbaum, B. Group therapy with LSD-25. *Dis. Nerv. Syst.,* **22,** 459–492, 1961.

Watt, N., & Maher, B. A. Prisoners' attitudes toward home and the judicial system. *J. Crim. Law., Criminol., Police Sci.,* **49,** 327–330, 1958.

Wheeler, S. Socialization in correctional communities. *Amer. Sociol. Rev.,* **26,** Pp. 697–712, 1961.

6

An Autobiographical Perspective of the CPE

The Effects of Consciousness-Expanding Drugs on Prisoner Rehabilitation

Timothy Leary

Although Leary left Harvard in 1963, he continued to write about his Harvard experiments for many years. "The Effects of Consciousness-Expanding Drugs on Prisoner Rehabilitation" appeared in Leary's book *High Priest* in 1968, and then the article was reprinted in *The Psychedelic Review* in 1969; it is his third article on the Concord Prison Experiment (CPE), which was conducted from 1961 to 1963. This original article of Leary's features various journalistic accounts of the CPE (*The Boston Herald* and *Traveler*). The newspaper accounts of the CPE are presented as marginal notes. The juxtaposition of various sources implies the multiple layers of the psychedelic experience. Leary's first person narrative conveys how the psilocybin researchers see and experience the world differently: their utopian optimism is contrasted with the media's rationalistic interpretation of the CPE.

"Effects of Consciousness Expanding Drugs . . ." can be read alongside Leary's two scientific accounts of the Concord Prison Experiment: "A New Behavior Change Program Using Psilocybin" (1965) and "Use of Psychedelic Drugs in Prisoner Rehabilitation" (1967). However, this article is fundamentally different from Leary's scholarly articles in that at this point in his career he is attempting to reach a much broader audience of readers. Thus, he employs colloquial language and a first-person narrative. Since Leary is no longer a practicing social scientist, he no longer feels obliged to offer scientific proof for all of his claims; he simply describes what happened when he and his graduate students took psilocybin with a group of inmates at the Concord Reformatory. This article does not contain an argument or a conclusion in the traditional sense. Instead, it ends with the prisoner's account of what happened during the Concord Prison Experiment:

> Did you hear? Some Harvard professors gave a new drug to some guys at Concord. They had a ball. It was great. It's a grand thing. It's something new. Hope. Maybe. Hope. Perhaps. Something new. We sure need something new. Hope.

Leary's straightforward, non-academic account of the CPE also represents the attempt to speak directly to his new audience of readers: the counterculture, and his stripped-down ending encourages the reader to identify with the prisoner's understanding of the psychedelic drug experience and its utopian potential.

Leary's interest in prisons and prisoners in 1961 could be interpreted as a bizarre example of Jung's notion of synchronicity. In 1970, some nine years after the inception of the Concord Prison Experiment, Leary was sent to the California Men's Colony in San Luis Obispo to serve a ten-year sentence for possessing a small amount of marijuana (less than an ounce). Leary discusses the experience of taking psychedelic drugs with prisoners in 1961 and 1962 in his autobiography: "[i]n some weird and ominous way, I may have been 're-imprinting' a prison mentality, a reality which I was forced to inhabit between 1970 and 1976"

(*Flashbacks* 90). Leary escaped from the California Men's Colony in 1970 and fled to Algeria and Switzerland. When he was eventually apprehended in Kabul in 1973, he was given a harsher sentence—twenty-five years—and sent to Folsom, a maximum-security prison, also in California. After six months in Folsom, Leary was transferred to the California Medical Facility in Vacaville in November of 1973. Leary was eventually released from prison in 1976 after serving a three-year sentence.

JAMES PENNER

REFERENCES

Leary, Timothy. *Flashbacks: A Personal and Cultural History of an Era.* New York: Jeremy Tarcher/Perigee, 1990.

THE EFFECTS OF CONSCIOUSNESS-EXPANDING DRUGS ON PRISONER REHABILITATION

From *High Priest* by Timothy Leary, published in 1968 by World Publishing Company: pages 174–89 ("Trip 9").

Timothy Leary

[Leary's narrative is flanked by official reports and newspaper accounts of the same story.]

◆ ◆ ◆

Second Annual Report; Psilocybin Rehabilitation Project:

All the professional work on this project was volunteer. The expenses for clerical assistance and salaries for ex-inmate workers were covered by generous donations from The Uris Brothers Foundation, New York, and the Parapsychology Foundation, Eileen Garrett, President.

During the fall and the winter of 1960, much of my time and energy was going into the study of the effects of the psychedelic mushrooms. I was also carrying on an active program of lecturing, teaching, and fieldwork in clinical psychology in the Harvard Graduate School. I had been brought to Harvard in 1959 in order to introduce existential-transactional methods for behavior change. After fifteen years practicing psychotherapy and about ten years of doing research on psychotherapy, I had come to the conclusion that there was very little that one person called a doctor could do for another person called a patient by talking to him across a desk, or listening to him as he lay on a couch. I developed a lot of theories and a lot of methods on how behavior change could be brought about in ways more effective than the standard clinical interview method.

There are two main points to the theories I developed; first, (transactional) I was convinced that the doctor had to suspend his role and status as a doctor, had to join the other person actively and collaboratively in figuring out the solution to his problem. As much as possible, the doctor had to turn over the responsibility to the man who knew the most about the problem at hand, namely, the patient. I developed many techniques for getting patients to help each other.

The second point in my theory (existential) was that the doctor has to leave the safety of his consulting room and get out there in the field where the so-called patient is having his unique problems and where he is going to solve his problems. I saw the role of the doctor as that of a coach in a game in which the patient was the star player. The coach can help, can point out mistakes, can share his wisdom, but in the last analysis, the guy who does the job is the guy out there in the field, the so-called patient.

I was enthusiastic about these theories because they worked, and because no joy in teaching can equal that thrill which comes when you watch someone who's been hung up, and blocked, and confused, and making a mess of things out there in the field suddenly learn how. All this had started happening before I got involved in the drug research, and I had

Applications to three offices of the U.S. Public Health Service requesting support for continuing this project were refused.

Exactly two years ago the Harvard Psilocybin Project initiated a research program at Massachusetts Correctional Institution, Concord, designed to test the effects of consciousness-expanding drugs on prisoner rehabilitation.

The project was designed as a pilot study—necessarily exploratory—since little was known about the long-range application of the substances.

The key issue was the use of a consciousness-expanding drug; but equally important was the philosophy underlying the research, which emphasized:

DEMOCRATIC COLLABORATION:

Inmates were given responsibility for planning and evaluating the work. This was seen as preparation for assuming roles as responsible citizens in a democratic society.

SHARING OF INFORMATION: The inmates were given all information relevant to their treatment. This was seen as a necessary step in increasing trust and self-respect.

SPIRITUAL INSIGHT: The transcendental experience provided by the drugs propels the subject beyond space, time, ego, culture, etc. The implications of this visionary experience were utilized in the program.

INTERPERSONAL TRUST AND CLOSENESS: Evidence shows that where subjects share an ego–shattering experience together they develop strong positive emotional bonds.

SELF-HELP AND MUTUAL HELP: The most successful rehabilitation methods (A.A., Synanon group dynamic T groups, etc.) seem to be those which turn over responsibility to the subjects themselves and which stimulate them to help each other. The drug experience facilitates this tendency.

already become a controversial figure around the Boston area, because everything that I was saying made a tremendous amount of sense to students and patients, but the doctors, the psychiatrists, the social workers, the professors, the psychologists, were not so quick to accept these theories. You see, I was asking them to give up the status and the omniscient position which they felt their training entitled them to. I asked them to turn over the authority and the star role in the game to the patient.

Times change, and with them their demands. Thus the seasons change in the course of the year. In the world cycle also there are spring and autumn in the life of peoples and nations, and these call for social transformations. (I Ching XLIX)

I was taking one day off a week to drive down with two or three graduate students to New Bedford, Massachusetts, where we were working in an orphanage, teaching social workers and nuns to set up groups in which older kids would help younger kids, and in which children at every age level were encouraged to take more responsibility for running the school and planning their lives.

We set up another project in a slum housing district in a Boston suburb. Here were hundreds of people who were bogged down socially and psychologically. They could not afford psychiatric help and there was none available for them. With another group of graduate students, I used to go down there one night a week with tape recorders and blackboards. We set up headquarters in one of the slum apartments and started teaching groups of the neighbors how they could help each other and become psychiatrists for each other and develop some facility for solving their own problems.

All this, of course, was very déclassé at Harvard. Universities are supposed to be research institutes, and if you get too involved in service functions or helping people, you're considered a bleeding heart. I was able to justify the work in the orphanage, the work with alcoholics, the work in the slum projects, by using the word methodology. We weren't really trying to help these people. No sir, not us. We were trying to develop new techniques and scientific methods for changing psychotherapeutic theory. Of course, if people enjoyed it and got help, that was an interesting by-product which supported the method and the theory. It was all experimental, you see. It became a tradition in the center where I worked that any time they got a call from a do-good social service agency requesting Harvard's help in curing any sort of social disease, the request was likely to get bucked to me because they knew that this was my vice and my eccentricity.

One day I got a note in my box saying that two men from the Department of Legal Medicine were interested in enlisting Harvard's help in the psychological rehabilitation of prisoners. Now prison work is considered to be the least interesting, lowest status work you can do in the field of psychology, psychiatry, and sociology. The problems are hopeless. Criminals never change. The atmosphere is dreary and the academic rewards are slim. But when I found this little piece of paper in my box requesting an appointment from two officials from the Department of Legal Medicine, I chuckled all the way to my office

EMOTIONAL AND PRACTICAL SUPPORT:
The model used was not doctor-patient or expert-client but that of human beings who believe in each other and want to help each other.

The project developed the model of friends who are available to help group members stay out of trouble and maintain a responsible role in society.

In our research we helped inmates get jobs, purchase union cards, made small loans and spent hours in friendly advising interaction.

PROCEDURES:
Since its initiation, the project has operated under the medical and psychiatric supervision of Dr. W. Madison Presnell.

Inmates received on the average four doses of psilocybin. Dosage ran from 20 mg. in early sessions to 70 mg. Now we employ 30 mg. as a standard, moderate dose.

Inmates were given personality tests before, and six month after, the program began. Significant decreases in hostility, cynicism, social delinquency and irresponsibility were registered.

There seems to be general agreement that the effects of the program *in-the-institution* were quite dramatic. The behavior and attitude of the project members became more mature and social.

The post-release events, however, involved a different set of factors and required several revisions in the program.

POST-RELEASE PROGRAM:
The main conclusion of our two-year pilot study is that institutional programs, however effective, count for little after the ex-convict reaches the street. The social pressures faced are so overwhelming as to make change very difficult.

We recognized very early in our work the advantages of a post-release program.

because this was just the chance I was looking for.

By this time, we had given the psychedelic mushrooms to about a hundred people in a wide variety of circumstances and we had learned a lot about the process. In spite of the bungling and the confusion, and our ignorance, we still hadn't caused any damage to anyone and there were a lot of mistakes that we'd never make again. By this time, we had learned a few things about how to run the sessions. About 90 percent of the people who were taking the magic mushrooms were reporting the most ecstatic and educational experience of their lives. The problem was, there was no way to get any measurement as to how much good we were doing. There was no way to keep score.

This of course is the main problem in the field of psychotherapy. You can develop a completely effective method of treating people's psychological problems and there is no way you can prove it. You can work with one thousand people and help every one of them change his way of thinking and his way of acting, but there are no statistics (like hits, runs, and errors) with which to tabulate your score. The problem is that half the people you help are going to get better jobs, and half of them are going to quit the jobs they have. Half of them may increase the intimacy and closeness and meaning in their marriages, but the other half may leave their wives. Changing a person's psyche is one thing, but measuring results in an observable way is another thing. Because who's to say which behavior reflects growth and change.

Here's where the prison came in. The prison is the ideal place to do a study in psychotherapy behavior change because when you try to rehabilitate prisoners, you've got an ironclad statistic you can work against. It's called the recidivism rate. When you are working with people outside, they may quit their job and join the Peace Corps, or they may quit their job and join the ministry, or they may quit the ministry and take up guitar, and *you* know about the growth of this person, but who else will believe it? But when you work with prisoners and you think you've helped them change, grow, and become more effective people, there's an easy way to tell. Where are they a year after you've finished with them? Are they back in jail, or are they making it on the outside? Prisoner rehabilitation presents the most objective check for someone who claims he can bring about change in behavior. In the prisons of Massachusetts the recidivism is about 70 percent. Seven out of every ten men who leave prison, return. If you develop a new and surefire way of changing man's mind, the prison presents the toughest and cleanest test of your effectiveness. Can you keep him out of jail? That's why I wanted to get into the prison.

Now, the reason why the prison psychologists wanted to get into Harvard is because everyone in any academic or professional activity in the Boston area has one way of measuring *his* success. Can he get on the Harvard payroll? The word Harvard in the Boston area is a powerful status symbol that operates at every level of society. There are several thousand janitors around the Boston area, but if you are a janitor at Harvard, you're a prince among custodians. The same with a cook, the same with a gardener, and the same with a psychologist.

A week later, I found myself host at a corner

Our philosophic and theoretical orientation led us to encourage inmates to plan and execute their own program.

We fondly hoped for a halfway house run by ex-inmates along the lines of the successful Synanon program.

In June, 1961, a non-profit organization, Freedom Center, was set up to administer the post-release program. Our hopes for a convict-run halfway house did not materialize.

We had too few men in the Boston area and they were too caught up in the desperate struggle to survive, to spare time, to help others.

In 1961, as a beginning step toward a halfway house, we began Project Contact. The purpose of this project was to keep in regular contact with all group members.

By these means we were able to reach ninety-one percent of ex-inmates living in Massachusetts.

A newsletter and personal letters also kept up contact and seemed to be effective in helping the rehabilitation spirit stay alive.

But increased contact only strengthened our convictions that an A.A.-type organization of ex-convicts is necessary.

The initial step of finding the small nucleus of men who are ready to make the dedication needed has not yet been taken.

As a possible solution we hope to be able to send two ex-inmates to spend a month living at Synanon House, Santa Monica.

The Director of Synanon, Mr. Chuck Dederich, has expressed interest in this project.

table in the Harvard Faculty Club with two officials from the Massachusetts prison system. What they wanted was simple. They wanted to have Harvard graduate students assigned to the prisons as psychology interns with a possible long-range hope of getting themselves clinical professorships at Harvard. And what I wanted was to get Harvard graduate students into the prisons because that's where I felt that all embryonic psychologists should be—out in the field, dealing with real people and real problems. But there was something else I wanted—and that was the chance to show that we could rehabilitate criminals by using the sacred mushrooms. And so the deal was made. I agreed to get Harvard approval to send graduate students to internships in the prison, and they agreed that if I could get the approval of the warden and the prison psychiatrists, I could give psychedelic mushrooms to prisoners.

About a week later I drove out to the prison. I wore my Harvard tweed suit and my button-down shirt. The warden was impressed and pleased. It wasn't often that Harvard professors came out to the prison to do research. But the whole thing hinged on the approval of the psychiatrists, because the sacred mushrooms were DRUGS and to work with DRUGS you had to have the medical Okay. So, we walked down the hallway to the metal cage that let us into the prison. We opened up the first steel door and we stood in the anteroom. Then we rang a bell, a slot opened, and a guard looked at us and opened up the second metal door. We walked into the middle of the guardroom, across the prison yard to the hospital where we rang the bell and got peered at through the slot, heard the metal hinges creak, and walked into the prison hospital. We walked down the corridor to the psychiatrist's office and knocked on the door. After a minute, out walked one of the most entertaining and interesting men in American psychiatry. The first thing that struck me about the prison psychiatrist was that he was the best-dressed man I had ever seen. He was short, graceful, like a ballet dancer. The first Negro psychiatrist I had ever met. I spent an hour talking with Dr. Madison Presnell. He was no intellectual; he mispronounced some of the polysyllabic words, but he had a twinkle in his eye and a wise, cool way of looking at you that told you he was a man who had seen a lot and suffered a lot, and was still looking for the funniest and wisest part of everyone he came in contact with.

In sizing up Dr. Presnell, I could say to myself a word which I had heard used quite often in recent months. He was hip. It was obvious too, that he had had some experience with psychedelic drugs. Which ones, he didn't make clear. He could have had LSD in medical school, or mescaline in psychiatric research, or maybe pot in the Village, but he knew what I was talking about.

A few days later Dr. Presnell came over to Harvard to meet some of my bosses, and the following Sunday, he brought his beautiful and intelligent wife over to my house for cocktails. He sat down on a chair in my study, thought for a minute and said, "Your plan to give psychedelic drugs to prisoners is the best idea I've ever heard for dealing with an impossible problem. If you're smart enough and dedicated enough to know how to do it, you could make it work. There's one

The next step of selecting two ex-inmates to make the trip is waiting to be taken.

Upon their return, Freedom Center is prepared to offer its resources to support a local self-help residence program.

RESULTS:

Plans and hopes are one thing, but the actual score card of accomplishments provides the crucial evidence. What are the available results?

PSILOCYBIN IS SAFE:

Thirty-five inmates and ten Harvard staff members have had group psilocybin experiences at Concord.

There were 131 inmate ingestions and 37 staff ingestions, a total of 168 experiences. There were no episodes of violence, lasting disturbances or negative after-effects.

Physically and psychologically there is clear-cut evidence that in a supportive environment the drug effect is safe and positive.

Those interested in using psilocybin for research or therapy purposes can proceed with confidence if their program is open, supportive, collaborative.

PSILOCYBIN PRODUCES TEMPORARY STATES OF SPIRITUAL CONVERSION, INTERPERSONAL CLOSENESS, AND PSYCHOLOGICAL INSIGHT

Forty-five percent of the entire inmate group clearly underwent a mystical, transcendent, death-rebirth experience.

This figure should be modified, however. The results for running sessions improved so that 100% of our *recent* groups were undergoing transcendent experiences.

The life-changing therapeutic effects of the psilocybin experience do not last for more than seventy-two hours unless the subject is in a situation which encourages him to maintain his emotional and spiritual insights.

chance in a hundred you can pull it off, but if you do, you will have accomplished more for American society and for prisoner rehabilitation than has been done in the last four thousand years since the code of Hammurabi. But it's risky business. You're bound to run into trouble. As a matter of fact, the more successful you are, the more trouble you're going to stir up. Because one thing I've learned as a prison psychiatrist is that society doesn't want the prisoner rehabilitated, and as soon as you start changing prisoners so that they discover beauty and wisdom, God, you're going to stir up the biggest mess that Boston has seen since the Boston Tea Party. I'll give you medical coverage and I'll be glad to serve as psychiatric consultant and I'll back you up all the way with the wardens, with the guards, with the mental health department, but sooner or later as soon as they see the thing you do is working, they're going to come down on you—the newspaper reporters, the bureaucrats, and the officials. Harvard gives drugs to prisoners! And you're going to have to do the impossible—you're going to have to cure prisoners with your left hand, and that's something that's never been done before, and you're going to have to hold off the entire bureaucracy of the state of Massachusetts with your right hand and that's never been done before, not even by Kennedy. So, I'll back you all the way, until you make a mistake, and when you make that mistake, and they all start coming down at you, exactly at that point, I'm going to walk out because I'm not you. I'm not the new Freud and I have no ambitions to play that game. I'm a Negro from the South with a degree from a second-class medical school, with a wife and two kids whom

I'm trying to support and educate in an insane society, and I'll help you all the way to win, but I'm not going to lose with you."

Political revolutions are extremely grave matters. They should be undertaken only under stress of direst necessity, when there is no other way out. Not everyone is called to this task, but only the man who has the confidence of the people, and even he only when the time is ripe. He must then proceed in the right way, so that he gladdens the people and, by enlightening them, prevents excesses. Furthermore, he must be quite free of the selfish aims and must really relieve the need of the people. Only then does he have nothing to regret. (I Ching XLIX)

And so it was settled. Dr. Presnell would line up volunteers in the prisoner population for the sacred mushroom project and I would go back to Harvard and get graduate students who would volunteer their time and energy and their nervous systems to take drugs with maximum security prisoners at the penitentiary.

A few days later I was in my office when a knock came on the door, and I was visited by a graduate student named Ralph Metzner. Metzner had a reputation for being one of the smartest students in the department. He was a graduate of Oxford, an experimentalist, a precise, objective, and apparently very academic young man. He said he had heard about the prison project and he wanted to work with me on it. My first reactions were that Metzner was too academic, too dainty-British, too bookish, too ivory tower, to walk into a prison and roll up his sleeves

Therefore, psilocybin must be used in on-going programs of therapy or self-help. When employed in such programs, psilocybin is a dramatically useful, educational, and rehabilitative instrument.

If the subject shares time and space subsequently with those who have had the experience, his chances of maintaining the insights are increased.

The actual scoreboard is difficult to interpret. The aims of this project were: 1) to help keep men on the street and 2) to help them in constructive contact with each other.

RESULT PERCENTAGES
January 15, 1963:

Percentage of men released who are now on street . . . 73.

Percentage of men now back for technical parole violation . . . 19

Percentage of men now back for new crimes . . . 8.

If ex-convicts who have had a psilocybin experience in a supportive environment meet regularly after release (these statistics suggest once a month), the chances of their remaining on the street will be dramatically improved.

The Harvard staff members—Dr. Ralph Metzner, Gunther Weil, Dr. Ralph Schwitzgebel, Jonathan Clark, David Kolb, Michael Hollingshead, Kathy Harris, Dr. Timothy Leary—who contributed several thousands of hours each to this work, cared deeply and suffered keen disappointments as they witnessed the failures.

But the results summarized in this report offer some consolation that the time shared in psilocybin experiences, and the meetings in and out of Concord were educational, and somewhat effective.

SUMMARY:

Thirty-one inmates of MCI Concord participated in a rehabilitation program combining:

. . . psilocybin administered in a supportive setting, and . . . volunteer contact of inmates after release.

and take drugs that would put him out of his mind, with rough and tumble prisoners. Metzner said he wanted to learn how. Then I said, Before you can give drugs and take drugs with anyone else, you have to have some experiences yourself. Are you ready to take mushrooms? He was ready. As a matter of fact, that's exactly what he wanted to do, to have a session.

And so it happened that on March 12, 1961, at my home in Newton, Massachusetts, I ran a session for Dr. Presnell and his beautiful wife, for Ralph Metzner and his girl friend and another graduate student, and Gunther Weil and his wife, Karen. This was the fifty-second time I had taken psilocybin with other people. The notes on the session say, This training session was designed to introduce several new subjects to the sacred mushroom experience under supportive circumstances.

The session took place in my study. Since this was an exploratory training session, I told the participants that they should relax, have a good time, be entertained, and learn what they could. Dr. Presnell was the dominating factor in this session. His joking and warm attitude created a benign atmosphere. Each new subject had his spouse or a trusted friend present. After a long period of happy, relaxed giggling, the joking became more and more philosophic. Members of the group would leave the room periodically to be by themselves or to talk in pairs, but my study operated as the center for the session. There were no discordant notes, no anxiety, depression, or friction. We were finally getting to the point where we knew how to set up a pleasant session. Each member of this six-person group reported a deep ecstatic, educational experience.

A few days after this session, Ralph Metzner, Gunther Weil, and I drove out to the concrete prison and met with the six volunteers who had been selected by Dr. Presnell. Sitting around a table in a dreary hospital room, with gray walls, black asphalt floor, bars in the windows, telling six skeptical and suspicious men about an experience which could change their lives.

The first psychedelic session in the prison was well-planned. The first thing we did was to tell the prisoners as much as we could about the psychedelic experience. We brought in books for them to read, reports by other subjects, articles which described the terrors as well as the ecstasies of the experience. We spent most of the time describing our own experiences and answering groping questions. We made it very clear to the prisoners that this was nothing *we* were doing to them. There was no doctor-patient game going here. We would take the drugs along with them. We were doing nothing to them that we wouldn't willingly, happily have done to ourselves. We also made a research contract with the prisoners. We said something like this, We want to find out how and how much you change during this experience. For this reason, we want you to take a battery of psychological tests before you eat the mushrooms. Then, after three or four sessions with the sacred mushrooms, we'll give you the tests again. The aim here is to find out how you change, like you weigh yourself on a scale before and after you go on a diet. After you've taken the tests, we'll give you the results. We'll go over the tests with you and explain how you were before and how you changed. Nothing in this project is going to be a secret. We've told you everything we know about

The evidence after two years of operation suggests that the drug is safe, that the experience temporarily provides personal and spiritual insight, and has some effect in keeping inmates out of prison.

A listing of the major mistakes and improvements in method will be found in two publications, one in press and one in preparation.

∞

From the *Boston Herald and Traveler*:

CONVICTS GAINS CITED BY STUDY

Insight drugs called boon

IFIF is the Internal Federation for Internal Freedom, a non-profit organization involving the use of conscious-expanding drugs.

The supply of the drug has, temporarily at least, been cut off because the medical supervision required by federal regulation in the administration of the drugs for research has been withdrawn.

the drugs before you take them and we'll tell you everything we know about you after you finish your sessions.

That sounded like a good deal to them and the following week, each prisoner was administered a long and complicated battery of psychological tests.

And it happened that on March 27, 1961, in the large ward room in the prison infirmary in Concord, Massachusetts, five prisoners and three Harvard psychologists met for a trip. In the morning I was to turn-on with three convicts, and the two other prisoners and the two graduate students would act as observers. Then in the afternoon, Gunther Weil and Ralph Metzner and the two observing prisoners were to take the drug, and the rest of us were to act as guides. We brought a record player, tape recorder, and some books of classical art with us. Otherwise the room was bleak in decor with four beds, a large table, and a few chairs. At 9:35 in the morning the bowl of pills was placed in the center of the table. I was the first one to turn-on in the prison project. I reached over, took fourteen milligrams of psilocybin. Then I handed the bowl to the prisoner next to me and he took twenty milligrams and passed it on to the guy next to him who took twenty, and the next man. Then we pushed the bowl to the middle of the table and sat back to see what would happen.

I'll never forget that morning. After about half an hour, I could feel the effect coming up, the loosening of symbolic reality, the feeling of humming pressure and space voyage inside my head, the sharp, brilliant, brutal intensification of all the senses. Every cell and every sense organ was humming with charged electricity. I felt terrible. What a place to be on a gray morning! In a dingy room, in a grim penitentiary, out of my mind. I looked over at the man next to me, a Polish embezzler from Worcester, Massachusetts. I could see him so clearly. I could see every pore in his face, every blemish, the hairs in his nose, the incredible green-yellow enamel of the decay in his teeth, the wet glistening of his frightened eyes. I could see every hair in his head, as though each was as big as an oak tree. What a confrontation! What am I doing here, out of my mind, with this strange mosaic-celled animal, prisoner, criminal?

I said to him, with a weak grin, How are you doing, John? He said, I feel fine. Then he paused for a minute, and asked, How are you doing, Doc? I was about to say in a reassuring psychological tone that I felt fine, but I couldn't, so I said, I feel lousy. John drew back his purple-pink lips, showed his green-yellow teeth in a sickly grin and said, What's the matter, Doc? Why you feel lousy? I looked with my two microscopic retina lenses into his eyes. I could see every line, yellow spider webs, red network of veins gleaming out at me. I said, John, I'm afraid of you. His eyes got bigger, then he began to laugh. I could look inside his mouth, swollen red tissues, gums, tongue, throat. I was prepared to be swallowed. Then I heard him say, Well that's funny Doc, 'cause I'm afraid of you. We were both smiling at this point, leaning forward. Doc, he said, why are you afraid of me? I said, I'm afraid of you, John, because you're a criminal. He nodded. I said, John, why are you afraid of me? He said, I'm afraid of you Doc because you're a mad scientist. Then our retinas locked and I slid down into the tunnel of

Beginning with six convicts, a senior investigator, and two graduate students, the study came to include 33 convicts and eight psychologists. All participated in the drug ingestion.

Test Called Success

In Dr. Leary's opinion, the experiment was an unqualified success. Ingestion of the drugs produced sudden insight that one has been living in a narrow space-time-self context.

"It's all a game, Doc, cops and robbers—we're such tough guys," he quotes one convict as saying. "We take it all so seriously as though that's all there is to life."

He reports also of frequent mystical insight among the convicts, particularly the death-rebirth experience.

"I felt helpless and wanted to murder you guys who did it to me; then I realized it was my own mind doing it; it's always been my own mind imagining troubles and enemies," he quotes one convict.

Over half the hard-bitten convicts displayed a sudden swing towards increased religious understanding and need, according to the study report.

Return Rate Drops

More important, perhaps, in the long run is the fact that the recidivism rate among the convicts who have been discharged dropped sharply.

"Seventy-five percent are holding their own against stiff winds and treacherous currents," Dr. Leary says.

The expected return rate of ex-convicts to the Concord reformatory would be between 50 and 70 percent.

But even in his claimed success among the convicts, Dr. Leary runs up against a doubting Thomas in the reformatory Superintendent Edward Grennan.

his eyes, and I could feel him walking around in my skull and we both began to laugh. And there it was, that dark moment of fear and distrust, which could have changed in a second to become hatred and terror. But we made the love connection. The flicker in the dark. Suddenly, the sun came out in the room and I felt great and I knew he did too.

Fire below and the lake above combat and destroy each other. So too in the course of the year a combat takes place between the forces of light and the forces of darkness, eventuating in the revolution of the seasons. Man masters these changes in nature by noting their regularity and marking off the passage of time accordingly. In this way order and clarity appear in the apparently chaotic changes of the seasons, and man is able to adjust himself in advance to the demands of the different times. (I Ching XLIX)

We had passed that moment of crisis, but as the minutes slowly ticked on, the grimness of our situation kept coming back in microscopic clarity. There were the four of us turned-on, every sense vibrating, pulsating with messages, two billion years of cellular wisdom, but what could we do trapped within the four walls of a gray hospital room, barred inside a maximum security prison? Then, one of the great lessons in my psychedelic training took place. One of the turned-on prisoners was a Negro from Texas, jazz saxophone player, heroin addict. He looked around with two huge balls of ocular white, shook his head, staggered over to the record player, put on a record. It was a Sonny Rollins record which he'd especially asked us to bring. Then he lay down on the cot and closed his eyes. The rest of us sat by the table while metal air from the yellow saxophone spinning across copper electric wires bounced off the walls of the room. There was a long silence. Then we heard Willy moaning softly and moving restlessly on the couch. I turned and looked at him and said, Willy, are you all right? There was apprehension in my voice. Everyone in the room swung his head anxiously to look and listen for the answer. Willy lifted his head, gave a big grin, and said, Man, am I all right? I'm in heaven and I can't believe it! Here I am in heaven man, and I'm stoned out of my mind, and I'm swinging like I've never been before and it's all happening in prison, and you ask me man, am I all right. What a laugh! And then he laughed and we all laughed, and suddenly we were all high and happy and chuckling at what we had done, bringing music, and love, and beauty, and serenity, and fun, and the seed of life into that grim and dreary prison.

Well, the session went on and on. There were high points and low points, ecstasies and terrors. My friend John, the Polish man, got sick and vomited. We all got pretty thoughtful. Why are there prisons? Why do some men put the warm cellular envelopes of their fellowmen in metal cages? What were we doing here? Then after a few hours, Ralph and Gunther and the other two convicts turned-on. Gunther was silly and acting like a hipster and Ralph fell down on the bed and experienced visions of Blakean terror. Two prisoners came and held his hand and guided him through. Dr. Presnell would check in every now and then, walk around the room like a dainty, graceful cat, not saying

Control Questioned

Grennan feels that study was done without a control and was therefore unscientific.

"These men received an extremely high degree of personal attention," he said. "The psychologists even set up a kind of criminal AA for the paroled prisoners in Cambridge. They made themselves available to them around the clock."

"I feel that the same rate of recidivism might have been achieved if the same concentration and attention were given to any parolee by highly placed members in any community."

∞

much, but taking it all in. And the guards came in bringing metal trays of food which we all looked at with disbelief, the way you'd look at a plate of worms or a pot of sawdust served up to you on a plate, and some said, Man, do they call that food? Since we Harvard people weren't allowed to eat prison food at the expense of the state, Dr. Presnell went out and got milkshakes and sandwiches which we all shared and never tasted food so good.

Then at five o'clock, there was a bang on the door, and we opened it and the guards came in and said, Time is up, men. Back to the prison ward. Ralph, Gunther, and I went with the five prisoners back to the lockup part of the hospital and sat there on beds, and smoked, and laughed, and compared notes on what we'd seen, and where we'd been. Then it was time for us to go. We shook hands, said we'd be back tomorrow, and Ralph and Gunther and I walked out of the prison, across the dark yard, rang the bell, and waited until the iron doors opened into the guardroom, and then across the guardroom, through the two metal doors, and down the metal stairs, past the clanking, steaming, old-fashioned radiators, and then we were outside. Ralph and Gunther got into their car and drove back to Cambridge, and I got in my car and drove to Newton.

As I rode along the highway, the tension and the drama of the day suddenly snapped off and I could look back and see what we had done. Nothing, you see, is secret in a prison, and the eight of us who had assembled to take drugs together in a prison were under the microscopic gaze of every convict in the prison and every guard, and within hours the word would have fanned through the invisible network to every other prison in the state. Grim Walpole penitentiary. Gray, sullen-walled Norfolk.

Did you hear? Some Harvard professors gave a new drug to some guys at Concord. They had a ball. It was great. It's a grand thing. It's something new. Hope. Maybe. Hope. Perhaps. Something new. We sure need something new. Hope.

PART 3

Psychedelic Drugs and Mysticism

The Good Friday Experiment of 1962

When Timothy Leary first experimented with mushrooms in Cuernavaca, he was an unlikely candidate for a religious experience. Before experimenting with psychedelic drugs, he described himself as "an atheist, a rationalist, skeptical of any sort of authority, ritual, tradition, faith, or magic . . ." (*High Priest* 282). Throughout his life, he had been a staunch critic of the faith of his upbringing, Roman Catholicism. Therefore, when the Harvard psychologist described his "religious turn," he often underscored the irony of the situation. It is therefore fitting that the opening sentence of "The Religious Experience: Its Production and Interpretation" makes references to both science and religion: "Three years ago, on a sunny afternoon in the garden of a Cuernavaca villa, I ate seven of the so-called 'sacred mushrooms' which had been given to me by a scientist from the university of Mexico. During the next five hours, I was whirled through an experience which could be described in many extravagant metaphors but which was above all and without question the deepest religious experience of my life."

Leary's opening paragraph is fascinating in the sense that it juxtaposes scientific rhetoric with religious rhetoric. The paragraph opens with a detached description of the mushrooms ("so-called 'sacred mushrooms'"). Leary's quotation marks imply his skeptical view of "ritual" and "magic." He also chooses to emphasize that the mushrooms were given to him by a "scientist from the University of Mexico" and not a shaman or a *curandera* (herb doctor or healer). However, Leary's first sentence also has a religious dimension: it invokes the biblical Garden of Eden and the eating of the forbidden fruit ("in the garden of a Cuernavaca garden I ate seven of the so-called 'sacred mushrooms'"). Leary's next sentence begins as an objective scientific statement about his experience with a psychotropic drug: "during the next five hours, I was whirled through an experience that could be described in many extravagant metaphors"). With this objective statement, Leary implies that the nature of the drug experience—what psychologists deem the "the expansion of consciousness"—is often described with hyperbolic language ("extravagant metaphors"). However, after emphasizing the importance of scientific detachment, Leary then chooses to end his paragraph with an "extravagant metaphor" of his own choosing: "it was . . . without question the deepest religious experience of my life." In short, Leary becomes a paradox: a scientist who speaks in religious metaphors.

Part 3 captures Leary's budding interest in mysticism and religious concepts (the beatific vision, ecstasy, satori, awe). Although Leary never abandoned his scientific perspective, he often used religious metaphors to convey his dichotomous understanding of the psychedelic experience. Leary's new-found interest in mysticism often brought him into direct contact with theologians and divinity graduate students while he was at Harvard. In the spring of 1962, Walter Pahnke, a medical doctor and a Ph.D. student in Harvard's Divinity School, approached Leary with an ambitious research project. Pahnke wanted to see if psilocybin could produce a genuine mystical experience. His select group—twenty Protestant divinity students—would gather in the Marsh Chapel on Good

Friday and ingest capsules that would be administered by Pahnke. The Good Friday Experiment would be a rigorous double-blind experiment: half of the students would receive a psilocybin extract and half would receive a placebo (nicotinic acid). Leary was chosen as a faculty sponsor because of his extensive research with psilocybin as well as the programming for positive psychedelic experiences.

After thirty minutes, it was easy to tell the difference between the psilocybin group and the control group who received the placebo. Those who received the psilocybin were thoroughly enraptured: they were lying on the floors and on the pews. Some of them wandered about the chapel murmuring prayers of wonderment: "God is everywhere." In contrast, the placebo group was largely unaffected by the experience; it was obvious that they had not received "the real thing." When the experiment concluded, the participants filled out an extensive questionnaire (over 150 questions) that attempted to identify if the psilocybin group had truly experienced "a classical mystical experience." The questionnaire featured nine categories that delineated a mystical experience (a sense of unity, transcendence to time and space, a sense of sacredness, a sense of objectivity and reality, a deeply felt positive mood, ineffability, paradoxicality, and transiency). Eight of the ten subjects in the experimental group experienced seven of nine categories. In contrast, all the members of the placebo control group had scores that were significantly lower than the experimental group.

Although the results from the experiment indicate that the experimental group experienced "mystical consciousness," the Good Friday Experiment (also called "The Marsh Chapel Miracle") was controversial in the 1960s and it remains so today. Religious and secular critics are skeptical of the experiment because the nature of a mystical experience is intrinsically difficult to define and measure. Moreover, many religious traditionalists are skeptical of the notion that a bona fide mystical experience can be stimulated by a pill. Others are alarmed by the suggestion that divine inspiration is merely the result of a change in brain chemistry.

The articles in Part 3 are loosely organized around the topic of psychedelic mysticism; each article places the reader in the social milieu of the early 1960s—the moment when psychedelic drugs—still legal—inspired moral debate and controversy. "The Religious Implications of Conscious-Expanding Drugs" was co-authored by Walter Houston Clark, a theologian at the Andover-Newton Theological School and an enthusiastic participant in the Good Friday Experiment (GFE). "The Religious Experience and Its Production" is Leary's famous account of GFE and its profound social and political repercussions; it concludes with the Harvard psychologist's attempt to deconstruct the anti-drug propaganda of the early 1960s. Part 3 also contains Leary and Alpert's Foreword to Alan Watts's *The Joyous Cosmology* (1962). Watts, a leading authority on Zen Buddhism, was a participant in the Harvard Psilocybin Project.

REFERENCES

Leary, Timothy. *High Priest*. New York: The World Publishing Company, 1968.

7

Leary's Mystical Turn

Religious Implications of Consciousness-Expanding Drugs

Timothy Leary and Walter Houston Clark

Aldous Huxley's *The Doors of Perception,* published in 1954, first introduced the notion that psychedelic drugs could, in some circumstances, induce mystical and religious experiences. When Huxley first made the argument in the early 1950s he was widely rejected in traditional religious circles. Theologians and religious thinkers were predictably uncomfortable with his suggestion that man-made substances—psilocybin pills and LSD—could produce authentic mystical experiences.

While many religious scholars objected to Huxley's ideas, some were eager to follow Huxley's footsteps. In 1962, Dr. Walter Clark was a sixty-two-year-old professor at the Andover Newton Theological School and a visiting scholar at Harvard University. Dr. Clark had heard about the Harvard Psilocybin Project from his colleague and friend Dr. Huston Smith, then a professor of philosophy at the Massachusetts Institute of Technology. Although Dr. Clark did not drink or smoke, he was very keen to try psilocybin. At first, Leary was reluctant to give psilocybin to Dr. Clark: "[t]o tell the truth I felt that Dr. Clark might be too academic and too conservative. But he kept insisting. As usual my apprehensions were unfounded. Clark had been searching for mystical experience for most of his life. After his first session, he became a committed project member" (*Flashbacks* 101). Dr. Clark was also a founding member of Leary's IFIF research project.

Leary and Clark's "Religious Implications of Consciousness Expanding Drugs" was one of the earliest articles that attempts to link psychedelic drugs to mystical experiences. The first two sections of the article were written by Leary and the final section ("Commentary") was written by Clark. Leary's two sections summarize his findings from the Harvard Psilocybin Project and the Concord Prison Experiment. While giving psilocybin pills to inmates, Leary discovered that Huxley's theory of drug-induced mysticism could be documented with his prison research. The authors also observed that intense bonds often emerged after the psychedelic sessions: "the most obvious result of these experiences is the closeness that develops among men who have been enlightened together. Even afterwards, in the somnambulance of normal reality, the bond remains." For Leary and Clark, the strong ties that emerged also resembled the notion of religious fellowship.

Many of Leary's colleagues in Harvard's psychology department were disturbed by Leary's sudden enthusiasm for religious mysticism. David McClelland, the chair of the Harvard Center for Research in Personality, remarked of Leary and Alpert's enthusiasm for psychedelic drugs: "They started out as good scientists. They've become cultists" (*Storming Heaven* 189). Before taking psychedelic drugs, Leary was a secular psychologist who was a staunch critic of religion, especially Roman Catholicism. However, Leary's growing interest in psychedelic drugs and Eastern thought, especially Tibetan Buddhism, led him to completely reconceptualize his secular and materialistic worldview. "Religious Implications . . ." captures Leary's initial turn toward mysticism and the attempt to link the psychedelic drugs to various religious impulses and the experience of transcendence.

JAMES PENNER

REFERENCES

Leary, Timothy. *Flashbacks: A Personal and Cultural History of an Era*. New York: Jeremy Tarcher/Perigee, 1990.

Stevens, Jay. *Storming Heaven: LSD and the American Dream*. New York: Harper and Row, 1987.

RELIGIOUS IMPLICATIONS OF CONSCIOUSNESS-EXPANDING DRUGS

From *Religious Education* 58, no. 3, 1963, pages 251–56.

Timothy Leary, Harvard University, and Walter Houston Clark, Andover Newton Theological School

The research reported in this paper was supported by grants from the Uris Brothers Foundation and the Parapsychology Foundation, Eileen Garrett, President. The first two sections of this article were written by Dr. Leary. The commentary is the work of Dr. Clark.

INTRODUCTION

Since the dawn of recorded history men have eaten vegetables to obtain religious visions. Indeed, there are some scholars of mysticism and ritual (Wasson, Graves, Watts) who suggest that the origins of most religions are based on experiences brought about by sacramental or visionary food. The words, soma, peyote, Hell's fire, divine mushrooms (in the Aztec dialect called God's flesh), are the most familiar reminders of this persisting correlation between spiritual ecstasy and sacred foods.

More recently William James, Aldous Huxley, Gerald Heard and Henri Bergson have seriously speculated about the metaphysical insights obtained by such substances as nitrous oxide and mescaline.

In 1943, a Swiss chemist, Albert Hofmann, accidentally discovered the properties of LSD (the most powerful consciousness-expanding drug known to man). Since then Hofmann and other bio-chemists have isolated and synthesized the active agents of several other flora— including the agent, psilocybin, in the sacred Mexican mushroom.

During 1960, psychologists at the Center for Research in Personality at Harvard University initiated a pilot study of the effects of psilocybin. Three general questions were posed: (1) Is the experience safe, physically and psychologically? (2) What are the range of reactions? (3) How is the experience effected by the *set* of the subject (his expectations and temperament) and the *setting* (the social atmosphere)?

Psilocybin was administered to over 400 volunteers—graduate students, professors, creative artists. Questionnaires were filled out by the subjects and analyzed. The results suggested tentative answers to these three inquiries.

1. No adverse physiological reactions were observed. About ten percent reported mild transient symptoms (nausea, headache, fatigue), but the majority claimed an increase in energy and heightened *élan* lasting several days afterward. No serious or enduring psychological symptoms were reported. The experience is dramatically intense, plunging the subjects into a realm of infinitely heightened reactivity and usually demanding a long period of reevaluation. No one seems to have been hurt by the experience.

2. Most subjects claimed to have been helped. 66 percent of the respondents found the experience pleasant and would be willing to try it again. 62 percent stated that their lives were changed for the better. 55 percent reported "learning a great deal" or "dramatic insights."

3. A definite relationship existed between set, setting, and the type of result. Those subjects who approached the experience with hopeful, serious intentions and who sensed a supportive environment learned more and changed the most.

These data supported the impressions of the research staff that generalizations about the "drug" were futile. We were dealing rather with the potentialities of expanded consciousness, the stare of ego-suspension or self-transcendence. Such ancient concepts as faith, belief, trust, served as the best predictors.

Another surprising result was the frequent use of religious terminology to explain the reactions. Less than ten percent of our original sample were orthodox believers or churchgoers, yet such terms as "God," "divine," "deep religious experience," "meeting the infinite," occurred in over half of the reports. This first naturalistic study of the effects of psilocybin left the research team with several unanswered questions. Were these insightful, life-changing, conversion-type reactions simply transient intoxications, or could they be made to stick? If the psilocybin experience were built into a systematic rehabilitation program, could we demonstrate enduring and measurable changes?

REHABILITATION FOR PRISON INMATES

To check on this possibility we undertook a rehabilitation project in the Massachusetts Correctional Institution, Concord. We selected a prison sample for three reasons. The prison provides an objective measure of success. Psychotherapy research is permanently plagued by the absence of a criterion. How should one measure improvement in mental health? The penitentiary recidivism rate is a clear irrefutable index. A second reason for working in a prison was the notorious resistance of inmates to conventional, verbal psychotherapy. And finally the strong religious tone to the experience suggested rehabilitative possibilities with that social group most reluctant to accept moral and religious blandishments.

A representative group of six maximum security inmates were originally selected by the correctional officials.* The Harvard personnel (one faculty member and two graduate students) outlined the project and offered the inmates the opportunity to volunteer or decline. Of thirty-eight inmates only two declined to participate. The original six inmates were then administered a battery of psychological tests and attended three orientation sessions.

---

*The Superintendent of Massachusetts Correctional Institution, Concord, Mr. Edward Grennan, provided interested and supportive counsel for this pilot project. Mr. William Ryan, Mr. Bernard Dee and Officer Stuart Scott provided energetic collaboration. Dr. W. Madison Presnell, prison psychiatrist, provided medical supervision and consultation.

The first psilocybin session was held on a gray, cloudy day in March, 1961. The setting was a hospital conference room equipped with six cots, a large table, and a record player. The surroundings were grim—barred windows, drab painted walls. The atmosphere (in spite of the encouraging orientation) was heavy and anxious. The first person to take the drug was the senior investigator.* Three inmates then followed. The two graduate students and the three remaining inmates acted as observers in the morning and switched roles in the afternoon.

After one hour the drug took effect and the nature of reality became sharp and microscopically clear. The nature of this particular reality was, however, painfully harsh—three criminals and a psychologist locked behind forbidding bars. Suddenly stripped of his ego protection—role, status, conceptual machinery—the psychologist felt frightened and helpless. With their ego defenses gone, the three prisoners were equally helpless. One inmate, a former jazz musician, murmured ecstatically and fell on a cot to listen to the recorded music. Melody was his trusted thread to the transcendent and he later reported the deepest aesthetic experience of his life, but his raptured gasps were interpreted by the others as discomfort.

The psychologist wanly asked another inmate how he felt. A weak forced smile, "O.K., I guess, Doc." The psychologist replied, "Well, I'm scared, I feel lousy!" The two pair of eyes met. "Well, Doc, now that you mention it, I'm scared, too!" Then laughter, relaxation, trust flooded the room. The oldest human experience—caught together in dark, limitless space and then the recognition of the basic paradox and the basic resolution—we are all one—we're all in it together—trust and share, it's the only way out. The sun was suddenly out and another long night of the soul was ended. The participants smiled at each other, closed their

---

*The practice of having the investigator "join the subject" in the experience is a hotly debated issue. Participation by the researcher is not necessary and in many cases not desirable. The general advantage of investigator's participation has to do with the ego-transcendental, expanded-consciousness state. A person operating on the level of routine space-time-conceptual reality is usually unable to communicate with the transcendent subject. In the prison situation where distrust, suspicion, and mutual manipulation are so intense, the deep empathetic rapport of mutual transcendence is particularly necessary.

eyes and moved on to their own form of transcendental experience.

Since that session, we have shared over one hundred individual ingestions with prisoners. While there have been rare moments of panic and distrust, the overall behavior of this group of maximum-security prisoners has been more serene, illuminated, and serious than any other occupational group with whom we have worked.

The most obvious result of these experiences is the closeness that develops among men who have been enlightened together. Even afterwards, in the somnambulance of normal reality, the bond remains. Another result is the collaborative honesty which developed. As the group grew to include 33 convicts and eight Harvard psychologists, there were men from both groups who rigidly protected their individuality and personal goals. Among the rest, commitment to the collaborative enterprise varied with ego defensiveness.

A classic aspect of the psilocybin experience is the awakening to broader perspectives: the sudden insight that one has been living in a narrow space-time-self context. "It's all a game, Doc, cops and robbers— we're such tough guys! We take it so seriously as though that's all there is to life." This illumination, when shared with other group members, becomes a powerful instrument for maintaining philosophic expansion. Men who have been through a psilocybin session together can perpetuate some of the transcendental flavor. Most of us would really prefer to operate with the selfless ecstatic freedom of a Buddha or a saint. We don't because we fear that the others won't take it as seriously, that they will continue their self-games, will ridicule or take advantage.

About half of the prisoners and psychologists in our experiment were able to keep ego-free moments going in subsequent group discussions, and a cult-like closeness and trust often developed. This development appears to have had significant measurable effects on objective test changes and on post-release behavior.

The phenomena of mystical insight occurred so frequently in our studies as to deserve brief illustration; for instance, death-rebirth experiences as illustrated by comments like these: "I went into the john and sat in the shower and died;" or "I was out there looking back at my body lying on the bed, free of that whole business;" or "I felt helpless and wanted to murder you guys who did it to me; then I realized it was my own mind doing it; it's always been my own mind imagining trouble and enemies;" or the semi-literate tough guy leaping off his cot shouting, "Doc, this is it! This is what life is all about! We'll never live more than we are right now, this minute!" or "I saw fire everywhere. All of life was fire, I was scared. Then I knew it was all right, I was part of it. I relaxed and went with it."

In their own words and without religious terminology, about one-half of these "hardened" cynics reported classic mystic, conversion reactions. "All is one." "Thy will be done." Many, of course, reached this point and drew back. *"My* mind. *My* will be done."

During the last three thousand years rebirth experiences have been induced by practitioners of every religious and therapeutic persuasion. The traditional appraisals are: How long does it last? What effects does it have on observable behavior?

The problem here is more social than individual. To those of us who became (somewhat accidentally) deeply identified with the rebirth and rehabilitation of thirty-six criminals, it became disturbingly clear that society is not ready for dramatic changes in our criminal class. Powerful forces operate to thrust the ex-convict back into the criminal role. However negative were the environmental pressures before incarceration, one can rest assured they are worse after release. When as thoughtful citizens we read about this situation in a sociology text or a *Harper's* article, we wince. When we see these pressures operating on comrades, on men who have become part of ourselves, in whom we have seen divinity reflected, then it really hurts. To ease these wounds we have worked to develop a post-release program, an Alcoholics Anonymous-type group, a "halfway" house, a readjustment program. Follow-up work to maintain the rebirth experience is necessary, and one should be cautious about providing a chemical mystic experience unless the preparation (set and setting) is conscientious and one is prepared to share in the rebirth pains.

With these frustrating limitations in mind, let us look at the objective results of our work. First, the psychological test changes: There were statistically significant increases in socialization, tolerance, responsibility, insight, and significant decreases in psychopathic tendencies, hostility, cynicism. Ratings by prison officers showed improvement in institutional adjustment.

More important than changes in test forms is the recidivism rate. Where are these prisoners located in space-time after their release? Back in prison? On the street? While it is premature to draw conclusions, the results so far look hopeful. Twenty-four men have been on the street an average of ten months. There have been no convictions for new crimes. Five men have been returned for technical parole violations: drinking, failure or inability to find or hold a job. Seventy-five percent are holding their own against stiff winds and treacherous currents.*

COMMENTARY

The student of religious behavior who studies phenomena such as those described in the foregoing cannot but be struck by similarities to intense religious groups of an evangelistic nature, such as Moral Rearmament or Alcoholics Anonymous. As with them, the experience tends to be dramatic; as with them, individuals are changed as to their life goals; as with them, the experience tends to be individualized, for while some are greatly helped, there are others on whom the experience seems to have very little permanent effect. However, it may not be without significance that sixty-two percent of one group, as indicated above, reported that their lives were changed for the better; for studies have indicated that roughly the same percentage find help in MRA or AA. Still another striking similarity is the depth of fellowship reported by participants both in the consciousness-expanding experience and in the intense religious groups. But, on the whole, results are dependent

---

*The expected return rate of ex-convicts to this prison after eight months would be between fifty and seventy percent. Of the twenty-five percent who actually did return, none was convicted of a new crime, but accused only of technical parole violation.

partly on the nature of surrounding circumstances, partly on follow-up, but chiefly on the essential nature of the person himself.

The exact nature of the experience is usually felt and reported to be ineffable, while the figures of speech used to describe it and the language used is reminiscent of the mystics. The question then arises whether an experience, apparently touched off by ingestion of a material substance, properly can be described as mystical. The observation and participation at least of this writer leads him to the conclusion that it is, confirming the opinion of a leading American authority on mysticism, W. T. Stace. At least, if the psilocybin experience is not at times mystical in nature, then the difference is so subtle as to be indistinguishable. Consequently (even though we are not ready to be categorical about the matter) the best assumption we can make at the moment is that some forms of the psilocybin experience and mysticism are identical. This raises some interesting and important issues for the student of religion and suggests several ways in which consciousness-expanding substances may be useful.

The chief and most obvious use to which they may be put is in the study of the nature of religious experiences and their sources. We note that psilocybin and its companion chemical, mescaline, have been used in esoteric religious rituals, both ancient and modern, presumably as a stimulus to religious experience. Also we know that any profound emotional experience, religious or otherwise, is accompanied by bodily changes, partly of a chemical or hormonal nature. Furthermore, we know that the natural chemistry of the body includes biochemical substances, known as the *indoles,* which are similar in structure to the consciousness-expanding chemicals and seem to be associated with some of the same psychological states as those produced by psilocybin. The question then immediately arises whether a naturally occurring excess of the indoles might not predispose some people to certain kinds of mystical experience or whether a mystical state of mind might not, on the other hand, stimulate chemical changes in the body. Scientific investigation into this problem may initially offend some religious persons. Nevertheless, if answers to questions of this kind are ascertainable through proper research, it is the duty of the scholar to pursue them.

It cannot be too strongly emphasized that these substances are *not in themselves* sacred or religious any more than organ music is. Given the proper setting and attitudes on the part of listeners, organ music *may be* a *means* to the stimulation of a religious experience on the part of some people. In much the same way, psilocybin, in conjunction with proper setting and preparation, accompanied by the fundamental willingness of the subject, may *release* latent religious sensitivities and so make possible what appears to be either a genuine religious experience or something so similar as to be indistinguishable from one. Like a true religious experience this may result in a profound change of attitudes and values. But also, like a religious experience, it requires discipline if wholesome results are to be permanent. The essential capacity to reach out toward or be "grasped by" the Divine resides within the person.

Other uses of psilocybin are more secular. The project with the convicts certainly suggests that it is useful in reform and rehabilitation to more wholesome life aims. Doubtless there are those willing to experiment further under appropriate conditions to discover whether the substance is helpful in the mitigation of crime, alcoholism, and other situations where pilot programs have indicated such possibilities. Such results would be hard for religion to ignore.

We have, then, the continuous reports that psilocybin seems to mediate an experience of self-discovery, an awareness of *who one is* to a degree never before enjoyed. "This is what life is all about!" we recall that one convict exclaimed. This has been the experience of many, and, furthermore, such insights often seem to have profound effects on conduct. This reminds one of Pascal's mystical experience, so influential in leading that genius to what he considered higher spiritual ground and which seemed to reflect itself in so much of his subsequent writing. It also recalls Socrates' conviction that the knowing of oneself was the beginning of an effective life. This certainly has religious significance. If it were to be proved that psilocybin, administered under serious conditions, is a safe and effective means toward self-discovery, this also would have religious significance.

In connection with the latter point, it is to be noted that many religious people who have participated in the Harvard psilocybin research have reported that their spiritual sensitivities have also been expanded. Biblical passages or religious terms formerly meaningless or pale have suddenly acquired vivid meaning. Like the renegade who, through conversion experience, suddenly finds himself in possession of the meaning of the term "salvation," so he who ingests psilocybin may find this or similar terms illuminated for him. All good education is punctuated by a repeated process of awakening— the student of a foreign language who suddenly finds himself thinking in the language, the scientific student cloyed with the acquisition of fact who unexpectedly has the joy of discovering something for himself, the obdurate Philistine despiser of all things literary who, despite himself, is seized by the surging passion of a great poem. It is in this way, only more poignantly and effectively, that the psilocybin experience might be found to be a powerful aid in religious instruction.

A final religious use of the substance is a social one. The account of the convicts mentioned the closeness that develops among those who have been illuminated together. This type of fellowship has long been known to be demonstrated among religious groups. However, this closeness has been dissipated or lost in most of our large religious institutions, where fellowship hardly exceeds that to be found in a Rotary club or a closely-knit business. For best results it is probably mandatory that a fellowship group be formed to follow up the experience of illumination, and such groups within a larger body could well become fertilizing and creative forces.

But this critique must end on a note of caution. We have been speculating quite freely, basing our speculations largely on the experiences of a few convicts. What may work with convicts may not be the best thing for the church. Furthermore, psilocybin is not a substance to be ingested for thoughtless fun or without skilled and experienced supervision. It requires also both careful preparation and highly disciplined follow-up. The experience will be pleasant for some and disagreeable for others. The use of the substance is still very much in the experimental stage. A considerable amount of experimentation has gone into both psilocybin and similar materials indicating they are relatively safe, but unfortunate side effects, both physiological and psychological, may yet appear. Certain unstable individuals, for example, should be screened and not permitted to use the substance in the ordinary experimental programs. Medical and psychological supervision is necessary at this stage of development.

But enough has been done with psilocybin, mescaline, and LSD to suggest creative possibilities of which the most constructive seem to lie in the field of religion and moral regeneration. There are some religious people averse to linking religion in any way to chemicals. But, because of the natural conservatism of religious bodies, are we to shrink from a thorough investigation of the legitimate uses of these substances? It might be recalled here that religious interests in Puritan New England put up great opposition to the then new practice of vaccination against smallpox. The hue and cry after the fluoridation of drinking water is a psychologically similar movement today. But with a cautious boldness religiously-minded scientists are experimenting with the relation of the consciousness-expanding substances and religion. The results cannot be ignored by scholars, theologians, or leaders of organized religion.

REFERENCES

R. DeRopp, *Drugs and the Mind*. New York: Grove Press, 1960 (paper). Biochemistry for the layman.

Jane Dunlap, *Exploring Inner Space*. New York: Harcourt, Brace, 1961. A subject describes experiences with LSD.

R. M. Featherstone and A. Simon, Eds., *A Pharmacologic Approach to the Study of the Mind*. Springfield, Ill.: Thomas, 1959. See especially the article by Sidney Cohen.

Aldous Huxley, *Doors of Perception*, and, *Heaven and Hell*, now issued together in the Colophon paperbacks, New York: Harper, 1963.

W. T. Stace, *Mysticism and Philosophy*. Philadelphia: Lippincott, 1960. The most penetrating study of mystical experience.

V. O. Wasson and R. G. Wasson, *Mushrooms, Russia, and History*. New York: Pantheon Books, 1957.

8

The Good Friday Experiment

The Religious Experience: Its Production and Interpretation

Timothy Leary

Many theologians were interested in Leary's Good Friday Experiment, which had been held at the March Chapel in Boston in 1962. As a result, in 1963, Leary was invited to speak to a group of Lutheran psychologists and theologians at the annual conference of the American Psychology Association (APA); his presentation would be sponsored by the Board of Theological Education. "The Religious Experience: Its Production and Interpretation," the address Leary would deliver, was composed in August of 1963 at Newton Center (Leary's home near Cambridge).

The timing was odd because Leary was in the middle of his *annus horribilis*. During the past four months, he had been fired by Harvard University and expelled from three countries—Mexico, Dominica, and Antigua. In each case, Leary's attempt to establish an independent psychedelic research center abroad had failed miserably. Although Leary had clearly reached a low point in his life, his address to Lutheran psychologists is anything but bitter. "The Religious Experience: Its Production and Interpretation" is a boldly speculative piece of writing that attempts to speak to psychologists, theologians, and scientists at the same time.* It includes an overview of Leary's research at Harvard and a descriptive account of the Good Friday Experiment.

Leary's appearance at the APA's annual conference was controversial because it was his first public appearance in the aftermath of the Harvard Drug Scandal. Leary spoke to a packed audience that included psychologists, Lutheran ministers, and members of the press and his passionate defense of academic freedom and the right to expand one's consciousness received a standing ovation.

In many respects, Leary's APA address can be considered the apex of Leary's academic career. His article poses philosophical questions that concern both scientists and religious thinkers. Leary's new found interest in religious mysticism and ecstasy is juxtaposed with a scientific view of the drug experience. Thus, Leary attempts to understand the drug experience from seemingly antithetical points of view ("I am going to advance the hypothesis that those aspects of the psychedelic experience which subjects report to be ineffable and ecstatically religious involve a direct awareness of the processes which physicists and biochemists and neurologists measure.")

Leary's essay also effectively deconstructs the rhetoric of the

---

*Leary's account of the essay "The Religious Experience: Its Production and Interpretation" in *Flashbacks* contains several factual errors (186–87). In *Flashbacks*, Leary actually describes his revised version of the essay ("Seven Tongues of God") that was published in *The Politics of Ecstasy* in 1968. "The Seven Tongues of God"—an expanded version of Leary's lecture to the Lutherans, which constitutes this article—includes eight philosophical questions rather than the four that appeared in the original version. Leary's original version ("The Religious Experience . . .") is intended for a scholarly audience while the expanded version is written with a wider audience in mind; it contains colloquial language ("turning on") and sound bites for the counterculture ("the only hope is dope"). From a rhetorical point of view, Leary's original version is a more effective piece of writing. "The Seven Tongues of God" is disappointing because it waters down the speculative grandeur of Leary's original article.

anti-drug propagandists. Leary urges his audience to approach the issue of consciousness expansion with a checklist of nine questions. Leary opts not to refute the opposition with a traditional rhetorical appeal for internal freedom and the right to expand one's consciousness; instead Leary urges the reader to consider a list of salient philosophical questions:

(7) If he is against what he calls "artificial methods of illumination," ask him what constitutes the natural. Words? Rituals? Tribal customs? Alkaloids? Psychedelic vegetables?

(8) If he is against biochemical assistance, where does he draw the line? Does he use nicotine? alcohol? penicillin? vitamins? conventional sacramental substances?

(9) If your advisor is against LSD, what is he for? If he forbids you the psychedelic key to revelation, what does he offer you instead?

"The Religious Experience: Its Production and Interpretation" is one of Leary's most impressive articles because he engages his skeptics and refutes their ill-informed objections to psychedelic drugs. This article can also be read as the swan song of Leary's controversial academic career. After his expulsion from Harvard and Mexico, Leary embraced his heretical status within the psychological community and assumed the role of rebel and icon.

JAMES PENNER

REFERENCES

Leary, Timothy. *Flashbacks: A Personal and Cultural History of an Era.* New York: Jeremy Tarcher/Perigee, 1990, 186–87.
Stevens, Jay. *Storming Heaven: LSD and the American Dream.* New York: Harper and Row, 1987.

THE RELIGIOUS EXPERIENCE: ITS PRODUCTION AND INTERPRETATION

From *Psychedelic Review* 1, no. 3 (1964): 324–46.

Timothy Leary

Lecture delivered at a meeting of Lutheran psychologists and other interested professionals, sponsored by the Board of Theological Education, Lutheran Church in America, in conjunction with the 71st Annual Convention of the American Psychological Association, Philadelphia, Bellevue Stratford Hotel, August 30, 1963.

◆ ◆ ◆

Three years ago, on a sunny afternoon in the garden of a Cuernavaca villa, I ate seven of the so-called "sacred mushrooms" which had been given to me by a scientist from the University of Mexico. During the next five hours, I was whirled through an experience which could be described in many extravagant metaphors but which was above all and without question the deepest religious experience of my life.

Statements about personal reactions, however passionate, are always relative to the speaker's history and may have little general significance. Next come the questions "Why?" and "So what?"

There are many predisposing factors—intellectual, emotional, spiritual, social—which cause one person to be ready for a dramatic mind-opening experience and which lead another to shrink back from new levels of awareness. The discovery that the human brain possesses an infinity of potentialities and can operate at unexpected space-time dimensions left me feeling exhilarated, awed, and quite convinced that I had awakened from a long ontological sleep.

A profound transcendent experience should leave in its wake a changed man and a changed life. Since my illumination of August, 1960, I have devoted most of my energies to try to understand the revelatory potentialities of the human nervous system and to make these insights available to others.

I have repeated this biochemical and (to me) sacramental ritual over fifty times personally and, almost every time, I have been awed by religious revelations as shattering as the first experience. During this period I have been lucky enough to collaborate in this work with more than 50 scientists and scholars who joined our various research projects. We have arranged transcendent experiences for over one thousand persons from all walks of life, including 69 full-time religious professionals, about half of whom profess the Christian or Jewish faith and about half of whom belong to Eastern religions.

Included in this roster are two college deans, a divinity college president, three university chaplains, an executive of a religious foundation, a prominent religious editor, and several distinguished religious philosophers. In our research files and in certain denominational offices there is building up a large and quite remarkable collection of reports which will be published when the political atmosphere becomes more tolerant. At this point it is conservative to state that over 75 percent of these subjects report intense mystico-religious responses, and considerably more than half claim that they have had the deepest spiritual experience of their life.[3]

The interest generated by this research led to the formation of an informal group of ministers, theologians and religious psychologists who have been meeting once a month (summers excepted) for over two years, with an average of 20 persons in attendance. In addition to arranging for spiritually oriented psychedelic sessions and discussing prepared papers, this group provided the supervisory manpower for the dramatic "Good Friday" study, and was the original planning nucleus of the organization which assumed sponsorship of our research in consciousness-expansion: IFIF (the International Federation for Internal Freedom). The generating impulse and the original leadership of IFIF came from a seminar in religious experience, and this fact may be related to the alarm which IFIF aroused in some secular and psychiatric circles.

THE "GOOD FRIDAY" STUDY, which has been sensationalized recently in the press as "The Miracle of Marsh Chapel," deserves further elaboration not only as an example of a serious, controlled experiment, involving over 30 courageous volunteers, but also as a systematic demonstration of the religious aspects of the psychedelic revelatory experience. This study was the Ph.D. dissertation research of a graduate student in the philosophy of religion at Harvard University, who is, incidentally, both an M.D. and a Bachelor of Divinity. This investigator set out to determine whether the transcendent experience reported during psychedelic sessions was similar to the mystical experience reported by saints and famous religious mystics.

The subjects in this study were 20 divinity students selected from a group of volunteers. The subjects were divided into five groups of four persons, and each group met before the session for orientation and preparation. To each group were assigned two guides with considerable psychedelic experience. The ten guides were professors and advanced graduate students from Boston-area colleges.

The experiment took place in a small, private chapel, beginning about one hour before noon on Good Friday. The Dean of the Chapel, who was to conduct a three-hour devotional service upstairs in the main hall of the church, visited the subjects a few minutes before the start of the service at noon, and gave a brief inspirational talk.

Two of the subjects in each group and one of the two guides were given a moderately stiff dosage (i.e., 30 mg.) of psilocybin, the chemical synthesis of the active ingredient in the "sacred mushroom" of Mexico. The remaining two subjects and the second guide received a placebo which produced noticeable somatic side effects, but which was not psychedelic. The study was triple-blind: neither the subjects, guides, nor experimenter knew who received psilocybin.

Because the dissertation describing this study has not yet been published,[1] any detailed discussion of the results would be premature and unfair to the investigator. I can say, however, that the results clearly support the hypothesis that, with adequate preparation and in an environment which is supportive and religiously meaningful, subjects report mystical experiences significantly more than placebo controls.

Our studies, naturalistic and experimental, thus demonstrate that if the expectation, preparation, and setting are spiritual, an intense mystical or revelatory experience can be expected in from 40 to 90 percent of subjects ingesting psychedelic drugs. These results *may be* attributed to the bias of our research group, which has taken the "far-out" and rather dangerous position that there are experiential-spiritual as well as secular-behavioral potentialities of the nervous system. While we share and follow the epistemology of scientific psychology (objective records), our basic ontological assumptions are closer to Jung than to Freud, closer to the mystics than to the theologians, closer to Einstein and Bohr than to Newton. In order to check on this bias, let us cast a comparative glance at the work of other research groups in this field who begin from more conventional ontological bases.

Oscar Janiger, a psychiatrist, and William McGlothlin, a psychologist, have reported the reactions of 194 psychedelic subjects. Seventy-three of these took LSD as part of a psychotherapy program, and 121 were volunteers. The religious "set" would not be expected to dominate the expectations of these subjects. The results, which are abstracted from a paper published in *The Psychedelic Review*,[2] are as follows:

ITEM	PERCENT Janiger-McGlothlin (non-religious setting) N = 194
Increased interest in morals, ethics . . .	35
Increased interest in universal concepts (meaning of life)	48
Change in sense of values	48
LSD should be used for	
becoming aware of oneself	75
giving new meaning to life	58
getting people to understand each other	42
An experience of lasting benefit	58

Two other studies, one by Ditman et al., another by Savage et al., used the same questionnaire, allowing for inter-experiment comparison. Both Ditman and Savage are psychiatrists, but the clinical environment of the latter's study is definitely more religious (subjects are shown religious articles during the session, etc.). Summarizing the religious items of their questionnaires:

	PERCENT	
ITEM	Ditman (supportive environment) N = 74	Savage (supportive environment & some religious stimuli) N = 96
Feel it [LSD] was the greatest thing that ever happened to me	49	85
A religious experience . . .	32	83
A greater awareness of God or a Higher Power or an Ultimate Reality	40	90

Here, then, we have five scientific studies by qualified investigators—the four naturalistic studies by Leary et al.,[3] Savage et al.,[4] Ditman et al.,[5] and Janiger-McGlothlin,[6] and the triple-blind study in the Harvard dissertation mentioned earlier—yielding data which indicate that (1) if the setting is supportive but not spiritual, between 40 to 75 percent of psychedelic subjects will report intense and life-changing religious experiences; and that (2) if the set and setting are supportive and spiritual, then from 40 to 90 percent of the experiences will be revelatory and mystico-religious.

It is hard to see how these results can be disregarded by those who are concerned with spiritual growth and religious development. These data are even more interesting because the experiments took place during an historical era when mysticism, individual religious ecstasy (as opposed to religious behavior), was highly suspect, and when the classic, direct, non-verbal means of revelation and consciousness-expansion such as meditation, yoga, fasting, monastic withdrawal and sacramental foods and drugs were surrounded by an aura of fear, clandestine secrecy, active social sanction and even imprisonment.[7] The 69 professional workers in religious vocations who partook of psychedelic substances (noted earlier), were responsible, respected, thoughtful, and moral individuals who were grimly aware of the controversial nature of the procedure and aware that their reputations and their jobs might be undermined (and, as a matter of fact, have been and are today being threatened for some of them). *Still* the results read: 75% spiritual revelation. It may well be that the most intense religious experience, like the finest metal, requires fire, the heat of external bureaucratic opposition, to produce the keenest edge. When the day comes—as it surely will—that sacramental biochemicals like LSD will be as routinely and tamely used as organ music and incense to assist in the attainment of religious experience, it may well be that the ego-shattering effect of the drug will be diminished. Such may be one aspect of the paradoxical nature of religious experience.

◆ ◆ ◆

THE RELIGIOUS EXPERIENCE. You are undoubtedly wondering about the meaning of this phrase which has been used so freely in the preceding paragraphs. May I offer a definition?

The religious experience is the ecstatic, incontrovertibly certain, subjective discovery of answers to four basic spiritual questions. There can be, of course, absolute subjective certainty in regard to secular questions: "Is this the girl I love? Is Fidel Castro a wicked man? Are the Yankees the best baseball team?" But issues which do not involve the four basic questions belong to secular games, and such convictions and faiths, however deeply held, can be distinguished from the religious. Liturgical practices, rituals, dogmas, theological speculations, can be and too often are secular, i.e., completely divorced from the spiritual experience.

What are these four basic spiritual questions? There is the Ultimate-Power question, the Life question, the Human-Destiny question, and the Ego question.

1. **The Ultimate Power Question:**
   What is the Ultimate Power or Basic Energy which moves the universe, creates life? What is the Cosmic Plan?
2. **The Life Question:**
   What is life, where did it start, where is it going?
3. **The Human-Destiny Question:**
   What is man, whence did he come, and where is he going?
4. **The Ego Question:**
   Who am I? What is my place in the plan?

While one may disagree with the wording, I think most thoughtful people—philosophers or not—can agree on something like this list of basic issues. Do not most of the great religious statements—Eastern or monotheistic—speak directly to these four questions?

Now one important fact about these questions is that they are continually being answered and re-answered, not only by all the religions of the world but also by the data of the natural sciences. Read these questions again from the standpoint of the goals of (1) astronomy-physics, (2) biochemistry, (3) genetics, paleontology, and evolutionary theory, (4) neurology.

We are all aware of the unhappy fact that both science and religion are too often diverted towards secular game goals. Various pressures demand that laboratory and church forget these basic questions and instead provide distractions, illusory protection, narcotic comfort. Most of us dread confrontation with the answers to these basic questions, whether these answers come from science or religion. But if "pure" science and religion address themselves to the same basic questions, what is the distinction between the two disciplines? Science is the systematic attempt to record and measure the energy process and the sequence of energy transformations we call life. The goal is to answer the basic questions in terms of objective, observed, public data. Religion is the systematic attempt to provide answers *to the same questions* subjectively, in terms of direct, incontrovertible, personal experience.

Science is a social system which evolves roles, rules, rituals, values, language, space-time locations to further the quest for these goals—these answers. Religion is a social system which has evolved its roles, rules, rituals, values, language, space-time locations to further the pursuit of the same goals—the revelatory experience. A science which fails to address itself to these spiritual goals, which accepts other purposes (however popular), becomes secular, political, and tends to oppose new data. A religion which fails to provide direct experiential answers to these spiritual questions becomes secular, political, and tends to oppose the individual revelatory confrontation. R. C. Zaehner,[8] whose formalism is not always matched by his tolerance, has remarked that "experience, when divorced from revelation, often leads to absurd and wholly irrational excesses." Like any statement of polarity the opposite is equally true: revelation, when divorced from experience, often leads to absurd and wholly rational excesses. Those of us who have been researching the area of consciousness have been able to collect considerable sociological data about the tendency of the rational mind to spin out its own interpretations. But I shall have more to say about the political situation in a later section of this paper.

◆ ◆ ◆

At this point I should like to present my main thesis. I am going to advance the hypothesis that *those aspects of the psychedelic experience which subjects report to be ineffable and ecstatically religious involve a direct awareness of the processes which physicists and biochemists and neurologists measure.*

We are treading here on very tricky ground. When we read the reports of LSD subjects, we are doubly limited. First, they can only speak in the vocabulary they know, and for the most part they do not possess the lexicon and training of energy scientists. Second, *we researchers* only find what we are prepared to look for, and too often we think in crude psychological-jargon concepts: moods, emotions, value judgments, diagnostic categories.

In recent months we have re-examined our data and have begun to interview subjects from the perspective of this present hypothesis. The results are interesting. To spell them out in brief detail I am going to review some of the current scientific answers to these four basic questions and then compare them with reports from psychedelic subjects.

(1) The Ultimate-Power Question

A. *The scientific answers* to this question change constantly—Newtonian laws, quantum indeterminacy, atomic structure, nuclear structure. Today the *basic energy* is located within the nucleus. Inside the atom,

> a transparent sphere of emptiness, thinly populated with electrons, the substance of the atom has shrunk to a core of unbelievable smallness: enlarged 1000 million times, an atom would be about the size of a football, but its nucleus would still be hardly visible—a mere speck of dust at the center. Yet that nucleus radiates a powerful electric field which holds and controls the electrons around it.[9]

Incredible power and complexity operating at speeds and spatial dimensions which our conceptual minds cannot register. Infinitely small, yet pulsating outward through enormous networks of electrical forces—atom, molecule, cell, planet, star: all forms dancing to the nuclear tune.

The *cosmic design* is this network of energy whirling through space-time. More than 15,000 million years ago the oldest known stars began to form. Whirling disks of gas molecules (driven of course by that tiny, spinning, nuclear force)—condensing clouds—further condensations—the tangled web of spinning magnetic fields clustering into stellar forms, and each stellar cluster hooked up in a magnetic dance with its planetary cluster and with every other star in the galaxy and each galaxy whirling in synchronized relationship to the other galaxies.

One thousand million galaxies. From 100 million to 100,000 million stars in a galaxy—that is to say, 100,000 million planetary systems per galaxy and each planetary system slowly wheeling through the stellar cycle that allows for a brief time the possibility of life as we know it.

Five thousand million years ago, a slow-spinning dwarf star we call the sun is the center of a field of swirling planetary material. The planet earth is created. In five thousand million years the sun's supply of hydrogen will be burned up, the planets will be engulfed by a final solar explosion. Then the ashen remnants of our planetary system will spin silently through the dark infinity of space. And then is the dance over? Hardly. Our tiny solar light, which is one of one hundred thousand million suns in our galaxy, will scarcely be missed. And our galaxy is one of a thousand million galaxies spinning out and up at rates which exceed the speed of light—each galaxy eventually burning up, to be replaced by new galaxies to preserve the dance equilibrium.

Here in the always changing data of nuclear physics and astronomy is the current scientific answer to the first basic question—material enough indeed for an awesome cosmology.

B. *Psychedelic reports* often contain phrases which seem to describe similar phenomena, subjectively experienced.

(a) I passed in and out of a state several times where I was so relaxed that I felt open to a total flow, over and around and through my body (more than my body). . . . All objects were dripping, streaming, with white-hot light or electricity which flowed in the air. It was as though we were watching the world, just having come into being, cool off, its substance and form still molten and barely beginning to harden.

(b) Body being destroyed after it became so heavy as to be unbearable. Mind wandering, ambulating throughout an ecstatically-lit indescribable landscape. How can there be so much light—layers and layers of light, light upon light, all is illumination.

(c) I became more and more conscious of vibrations—of the vibrations in my body, the harp-strings giving forth their individual tones. Gradually I felt myself becoming one with the Cosmic

Vibration. . . . In this dimension there were no forms, no deities or personalities—just bliss.

(d) The dominant impression was that of entering into the very marrow of existence. . . . It was as if each of the billion atoms of experience which under normal circumstances are summarized and averaged into crude, indiscriminate wholesale impressions was now being seen and savored for itself. The other clear sense was that of cosmic relativity. Perhaps all experience never gets summarized in any inclusive overview. Perhaps all there is, is this everlasting congeries of an infinite number of discrete points of view, each summarizing the whole from its perspective.

(e) I could see the whole history and evolution along which man has come. I was moving into the future and saw the old cycle of peace and war, good times and bad times, starting to repeat, and I said, "The same old thing again, oh God! It has changed though, it is different," and I thought of the rise of man from animal to spiritual being. But I was still moving into the future and I saw the whole planet destroyed and all history, evolution, and human efforts being wiped out in this one ultimate destructive act of God.

Subjects speak of participating in and merging with pure (i.e., content-free) energy, white light; of witnessing the breakdown of macroscopic objects into vibratory patterns, visual nets, the collapse of external structure into wave patterns, the awareness that everything is a dance of particles, sensing the smallness and fragility of our system, visions of the void, of world-ending explosions, of the cyclical nature of creation and dissolution, etc. Now I need not apologize for the flimsy inadequacy of these words. We just don't have a better experiential vocabulary. If God were to permit you a brief voyage into the Divine Process, let you whirl for a second into the atomic nucleus or spin you out on a light-year trip through the galaxies, how on earth would you describe what you saw, when you got back, breathless, to your office? This metaphor may sound far-fetched and irrelevant, but just ask someone who has taken LSD in a supportive setting.

(2) The Life Question
A. *The Scientific Answer:*

Our planetary system began over five billion years ago and has around five billion years to go. Life as we know it dates back to about one billion years. In other words, the earth spun for about 80 percent of its existence without life. The crust slowly cooled and was eroded by incessant water flow. "Fertile mineral mud was deposited . . . now giving . . . for the first time . . . the possibility of harboring life." Thunderbolts in mud produce amino acids, the basic building blocks of life. Then begins the ceaseless production of protein molecules, incalculable in number, forever combining into new forms. The variety of proteins "exceeds all the drops of water in all the oceans of the world." Then protoplasm. Cell. Within the cell, incredible beauty and order.

> When we consider the teeming activity of a modern city it is difficult to realize that in the cells of our bodies infinitely more complicated processes are at work—ceaseless manufacture, acquisition of food, storage, communication and administration. . . . All this takes place in superb harmony, with the cooperation of all the participants of a living system, regulated down to the smallest detail.[9]

Life is the striving cycle of repetitious, reproductive energy transformations. Moving, twisting, devouring, changing, the unit of life is the cell. And the blueprint is the genetic code, the two nucleic acids—the long, intertwined, duplicating chains of DNA and the controlling regulation of RNA—"which determine the structure of the living substance."

And where is it going? Exactly like the old Hindu myths of cyclical rotation, the astrophysicists tell us that life is a temporary sequence which occurs at a brief midpoint in the planetary cycle. Terrestrial life began around four billion years A.B. ("after the beginning" of our solar cycle) and will run for another two billion years or so. At that time the solar furnace will burn so hot that the minor planets (including Earth) will boil, bubble and burn out. In other planetary systems the time spans are different, but the cycle is probably the same.

There comes an intermediate stage in the temperature history of a planet which can nourish living forms, and then life merges into the final unifying fire. Data here, indeed, for an awesome cosmology.

B. *The psychedelic correlates* of these biological concepts sound like this: confrontation with and participation in cellular flow; visions of microscopic processes; strange, undulating, multi-colored, tissue patterns; being a one-celled organism floating down arterial waterways; being part of the fantastic artistry of internal factories; recoiling with fear at the incessant push, struggle, drive of the biological machinery, clicking, clicking, endlessly, endlessly—at every moment engulfing you. For example:

(a) My eyes closed, the impressions became more intense. The colors were brilliant blues, purples, and greens with dashes of red and streaks of yellow-orange. There were no easily identifiable objects, only convolutions, prisms, and continuous movement.

(b) My heart a lizard twitching lithely in my pocket, awaiting the wave again, my flesh sweating as it crawled over my bones, the mountains curved around my heart, the surf crashing against my mucoused lungs, coughing into heart beats, pulsing death to scare me. Futile body. Awaiting the undertow escaping under the wave which crashed so coughingly over my heart, blue lighted into YES. An undertow going UP. . . . The universe has an axis which is not perpendicular, and round it flock the living colors, pulsing eternal involutions.

(c) I then gradually became aware of movement, a rocking type of movement, like on a roller-coaster, yet I did not move my body at all. . . . With an overwhelming acceleration I was turning around and around, swirling, then shuttling back and forth, like a piece of potassium on water, hissing, sparkling, full of life and fire.

(3) The Human-Destiny Question

A. *The Scientific Answer:*

The flame of life which moves every living form, including the cell cluster you call *yourself,* began, we are told, as a tiny single-celled spark in the lower pre-Cambrian mud; then passed over in steady transformations to more complex forms. We like to speak of higher forms, but let's not ignore or patronize the single-cell game. It's still quite thriving, thank you. Next, your ancestral fire glowed in seaweed, algae, flagellate, sponge, coral (about one billion years ago); then fish, fern, scorpion, milliped (about 600 million years ago). Every cell in your body traces back (about 450 million years ago) to the same light-life flickering in amphibian (and what a fateful and questionable decision to leave the sea—should we have done it?). Then forms, multiplying in endless diversity—reptile, insect, bird— until, one million years ago, comes the aureole glory of Australopithecus.*

The torch of life next passes on to the hand-axe culture (around 600,000 years ago) to Pithecanthropus (can you remember watching for the charge of Southern elephants and the sabre-tooth tiger?); then blazing brightly in the radiance of our great-grandfather Neanderthal man (a mere 70,000 years ago), suddenly flaring up in that cerebral explosion that doubled the cortex of our grandfather Cro-Magnon man (44,000 to 10,000 years ago), and then radiating into the full flame of recent man, our older Stone Age, Neolithic brothers, our Bronze and Iron Age selves.

What next? The race, far from being culminated, has just begun:

---

*The fossils of the newly discovered "Homo Habilis" from East Africa are estimated to be 1,750,000 years old. (*N.Y. Times,* March 18, April 3 & 4, 1964. Another estimate traces human origins back about 15 million years. *N.Y. Times,* April 12, 1964.)

The development of Pre-hominines Australopithecus . . . to the first emergence of the Cro-Magnons lasted about . . . fifteen thousand human life spans. . . . In this relatively short period in world history the hominid type submitted to a positively hurricane change of form; indeed he may be looked upon as one of the animal groups whose potentialities of unfolding with the greatest intensity have been realized. It must, however, by no means be expected that this natural flood of development will dry up with *Homo sapiens recens*. Man will be unable to remain man as we know him now, a modern sapiens type. He will in the courses of the next hundreds of millennia presumably change considerably physiologically and physically.[10]

B. *The Psychedelic Correlate:*

What does all that evolutionary business have to do with you or me or LSD or the religious experience? It might, it just might, have a lot to do with very current events. Many, and I am just bold enough to say most, LSD subjects say they experience early forms of racial or subhuman species evolution during their sessions. Now the easiest interpretation is the psychiatric: "Oh yes, hallucinations. Everyone knows that LSD makes you crazy, and your delusions can take any psychotic form." But wait; not so fast. Is it entirely inconceivable that our cortical cells, or the machinery inside the cellular nucleus, "remembers" back along the unbroken chain of electrical transformations that connects every one of us back to that original thunderbolt in the pre-Cambrian mud? Impossible, you say? Read a genetics text. Read and reflect about the DNA chain of complex protein molecules that took you as a uni-celled organism at the moment of your conception and planned every stage of your natural development. Half of that genetic blueprint was handed to you intact by your mother, and half from your father, and then slammed together in that incredible welding process we call conception.

"You," your ego, your good-old American-social-self, have been trained to remember certain crucial secular game landmarks: your senior prom, your wedding day. But is it not possible that others of your ten billion brain cells "remember" other critical survival crossroads like conception, intra-uterine events, birth? Events for which our language has few or no descriptive terms? Every cell in your body is the current-carrier of an energy torch which traces back through millions of generation-transformations. Remember that genetic code?

You must recognize by now the difficulty of my task. I am trying to expand your consciousness, break through your macroscopic, secular set, "turn you on," give you a faint feeling of a psychedelic moment, trying to relate two sets of processes for which we have no words—speed-of-light energy-transformation processes and the transcendent vision.

I'm going to call for help. I could appeal to quotes from Gamow the cosmologist, or Eiseley the anthropologist, or Hoyle the astronomer, or Teilhard du Chardin the theological biologist, or Aldous Huxley the great visionary prophet of our times, or Julian Huxley whose pharmacological predictions sound like science-fiction. I could call upon a hundred articulate scientists who talk in dazed poetry about the spiritual implications of their work. Instead, I am going to read a passage by the German anthropologist Egon Freiherr von Eickstedt. The topic is the spiritual attitude of Australopithecus. The point is that this description of the world-view of a tiny monkey-man who lived a million years ago could be a quote from any one of a hundred LSD reports I've read in the last three years. Von Eickstedt's research leads him to say that,

> In the way of experience there is dominant, throughout, a kaleidoscopic interrelated world. Feeling and perception are hardly separated in the world of visions; space and time are just floating environmental qualities . . . Thus the border between I and not-I is only at the border of one's own and actually experienced, perceptible world . . . But this by no means denotes merely bestial brutality and coarseness which is so erroneously and often ascribed to the beginnings of humanity. Quite the reverse. The thymality within his own circle means just the opposite, tenderness, goodness and cheerfulness, and allows with complete justification the presumption of a

picture of intimate family life and the specific teaching of the children, also need of ornament, dance and much happiness. Thus the extremes of feeling swing with the mood between fear and love, and the dread of the unknowable . . .[11]

We have in our files an LSD report from a world-renowned theologian with astonishing parallels to this quotation.

The best way I can describe the experience as a whole is to liken it to an emotional-reflective-visual kaleidoscope. . . . Experiences involving these three components kept dissolving continuously from one pattern into another. Emotionally the patterns ranged from serene contentment and mild euphoria to apprehension which bordered on, but never quite slipped into, alarm. But overwhelmingly they involved (a) astonishment at the absolutely incredible immensity, complexity, intensity and extravagance of being, existence, the cosmos, call it what you will. Ontological shock, I suppose. (b) The most acute sense of the poignancy, fragility, preciousness, and significance of all life and history. The latter was accompanied by a powerful sense of the responsibility of all for all. . . . Intense affection for my family. . . . Importance and rightness of behaving decently and responsibly.

(4) The Ego Question

A. *The Scientific Answer:*

The question "Who am I?" can be answered at many levels. Psychologists can describe and explain your psychogenesis and personal evolution. Sociologists and anthropologists can explain the structure of the tribal games which govern your development. Biologists can describe your unique physical structure. But the essence of you and "you-ness" is your consciousness. You are not a psychological or social or bodily robot. No external description comes close. What cannot be measured, replaced, understood by any objective method is your consciousness. And where is this located? In your nervous system. The secular-game engineers can entertain you with their analyses of your macroscopic characteristics, but the biochemical neurologist is the man to listen to. He is the person who can locate "you" in the five-billion-year sequence by describing the capacities of your cortex. Your consciousness is a biochemical electrical process.

The human brain, we are told,

> is composed of about 10 billion nerve cells, any one of which may connect with as many as 25,000 other nerve cells. The number of interconnections which this adds up to would stagger even an astronomer—and astronomers are used to dealing with astronomical numbers. The number is far greater than all the atoms in the universe. . . . This is why physiologists remain unimpressed with computers. A computer sophisticated enough to handle this number of interconnections would have to be big enough to cover the earth.[12]

Into this matrix floods "about 100 million sensations a second from . . . [the] various senses." And somewhere in that ten-billion-cell galaxy is a tiny solar system of connected neurons which is aware of your social self. Your "ego" is to your cortex what the planet Earth is to our galaxy with its 100,000 million suns.

B. *The psychedelic answer* to the "I" question is the crux of the LSD experience. Most of the affect swirls around this issue. As Erik Erikson reminds us, it's hard enough to settle on a simple tribal role definition of "Who am I?" Imagine the dilemma of the LSD subject whose cortex is suddenly turned on to a much higher voltage, who suddenly discovers his brain spinning at the speed of light, flooded by those 100 million sensations a second. Most of the awe and reverent wonder stems from this confrontation with an unsuspected range of consciousness, the tremendous acceleration of images, the shattering insight into the narrowness of the learned as opposed to the potentiality of awareness, the humbling sense of where one's ego is in relationship to the total energy field.

(a) I was delighted to see that my skin was dissolving in tiny particles and floating away. I felt as though my outer shell was disintegrating, and the 'essence' of me was being liberated to join the 'essence' of everything else about me.

(b) Two related feelings were present. One was a tremendous freedom to experience, to be I. It became very important to distinguish between 'I' and 'Me,' the latter being an object defined by patterns and structures and responsibilities—all of which had vanished—and the former being the subject experiencing and feeling. My normal life seemed to be all Me, all demands and responsibilities, a crushing burden which destroyed the pleasure and freedom of being 'I.' Later in the evening the question of how to fit back into my normal life without becoming a slave of its patterns and demands became paramount. The other related feeling was one of isolation. The struggle to preserve my identity went on in loneliness; the 'I' cannot be shared or buttressed. The 'Me,' structured as it is, can be shared, and is in fact what we mean when we talk about "myself," but once it is thus objectified it is no longer *I,* it has become the known rather than the knower. And LSD seemed to strip away the structure and to leave the knowing process naked—hence the enormous sense of isolation: there was no Me to be communicated.

(c) All this time, for about 2–3 hours, although there was thinking, talking going on, my mind was being used, yet there was no ego. . . . I could with total dispassion examine various relationships that 'I' had with parents, friends, parts of 'myself,' etc. People who walked into the room were accepted with the same serene equanimity that I felt about accepting my own mental products; they were really walking around in my mind.

(d) I was entering into another dimension of existence. 'I' was not. Everything was totally dissolved into a flow of matter continuously moving. No time, no space. A feeling of color, but indescribable. Feeling of movement mainly. Awareness that I, the others, are only collections of clusters of molecules, which are all part of the same stream.

For the small percentage of unprepared subjects who take LSD in careless or manipulative settings and experience terror and paranoid panic, their misery invariably centers around the struggle to reimpose ego control on the whirling energy flow in them and around them. Theirs is the exhausting and sad task of attempting to slow down and limit the electrical pulse of the ten-billion-cell cerebral computer. Thorazine, alcohol and narcotics help apply the brakes. So, I fear, do words.

◆ ◆ ◆

When we read about the current findings of the energy sciences such as those I have just reviewed, how can our reaction be other than reverent awe at the grandeur of these observations, at the staggering complexity of the design, the speed, the scope? Ecstatic humility before such Power and Intelligence. Indeed, what a small, secular concept—intelligence—to describe that Infinitude of Harmonious Complexity! How impoverished our vocabulary and how narrow our imagination!

Of course, the findings of the pure sciences *do not* produce the religious reaction we should expect. We are satiated with secular statistics, dazed into robot dullness by the enormity of facts which we are not educated to comprehend. Although the findings of physics, genetics, paleontology and neurology have tremendous relevance to our life, they are of less interest than a fall in the stock market or the status of the pennant race.

The message is dimly grasped hypothetically, rationally, but never experienced, felt, known. But there can be that staggering, intellectual-game ecstasy which comes when you begin to sense the complexity of the Plan. To pull back the veil and see for a second a fragment of the energy dance, the life power. How can you appreciate the Divine unless you comprehend the smallest part of the fantastic design? To experience (it's always for a moment) the answers to the four basic spiritual questions is to me the peak of the religious-scientific quest.

But how can our ill-prepared nervous systems grasp the message? Certainly the average man cannot master the conceptual, mathematical bead game of the physics graduate student. Must his experiential contact with the Divine Process come in watered-down symbols, sermons, hymns, robot rituals, religious calendar art, moral-behavior sanctions eventually secular in their aim? Fortunately the Great Plan has produced a happy answer and has endowed every human being with the equipment to comprehend, to know, to experience directly, incontrovertibly. It's there in that network of ten billion cells, the number of whose interconnections "is far greater than all the atoms in the universe."

If you can, for the moment, throw off the grip of your learned mind, your tribal concepts, and experience the message contained in the ten-billion-tube computer which you carry behind your forehead, you would know the awe-full truth. Our research suggests that even the uneducated layman can experience directly what is slowly deduced by scientists—for example physicists, whose heavy, conceptual minds lumber along at three concepts a second, attempting to fathom the speed-of-light processes which their beautiful machines record and which their beautiful symbols portray.

But the brakes can be released. Our recent studies support the hypothesis that psychedelic foods and drugs, ingested by prepared subjects in a serious, sacred, supportive atmosphere, can put the subject in perceptual touch with other levels of energy exchanges. Remember the data—the Good Friday study, the Savage study, the 69 religious professionals. Forty to ninety percent telling us they experienced "a greater awareness of God, or a Higher Power, or an Ultimate Reality."

But to what do these LSD subjects refer when they report spiritual reactions? Do they obtain specific illuminations into the four basic questions, or are their responses simply awe and wonder at the experienced novelty? Even if the latter were the cause, could it not support the religious application of the psychedelic substances and simply underline the need for more sophisticated religious language coordinated with the scientific data? But there is some evidence, phenomenological but yet haunting, that the spiritual insights accompanying the psychedelic experience might be subjective accounts of the objective findings of astronomy, physics, biochemistry, and neurology.

Now the neurological and pharmacological explanations of an LSD vision are still far from being understood. We know almost nothing about the physiology of consciousness and the body-cortex interaction. We cannot assert that LSD subjects are directly experiencing what particle physicists and biochemists measure, but the evidence about the detailed complexity of the genetic code and the astonishing design of intra-cellular communication should caution us against labeling experiences outside of our current tribal clichés as "psychotic" or abnormal. For three thousand years our greatest prophets and philosophers have been telling us to look within, and today our scientific data are supporting that advice with a humiliating finality. The limits of introspective awareness may well be sub-microscopic, cellular, molecular and even nuclear. We only see, after all, what we are trained and predisposed to see. One of our current research projects involves teaching subjects to recognize internal physical processes much as we train a beginning biology student to recognize events viewed through his microscope.

No matter how parsimonious our explanations, we must accept the fact that LSD subjects do claim to experience revelations into the basic questions and do attribute life-change to their visions.

We are, of course, at the very beginning of our research into these implications. A new experiential language and perhaps even new metaphors for the Great Plan will develop. We have been working on this project for the past two years, writing manuals which train subjects to recognize energy processes, teaching subjects to communicate via a machine we call the experiential typewriter, and with movies of microbiological processes. And we have continued to pose the question to religious and philosophic groups as I am doing tonight. What do you think? Are these biochemical visions religious?

Before you answer, remember that God (however you define the Higher Power) produced that wonderful molecule, that extraordinarily powerful organic substance we call LSD, just as surely as "He" created the rose, or the sun, or the complex cluster of molecules you insist on calling your "self."

Among the many harassing complications of our research into religious experience has been the fact that few people, even some theological professionals, have much conception of what a religious experience really is. Few have any idea how the Divine Process presents Itself. If asked, they tend to become embarrassed, intellectual, evasive. The adored cartoonists of the Renaissance portray the Ultimate Power as a Dove, or a Flaming Bush, or as a man—venerable, with a white beard, or on a Cross, or as a Baby, or a Sage seated in the Full Lotus Position. Are these not incarnations, temporary housings, of the Great Energy Process?

Last fall a minister and his wife, as part of a courageous and dedicated pursuit of illumination, took a psychedelic biochemical called dimethyltryptamine. This wondrous alkaloid (which closely approximates serotonin, the natural "lubricant" of our higher nervous system) produces the most intense psychedelic effect of any sacramental food or drug. In 25 minutes (about the duration of the average sermon), you are whirled through the energy dance, the cosmic process, at the highest psychedelic speed. The 25 minutes are sensed as lasting for a second and for a billion-year Kalpa. After the session, the minister complained that the experience, although shattering and revelatory, was disappointing because it was "content free"—so physical, so unfamiliar, so scientific, like being beamed through microscopic panoramas, like being oscillated through cellular functions at radar acceleration. Well, what do you expect? If God were to take you on a visit through His "workshop," do you think you'd walk or go by bus? Do you really think it would be a stroll through a celestial Madame Tussaud waxworks? Dear friends, the *Divine Product* is evident in every macroscopic form, in every secular event. The Divine Product we can see. But the *Divine Process* operates in time dimensions which are far beyond our routine, secular, space-time limits. Wave vibrations, energy dance, cellular transactions. Our science describes this logically. Our brains may be capable of dealing with these processes experientially.

So here we are. The Great Process has placed in our hands a key to this direct visionary world. Is it hard for us to accept that the key might be an organic molecule and not a new myth or a new word?

◆ ◆ ◆

And where do we go? There are in the United States today several hundred thousand persons who have experienced what I have attempted to describe to you tonight—a psychedelic, religious revelation. There are, I would estimate, several million equally thoughtful people who have heard the joyous tidings and who are waiting patiently but determinedly for their psychedelic moment to come.

There is, of course, the expected opposition. The classic conflict of the religious drama—always changing, always the same. The doctrine (which was originally someone's experience) now threatened by the *new* experience. This time the administrators have assigned the inquisitorial role to the psychiatrists, whose proprietary claims to a revealed understanding of the mind and whose antagonism to consciousness-expansion are well known to you.

The clamor over psychedelic drugs is now reaching full crescendo. You have heard rumors and you have read the press assaults and the slick-magazine attacks-by-innuendo. As sophisticated adults you have perhaps begun to wonder: why the hysterical outcry? As scientists you are beginning to ask: where is the evidence? As educated men with an eye for history, you are, I trust, beginning to suspect that we've been through this many times before.

In the current hassle over psychedelic plants and drugs, you are witnessing a good-old-fashioned, traditional, religious controversy. On the one side the psychedelic visionaries, somewhat uncertain about the validity of their revelations, embarrassedly speaking in new tongues (there never is, you know, the satisfaction of a sound, right academic language for the new vision of the Divine), harassed by the knowledge of their own human frailty, surrounded by the inevitable legion of eccentric would-be followers looking for a new panacea, always in grave doubt about their own motivation—(hero? martyr? crank? crackpot?)—always on the verge of losing their material achievements—(job, reputation, long-suffering wife, conventional friends, parental approval); always under the fire of the power-holders. And on the other side: the establishment (the administrators, the police, the fund-granting foundations, the jobgivers) pronouncing their familiar lines in the drama: "Danger! Madness! Unsound! Intellectual corruption of youth! Irreparable damage! Cultism!" The issue of chemical expansion of consciousness is hard upon us. During the next months, every avenue of propaganda is going to barrage you with the arguments. You can hardly escape it. You are going to be pressed for a position. Internal Freedom is becoming a major religious and civil-rights controversy.

How can you decide? How can you judge? Well, it's really quite simple. Whenever you hear anyone sounding off on internal freedom and consciousness-expanding foods and drugs—whether pro or con—check out these questions:

(1) Is your advisor talking from direct experience, or simply repeating clichés? Theologians and intellectuals often deprecate "experience" in favor of fact and concept. This classic debate is falsely labeled. Most often it becomes a case of "experience" versus "inexperience."

(2) Do his words spring from a spiritual or from a mundane point of view? Is he motivated by a dedicated quest for answers to basic questions, or is he protecting his own social-psychological position, his own game investment?

(3) How would his argument sound if it were heard in a different culture (for example, in an African jungle hut, a ghat on the Ganges, or on another planet inhabited by a form of life superior to ours); or in a different time (for example in Periclean Athens, or in a Tibetan monastery, or in a bull-session led by any one of the great religious leaders—founders—messiahs); or how would it sound to other species of life on our planet today—to

the dolphins, to the consciousness of a redwood tree? In other words, try to break out of your usual tribal game-set and listen with the ears of another one of God's creatures.

(4) How would the debate sound to you if you were fatally diseased with a week to live, and thus less committed to mundane issues? Our research group receives many requests a week for consciousness-expanding experiences, and some of these come from terminal patients.[13]

(5) Is the point of view one which opens up or closes down? Are you being urged to explore, experience, gamble out of spiritual faith, join someone who shares your cosmic ignorance on a collaborative voyage of discovery? Or are you being pressured to close off, protect your gains, play it safe, accept the authoritative voice of someone who knows best?

(6) When we speak, we say little about the subject-matter and disclose mainly the state of our own mind. Does your psychedelic advisor use terms which are positive, pro-life, spiritual, inspiring, opening, based on faith in the future, faith in your potential, or does he betray a mind obsessed by danger, material concern, by imaginary terrors, administrative caution or essential distrust in your potential. Dear friends, there is nothing in life to fear, no spiritual game can be lost. The choice is not double-bind but double-win.[14]

(7) If he is against what he calls "artificial methods of illumination," ask him what constitutes the natural. Words? Rituals? Tribal customs? Alkaloids? Psychedelic vegetables?

(8) If he is against biochemical assistance, where does he draw the line? Does he use nicotine? alcohol? penicillin? vitamins? conventional sacramental substances?

(9) If your advisor is against LSD, what is he for? If he forbids you the psychedelic key to revelation, what does he offer you instead?

SUMMARY

The outline of this paper can be summarized as follows:

(1) Evidence is cited that, depending on the set and setting, from 40 to 90 percent of psychedelic subjects report intense religious experiences.

(2) The religious experience was defined as the ecstatic, incontrovertibly certain, subjective discovery of answers to four basic questions which concern ultimate power and design, life, man and self. It was pointed out that science attempts to provide objective, external answers to these same questions.

(3) We considered the hypothesis that the human being might be able to become directly aware of energy exchanges and biological processes for which we now have no language and no perceptual training. Psychedelic foods and drugs were suggested as one key to these neurological potentials, and subjective reports from LSD sessions were compared with current findings from the energy sciences.

(4) The current controversy over the politics of the nervous system (which involves secular-external versus spiritual-internal commitments) were reviewed, and a checklist for the intelligent voter was presented.

REFERENCES

1. Walter N. Pahnke, *Drugs and Mysticism: An Analysis of the Relationship between Psychedelic Drugs and the Mystical Consciousness.* A thesis presented to the Committee on Higher Degrees in History and Philosophy of Religion, in partial fulfillment of the requirements for the degree of Doctor of Philosophy, Harvard University, Cambridge, Mass., June, 1963.
2. "The Subjective After-Effects of Psychedelic Experiences: A Summary of Four Recent Questionnaire Studies." *The Psychedelic Review,* Vol. I, No. 1 (June 1963), 18–26.

3. Leary, T., Litwin, G. H., and Metzner, R., "Reactions to Psilocybin Administered in a Supportive Environment." *J. Nervous & Mental Disease,* Vol. 137, No. 6, (December 1963), 561–573.

4. Savage, C., Harman, W. W., Fadiman, Jr., and Savage, E., "A Follow-up Note on the Psychedelic Experience." [Paper delivered at a meeting of the American Psychiatric Association, St. Louis, Mo., May, 1963.]

5. Ditman, K. S., Haymon, M., and Whittlesey, J. R. B., "Nature and Frequency of Claims Following LSD." *J. Nervous & Mental Disease,* Vol. 134 (1962), 346–352.

6. McGlothlin, W. H., *Long-Lasting Effects of LSD on Certain Attitudes in Normals: An Experimental Proposal.* [Privately printed, The Rand Corporation, Santa Monica, California, June 1962. Pp. 56.] Cf. McGlothlin, W. H., Cohen, S., & McGlothlin, M. S., *Short-Term Effects of LSD on Anxiety, Attitudes, and Performance. Ibid.,* June 1963. Pp. 15.

7. A continuing present-day instance is the case of members of the Native American Church, a duly constituted and recognized religious denomination numbering almost a quarter of a million adherents. A good popular account of their situation is presented in "Peyote," by A. Stump, in *Saga,* Vol. 26, No. 3 (June 1963), 46–49, 81–83. Cf. the Supreme Court's decision, *Oliver v. Udall,* 306 F2d 819 (1962). The most recently proposed legislation against peyote is seen in the *Congressional Record* (House) for Dec. 13, 1963. W. La Barre's famous book, *The Peyote Cult,* will be reprinted in an enlarged edition in August, 1964, by the Shoe String Press (Hamden, Conn.) and will bring the entire discussion up to date. For a good general statement in another area of research, see "The Hallucinogenic Drugs," by Barron, Jarvik, and Bunnell. *Sci. Amer.,* Vol. 210, No. 4 (April 1964), 29–37.

8. Zaehner, R. C., *At Sundry Times.* An Essay in the Comparison of Religions. London: Faber & Faber, 1958, p. 57.

9. Woltereck, H., *What Science Knows About Life.* N.Y.: Association Press, 1963.

10. Schenk, G., *The History of Man.* Phila., N.Y.: Chilton Co., 1961, pp. 56–57.

11. *Ibid.,* p. 238.

12. Campbell, R., "The Circuits of the Senses," in a series on "The Human Body" (Part IV). *Life,* Vol. 54, No. 27 (June 27, 1963), 64–76b.

13. The medical press has recently reported on the analgesic use of LSD with terminal cancer patients. Cf. *Medical World News,* Aug. 30, 1963, *Medical Tribune,* April 8, 1963, and *J. Amer. Med. Assoc.,* Jan. 4, 1964.

14. Levitsky, A.—Personal communication.

9

The World Beyond Words

Foreword to Alan Watts's
The Joyous Cosmology

Timothy Leary and Richard Alpert

Interest in Zen Buddhism was growing in the United States in the early 1960s, and for many followers, Alan Watts was its most articulate spokesperson. In 1961, Aldous Huxley, a friend of Watts's and a fellow expatriate from the British Isles, encouraged Watts to contact Timothy Leary, a Harvard psychologist who was doing important research with psilocybin. Watts was quite surprised when he met Leary for the first time because he was expecting to meet a stuffy academic: "[f]rom the detached and scholarly flavor of Aldous's account of this work I was expecting Timothy Leary to be a formidable pandit, but the man I first met in a New York restaurant was an extremely charming Irishman who wore a hearing-aid as stylishly as if it had been a monocle. Nothing could then have told me that anyone so friendly and intelligent would become one of the most outlawed people in the world, a fugitive from justice charged with the sin of Socrates, all upon the legal pretext of possessing trivial amounts of marijuana" (*In My Own Way* 327–28).

In 1962, Watts was a visiting professor at the Harvard

Divinity School. While living in Cambridge, he became close friends with Leary and Alpert, and when he finished his book on psychedelic drugs, he asked them to write its Foreword. Leary and Alpert's enthusiasm about *The Joyous Cosmology,* conveyed in their Foreword, makes it an important piece of writing in that it reflects the convergence of three important thinkers who would profoundly influence the counterculture of the late 1960s. Leary and Alpert's essay is utopian in the sense that it posits the notion that hallucinogenic drugs could transform American society and infuse it with a more vibrant form of spirituality.

In their collaborative essay on Watts, Leary and Alpert recognized that the right to expand consciousness is inherently political: "we speak here (and Alan Watts speaks in this book) about the politics of the nervous system—certainly as complicated and certainly as important as external politics. The politics of the nervous system involves the mind against the brain, the tyrannical verbal brain disassociating itself from the organism and world of which it is a part, censoring, altering, evaluating." In this passage, Leary and Alpert identify a key tenet in early psychedelic thought and '60s utopianism: the critique of learned or acquired behavior. For the Harvard psychologists, this tyrannical verbal brain was the powerful influence of social conditioning. Psychedelic drugs were revered precisely because they seem to allow the subject to detach from the socialization process. At this point in the 1960s, Leary and Alpert have tremendous faith in non-verbal behavior, which for them was the gateway to Dionysian impulses and unmediated experience.

Thus, Leary and Alpert formulate their earliest conception of the "fifth freedom": "[t]he freedom to expand one's consciousness beyond artifactual cultural knowledge. The freedom to move from constant preoccupation with the verbal imprints—the social games, the game of the self." In the psychedelic revolution of the early 1960s, Watts was a crucial ally because he was an articulate spokesperson of the transcendent experience that psychedelic drugs often induce ("the joyous unity of what exists beyond").

Although Watts was a proponent of enlightenment through chemical consciousness in the early 1960s, he also suggested that hallucinogenic drugs had clear limitations: "My retrospective attitude to LSD is that when one has received the message, one hangs up the phone." Watts also believed that psychedelic drugs should "serve as medicine rather than diet" (*In My Own Way*, 327).

JAMES PENNER

REFERENCES

Watts, Alan. *In My Own Way*. Novato, Calif.: New World Library, 1972.

FOREWORD
to Alan Watts's *The Joyous Cosmology:*
Adventures in the Chemistry of Consciousness

From *The Joyous Cosmology: Adventures in the Chemistry of Consciousness* by Alan Watts, published in 1962 by Pantheon Books: pages ix–xv.

Timothy Leary, Ph.D., and Richard Alpert, Ph.D.

The Joyous Cosmology is a brilliant arrangement of words describing experiences for which our language has no vocabulary. To understand this wonderful but difficult book it is useful to make the artificial distinction between the external and the internal. This is, of course, exactly the distinction which Alan Watts wants us to transcend. But Mr. Watts is playing the verbal game in a Western language, and his reader can be excused for following along with conventional dichotomous models.

External and internal. Behavior and consciousness. Changing the external world has been the genius and the obsession of our civilization. In the last two centuries the Western monotheistic cultures have faced outward and moved objects about with astonishing efficiency. In more recent years, however, our culture has become aware of a disturbing imbalance. We have become aware of the undiscovered universe within, of the uncharted regions of consciousness.

This dialectic trend is not new. The cycle has occurred in the lives of many cultures and individuals. External material success is followed by disillusion and the basic "why" questions, and then by the discovery of the world within—a world infinitely more complex and rich than the artifactual structures of the outer world, which after all are, in origin, projections of human imagination. Eventually, the logical conceptual mind turns on itself, recognizes the foolish inadequacy of the flimsy systems it imposes on the world, suspends its own rigid control, and overthrows the dominance of cognitive experience.

We speak here (and Alan Watts speaks in this book) about the politics of the nervous system—certainly as complicated and certainly as important as external politics. The politics of the nervous system involves the mind against the brain, the tyrannical verbal brain disassociating itself from the organism and world of which it is a part, censoring, alerting, evaluating.

Thus appears the fifth freedom—freedom from the learned, cultural mind. The freedom to expand one's consciousness beyond artifactual cultural knowledge. The freedom to move from constant preoccupation with the verbal games—the social games, the game of self—to the joyous unity of what exists beyond.

We are dealing here with an issue that is not new, an issue that has been considered for centuries by mystics, by philosophers of the religious experience, by those rare and truly great scientists who have been able to move in and then out beyond the limits of the science game. It was seen and described clearly by the great American psychologist William James:

> . . . our normal waking consciousness, rational consciousness as we call it, is but one special type of consciousness, whilst all about it, parted from it by the filmiest of screens, there lie potential forms of consciousness entirely different. We may go through life without suspecting

their existence; but apply the requisite stimulus, and at a touch they are there in all their completeness, definite types of mentality which probably somewhere have their field of application and adaptation. No account of the universe in its totality can be final which leaves these other forms of consciousness quite disregarded. How to regard them is the question—for they are so discontinuous with ordinary consciousness. Yet they may determine attitudes though they cannot furnish formulas, and open a region though they fail to give a map. At any rate, they forbid a premature closing of our accounts with reality. Looking back on my own experiences, they all converge toward a kind of insight to which I cannot help ascribing some metaphysical significance.

But what are the stimuli necessary and sufficient to overthrow the domination of the conceptual and to open up the "potential forms of consciousness"? There are many. Indian philosophers have described hundreds of methods. So have the Japanese Buddhists. The monastics of our Western religions provide more examples. Mexican healers and religious leaders from South and North American Indian groups have for centuries utilized sacred plants to trigger off the expansion of consciousness. Recently our Western science has provided, in the form of chemicals, the most direct techniques for opening new realms of awareness.

William James used nitrous oxide and ether to "stimulate the mystical consciousness in an extraordinary degree." Today the attention of psychologists, philosophers, and theologians is centering on the effects of three synthetic substances—mescalin, lysergic acid and psilocybin.

What are these substances? Medicines or drugs or sacramental foods? It is easier to say what they are not. They are not narcotics, nor intoxicants, nor energizers, nor anaesthetics, nor tranquilizers. They are, rather, biochemical keys which unlock experiences shatteringly new to most Westerners. For the last two years, staff members of the Center for Research in Personality at Harvard University have engaged in systematic experiments with these substances. Our first inquiry into the biochemical expansion of consciousness has been a study of the reactions of Americans in a supportive, comfortable naturalistic setting. We have had the opportunity of participating in over one thousand individual administrations. From our observations, from interviews and reports, from analysis of questionnaire data, and from pre- and post-experimental differences in personality test results, certain conclusions have emerged. (1) These substances do alter consciousness. There is no dispute on this score. (2) It is meaningless to talk more specifically about the "effect of the drug." Set and setting, expectation, and atmosphere account for all specificity of reaction. There is no "drug reaction" but always setting-plus-drug. (3) In talking about potentialities it is useful to consider not just the setting-plus-drug but rather the potentialities of the human cortex to create images and experiences far beyond the narrow limitations of words and concepts. Those of us on this research project spend a good share of our working hours listening to people talk about the effect and use of consciousness-altering drugs. If we substitute the words *human cortex* for *drug* we can then agree with any statement made about the potentialities of the cortex, not of the drug. The drug is just an instrument.

In analyzing and interpreting the results of our studies we looked first to the conventional models of modern psychology—psychoanalytic, behavioristic—and found these concepts quite inadequate to map the richness and breadth of expanded consciousness. To understand our findings we have finally been forced back on a language and point of view quite alien to us who are trained in the traditions of mechanistic objective psychology. We have had to return again and again to the non-dualistic conceptions of Eastern philosophy, a theory of mind made more explicit and familiar in our Western world by Bergson, Aldous Huxley, and Alan Watts. In the first part of this book Mr. Watts presents with beautiful clarity this theory of consciousness, which we have seen confirmed in the accounts of our research subjects—philosophers, unlettered convicts, housewives, intellectuals, alcoholics. The leap across entangling thickets of the verbal, to identify with the totality of the experienced, is a phenomenon reported over and over by these persons.

Alan Watts spells out in eloquent detail his drug-induced visionary moments. He is, of course, attempting the impossible—to describe in words (which always lie) that which is beyond words. But how well he can do it!

Alan Watts is one of the great reporters of our times. He has an intuitive sensitivity for news, for the crucial issues and events of our century. And he has along with this the verbal equipment of a poetic philosopher to teach and inform. Here he has given us perhaps the best statement on the subject of space-age mysticism, more daring than the two classic works of Aldous Huxley because Watts follows Huxley's lead and pushes beyond. The recognition of the love aspects of the mystical experience and the implications for new forms of social communication are especially important.

You are holding in your hands a great human document. But unless you are one of the few Westerners who have (accidently or through chemical good fortune) experienced a mystical minute of expanded awareness, you will probably not understand what the author is saying. Too bad, but still not a cause for surprise. The history of ideas reminds us that new concepts and new visions have always been non-understood. We cannot understand that for which we have no words. But Alan Watts is playing the book game, the word game, and the reader is his contracted partner.

But listen. Be prepared. There are scores of great lines in this book. Dozens of great ideas. Too many. Too compressed. They glide by quickly. Watch for them.

If you catch even a few of these ideas, you will find yourself asking the questions which we ask ourselves as we look over our research data: Where do we go from here? What is the application of these new wonder medicines? Can they do more than provide memorable moments and memorable books?

The answer will come from two directions. We must provide more and more people with these experiences and have them tell us, as Alan Watts does here, what they experienced. (There will hardly be a lack of volunteers for this ecstatic voyage. Ninety-one percent of our subjects are eager to repeat and to share the experience with their family and friends.)

We must also encourage systematic objective research by scientists who have taken the drug themselves and have come to know the difference between inner and outer, between consciousness and behavior. Such research should explore the application of these experiences to the problems of modern living—in education, religion, creative industry, creative arts.

There are many who believe that we stand at an important turning point in man's power to control and expand his awareness. Our research provides tentative grounds for such optimism. *The Joyous Cosmology* is solid testimony for the same happy expectations.

TIMOTHY LEARY, PH.D.—RICHARD ALPERT, PH.D.

HARVARD UNIVERSITY, JANUARY, 1962

PART 4

Bold New Frontiers

Leary's Early Writing on LSD and DMT

Few people realize that Timothy Leary, LSD's most famous proselytizer, was initially reluctant to try the drug. In *High Priest,* Leary describes his resistance: "[e]verything I had heard about lysergic acid sounded ominous to me. The mushrooms and peyote had grown naturally in the ground and had been used for thousands of years in wise Indian cultures. LSD, on the other hand, was a laboratory product and had quickly fallen in the hands of doctors and psychiatrists" (244). Leary had also heard that LSD was stronger than mushrooms, and this scared him as well: "The sacred mushrooms were my familiar territory. I had them harnessed up to my brand of revelation and ecstasy. It was obvious that LSD swept you far beyond the tender wisdom of psilocybin" (244).

Leary eventually succumbed to the chemical temptation in November of 1961. In *High Priest,* Leary describes his virginal LSD trip, and how it altered his life:

> I have never forgotten [my first LSD trip] . . . [n]or has it been possible for me to return to the life I was leading before that session. I have never recovered from that shattering ontological confrontation.

I have never been able to take myself, my mind, and the social world as seriously. Since that time five years ago I have been acutely aware of the fact that everything I perceive, everything within and around me is a creation of my own consciousness." (256)

The latter discovery—what might be termed Leary's LSD epiphany—would change the course of his career and personal life. In the coming months, Leary would become increasingly nonchalant about his academic career and his commitment to Harvard.

When the Harvard drug scandal of 1963 hit in May of 1963, Leary seemed to be curiously unfazed by his dismissal from America's oldest and most revered university. Reporters covering the scandal believed that Leary's professional career would certainly be ruined. However, Leary seemed to know otherwise. In the aftermath of the scandal, the ex-Harvard professor was slowly reinventing himself. During the next five years, he would become an iconic figure for the counterculture and the leading spokesperson for the right to expand one's consciousness.

Part 4 presents Leary's earliest writings on LSD and DMT. Each of these essays was written when Leary was no longer a part of the academic community of Harvard. The first essay, "Introduction to LSD: The Conscious-Expanding Drug," was written for David Solomon's impressive collection of essays on LSD that appeared in 1964.* This essay marks Leary's ascendance in the nascent psychedelic movement of the mid-1960s. This piece of writing is also symbolic in the sense that it was written from Leary's new residence in Millbrook, New York. Peggy and Billy Hitchcock, heirs to the Gulf Oil fortune and psychedelic enthusiasts, agreed to rent the baronial mansion to Leary and Richard Alpert for a nominal fee (one dollar a year). Millbrook became the home of the Castalia Institute, a research center that promoted psychedelic research and weekend retreats for artists, musicians, and psy-

*LSD: The Consciousness-Expanding Drug. Edited by David Solomon. New York: G. P. Putnam and Sons, 1964.

chologists. Throughout the mid-1960s (1963 to 1967), Millbrook was an ongoing social experiment in utopian living and a cultural incubator for the emerging counterculture and its growing interest in mind-expanding drugs and Eastern thought.

Part 4 also contains two other important articles from the Millbrook years: "Programming Communication During Experiences with DMT" and "Languages: Energy Systems Sent and Received." The former article was based on Leary's early experiences with DMT (dimethyltryptamine) in 1962 and 1963 in California and Cambridge. In an attempt to express the mind-blowing intensity of DMT, Leary employs a highly experimental prose style that is quite distinct from his scholarly writings. "Languages: Energy Systems and Sent and Received" also represents a clean break from Leary's Cambridge writings. This complex piece of writing is arguably Leary's most revolutionary attempt to theorize the meaning of the LSD experience. It also contains a detailed description of one of Leary's most controversial concepts: "re-imprinting."

REFERENCES

Leary, Timothy. *High Priest*. New York: The World Publishing Company, 1968.

10

Leary's First Article on LSD

Introduction to
LSD: The Consciousness-Expanding Drug

Timothy Leary

Leary's writings on psychedelic drugs typically feature two rhetorical modes: the scientific and the religious. Leary's Introduction to *LSD: The Consciousness-Expanding Drug** contains both appeals. It begins with a religious appeal that stresses the theme of spiritual rebirth through the lived experience of ecstasy. Leary translates ecstasy as "ex-stasis," which means "literally out of, or released from an unmoving experience." Leary's essay then morphs into scientific appeal that emphasizes the drug's ability to unlock the untapped potential of the human mind. In the Introduction, Leary argues that "we are aware of only the millionth fraction of our own cortical signaling. Huge areas of the brain—neurologists call them 'silent areas'— are blocked off from consciousness." For Leary and other pro-

---

**LSD: The Consciousness-Expanding Drug* was edited by David Solomon (an editor for *Playboy*) and published by G. P. Putnam's Sons in 1964. The collection featured articles and essays by various intellectual luminaries of the early 1960s: Aldous Huxley, Alan Watts, William S. Burroughs, Huston Smith, and Humphrey Osmond.

gressive thinkers, LSD is a scientific breakthrough because it enables the user to tap into greater awareness and a higher state of consciousness. Leary even suggests that the human brain is analogous to a "powerful engine [that has been] installed in a decrepit automobile which can never utilize more than a fraction of the available horsepower."*

In the Introduction, Leary also provides a brief socio-historical view of consciousness-expanding drugs. The reference to Thomas Kuhn's *The Structure of Scientific Revolutions* is central to his argument. Kuhn suggests that scientific activities are determined by what he calls "the paradigm of any period." Kuhn also argues that "[c]onventional science cannot go beyond the risk of being seen as eccentric or even 'unscientific.'" Thus, Leary implies that the current debate over psychedelic drugs is evidence of another paradigm shift in the scientific world. According to Leary, psychedelic drugs are demonized by moralists and conservative scientists because they unveil a new way of interpreting and understanding human consciousness. Throughout the essay, Leary urges the reader to break with the status quo and embrace the new paradigm of consciousness expansion.

Leary's Introduction is also important because it presents his radical theory of re-imprinting. Prior to 1964, Leary's central metaphor for the psychedelic experience was the game metaphor. Leary maintains that psychedelic drugs are illuminating because they make the user aware of the various cultural games he/she is playing in life (the ego game, the teacher-student game, the doctor-patient game, etc.). Leary notes that cultural stability is attained by everyone's adherence to their respective game or games. Thus, for Leary psychedelic drugs have a powerful

---

*Leary's engine metaphor is taken from Robert S. De Ropp's *Drugs and the Mind*. New York: Grove Press, 1961.

demystifying effect: the user is able to disentangle himself/herself from the grip of social conditioning.

However, Leary's theory of re-imprinting goes further than the game metaphor. Re-imprinting suggests that the user taking psychedelic drugs can undergo a form of "rapid learning." With this metaphor, Leary attempts to re-appropriate Conrad Lorenz's term ("imprinting"). Many scientists, of course, objected to Leary's use of the term imprinting and maintained that only animals in a neonatal state (i.e., goslings) could undergo rapid learning. Leary was well aware of the differences between Lorenz's theory ("imprinting") and his theory ("re-imprinting"). Nonetheless, he re-appropriates the term to provoke his academic readers, especially the ones who were not predisposed to taking psychedelic drugs.*

Leary's Introduction is also significant because in it he moves away from psilocybin and embraces LSD as the central drug of the psychedelic era. If psilocybin was associated with illumination, the rebirth experience, and the possibility of behavior change, LSD went further than psilocybin in the sense that it facilitated the possibility of re-imprinting. In short, re-imprinting becomes Leary's most grandiose metaphor for the chemical remaking of human nature.

In addition to re-imprinting, Leary also employs other metaphors that are designed to shake up the status quo: "you need to go out of your mind to use your head." Leary knows that this aphorism will shock the non-users of LSD because it associates the drug with temporary insanity. By employing such metaphors, Leary is speaking to the adventurous members of the younger generation and tacitly urging them to break with their parents' mores and worldview. Leary's Introduction marks

---

*A more detailed description of imprinting and re-imprinting can be found in "Languages: Energy Systems Sent and Received" (1965): chapter 11 of this book.

his departure from the academic world and his attempt to find a larger audience for the emerging psychedelic revolution.

JAMES PENNER

INTRODUCTION
to *LSD: The Consciousness-Expanding Drug*

From *LSD: The Consciousness-Expanding Drug* by David Solomon, published in 1964 by G. P. Putnam's Sons: pages 1–19.

Timothy Leary, Ph.D.

You hold in your hand a book shot through with paradox and controversy.

The subject matter is consciousness—the expansion of consciousness by means of foods and drugs.

Neither the foods and drugs nor the controversy are new. Visionary plants (such as the peyote cactus, the divine mushroom of Mexico, the soma of ancient Vedic pre-Hindu philosophers, divinatory vines and roots) have been used for thousands of years by medicine men, soothsayers, priest-philosophers, mystic brotherhoods. Today our technology provides us with chemical synthetics of the active ingredients of these ancient and venerable concoctions: lysergic acid diethylamide (LSD-25), mescaline, psilocybin and a host of lesser-known consciousness-expanding substances.

These foods and drugs have always been shrouded in mystery, misunderstanding and controversy because they produce that most sought-after and yet most dread experience known to man. They produce ecstasy. *Exstasis,* literally, out of, or released from a fixed or unmoving condition. They propel awareness out beyond normal modes of consciousness. They are properly called psychedelics—i.e., mind-opening substances.

The ecstatic, expansion process is neither new nor limited to the psychedelics. Many philosophers—Heard, Teilhard de Chardin and Heidegger, among others—have pointed out that human evolution seems to be characterized by alterations in consciousness.

Some theorists like to suppose a steady growth in consciousness; others, especially the Eastern philosophers, point to alternating cycles of expansion and contraction of consciousness and warn that man may be in danger of contracting awareness down to the robot-narrow precision of certain overorganized species of life which we see around us. One of the many paradoxes about consciousness is that increased motor or social efficiency does not necessarily mean expanded awareness. The anthill and the computer remind us of this sober fact.

The explosion of scientific knowledge which began in modern times in the Renaissance has reached atomically accelerated proportions in our own day. We have learned that the structure of the entire physical universe is emergent and expanding. Along with the existential dangers of the destruction of consciousness by a nuclear holocaust, our era seems to offer the hope of an unparalleled expansion of man's untapped mental capacities. We are witnessing an exponential increase in time-space perspectives, esthetic and deliberate shatterings of classical symmetries. I believe the general topic of the psychedelic drugs and the specific interpretations of their effects, as presented in this book, should be viewed in the general context of this emergent scientific philosophy of expansion.

First we note that the scientific instrumentation developed in the last few decades has confronted man with visions, vistas and processes which have thoroughly dissipated his philosophic and social securities and, in addition, and most painfully, his views of himself and his nature.

The consistent message inherent in the data from every branch of science these days propels our imagination out beyond man's limited and transient position in the natural order.

Astronomers speak of billions of light years. Physicists speak of critical nuclear-process structures which last only microseconds. Biochemists and microgeneticists remind us that the genetic material—those strands of blueprinting intelligence—are so compact that the essence and seed of every human being on earth today could be contained in a cubical box one-eighth of an inch on a side.[1]

The speeds, complexities, spatial dimensions, durations of these basic energy transformations demand a revision of our illusions about man's pre-eminence and dominance. The Renaissance-Reformation mythos would have us believe that man is the chosen vehicle, lord of all species. It may be closer to the data to see man as an animal who is only dimly aware of the powers, energies, plannings and wisdom that surround him and radiate through him.

As if the findings of physics, astronomy and biochemistry were not awesome enough, next come data from two fields more directly connected with man's psychological core: neurology and psychopharmacology.

Neurology sketches out the existence of undreamed of structural and phenomenological galaxies within. And pharmacology provides new means for altering consciousness, for propelling us into new dimensions of awareness.

We have moved into a challenging, upsetting stage of the science drama. The awesome speeds and spaces of the energy sciences are humbling to our self-image, but at least they are attributes of forces external to our cognitions. We can use our rational faculties to change our instruments, change our language, invent new mathematics and new symbols to deal with processes beyond our neurological scope. But then comes the neurological implosion. Rational consciousness itself is seen as a fragile, tissue-thin artifact easily blown away by the slightest alteration of our biochemistry, by the simplest forms of external stimulation—for example, a few microvolts strategically introduced into specific areas of the brain, or the removal of accustomed stimulation.

We discover that our brain works with a velocity and scope which far surpasses our mental operations. The potential of cerebral association is of the order of thirteen billion to the twenty-five-thousandth power per second. But we think; we experience rationally at a maximum rate of three concepts—ten phonemes—a second. Our present mental machinery cannot possibly handle the cerebral potential. Our rational instrumentation is to our cerebral capacities as Eratosthenes's shadow pole is to the radiation from the sun. Most distressing is this fact: the instrumental inadequacy is not external but internal. The whirling, speed-of-light, trackless processes are properties of our brain, our organ of consciousness itself.

The paradox may be stated as follows: *it becomes necessary for us to go out of our minds in order to use our heads.*

It is much easier to give up our shadow poles and our hand telescopes than to go beyond what we generally consider our rational minds in order to experience, describe and measure new levels of consciousness.

This book is an early exploratory probe into the area of accelerated and expanded consciousness opened up by psychedelic drugs. Each chapter takes up in turn a different interpretation and a different social rationalization of the process of ecstasy. Most of the contributors to this volume have experienced the psychedelic effect themselves and have dedicated considerable thought and time to the empirical study of their effects. Each author uses his own model, his own concepts to explain what happens when we push out beyond the unexpended boundaries of our minds, beyond words, space-time categories, beyond social identifications, beyond models and concepts.

If the authors at times seem uncertain, if they seem to grope for words, if they seem too ready to spin out unproven hypotheses, if they seem to be going off in different directions, this is not a sign of disorganization but rather of the preliminary, rapidly changing speculation which inevitably characterizes a new breakthrough in the realm of ideas.

And the fact that research in this area provokes fierce controversy does not diminish but indeed strengthens the suggestion that we may be at another one of those wrenching transition points in intellectual history when the accepted ontological and mythological fundaments of society and of man's view of himself come into uneasy collision with new concepts.

THE STABLE WORLD THAT USED TO BE

To understand the meaning of any cultural development, it is useful to locate it in relationship to the dominant themes or mythos of its era. It is possible and sometimes useful to see all institutions—scientific, political, religious, economic—as differing expressions of the basic mythos of the epoch. This viewpoint perceives that each discipline simply rewords, reorchestrates certain underlying themes of the age. A profession or discipline which fails to fit into the mythic harmonic tends to be heard as a disruptive dissonance.

Thomas S. Kuhn has recently published a thought-provoking book which describes how scientific activities are determined by what he calls the paradigm of any period.[2] The paradigm is a distinctive world view which defines the sorts of problems and methods used in any era. Conventional science cannot go beyond the limits set by the paradigm without running the risk of being seen as eccentric or even "unscientific."

During the last fifty years our basic view of the world seems to have been undergoing another one of these revolutions, a gigantic struggle of ideologies of which the current controversy over psychedelic drugs is but a minor skirmish. The older, classic world view (which is now being outgrown) concerns itself with equilibria among forces which are visible, external, predictable, measurable, manageable by man, within the realm of macroscopic consciousness. The religious expression of this mythos is Protestantism, with its emphasis on behavior, achievement, work, balancing and rationality. The current political forms (socialism, democracy, communism, parliamentarianism) are again anthropocentric, oriented toward man, either the individual man or the man-state, and all emphasize a balance among a limited set of external factors, resources, territories. Again the macroscopic, visible, man-age-able aspects of behavior are stressed.

It is interesting to note how the scientific ideology of the last three centuries is seen to be symmetrical with the other institutions just listed. Classic physical science was almost exclusively a Protestant affair; the emphasis was on the orderly, clockwork equilibrium of external, material, visible macroscopic forces: God the master engineer, God the cosmic cost accountant balancing the natural books. Note for example how the mantra, the sacred motto of classic physics, is expressed in terms of conservation. Empirical facts stand as measured but the metaphorical interpretations we impose on the measures simply betray our basic (and usually unconscious) mythic commitments. Energy transformations measured by physicists could just as well be verbalized in other terms. Instead of talking about the Laws of Conservation we could just as well speak of the Orderly Sequence of Transformation—a metaphor which probably would be more productive of original thinking in the physical sciences. The conservation principle is, I submit, an implicit commitment to the mythos of the times. God runs the universe the way a good Christian runs his business and the way Andrew Mellon ran the country.

The *psychological* expressions of the anthropocentric mythos again fit the dimensions of the myth. Behaviorism (again a scientific movement invented and manned by men of the Protestant faith) recognizes only visible actions. Experimental psychology (in direct defiance of Fechner, the so-called Father of psychophysics) defines consciousness in terms of physical changes—much to the distress of Fechner himself, who was completely committed to a spiritual, expansive conception of consciousness, a hundred years or more ahead of his time. Freudian psychology has become the platform for a psychology of adjustment. The human personality is pictured as a miniature universe ruled by conservation principles—ego, id, superego—pushing toward equilibrium. There was much more to Freud than this; but the post-Freudian history of psychoanalysis clearly reflects the protestantization of the theory. The Hassidic, expansive and mystical aspects of Freud's thinking have not been able to survive the inevitable pressure of the contemporary mythos.

THE EMERGENT-ROOT MYTH

Evidence from every branch of science—physical, biological and social—testifies to the humiliating inadequacy of the anthropocentric pattern of our time. The dimensions of the emerging vision are explosively expansive and deal with energies and structures which though fantastically potent are microscopic and, indeed, invisible. The good old macroscopic world is seen to be one level of conception, and a rather clumsy, robot-like conception at that. The orientation becomes internal, i.e., nuclear.

I have previously referred to the space-time parameters of astronomy, microphysics, and genetics, and noted the seemingly endless sequence of exponential transformations of speeds and complexities.

The sacred mantra of these new sciences seems to be best expressed in the Einsteinian conversion equation: $E = MC^2$. Here is a truly ecstatic logos—a shattering, vision-challenging motto. Structure becomes process. Matter becomes a transient state of energy. Stasis becomes ex-stasis.

It would be inappropriate and probably unnecessary to spell out at this time the obvious and varied ways in which the same exponential mythos begins to appear in other institutions. Overproduction, over-killing, overpopulation, automation are a few of the new terms which remind us that man's body and man's rational mind are becoming outmoded by social and technical explosions. The older view of man (economic, political, religious, artistic, psychological) defined in terms of externals and behaviorals is reaching an agonizing endpoint.

Psychology, that discipline which treats of man's nature, man's view of himself, is always the last to adapt to a new world view. As my ex-colleague, Harvard's Jerome Bruner, points out:

> . . . the view one takes of man affects profoundly one's standard of what is humanly possible. And it is by the measure of such a standard that we establish our laws, set our aspirations for learning, and judge the fitness of men's acts. It is no surprise, then, that those who govern must perforce be jealous guardians of man's ideas about man, for the structure of government rests upon an uneasy consensus about human nature and human wants. The idea of man is of the order of *res publica,* and, by virtue of its public status, it is an idea

that is not subject to change without public debate. The behavioral scientist, as some insist on calling him, may propose, but it is the society at large that disposes. Nor is it simply a matter of public concern. For man as individual has a deep and emotional investment in his image of himself. If we have learned anything in the last half-century of psychology, it is that man has powerful and exquisite capacities for defending himself against violations of his cherished self-image. This is not to say that Western man has not persistently asked: "What is man that thou art mindful of him?" It is only that the question, when pressed, brings us to the edge of anxiety where inquiry is no longer free.[3]

While not addressed specifically to the issue of psychedelic drugs, this frank statement by a prominent member of the psychological orthodoxy speaks directly to the psychedelic paradox. From the standpoint of the established values of the older world, the psychedelic process is dangerous and insane—a deliberate psychotization, a suicidal undoing of the stability, conformity and equilibrium which man should be striving for. With its emphasis on consciousness, on internal, invisible, indescribable phenomena, with its multiplication of realities, the psychedelic experience is dreadfully incomprehensible to one committed to a rational, Protestant, achievement-oriented, behaviorist, equilibrated, conformist philosophy. But it makes perfect sense to one who is ready to experience the world in terms of the Einsteinian exponential view of the universe. The psychedelic experience is exquisitely effective preparation for the inundation of data and the problems to come.

In the last few pages I have been sketching in the outline of the over-all cultural mythos, the world view of which the new neurology and psychedelic pharmacology seem to be parts. The reader's reaction to this book and his position vis-à-vis the psychedelic drugs will depend, to a great extent, on his orientation to this general struggle of ideologies which characterize our times. Little has been said, so far, about the ecstatic process initiated by the consciousness-expanding drugs. The reader's understanding of the diverse essays presented in this book will be facilitated by a brief examination of three important aspects of the psychedelic process: (1) the neurological situation; (2) the pharmacological situation; (3) the psychological factors.

THE NEUROLOGICAL SITUATION

The facts of the neurological capacities of the human being are simply astronomical. We possess, each of us, around 10 billion brain cells. This is several times the number of human beings in the world. Any one brain cell can be in relationship with as many as 25,000 others. The number of possible associations is of the order of 10 billion to the twenty-five-thousandth power, a quantity larger than the number of atoms in the universe.[4] This electrical-chemical network, inconceivable in its complexity, is the anatomical structure of consciousness.

Into the brain, at each second, there pours something like 100 billion sensations. The brain itself fires off around 5,000 million signals a second.[5]

In contrast to the incredible potentialities of the brain is the obvious fact that we are aware of only the millionth fraction of our own cortical signaling. Huge areas of the brain (neurologists call them "silent areas") are blocked off from consciousness. Neurologists in their reflective moments pose disturbing questions: ". . . has man, perhaps, more brain than he knows what to do with? Is his huge 'neo-pallium' merely a wasted asset, like a powerful engine installed in a decrepit automobile which can never utilize more than a fraction of the available horsepower?"[6]

How can we explain this extraordinary discrepancy between the potentials of the cortical computer and the poverty of the programs we impose upon it? There is little known about the function of the brain and about the learning processes by means of which the brain's enormous potential is limited and contracted. The term which seems most adequate to describe this process is *imprinting*.

What is imprinting? According to psychologist Clifford Morgan it is "very rapid learning that takes place in some animals . . . at a certain early state of development." Morgan goes on to describe this fascinating process.

> One investigator hatched out some goose eggs in an incubator and happened to be present when the eggs hatched. For this reason he was the first large moving object that the goslings saw. Much to his surprise, the goslings began following him about and acted as though he, rather than the mother goose, were their parent. The young goslings, in fact, would have nothing to do with their mother and insisted on having his constant company. *This learning, which takes place very rapidly and without any specific reward, is called imprinting.*
>
> We have not yet fully explored the phenomenon of imprinting. We already know, though, that it is fairly widespread among birds. We know too that it can take place only *during a short interval* (a few hours or a day or two) and *at a certain time* (usually shortly following birth) in the life of an animal. It also seems to be *irreversible;* once it has taken place, it is difficult to alter through subsequent learning. There may, however, be some true learning connected with it. Young goslings, for example, at first follow any person if a human being has been the first object with which they have contact after hatching. A few days later, however, they learn the individual characteristics of the person who ordinarily leads them to food and shelter, and then they will follow no one else. Thus imprinting may be a natural stage in the maturation of an animal.[7]

The exact biochemical, neurological mechanism which produces imprinting is not yet known but the process exists and poses some challenging problems for psychological theory. Here is a sudden irreversible type of learning which seems independent of the laws of motivation, reward, conditioning. It is a rapid structuring of the nervous system, a sudden, shutterlike fixing of neurological film. The picture once taken, the structure once established, then determines the scope and type of subsequent "lawful learning." Imprinting is a biochemical event which sets up the chess board upon which the slow step-by-step learning of conditioning takes place. A major, perhaps the most important, aspect of learning thus eludes psychology and is located in the mysteries of neurology. Imprinting is an embarrassing topic to the conventional psychologist.

Another awesome aspect of the imprinting process is its unpredictable and accidental quality. Because Conrad Lorentz happened to be present at the right moment, the goslings "imprinted" him as the protective, maternal object. In another experiment young birds were presented with a Ping-Pong ball at the critical moment and spent their remaining life pursuing and making love to the plastic globes. This experiment is both amusing and frightening. It reminds us that each of us sees the world through perceptual structures (biochemical-neurological) which were laid down accidentally in our earliest moments. It raises the uneasy suspicion that, in spite of our vaunted rationality and conditioned certainty, we may be simply chasing the particular Ping-Pong balls which, at those sensitive shutter moments, had been imprinted on our cortical film.

These two neurological findings, the astronomical amplitude of the brain and its susceptibility to sudden fixated contraction, have implications for our understanding of the effect of psychedelic drugs.

THE PHARMACOLOGICAL SITUATION

Certain alkaloid molecules possess the power of dramatically suspending the familiar, learned structural aspects of the nervous system. Consciousness is suddenly released from its conditioned patterning and flung into a flashing loom of unlearned imagery. However heatedly scientists may disagree about the value and social meaning of the psychedelic drugs, there is one point upon which they concur: the drugs do propel awareness into an eerie, novel landscape in which everything seems possible and nothing remains fixed.

As in the case of the imprinting process, research on the psychedelic drugs has not yet discovered a neurological explanation of how this comes about. Just as the term *imprinting* defines an as yet unexplained, sudden biochemical fixing of a structure upon the nervous system, so might we consider the effect of psychedelic drugs as a temporary suspension of imprinting—an as yet unexplained sequence of sudden biochemical "unfixing" of perceptual constancies.

This metaphor is offered as assistance to the reader who will find himself intrigued and fascinated by the varied interpretations, literary and clinical, presented by the authors of this book. How do we develop our strange, unyielding modes of perceiving ourselves and the world which we call normal? How are they so awesomely altered upon the ingestion of a psychedelic food or drug?

This hypothesis of the psychedelic effect as a suspension of imprinting may be more than just an aid to comprehension. Hypotheses do not present themselves for approval or rational agreement. They define experimental questions. The imprinting hypothesis, relating as it does two hitherto separate fields of research, may suggest new empirical tests. Psychedelic drug states may throw light upon basic neurological theories of learning. More relevant to this volume, the imprinting theory may provide a more coherent explanation of the psychedelic state.

Some suggestive evidence already exists: current neurological research indicates that serotonin is a key factor in the transmission of nerve impulses. It has been shown that there is a difference in serotonin metabolism between infants and adults and between "normal" and schizophrenic persons. It is also known that LSD effects serotonin metabolism.[8] Marplan, a drug which "builds up the brain's stockpile of serotonin" and which has a tranquilizing effect on mental patients, blocks the action of LSD.[9]

Serotonin, in the light of this metaphor, might be seen as contributing to the fixing or imprinting process which is necessary for "normal" perception. The fluid, shifting, unfixed imagery of the involuntary and unpleasant psychotic state, the voluntary, ecstatic psychedelic state and the preimprinted period of infancy are associated with a change in the body's level of serotonin.

To carry the metaphor to its next logical position, psychedelic drugs may not only suspend old imprinted patterns, they may also provide the possibility of *reimprinting.*

The concept of reimprinting is, of course, a neurological restatement of the "death-rebirth" experience which is so often reported during psychedelic moments.[10, 11, 12] Reimprinting means that during the psychedelic session the subject's nervous system is in a state of disorganized flux closely analogous to that of infancy. The planned, voluntary release of fixed perceptual patterns and the temporary opening up of fluid, boundaryless awareness suggests the hope of controlled, self-controlled reimprinting. And here we come to the psychological implications of the psychedelic experience. The accelerated personality change, the rapid learning, the sudden life changes so regularly reported by psychedelic researchers.[11, 12, 13, 14, 15, 16]

THE PSYCHOLOGICAL SITUATION

One of the most confusing aspects of psychedelic phenomena is the wide variation of response. There is the common factor of going out of your mind, out beyond the imprinted, learned structure, but the specific content of what comes next is always different. Heaven or Hell. Buddha or Babbitt. It is this fantastic range of novel possibilities which has contributed to the controversy and confusion. This interpretative chaos is resolved by the set-setting hypothesis. One simply cannot make any sense of the psychedelic literature if one thinks of LSD, mescaline and psilocybin merely as drugs, as pharmacological agents which produce a generally predictable sequence of responses such as aspirin, morphine or insulin. The psychedelic substances have negligible somatic effects. Their site of action is the higher nervous system. They affect consciousness. Once the "normal" modes of awareness are suspended, the specific changes in consciousness which occur are due to set and setting.[13]

Set refers to that which the subject brings to the situation, his earlier imprinting, his learning, his temperament, his emotional, ethical and rational predilections and, perhaps most important, his immediate expectations about the drug experience.

Setting refers to the environment, social, physical, emotional, to the milieu of the session. The most important aspect of setting is the behavior, understanding and empathy of the person or persons who first administer the drug and who remain with the taker for the period that the drug is in effect.

Set and setting are psychological terms. The explanatory value of these concepts has been demonstrated in many studies[14, 17] and, indeed, one can say that the psychedelic controversy itself, that phenomenon of serious, honest, dedicated scientists heatedly making conflicting reports about LSD and other psychedelic substances, is nothing more than a broad social confirmation of the set-setting hypothesis.

Another psychological interpretation of the psychedelic effect which fits the set-setting hypothesis is the extreme *suggestibility* which characterizes the experience. The heightened vulnerability to internal or external stimuli—which leads some to paranoia and others to cosmic ecstasy—points to the critical importance of expectation and environmental pressure. Set and setting determine the direction in which suggestibility is pushed.

In the past few pages we have reviewed three areas which must be taken into account if one wishes to understand the psychedelic effect— the neurological, the pharmacological and the psychological. The concepts presented (imprinting, reimprinting, and set-setting-suggestibility) are broad, noncommittal metaphors—flexible enough to allow for a wide range of specifications and essentially heuristic, that is, a valuable guide capable of and indeed provocative of direct empirical check.

The most useful aspects of these broad concepts is that they allow for a cross-disciplinary articulation. The psychological metaphor translates directly to the neurological-pharmacological. This is to say that set-setting can be said to define the conditions for the reimprinting which can take place during the period of pharmacological heightened suggestibility.

A psychedelic session is a planned, temporary suspension of old imprinting, an opportunity for planned reimprinting, the structure of which should be determined by carefully planned set and setting.

THE PROBLEM OF COMMUNICATION

Such terms as "imprinting," "set-setting-suggestibility," "going out-of-your-mind," indeed, the term "psychedelic" itself, are static structural notions. They provide an outline within which we can think and talk about the psychedelic effect. But they do not attempt to communicate the speed, breadth and shuttling flow of the experience. Communication is blocked because words are inadequate to describe the shuttling web of a thirteen-billion-cell cerebral computer pharmacologically released from imprinted constancies.

Communication is also blocked because of the fears which are aroused by the very nature of the topic—"suspension of imprinting," "going out of your mind."

A case history anecdote may illustrate this point.

Not long ago I spent an afternoon with Dr. Richard Alpert and Dr. Ralph Metzner lecturing to the staff of one of the country's most respected scientific institutes. About thirty-five scientists were present, and after the formal lectures almost two hours of questions and discussion ensued. In closing the meeting the chairman, a well-known physicist who had taken LSD several times, made two rather pessimistic appraisals. He doubted whether any of the audience would retain more than a most fragmentary and distorted memory of the meeting and he questioned the possibility of verbal communication about the psychedelic experience. "Those who have taken a psychedelic drug realize it can't be talked about and those who haven't naïvely assume that it can be talked about with the current vocabulary."

After the meeting adjourned, we met in an office with four members of the institute who had previous experience with psychedelic drugs. Three of these men were strangers, but this did not prevent a most intimate evaluative discussion. Without any attempt at social niceties, these men immediately plunged into a frank, avuncular coaching process—ruthlessly critical and completely accepting.

It was as though Alpert, Metzner and I were rookie pitchers who had just been batted out of the box and were being instructed by four veterans of the same team. It was as though all seven of us were visitors from another planet meeting to figure out how to explain to earthlings, how to translate into English, the procedures and events of our totally different world.

It was interesting to note that each one of our coaches had a different strategy to suggest. One said we should make our psychedelic lectures completely personal. "Tell concretely what happened to you."

"Nonsense," said another. "You should be strictly objective and scientific. Rely only on published data."

A third advisor disagreed: "Make it practical. Tell the audience about the pragmatic details—dosage, how long it lasts, what people say and do during sessions."

The fourth advisor was the most psychological. "In discussing psychedelic drugs you must recognize the fears of the listener. Anticipate his objections. Be humble. Stress the dangers and problems. Don't put him on the defensive."

One of the advantages of the book you are now reading is that the editor, David Solomon, has skillfully selected essays which follow all these discrepant counsels. But while sensitive editing may solve the problem of dialect and rational approach, it does not resolve the emotional reactions which are usually generated by the topic of consciousness expansion.

Although our four fatherly advisors could not agree on strategy for communicating knowledge about psychedelics, they were unanimous in criticizing the central metaphor which I have employed here to prepare the reader for a better understanding of the psychedelic effect: *You have to go out of your mind to use your head.*

"This is guaranteed to scare people," we were told, "especially rational, intellectual people. You just can't go around telling persons that they are going to go out of their minds and expect a sympathetic response. Use a positive language. Use familiar jargon. Talk about creative reorganization or perceptual reintegration."

But this advice we cannot take. The message cannot be toned down. We are going to have to face the fact that psychedelic drugs do take us fast and far beyond our normal conceptual framework. But the term "going out of your mind" shouldn't really be that disturbing. We recall that most of the great religions have taken this goal, *ex-stasis,* the going beyond the rational, as their central program. The fact that we now possess the chemical means for guaranteeing this process should be a cause for rejoicing— for those who take their religion or their neurology seriously.

No, the point cannot be toned down. In preparing subjects for a psychedelic session or in preparing society for what is happening during this period of the psychedelic explosion, we cannot responsibly avoid confronting the paradox: you have to go out of your mind to use your head.

THE FEAR OF THE POTENTIAL

All of us, and I include here the most experienced psychedelic veterans, must recognize certain fears which are generated by the psychedelic process. The recognition of the type and source of tenor is the first step in dealing with it constructively.

Five most common fears provoked by the notion of consciousness expansion can now be listed:

1. *Cognitive*: the terror of the loss of rational control; the fear of disorientation and confusion.
2. *Social*: the terror of doing something shameful, or ludicrous; the loss of social inhibitions.
3. *Psychological*: the terror of self-discovery; of finding out something about yourself that you do not want to face.

4. *Cultural*: the terror of discovering the painful truth about the institutions with which one is identified; of seeing through the tribal shams; of becoming disillusioned with one's social commitments and thus an irresponsible person.

5. *Ontological addiction*: the terror of finding a realm of experience, a new dimension of reality so pleasant that one will not want to return. This fear is probably based on the unconscious hunch, shared by perhaps all men and dramatically expressed by a leading theoretician and practitioner of consciousness-expansion techniques, the late Georges I. Gurdjieff, that normal consciousness is a form of sleepwalking and that somewhere there exists a form of awakeness, of reality from which one would not want to return.

All these fears are frequently equated to fear of death. Each of the five elements of the ego structure are built up out of teaching, experience and habit to the point that each is taken as a part of identity. The respective fears are of a shattering, a fragmentation of this identity. And the fear of such shattering is the equivalent of, and indistinguishable from, the fear of death. But this construct of the identity is found to be an illusion. One who has the courage to undergo the shattering of the illusion will die, but will die in the mystical sense, ". . . so that he may live again." A Zen couplet says: "Be dead, thoroughly dead, and do as you will." It is the healing process which Tillich describes as "taking a walk through hell." To have courage to walk through this hell brings the transcendence that lies beyond.

Like other forms of anxiety, these five fears are related to deep yearnings and potentials in man. For each terror there is a corresponding liberation.

The cognitive terror is a negative interpretation of the desire to go out of your mind to gain your head. Transcendence of mind makes possible new realms of insight.

The social terror of "acting out" is a negative interpretation of the ancient axiom (Taoist, Zen, Buddhist) that you must go out of your mind to reach that creative quietude which is open to enriched experience.

The terror of seeing yourself is the negative aspect of the possibility of seeing beyond yourself.

The fear of cultural disillusionment is the negative aspect of the possibility of seeing into new institutional solutions.

The terror of ontological addiction is the static and negative interpretation of the goal of internal freedom, the ability to move voluntarily from one level of consciousness to another, just as the scientist focuses his vision from the microscopic to the telescopic.

This book, on the Consciousness Expanders, written by scientist-scholars, is another episode in the endless round of communication, the reading-writing game. There are the authors trying to explain and describe experiences which they recognize to be beyond the range of words and there are the readers, each one of whom brings to the book his own expectations and experiential background.

Let us plan the reading of this book as we would plan a psychedelic session itself. Like the taking of LSD, the reading experience depends upon set and setting. The setting is, of course, provided by the fifteen chapters which are about to present themselves to your nervous system. Committed to printers' type there is nothing more that can be done about the setting (which points to the static inefficiency of the written word). The rest is up to you, the reader. To get the most from this book (as in the psychedelic session) you should approach it with an open mind. Let it be said directly that unless you have had a psychedelic experience, great portions of this book will be beyond your present mental categories. If you plan to impose your own rational structure on this book, you will end up with, and within, the limits of your own categories. And that will be everyone's loss.

Like a psychedelic session, this book can, if you let it, startle, excite and even frighten you. But if you are prepared, if you are able to let your rational categories stretch and become permeable, you may sense some of the potentials—social, creative, psychological, cultural and ontological—which may be experienced by means of the consciousness-expansion process.

The study of psychedelic drugs has in the last ten years engendered an enormous emotional reaction from society. Each of the "consciousness expanders" who contribute to this book has risked two dangers, one personal and one social.

First of all, they have all gone out of their minds voluntarily and creatively for the furtherance of their work. Next, they have all risked social sanction to write about their experiences. Some have lost their jobs, many have risked their reputations, all of them have had to steer head on against the winds of orthodoxy at a time when it would have been easier to trim sails.

Theirs has been the fun of the adventure, the excitement of the discovery, the fascination of the paradox.

May it, reader, be yours as well.

MILLBROOK, N.Y.

MAY 1964

REFERENCES

1. Beadle, George W. *The New Genetics: The Threads of Life.* Britannica Book of the Year. Chicago: 1964.
2. Kuhn, Thomas S. *The Structure of Scientific Revolution.* Chicago: University of Chicago Press, 1964.
3. Bruner, Jerome S. *On Knowing: Essays for the Left Hand.* Cambridge: Belknap Press, 1963: 150–151.
4. Campbell, Robert. "The Circuit of the Senses," in a series on "The Human Body" (Part IV). *Life Magazine.* Vol. 54: 26 (June 28, 1963).
5. Pfeiffer, John. *The Human Brain.* New York: Harpers, 1955.
6. De Ropp, Robert. S. *Drugs and the Mind.* New York: Grove Press, 1961.
7. Morgan, Clifford T. *Introduction to Psychology.* New York: McGraw-Hill, 1956: 588.
8. Siva Sankar, D. V. and Sankar, D. Barbara, Phipps, Edward, and Gold, Eleanor. "Effects of Administration of Lysergic Acid Diethylamide on Serotonin Levels in the Body." *Nature* (London), 1961: 191.

9. Rednick, Oscar, Krus, Donald M., and Raskin, Milton. Paper read at Federation of American Societies for Experimental Biology, 1964.

10. Leary, Timothy, Metzner, Ralph, and Alpert, Richard. *The Psychedelic Experience*. New Hyde, New York: University Books, 1964. See also Editors. "The Subjective After-Effects of Psychedelic Experience: A Summary of Four Recent Questionnaire Studies," *The Psychedelic Review*. Vol 1: 1 (1963); Savage, Charles, Jackson, Donald D., and Terrill, James. "LSD, Transcendence and the New Beginning." *LSD: The Consciousness-Expanding Drug*. Ed. David Solomon. New York: Putnam, 1964: 174–199.

11. Ibid, Leary et al., Savage et al., Leary, Timothy, Litwin, George H., and Metzner, Ralph. "Reactions to Psilocybin Administered in a Supportive Environment." *J of Nervous & Mental Diseases*. December, 1963 Vol. 137: 6; Unger, Sanford. "Mescalin, LSD, Psilocybin on Certain Attitudes in Normal." Santa Monica: RAND Corporation (reprint), 1963; McGlothlin, W. M. "Long-lasting Effects of LSD on Certain Attitudes in Normals." Santa Monica: RAND Corporation (reprint), 1963; Sherwood, J. N., Stoloroff, M. J., and Harmon, W. "The Psychedelic Experience—a New Concept in Psychotherapy," *Journal of Neuropsychiatry*. 1962, vol. 3.

12. Savage et al.

13. Unger, Sanford. "Mescalin, LSD, Psilocybin and Personality Change"; see also Pahnke, Walter. *Drugs and Mysticism: An Analysis of the Relationship between Psychedelic Drugs and the Mystical Consciousness*. Ph.D. thesis, Harvard University, 1963.

11

Leary's Radical Theory of Reimprinting

Languages: Energy Systems Sent and Received

Timothy Leary

Leary's "Languages: Energy Systems Sent and Received" is perhaps Leary's most complex piece of writing. It was originally published in *ETC: A Journal of General Semantics* and has never been reprinted in its entirety.* It is also Leary's most radical attempt to theorize the meaning of the LSD experience. Anyone attempting to understand Leary's utopian understanding of the LSD experience needs to read it. "Languages . . ." is also crucial in Leary's *oeuvre* because it represents his last serious attempt to write for an audience of scholars; later he would adopt a more colloquial style that often eschews rigor and complexity. Leary's populist style can be found on display in *The Politics of Ecstasy,* his collection of writings on the psychedelic experience, published in 1968.

"Languages . . ." is also important because it contains the most detailed description of Leary's theory of imprinting

---

*Leary published an abridged version of the article in *Changing My Mind, Among Others.* Englewood Cliffs, N.J.: Prentice Hall, 1982.

and reimprinting. While interpreting the uniqueness of the LSD experience, Leary optimistically argues that the negative imprinting process (social conditioning) can be reversed through psychedelic drugs and through reimprinting: "these compounds not only temporarily suspend old imprints—they produce new imprints. During a psychedelic session, the nervous system, stripped of all previous learning and identity, is completely open to stimulation (and here is the joy, the discovery, the revelation), but it also completely vulnerable. Naked suggestibility. Powerful attachments and repulsions develop during psychedelic sessions. All known relationships are transcended. New ones are possible." This passage expresses Leary's most utopian interpretation of the LSD experience: the notion that human nature can be altered and remade through the drug experience. However, Leary's radical interpretation of the LSD experience—naked suggestibility—is also a double-edged sword because it often instills fear in the non-users of LSD. Opponents of LSD feared naked suggestibility because it conveys the possibility of cultic brainwashing.

Leary's article concludes with his attempt to theorize the LSD experience in aesthetic terms. To do this, Leary constructs three distinct forms of aesthetic representation: reproductive art, visionary art, and transcendental art ("Tranart"). In Leary's aesthetic system, Tranart is the highest form of representation because it "avoids any connection with symbol or external form and directly represents the energy dance." The latter is ultimately concerned with Direct Process Images (DPIs) or "externalized representations of the flow of direct sensation—experience." For Leary, "physics, biology, biochemistry, [and] genetics" all coalesce in Tranart: "[b]eyond the imprint all is one dance of electrical energy; one flow of cellular process." Leary insists that there need not be any conflict between science and art; both attempt to "record the process."

"Languages . . ." can be regarded as Leary most far-reaching attempt to theorize the LSD experience and the drug's unique effect on the human mind. Leary's article is ambitious in the sense that it attempts to synthesize the scientific view of LSD with an aesthetic understanding of the drug experience. The ultimate aim of Leary's article is to find ways to increase receptivity in the subject during the LSD experience. In doing so, the user becomes an artist who attempts to record the ceaseless flow of energy. Within Leary's interpretation, language—especially the written word—is less effective at recording the complex totality of the LSD experience. Leary's interest in new aesthetic mediums signifies his search for new ways to elucidate the elusive nature of the psychedelic experience.

JAMES PENNER

LANGUAGES: ENERGY SYSTEMS SENT AND RECEIVED

From *ETC: A Journal of General Semantics* volume 22, no. 4 (1965): 431–60.

Timothy Leary

To understand language you must have some experiential feeling for energy and how energy is packaged and how energy is sent and received by energy packages.

You must understand that consciousness is the decoding of energy patterns and that consciousness exists at all levels of energy structures. And that the evolution of life on this planet is a long-standing conversation, a transmission of coded energy messages.

To understand language you must have experienced that your body is a galaxy of linguistic systems, the dialects of which you can learn. And that symbols (which may be all you think of when you think of language) are the most frozen and inefficient form of communication and that the symbol system which you use is based on an accidental freezing of your nervous system in your young and formative days—a freezing which is chemical in nature.

When you understand these basic ideas you will know why men have always and everywhere found it necessary and pleasant to escape from imprinted symbol systems into touch with other energy exchanges by means of chemicals.

And you will be able to understand the proposals which are made in this article for improving man's linguistic capacities—which is to say, improving man's ability to receive and send more types of energy. You will be ready to understand why improvement in man's language means expansion and control of man's consciousness.

Energy is structure times the speed of light squared. Energy is trapped momentarily in structures which vary in complexity, duration and mass. All structures—atomic, molecular, cellular—are transient energy packages, energy transformers.

Energy is trapped in the atomic structure—the tiny nucleus and its far-flung electrons.

At a more complex, ponderous and slower, level we have the protein molecule—a gigantic and elaborate station for packaging and transforming nuclear and atomic energy.

Life. The cell houses the more basic, faster, and freer energies of proteins, and other molecules. Multi-cellular organisms are even more complicated housings for energy.

We possess only a crude, external intellectual language for describing energy packages—molecule, atom, nucleon, meson.

At the speed of light energy dances through patterns which physicists record and attempt to describe.

Communication is energy sent or received by a structure, by a temporary energy package. Language is the pattern of energy sent or received by a temporary energy package. There are as many languages as there are systems of energy packaging. Each living cell, for example, houses an astronomical number of dialects and linguistic systems—coded and decoded energy exchanges.

Each type of energy package has a system of internal communication—messages concerned with maintenance of the structure. And each structure has its external communication system for exchanging messages with other energy packages. This distinction (internal-external) is usually overlooked in the case of human consciousness.

While all energy packages send and receive messages—only a millionth fraction of the energy received can be registered, decoded, or used. Energy decoding is thus drastically limited—this is to say, communication among levels of energy structure is drastically limited by the ability of the receiving package to *be aware* of the incoming.

Consciousness, or decoding, is the registration of incoming energy by the energy structure or that specialized part of the energy structure designed to decode.

The human body, for example, is engaged in an enormous number of communications. Millions of signals flood into the brain each second, which are decoded but not in symbolic terms. Thousands of levels of energy are being consciously registered by different levels of the bodily structure—but not by that limited level of structure which we call our "waking consciousness."

LIFE AS A LINGUISTIC SYSTEM

The linguistic system of life, the blueprint, is the DNA code. The time span of the genetic material is long—that of the individual body is short. The body of every member of every species is designed as a seed-carrying package. The function of the body is to pass on the seed (i.e., the DNA code) and to stay about long enough to protect the young seed-carrying packages. Genetics plays a statistical game. Each species is the current experimental model of packaging design—the newest product in an industry that dates back two billion years.

In this design-sequence, species are more of minor importance. In the genetic game, the more important issues are vegetable-animal or aquatic-terrestrial.

The two billion year old chain of life is a long conversation-system. A direct line of communication (energy contact, energy exchange) traces back unbroken from every currently living creative to the original forms of life on this planet.

To understand language, indeed to understand any aspect of human affairs, we do well to look at nature. The evolutionary process has been dealing with all the basic issues for eons. The answers to problems of communication have been worked out over and over again and are there to be learned by those who can interpret scientific data.

The communication situation in living forms, for example, is extraordinarily complex. The single cell is a communication center of bewildering activity, incredible beauty and order.

> When we consider the teeming activity of a modern city, it is difficult to realize that in the cells of our bodies infinitely more complicated processes are at work—ceaseless manufacture and acquisition of food, storage communication and administration. . . . All this takes place in superb harmony with the co-operation of all the participants of a living system regulated down to the smallest detail.[1]

LINGUISTIC SYSTEMS OF THE BODY

Mammals are currently the most complex form of energy structure. The communication network in the mammal is staggeringly varied. In addition to each cell in the body conducting its own energy exchanges, there are organs, tissue systems, numerous biochemical networks, all in addition to the nervous system which is the major system for receiving, coordinating, storing, and relaying messages.

The mammalian brain contains an astronomical number of cells.

In the human being, these number between ten and thirteen billion. Around one hundred million sensations a second flood into the cortex. The mammalian nervous system is competently organized into subsystems to handle all these data, and an extraordinary division of labor and intercoordination exist. Thus, we see that there are thousands of levels of consciousness, thousands of language systems operating in the human body. These are all chemical in nature—the word "chemical" denoting a universe of energy exchanges which is still dimly understood.

The mammalian body is thus a galaxy of communication systems, each operating in exquisite harmony, both inter-system and intra-system. Billions of messages a minute are received from without and within the body and are woven into a harmonious flow of messages, coded in thousands of coordinated languages.

The mammalian body moves through the environment, a mobile communication center—with billions of messages a minute alerting it to the issues of intake, reproduction, survival. All of the instinctual machinery is geared to work perfectly, ready to flick on in response to the triggered stimuli from without. Each member of every species is essentially a structural duplicate of every other member of the species.

What varies, however, in the case of mobile, far-ranging mammals is the learning process. Learning the neighborhood and learning which cues in the environment trigger off which instinctual responses. Mammals have to learn how to pilot themselves through widely differing environments. Their complex machineries depend upon discrimination of cues and the learning of elaborate behavior sequences.

While millions of signals flood into the mammalian cortex each second from all parts of the nervous system, there has to be one level of awareness which is directed externally to changes in the immediate environment. One level of consciousness has to be alerted to neighborhood changes, to learn to distinguish between rewards and punishments, to select what is to be avoided and what is to be pursued in the service of each instinctual system.

Consider the mammalian body as an enormous ocean liner with

billions of passengers and crew all happily engaged in ship activities—a completely self-contained, integrated, harmonious system of energy exchanges and communication. But one thing is required—a watch-out. The task of the look-out is simple. He watches for the red light and the green light—for the cues of approach and avoidance, of desire or repulsion. This look-out is, of course, the so-called "waking conscious-ness." The cues which are learned through conditioning to be associated with red and green make up the entire mental life of man. The process by which this neurological "fixing" on external cues is accomplished, is called imprinting.

SYMBOLS—THE LANGUAGE OF IMPRINTS

Imprinting is a biochemical freezing of external awareness to stimuli which are presented at a *critical* period of neurological vulnerability which occurs very early in the life of fowl and mammal, and which probably occurs at critical hormonal, biochemical stages in the life of the human being.

1. The process (of imprinting) is confined to a very definite and very brief period in individual life and possibly also to a particu-lar set of environmental circumstances.
2. Once accomplished, it is often very stable—in some cases, per-haps totally irreversible.
3. It is often completed long before the very specific reactions to which the imprinted pattern ultimately becomes linked or established.
4. It is supra-individual learning—a learning of the broad charac-teristics of the species. . . . [2]

As the result of early imprinting, fowl attempt to court members of other species including humans; lambs desert the flock and follow their keepers; goslings sit on and attempt to hatch watermelons; buffalo calves attempt to mate with huntsmen's horses; zebra foals attach themselves to moving cars, refusing to be chased away; ducklings reject the mother in favor of orange basketballs.

There are other characteristics of imprinting which are implied but not emphasized in the research literature.

The first is the rather terrifying implication that early, accidental, and involuntary external events can blindly and tenaciously couple the instinctual machinery to entirely inappropriate stimuli. It raises the disturbing question for each individual—which orange basketballs imprinted you?

Another issue is the relationship of conditioning and learning to imprinting. One possibility is that imprinting sets up the basic attachment-avoidance of stimuli and that all subsequent learning is accomplished by means of association to the original imprint.

Before imprinting, we assume that the organism is fully conscious of the rich and ever-changing flow of neurological signals within and without. The brain of the human neonate is a ten billion celled machine with an infinity of interrelated sensations, dealing with an external world, infinitely changing and variable. Two infinitely complex energy fields interact—the free-flowing nervous system and the free-flowing external world. Imprinting freezes awareness to one aspect of the environment and cuts off consciousness from all internal, intrabody sensations except those associated with the imprint.

Imprinting sets up a chessboard—originally with one white and one black piece, and upon this static board and around its basic approach and avoidance cues all subsequent learning and awareness take place.

Another aspect of imprinting is its addictive quality. The human being is "hooked" to the external world. Sensory deprivation experiments suggest that when the human being is cut off from his "supply" of external stimuli, he shows all the symptoms of a "dope-fiend"—restlessness, discomfort, anxiety.

THE IMPRINTED COMMUNICATION SYSTEM

I have suggested that thousands of communication systems exist within the human body, mediated by the nervous system. In addition to the countless coded energy exchanges operating in blissful harmony—imprinting sets up a new and very different language.

The mental life of the human being is limited by and tied to associations relating back to the original imprint. Every level of communication is different from other energy exchanges. The communication system set up within the imprint structure differs from other languages in the nervous system in that it is the newest, it is tied to parochial externals, it is static and cut off from the flow of energy which characterizes other systems.

The brain is a billion lens motion picture camera shooting and coordinating billions of frames a second. The imprint system is one of these frames—stopped—upon which man's perception and symbolic thinking develops. Man's mind imposes upon the variegated flow of energy one static model—years out of date, kept current only by the slow process of conditioning and association.

The "dead," removed quality of man's thinking and communicating has interested philosophers for centuries, and has been described most effectively by linguists and semanticists, especially Wittgenstein, Sapir, and Korzybski.

What happens outside or inside, we perceive in terms of our mental imprinting system. We live in a dead world—cut off from the flow of life and energy.

Imprinting allows us to maneuver around the neighborhood, keeps us busy by determining the attractions and repulsions that pull and repel us. From the standpoint of the genetic blueprint, imprinting works. DNA plays a statistical game. In spite of the freaky nature of many early imprints to which our instincts are hooked, enough of us *do* imprint biologically appropriate stimuli such that we do reproduce and care for our young. That, after all, is the crucial genetic issue. The fact that man's consciousness is limited to a static field may be of no consequence to the genetic blueprint.

SUSPENSION OF IMPRINTS

Imprintings, indeed, all mental, neurological processes are biochemical. Even at the grossest level of the synapse, communication takes place chemically. A squirt of alkaloid keeps the message going. Other chemical processes can block the message.

Many experiments have demonstrated that the imprinting process can be postponed, altered, or prevented entirely by means of tension-reducing or tranquillizing drugs.

Then there are the psychedelic chemicals—alkaloid molecules possessing the power of dramatically suspending imprinting. Compounds such as LSD whirl the subject into a completely new realm far removed from learned categories and associations. Underlying the current controversy about drugs—their dangers or values—is the unanimous agreement that they do cause subjects to go out of their minds, i.e., out of their imprinted chessboards.

The chemical attack on the lifeless nature of symbol systems is not a recent development.

In every culture and in every century of recorded history, men have used chemicals of vegetable origin to alter consciousness. In most tribes (our own included) the "high points" of cultural life revolve around the imbibing or eating of mind-changing substances.

In cultures where primitive technologies and distribution systems make it difficult to obtain mind-changing potions, it is a commonplace observation that the members of the culture will drop any activity in order to "get high." The same is true of cultures where primitive legal or moral sanctions make it difficult to obtain mind-changers. During American prohibition a mass-mania sprang up around liquor. The same is true in penitentiaries or in military servitudes.

The drive to alter consciousness chemically is one of the strongest human characteristics.

Aldous Huxley has described the planetary extent of chemical methods of expanding consciousness:

> The urge to transcend self-conscious selfhood is ... a principal appetite of the soul. When, for whatever reason, men and women fail to transcend themselves by means of worship, good works and spiritual exercises, they are apt to resort to religion's chemical surrogates— alcohol and "goof pills" in the modern West, alcohol and opium in the East, hashish in the Mohammedan world, alcohol and marijuana in Central America, alcohol and cocoa in the Andes, alcohol and the barbiturates in the more up-to-date regions of South America. In *Poisons Sacrés, Ivresses Divines* Phillippe de Félice has written at length and with a wealth of documentation on the immemorial connection between religion and the taking of drugs. Here, in summary or in direct quotation, are his conclusions. The employment for religious purposes of toxic substances is "extraordinarily widespread." ... The practices studied in this volume can be observed in every region of the earth, among primitives no less than among those who have reached a high pitch of civilization. We are, therefore, dealing not with exceptional fads, which might justifiably be overlooked, but with a general and, in the widest sense of the word, a human phenomenon, the kind of phenomenon which cannot be disregarded by anyone who is trying to discover what religion is, and what are the deep needs which it must satisfy.[3]

Cultures vary, it is true, in the efficiency or toxicity of their mind-changers. Alcohol is a most primitive, crude, and dangerous mind-changing agent. Its world-wide popularity is probably due to the fact that European engineering developed methods for mass-production and distribution. Alcohol, by the eighteenth century, was available and dependable. Other competing mind-changers were relatively rare, dependent on inefficient means of preparation and distribution.

The global popularity of chemical mind-changers, intoxicants, euphoriants, hallucinogens, phantastics and vision-producing plants is due to their property of producing ecstasy.

Ecstasy means to go out of your mind; to break out of the verbal prisons; to suspend your imprints; to see things afresh; to perceive directly. With the freshened perception goes the feeling of liberation; the exultant sense of having escaped the lifeless net of symbols.

Men seek chemical liberation to regain what they have lost in the socialization process. They drink, smoke, chew, or they fast in order to escape from the tyranny of words, the limits of the imprint.

The ecstatic is wordless. Try to describe an orgasm. Try to describe the thrill of the "peak moment," the game ecstasy. Try to describe even the mundane effect of getting "tight" at a cocktail party. Look up the word "ecstasy" in the dictionary.

REIMPRINTING

Ecstasy has always been a central goal of human life and the psychedelic experience has been sought by mystics and visionaries who have struggled for decades to go out of their minds. But why and so what? What happens after the neurological liberation? How is it integrated back into life?

Many philosophers have argued that "staying high" is the highest goal of life. Hinduism and Hinayana Buddhism, for example, flatly turn their backs on social reality and urge their devotees to reach a state of nirvana and stay there.

Other philosophers of ecstatic consciousness have argued that the ecstasy must lead to a liberated return. Christian mystics, Mahayana Buddhists, and many Hindu sects insist that the person who has been liberated from his neurological strait-jacket will be known by his works and his actions.

This issue has remained academic until recently because very few persons, regardless of which method they have used to reach psychedelic experiences, have ever actually attained the psychedelic state, the freedom from imprints. Breathing exercises, monastic withdrawal, prolonged meditation, mantras, madras, mandalas can produce a state of quietude and serenity but only rarely do their adepts report a blinding illumination, a whirling inundation of sensation, the unity through multiplicity, which characterize the direct neurological confrontation with energy processes outside the imprint. Today, anyone can have this experience by ingesting a psychedelic drug. Temporary freedom from imprints is almost guaranteed.

But again, so what? And then what?

An exciting and frightening aspect of psychedelic drugs is just this—that these compounds not only temporarily suspend old imprints—they produce new imprints. During a psychedelic session the nervous system, stripped of all previous learning and identity, is completely open to stimulation (and here is the joy, the discovery, the revelation), but it is also completely vulnerable. Naked suggestibility, powerful attachments and repulsions develop during psychedelic sessions. All known relationships are transcended. New ones are possible.

New neurological chessboards can be set up which do not eliminate the old associative network, but do change the attraction-repulsion foci. Powerful new attraction-repulsion networks are formed. Zebra foals chase after the automobiles to which they have been exposed in their psychedelic session. Here is the danger and the promise of psychedelic drugs reimprinting the development of new symbol systems and the refocusing of old systems.

LANGUAGE SYSTEMS AVAILABLE TO MAN

In the preceding pages man's mental-linguistic system has been defined neurologically (imprinting) and located in relation to other systems of communication within and without the body.

A sad situation unfolds. We see that the human nervous system is very limited in the range of energy it can decode (become aware of). Our bodies plod through complex energy fields, blind to, and incapable of absorbing the largest part of messages surrounding us.

But even though we are cut off from most of the exciting conversations around us, the human nervous system is still capable of a much wider range of awareness than we tune in to, billions of messages and thousands of communication systems operating each minute in our cortex.

Eastern psychologists are aware of this potential. Tantric Hinduism, for example, defines seven chakras or nerve centers in the body and suggests that a universe of awareness exists at each chakra. For centuries oriental psychologists have been developing and testing methods for freeing man's connection to the external imprint so that these other levels can be decoded. While Western philosophy and Western psychology remain trapped in the rational imprint board, Eastern scholars never tire of reminding us of the crippling bargain that has been made for us.

Surrounded by networks of external energy and lugging around countless flashing message centers within our bodies, we perceive only in terms of static pieces. Our restriction of consciousness is, of course, no setback to the genetic blueprint. Life goes on in us and is transmitted by us, even though we sleepwalk. It may be that procreation and rearing of the young require a blindness to the broader meanings and processes of life and a deafness to the rapturous vibrations around us. G. I. Gurdjieff, perhaps the greatest psychologist the West has produced in two thousand years, reviewed these issues in a biblical text called *All and Everything*. In this book he considers the problem of the evolutionary process. If man saw his true position in the long evolutionary sequence he mighty sit down and quit playing his role. In order to keep man occupied chasing externals, Gurdjieff speculates, the legendary organ, Kundabuffer, was introduced into the human nervous system. This organ allegedly keeps man attached to external striving and causes him to see reality upside-down. The organ Kundabuffer is clearly a metaphorical reference to the imprinting process—a brilliant anticipation of current neurological findings.

The absurdity of man's language exchanges is now clear. Each of us has a static picture of the world—accidentally imprinted and elaborated by means of chains of conditioned associations—themselves arbitrary and parochially accidental.

Each of us labors under the illusion that our imprint board is reality—a situation beautifully described in Plato's analogy of the cave. When two human beings attempt to communicate the absurdity is compounded—my chessboard interacting with your Monopoly game.

We live as sleeping robots, cut off from life, from our own brains, and from each other.

Those of us who live at the same time and in the same neighborhood do share enough consensual codes to allow an alienated social life and to preserve the illusion of real communication. In particular, that fraction of our language system which refers to visible events, movements in space-time is reasonably efficient. We can communicate about static externals and materials, but little else. Not only do we not use the energy which is available, we do not know what we have lost.

THREE POSSIBILITIES FOR IMPROVING MAN'S LINGUISTIC SYSTEM

1. We can increase the efficiency of our current imprint by recognizing clearly what we have imprinted, recognizing the limitations and dimensions of our chessboards, by developing new chains of association which will open up the imprint board, by semantic analysis of the relation of our imprints to events in space-time.

2. We can suspend the imprint, move off the mental chessboard, and tune in on that range of energy flow, internal and external, which is accessible to that transient receiving instrument called the human nervous system. The problem here is that our present network of imprint-based associations must contain the possibility of getting off the board. *The error of Western psychology*

lies exactly here: no methods or possibilities for getting off the imprint board are recognized. Western psychology and philosophy assume that we must work within the limits which are tribally, temporarily, accidentally presented.

Note that suspension of imprint is a temporary event. No one has yet demonstrated the possibility of remaining in satori or "high" indefinitely.

Psychedelic drugs make it possible to move out beyond your mental structure for a period of hours—to escape from the addictive grasp of the external, to voyage through the internal galaxy, to wander through your chakras. But the problem of re-entry, return to externals, must always be met.

3. We can reimprint. We can reimprint carefully, selecting the new chessboard, the new mental game, carefully choosing the persons and the externals to which we will become voluntarily hooked.

Let us consider in detail some of these possibilities for improving our "language."

SEMANTICS AS THE FIRST STEP
FOR IMPROVING OUR OLD
IMPRINTED LINGUISTIC SYSTEM

Before the "dope-fiend" or the addicted alcoholic can be cured, he must recognize his affliction. Before the prisoner can escape, he must see that he is in prison.

The first step, therefore, is to recognize that we are hooked to certain externals. We must analyze the fabric of attraction and repulsion.

Since our consciousness is totally hooked to externals (and internal images and representations of externals), it is useful to clarify the exact nature of the externals we have become attached to.

The prisoner who has examined carefully the nature of his cell must consider the way out. He must distinguish between the limits of his cell and what is outside. He must recognize the limits and directions of his own and other people's imprints.

Some forms of psychoanalysis aim to do just this. The long chain of associations is laboriously traced back, step by step, to the original imprint situation. An attempt is made to set up a new sequence of relationships and associations, centering first on the person of the analyst. This is called the transference neurosis. But, imprinting is a biochemical event, as Freud recognized. And, as Freud also saw, the verbal interaction in the consulting room cannot duplicate the impact of the original physiological structuring.

In thinking and communicating about external events, it is important to recognize the semantic lesson that each external imprint is uniquely located in space and time. Here we can learn from the example of the physical sciences—which have solved the problem of keeping their language system flowing and in tune with the processes they measure.

The physical sciences languished as long as the verbal games of Aristotle cast the mold of investigation, the dualities, the poetic metaphors, the fourfold symmetries. Charming constructions with no relationship to the way things really move in nature. Science began to move when the language and grammar of philosophy were shelved and new concepts began to chase after the specific reactions. The chemical element became defined, not on the basis of a verbal game, but because the measuring operations reduced it to that point where it could be reduced no more.

And when technology was able to demonstrate that elements could be reduced to nuclear structures, then the language and grammar changed to keep up.

Physics and chemistry have flourished because they developed new languages, nonverbal systems, that could keep up with the observed phenomena. A chemical formula is a beautiful, functional shorthand which words can never hope to reproduce. Nature is an open system, and the denotation system describing nature should strive for openness as well. The linguistics of the chemical formula allow us to make changes in the formula which parallel changes in molecular structure. You can't do that to words.

The language of physical science is a language of objective records of movements in space-time. Psychology and the so-called behavioral sciences can, and inevitably will imitate the linguistic pattern of chemistry.

The behavior of the human being, like the behavior of a particle, is movement in space-time. The *ontological* problem of behavior is solved by recognizing that "reality" is subjective and that we can only agree upon and study the "subject matter" i.e., the movements in space-time we have specifically included within the scope of inquiry. The *epistemological* problems of behavior are solved by recognizing that "truth" is always subjective and that we can only talk in terms of "facts," i.e., consensually agreed upon records of movements in space-time. The *logical* problems of behavior are solved by recognizing that associations are always subjective but that standard methods of relating symbols can be agreed upon.

THE LANGUAGE OF EXPERIENCE AS A STEP IN IMPROVING OUR LINGUISTIC SYSTEM

The philosophic and technical advances of the physical sciences will inevitably be understood and incorporated into the game communication of a semantically oriented culture. This will straighten out our communication about external affairs but does not solve the problem of communicating the internal, the experiential.

Whether you are recording the spin of a nuclear particle or observing objects or human behaviors, you are dealing with movements in space-time which can be measured in terms of extension and duration. "Subject matter" can be defined and "fact" can be legislated.

But when we deal with the internal we dip our cups into the rushing stream of experience. "Reality" is always subjective, unique, and irreplicable and "truth," subjective, unique, and fleeting.

The science of internal process poses problems quite distinct from the science of the external process. A different ontology (subjective "reality" vs. consensual subject matter), epistemology (subjective "truth" vs. external "fact"), ethic, and politic are required. Very different communication techniques are necessary.

New and different languages which distinguish the external from the experiential will inevitably be developed. Since language determines experience, we must be attentive to design a language which keeps perception open. If our language is closed our experiencing and thinking will be closed.

But it is necessary to build in some system. If our linguistic structure is chaotic or haphazard, then our thinking and experiencing will be chaotic and haphazard.

THE VARIETIES OF EXPERIENTIAL LANGUAGE

To describe *external events* we use a symbol system. A chemical formula is one such denotative symbol. Verbal symbols are another form of denotation—less precise, but capable of semantic purification.

To describe *internal events,* three types of experiential languages are possible.

1. We can use external symbols to describe our experiential languages, but only when our consciousness is completely externalized—tied to the external game reference. But that is only one very limited and robot type of experiencing.

2. Awareness can combine external symbols in novel forms, e.g., thinking which is creative, imaginative, fantasied, visionary. Such experiencing is pathological if involuntary. Hallucinations. Delusions. Such experiencing is highly valued if it is voluntary. We experience in terms of symbols but we combine them in novel ways.

3. The third mode of experiencing bypasses symbols completely. We are directly aware of the energy being recorded by our nervous system. We communicate these experiences by selecting and directing energy sources which stimulate the nervous system of the person to whom we are communicating.

THE EXPERIENTIAL LANGUAGE CAN INCLUDE THE EXTERNAL IMPRINTED BEHAVIORAL LANGUAGE

We can experience in terms of the denotative symbols of our culture or we can bypass them. Much of our experiencing is in terms of external symbols. Thus, the experiential language must allow us to use external modes of awareness.

We include in the experiential vocabulary all of the terms in the "old language." But we no longer treat words as denoting external movements in space-time. They have no external reference. They are just noises, pencil-sketches which express an experience and which hopefully can communicate the experience of someone else. We must teach people the difference between using words to discuss externals and internals. Don't worry about external logic when you are describing experience. (If you are describing an external game sequence you must, on the contrary, be prudishly conscientious about the semantics of the movements in space-time.) If you plan to communicate internal states using external symbols (including words) you must smash through the external linguistic conventions. Alter sequences. Turn words upside down. Cut up and reassemble verbal sequences from all the relevant sources.

To describe externals you must become a scientist. To describe experience you must become an artist. The old distinction between people and artists and scientists must vanish. Linguistic education involves teaching our children the two philosophies and the two modes of communication for external and internal. We must teach our children to be free to create new images to express their unique experiences.

The rule of fifty-fifty might well prevail. Every time we teach a child correct usage and semantic convention for static external symbols, we must spend as much time teaching him how to dismantle and reassemble the external dialect to experience and communicate the internal.

The training of artists and creative performers could become a straightforward, mechanical process. When you teach someone how to perform creatively (i.e., associate dead symbols in a new combination) you are expanding his potential for experiencing more widely and richly.

Jonny is assigned the task of writing an essay on "A Day at the County Fair." He writes an essay describing what he observed about the external movements. By counting and accurate observation he tells us what happened on the fairgrounds. He must then be assigned the task of describing "My Experiences at the County Fair." Here he learns to reassemble the jumble of smells, sounds, memories, images in the style of James Joyce or William Burroughs. It is a simple task to teach a child to write experientially like Joyce. It is a simple task to teach him how to recount objectively the movement of people and things.

Every word in the dictionary becomes a counter which can be combined in endlessly new sequences. Every paragraph in the encyclopedia or any other publication becomes a paint pot in which we can dip our experiential brush.

The same is true of the plastic forms of communication.

Photographs, paintings, objects can be reassembled, combined into a new form, not to reproduce the external situation, but to express an experience. The work of Bruce Conner, the eccentric, garbage-can assembler is a good example of how experience can be communicated nonverbally. Conner nails on his painting board a burlesque poster, a worn-out brassiere, a faded hat feather, a tattered perfume ad. He covers the whole with transparent nylon hosiery and he communicates his image of the poignancy of sexual disillusionment in a powerful emotive cry.

This technique could be taught in primary school. In the art class

Jonny is told to reproduce the flowers; then he is asked to cut-up and reassemble in order to communicate his experience of the flower. This binocular approach to education teaches the basic philosophic distinction between "subject matter" and "reality." Between "fact" and "truth."

THE EXPERIENTIAL LANGUAGE MUST GO BEYOND THE EXTERNAL BEHAVIORAL LANGUAGE

The vocabulary of external reference covers a small fragment of experience and the most prosaic and game-limited fragment at that. We play with a very limited set of symbols. Korzybski suggested a method for increasing our semantic breadth and accuracy by using a numerical code; instead of "apple," we have apple[1], apple[2], etc. Combining and reassembling words is another way of multiplying the expressive potential of words, but we are still left with a lexicography which is basically designed for describing movements in space-time.

We need a vocabulary which is designed to reflect experience and which is not limited by external dimensions.

But what frame of reference to use? What general categories?

External referents belong to families; each game has its own cluster of terms. We relate and organize words by the game family.

But one of the characteristics of experience is that it is wildly subjective, it transcends games. In constructing a vocabulary and grammar of internal reactions we do not know where to begin. Do we have a game of non-game?

One starting place is the language of games which claim to be transcendental or experiential. Most religious languages refer to the external, ritualistic aspects of the creed. The holy books and prayers. But mystical religions deal with experience and we can find in the outpourings of the prophets and the mystical scholars a vocabulary for the transcendental.

We can look as well to the languages of cultures which have stressed or even been based on transcendental experiences. Sanskrit, compared to English, contains about forty times the number of references to experiential events.

Most of the non-psychiatric researchers in the psychedelic field have found it useful to borrow the terminology of oriental philosophy. This is no accident. In the west we have no game whose goals, roles, and languages are designed to produce the transcendental experience. In the East the major religious and intellectual games are so oriented.

The philosophies of the East are concerned with the internal. Their ontologies are experiential; so are their epistemologies and logics. This is the despair of the Western scholar who is attuned to an external philosophy. Oriental philosophies are of no help in setting up a contractual definition of fact. They do not lead to new methods for moving things around in space-time or for recording such movements. But they make experiential sense, representing three thousand years of careful exploration of experience and its description and change.

But the solution to the problem of a new experiential language is not going to come from oriental sources. It is impractical to teach our children Sanskrit and pointless, because no matter how superior Sanskrit may be as an experiential tongue, it is still a language of words and words are far removed from the speedy flash and flow of experience.

THE EXPERIMENTAL LANGUAGE WILL BE BASED ON THE TERMS AND ENERGIES OF THE PHYSICAL-BIOLOGICAL SCIENCES

To experience directly we must move out of the static lifeless imprint. Transcend symbols. Experience energy flow directly. Decode energy messages directly.

The future language of experience will bypass symbols and will be based directly on the concepts and technology of the physical and biological sciences.

The energies decoded will not be symbolic but light, sound, cellular movement, sympathetic and parasympathetic nervous system imagery. Direct awareness of energy flow.

Consciousness is a biochemical neurological decoding. This process takes place at many levels of the nervous system.

The units of the language of consciousness are going to be based on the units for measuring and describing these energy transformations.

THE COMMUNICATION OF EXPERIENCE IS ART

Communication about external events is science. All men are scientists (good scientists or bad) when they describe external events.

Communication of inner experience is art. All men must become artists to describe internal events.

In developing systems for communicating experience we are confronted with two problems. There is the problem of sending. How can we select and transmit those energy patterns which "turn on" the receiver—i.e., directly stimulate the nervous system of the receiver bypassing his symbol system?

Then there is the problem of the receiver. Most of us are terrified by the energy process. The consensual symbolic hallucination must be maintained constantly. Any rent in the verbal structure, the protective symbol system, threatens the perpetuation of the structural delusion.

We all resent confrontation with the energy process. We resist being turned on. We ostracize those who try to turn us on—by social isolation, censorship, and legal restriction.

While the illustrator is welcomed, the artist—he who turns you on—is anathematized.

The aim of the creative artist is the same as that of the scientist. The recording of the energy dance and the cycle of energy transformations. The scientist observes and records the external. The artist experiences and records the experienced. The engineer manipulates the external. The illustrator portrays the external. Neither are artists.

THREE ARTISTIC
LANGUAGE SYSTEMS

Reproductive art focuses only on the external, the consensual, static symbolical structure. Portrays the game. Great illustrators succeed in representing, communicating the revealing moment of game culmination.

Visionary art (or neo-symbolic art) attempts to translate the energy dance in terms of unique combinations of static symbols. Hieronymus Bosch. Lenora Carrington. The Surrealists. Goya. John Cage. Gaudi.

Transcendental art (Tranart) avoids any connection with symbol or external form and directly represents the energy dance. Closest to the life process. Abstract art is a step in this direction. This attempt to represent and communicate energy processes is called *Tranart*.

Physics, biology, biochemistry, genetics and Tranart—all express the same message: *Beyond the imprint all is one dance of electrical energy; one flow of cellular process.* The aims of science and of art are the same. To record the process.

We have been taught to think and perceive in terms of macroscopic static physics. Symbolic game structures.

Immersed in a process which moves at the speed of light, we narrow our awareness to a fantasy world of symbol solids. All matter is energy—but we are trained to forget this. The process which imposes simple, static, printed circuits on the nervous system is called imprinting. Education, acculturation builds up a network of associations around the imprint.

But that's not how it really is. Everything is whirling change. Even the self. *You.* You are a dramatically changing process. Look at your baby pictures. Look in the mirror. Imagine a mile-high camera which takes a picture of your city every six months. Run six hundred frames through your projector. Moving pictures.

REPRESENTATION OF THE ENERGY PROCESS

Representative Art plays the delusionary game. Visionary art invents its own categories. Tranart attempts to get back to the cortical flash. Abstract painting, for example, attempts to get back to the retina, freezing the naked, patternless mosaic. The Islamic artist is forbidden to reproduce forms. Glance down at your Persian rug. You are looking at static *Tranart*. A microbiological representation. It's an unstained experiential slide of retinal sensation.

Have you even seen a cross-section of retinal tissue? A many-layered technicolor swamp of rods and cones, interlaced with capillaries dancing the electrical tempo. No structured images there. Imagine your Persian rug undulating, each unit in motion, a swirling rock-and-roll of color. That's what the original rug designers had in mind. The rug is not to walk on. It tells the story of life. Contains the message, the reminder.

Reproductive art reminds only that man can share static symbols.

THE CREATIVE EXPERIENCE

There is the creative performance and the creative experience. Creative performance is the new combination of communicative symbols, the breaking through expressive set. Creative experience is awareness of the infinitely changing electrical network outside and apart from the imprinted categories. The creative experience is the passive registering of the process, the breaking through the perceptual set.

The rational mind "damages" the brain. The cortex is physiologically restricted by narrow learned printed circuits. Consciousness-expanding drugs suspend, loosen, the patterned flow of the expected and guarantee the creative experience.

Illustrative painting and photography freeze the symbolic. Abstract painting and microscopic photographs freeze the process. Moving pictures help keep the hallucinatory process going. Moving pictures duplicate the imprinted "reality" delusion.

The communication of experience is art. In the last few years we have witnessed the emergence of psychedelic art, Transart. Attempts to communicate non-symbolically, to cut through the hallucinations to the direct sensation. To produce the direct sensation of the flowing process. Molecular sensations. A reproduction of the microscopic event.

Psychedelic drugs provide the creative experience—suspend the verbal governors so that the neurological motor operates at full blast. To communicate a psychedelic experience, you require psychedelic art, Tranart, an artform which tries to keep up with the speed and breadth of the direct sensation. After psychedelic training, we accustom ourselves to the pace of the nervous system. We experience a flood of new words.

THE TECHNICAL PROBLEM

How can we express it? How can we communicate the flowing process? Tranart requires new technical means of communication. These will be based on the machines now used by scientists to record (1) the life process, (2) the energy dance. Instead of the brush and the Leica, psychedelic artists use the electromicroscopic camera, random analogue projectors, multiple films and tapes, polarized light, chemically treated slides, the oscilloscope, the telescopic camera, and scientific instruments not yet dreamed of.

Visual technique involves three media—the surface; the paint (or covering substance); the instruments to shape the design (pallet knife, brush). Tranart employs the same three media—(1) the screen which can vary in shape and texture; (2) the energy source, always changing these energy patterns are called Direct Process Images (DPI's); (3) symbolic representations, which are called Learned Form Images (LFI's) and which are used for visionary communication.

Direct Process Images (DPI's) are externalized representations of the flow of direct sensation—experience. They must be flowing, unstructured, unidentifiable. They are communications of the experience of direct energy.

Learned Form Images (LFI's) are representations of perceptual forms which are learned and artifactual. Objects, things, organisms, events, bodies, chairs, flowers.

Both *DPI's* and *LFI's* may be auditory or visual, as in terms of other uses. DPI's and LFI's may be internal or external, depending on whether they represent experiences bubbling out of the lower nervous system or coming from without.

Thus, visual internal DPI's are moving pictures of microscopic magnifications of retinal processes. Cellular or subcellular events (organic DPI's). Visual external DPI's are moving pictures of energy processes at the atomic or subatomic level. Waves, interacting planes of light. Images of inorganic processes photographed by observation instruments. Continually moving, flowing, dancing.

There are also auditory DPI's. Recordings of sounds heard from the inside of the body (internal). Recordings of sounds registered in the brain without cognitive patternings, unstructured natural noises, white noise (external).

Visual LFI's are representations of "things" if they are consensual, of "hallucinations" if they are idiosyncratic. Moving pictures of the traditional variety are visual LFI's. Filmed sequences of the traditional variety are visual LFI's. Filmed sequences of game life. Symphonies are auditory LFI's, game sequences for the trained ear. Auditory internal LFI's are representations of experiences generally considered psychotic: hearing "voices" or "meaningful" sounds inside your head.

DEFINITION OF THE THREE
KINDS OF ART

Thus, we have three kinds of art, communicating three types of experiences. 1. Art which uses "reality-oriented" symbol is story-telling art, reproductive, realistic art. 2. Creative performers combine old images into new patterns, blend incongruous sequences. Montage, assemblage. The movie "cut-up" method used by Bruce Conner in which he recombines dozens of old newsreels, Salvador Dali's surrealistic combinations of organic and inorganic forms, John Cage's composition by chance combinations of sounds and noises.

Art which records the mixture and interweaving of direct process with learned game form—we call *visionary tranart.* Van Gogh's skies contain perhaps stars or perhaps just inconceivable energy vortices. Tchelitchew's "Hide and Seek" has mysterious faces moving almost magically out of patterns of capillary streams and organic networks. The Sufi painters of visionary miniatures had rocks in the backgrounds of their pictures which when you look closely seem to have mysterious faces hidden. Bruce Conner's "Cosmic Ray" movie has pulsing rhythm of abstract forms out of which emerge now a naked woman, now marching soldiers, now parachutes, now Mickey Mouse. Visionary Tranart is LFI's imposed on or woven into DPI's. Game concepts superimposed on the energy process.

3. Art which attempts to record the experience of pure symbol-free energy we call Tranart. Jackson Pollock's paintings are indistinguishable from retinal cross-sections. Persian rugs are only slightly more symmetrical. To represent visual internal DPI's we have used recurrent film loops of microbiological processes. When these are projected they uncannily reproduce the psychedelic vision. They break through learned sets and structures. Cells dance through technicolor swamps. Ciliated protoplasm flails down undulating channels. Membrane spheres bounce across vague tissue landscapes. Flowing, flowing, flowing without cease. "What is it?" That's the point of course. You can't label the microscopic process. It's no thing you recognize. It's the cellular life process. It never stops. The film keeps moving. Life.

THE DPI LIBRARY

Tranart requires a wide variety of paint-color or sound-notes, i.e., a wide variety of DPI's. A library of visual DPI's is a classified collection of slides and films of energy and microbiological life processes. Just as the painter knows the range of available pigments, so does the Tranartist know the range of available DPI's—of images representing the flow of direct, formless sensations. He cannot express them in words. Our greatest artists have attempted to reproduce these basic energy flashes in their music or painting. The library of DPI films provides the nucleus of a transcendental language. After your vision, after your formless insight, you select from the DPI film catalogue the closest representation. Of course, no DPI comes close to the direct sensation, but it comes closer than words. The very existence of a DPI lexicon, a classification of images, makes possible expansion and increased specification. You find in the DPI library the closest representation, and then you know where to look for a more exact representation. You go to a microbiologist or a physics technician and he knows where to film your vision or how to prepare your slides. Microbiological film technicians and physics-lab technicians thus become the philologists of the new language of DPI's.

THE LFI LIBRARY

We have discussed two of the three aspects of art—i.e., a communication of experience: (1) the screen, (2) the plastic media, DPI's. We shall now consider (3) symbols. The structure in easel painting is provided by the brush or palette knife. The structure in neo-symbolic or visionary Tranart is provided by LFI's—films or tape-recordings of structured events, objects, people.

Just as we assemble a classified library of DPI's, so do we collect a classified library of LFI's—visual, auditory, tactual. Researchers at the Castalia Foundation have developed a code system for every cultural, personal, biological, and chemical event. When a structured (consensual hallucination) sequence is needed to add form to a Tranart communication, a filmstrip is located in the LFI library, or, if not in the library, it is filmed.

An ever-increasing library of catalogued DPI's and LFI's is thus assembled. It is even possible to play an experiential Hessean bead game with infinite combinations of images. More important, it is possible to express any experience—either of a non-cultural energy or life process or a visionary creation.

A subject wishes to record a visionary experience—a mixture of primary process and cultural sequence. This requires visionary Tranart—LFI's imposed on or woven into DPI's.

There comes a vision of undulating streams of bouncing spheres (not recognized as blood cells) which convert (as an LFI is imposed on the DPI, or as a hallucination is imposed on the primary processes) into uncoiling serpent-flow which changes to an insidious network of Chinese Communist soldiers which shifts into the pink florid, pulsating face of a leering oriental dictator which flickers into the portrait of one's feared stepmother, etc., etc. That's the vision sequence.

To express this the subject sorts through the DPI library until he locates a blood-circulation DPI. This stored film loop is set running on one projector. Then the subject finds an LFI sequence of uncoiling serpents. They are green, so he imposes a red filter. The DPI projector starts running; after a minute the red filter serpent LFI projector is snapped on—out of focus. Gradually, the LFI strip is brought into focus and the vision slowly shifts from pure DPI to DPI-LFI vision. The LFI film-strip is then spliced to newsreel film of marching Chinese columns and then the picture of Chou En Lai. A still photo of the stepmother is inserted in a slide projector with a veined red filter completely out of focus and slowly focused at the appropriate second.

The Tranartist then experiments with his material until he gets the flowing sequence he wants, LFI's fading in and out of focus—with the pulsing DPI stream always flowing, flowing in the background. He speeds up the sequence many times, then he adds sound. The pump, pump, pump of a heartbeat fades into the thud, thud of marching feet, to the shouted commands in Chinese, to stepmother's voice screaming. "You bad boy, you'll never amount to anything." The sound sequence is adjusted to the visual barrage and speeded up. That's one minute or thirty seconds of the Tranart representation of a psychedelic vision.

TRANART AS A NEW LANGUAGE

Perceived forms swim into focus out of swirling, unformed wave process. That's the fact of perception. Visionary Tranart makes it possible to duplicate this as an expressed communication. In principle, there is no limit to the range of experience and to the range of DPI-LFI communication. A new language is available. Since our language determines how we experience, the development of a new and vastly expanded range of experience becomes available.

Children who are educated in terms of a DPI-LFI language would possess a solid, realistic epistemology and a flexible conceptual structure which would begin to tap the potentialities of the cortical computer.

Tranart is based on the raw records of science and the film-taped portraits of the tribal sequence. The records of science become part of the basic language of experience.

Language approaches the speed and extension of the neural network.

An increasing percentage of the neural network becomes available to consciousness and to communication and to conceptualization.

Art becomes accurate communication of experiences.

Consciousness is expanded.

SUMMARY

1. Communication is energy sent or received by structure. Structure (or mass) is energy temporarily bound.
2. Consciousness is the decoding of energy patterns.
3. An infinite number of languages exist in nature and an enormous number of linguistic systems operate within the body.
4. Consciousness, i.e., decoding of energy in the living form is chemical.
5. The language system used by fowls and mammals to communicate with the outside world is based on imprinting. Imprinting is the sudden, accidental, chemical freezing of the nervous system early in

the life of the organism. A hooking of consciousness to specific cues for approach and avoidance.

6. The static symbolic limits of imprinted consciousness can be suspended by the use of chemicals—called psychedelic drugs.

7. New imprints are formed during a psychedelic drug session.

8. Some philosophic and linguistic differences between internal (experiential) and external (behavioral) were outlined.

9. The communication of experience was defined as art. The aim of art is to "turn on" the receiver—to induce in the receiver the experience of the sender.

10. Three methods of communicating experience, which is to say three types of "art," were described:

    a. Reproductive art uses external symbols and implies that consciousness is completely tied to externals.

    b. Visionary art or neo-symbolic art arranges external symbols in novel combinations.

    c. Tranart bypasses symbols entirely and uses direct energy messages to induce the experience in the receiver.

REFERENCES

1. H. Woltereck, *What Science Knows About Life* (New York: Association Press, 1963).

2. W. Sluckin, *Imprinting and Early Learning* (Chicago: Aldine, 1965).

3. Aldous Huxley, *The Doors of Perception* (New York: Harper, 1954): pp. 67–68.

12

Leary and the Psychedelic "Nuclear Bomb"

Programmed Communication during Experiences with DMT

Timothy Leary

Although this article was published in the *Psychedelic Review* in 1966, it was based on research that was conducted in the early 1960s while Leary was at Harvard. He had become curious about dimethyltryptamine (DMT) and its allegedly intense and shattering effects on sober consciousness. Some researchers claimed DMT was much stronger than LSD and psilocybin. For this reason, DMT was labeled "the nuclear bomb of the psychedelic family." Leary was also curious about DMT's short duration (twenty to thirty minutes). A DMT session was humorously described as a "businessman's lunch": the user could take DMT at lunch and then return to work for the rest of the afternoon.

Leary's first experience with DMT came in the fall of 1962. While attending a conference sponsored by the Southern California Society of Clinical Psychologists, Leary met up with a psychiatrist who was conducting research on DMT. The unnamed psychiatrist told Leary that DMT was an intensely powerful drug that mostly produced negative reactions (only four percent of his subjects reported a positive experience). However, because Leary was a staunch believer in set and setting theory, he was eager to disprove the researcher's hypothesis. Thus, Leary volunteered to test the drug himself, and a session was quickly arranged for the next day.

Leary's initial experience with the drug produced an enthusiastic response. Leary felt the drug had enormous potential: "I am left with the conviction that DMT offers great promise as a transcendental trigger. The brevity of the reaction has many advantages—it provides a security in the knowledge that it will be over in a half hour and should make possible precise explorations of specific transcendental areas."

When Leary returned to Harvard, he ordered samples of the drug from a pharmaceutical company—probably Sandoz—and began running DMT sessions with "experienced researchers" in Cambridge. Leary ran numerous sessions during 1962 and the spring of 1963. His results were dramatically different from the DMT research that was conducted by his colleague in California: "the percentage of successful, ecstatic sessions ran high—over ninety per cent. The set and setting hypothesis clearly held for DMT in regard to positive experiences."

"Programmed Communication during Experiences with DMT" is one of Leary's most experimental pieces of writing. The article contains two different reactions to the drugs and is written in a highly unconventional prose style. The second trip becomes increasingly unintelligible. In the second session, Leary's prose style seems to mimic the shattering effects of the drug: he gradually abandons grammar and syntax and proceeds to communicate in fragmentary phrases and non-sequiturs (. . . the void-white-light-contentless, meta-life-inorganic ecstasy . . . the kundalinie-lifeforce-biological-squirming-moist-sexual organic ecstasy . . . the singing genetic code-blueprint-temporary-structuring-of-form ecstasy and the . . .")

During the second report, the most striking technique is Leary's gratuitous use of the ellipsis. As the effects of the drug take hold, Leary's prose becomes untethered from rational discourse and the ellipsis seems to replace the period. In other places, Leary indulges in neologisms as he frantically hits the keys of the "experiential typewriter": "EXTERNAL PROCESS IMAGES . . . yes . . . hit the key timble back to Persopolic pulse." Leary, an admirer of *Finnegan's Wake*, was eager to emulate Joyce's penchant for wordplay and elastic prose. Leary's DMT narrative is also influenced by the futuristic imagery of science fiction novels—the DMT trip is analogous to a trip to outer space. As Leary drifts in mental outer space, the sitter (Ralph Metzner) constantly attempts to bring him back to earth: "TIM, WHERE ARE YOU NOW?" In certain moments, the "experimental typewriter" acts as an anchoring device and Leary's only connection to rational intelligibility.

As the effects of the drug subside, conventional syntax and punctuation reappear again. Leary opts to use metaphors from science fiction to convey his altered state of consciousness: "The session was a continual, serial 'comedown'. I repeatedly had to stop the flow in order to respond. My cortex was receiving hundreds of thousands of impulses a second; but in order to respond to ground control's questions I had to grind the ship to a slow stall to say, at the moment, 'I am here.'" Leary's article concludes not with his own subjective response, but with the statistics gathered from the "experimental typewriter." At times, "Programmed Communication . . . " seems to demonstrate a preference for the experiential typewriter and its ability to transcend the one-dimensional aspects of conventional written expression. The experiential typewriter is Leary's attempt at describing multiple modes of consciousness.

Taken as a whole, "Programmed Communication . . ." is a meditation on the inadequacy of human language in relation to the DMT experience. Leary desperately gropes for new forms and new modes of discourse to convey the ineffable.

JAMES PENNER

PROGRAMMED COMMUNICATION DURING EXPERIENCES WITH DMT (DIMETHYLTRYPTAMINE)

From *Psychedelic Review* 8 (1966): 83–95.

Timothy Leary

During the first two years of the Harvard Psychedelic Research Project rumors circulated about a "powerful" psychedelic agent called dimethyltryptamine: DMT. The effect of this substance was supposed to last for less than an hour and to produce shattering, terrorizing effects. It was alleged to be the nuclear bomb of the psychedelic family.

The Hungarian pharmacologist, Stephen Szara, first reported in 1957 that N,N-Dimethyltryptamine (DMT) and N,N-Diethyltryptamine (DET) produced effects in man similar to LSD and mescaline. The only difference was in duration: whereas LSD and mescaline typically last 8 to 10 hours, DMT lasted from 40 minutes to 1 hour and DET from 2 to 3 hours. The higher homologues, dipropyltryptamine and dibutyltryptamine, were also said to be active but less potent. The parent substance, tryptamine, by itself has no effect. Chemically, DMT is closely related to psilocybin and psilocin (4-hydroxy-N-dimethyltryptamine), as well as to bufotenine (5-hydroxy-N-dimethyltryptamine). The mechanism of action of DMT and related compounds is still a scientific mystery. Like LSD and psilocybin, DMT has the property of increasing the metabolic turnover of serotonin in the body. An enzyme capable of converting naturally occurring tryptamine to DMT has recently been found in some mammalian tissue; this suggests that mechanisms may exist whereby the body converts normally occurring substances to psychedelic compounds.[1, 2, 3, 4, 5]

DMT has been identified as one of the ingredients in the seeds of *Mimosa hostilis,* from which the Pancaru Indians of Pernambuco, Brazil, prepare an hallucinogenic beverage they call *vinho de Jurumena*. It is also, along with bufotenine, one of the ingredients in the seeds of *Piptadenia peregrina,* from which the Indians of the Orinoco Basin and of Trinidad prepare an hallucinogenic snuff they call *yopo*.[6]

William Burroughs had tried it in London and reported it in the most negative terms. Burroughs was working at that time on a theory of neurological geography—certain cortical areas were heavenly, other areas were diabolical. Like explorers moving into a new continent, it was important to map out the friendly areas and the hostile. In Burroughs' pharmacological cartography, DMT propelled the voyager into strange and decidedly unfriendly territory.

Burroughs told a gripping tale about a psychiatrist in London who had taken DMT with a friend. After a few minutes the frightened friend began requesting help. The psychiatrist, himself being spun through a universe of shuttling, vibratory pigments, reached for his hypodermic needle (which had been fragmented into a shimmering assemblage of wave mosaics) and bent over to administer an antidote. Much to his dismay his friend, twisting in panic, was suddenly transformed into a writhing, wiggling reptile, jewel-encrusted and sparkling. The doctor's dilemma: where to make an intravenous injection in a squirming, oriental martian snake? . . .

Alan Watts had a DMT story to tell: He took the drug as part of a California research [project] and had planned to demonstrate that he could maintain rational control and verbal fluency during the experience. The closest equivalent might be to attempt a moment-to-moment description of one's reactions while being fired out the muzzle of an atomic cannon with neon-byzantine barreling. Dr. Watts gave an awefull description of perceptual fusion.

In the fall of 1962, while giving a three-day series of lectures to the

Southern California Society of Clinical Psychologists, I fell into discussion with a psychiatrist who was collecting data on DMT. He had given the drug to over a hundred subjects and only four had reported pleasant experiences. This was a challenge to the set-setting hypothesis. According to our evidence, and in line with our theory, we had found little differentiation among psychedelic drugs. We were skeptically convinced that the elaborate clinical differences allegedly found in reactions to different drugs were psychedelic folk tales. We were sticking to our null hypothesis that the drugs had no specific effect on consciousness but that expectation, preparation, emotional climate, and the contract with the drug-giver accounted for all differences in reaction.

We were eager to see if the fabled "terror-drug," DMT, would fit the set-setting theory.

A session was arranged. I came to the home of the researcher, accompanied by a psychologist, a Vedanta monk and two female friends. After a lengthy and friendly discussion with the physician, the psychologist lay down on a couch. His friend's head rested on his chest. I sat on the edge of the couch, smiling in reassuring expectation. Sixty mg. of DMT were administered intramuscularly.

Within two minutes the psychologist's face was glowing with serene joy. For the next twenty-five minutes he gasped and murmured in pleasure, keeping up an amused and ecstatic account of his visions.

The faces in the room had become billion-faceted mosaics of rich and vibrant hues. The facial characteristics of each of the observers, surrounding the bed, were the keys to their genetic heritage. Dr. X (the psychiatrist) was a bronzed American Indian with full ceremonial paint; the Hindu monk was a deep soulful middle-easterner with eyes which were at once reflecting animal cunning and the sadness of centuries; Leary was a roguish Irishman, a sea captain with weathered skin and creases at the corners of eyes which had looked long and hard into the unsee-able, an adventurous skipper of a three-masted schooner eager to chart new waters, to explore the continent just beyond, exuding a confidence that comes from a humorous cosmic awareness of his predicament—genetic and immediate. And next to me, or rather on me, or rather in me, or rather more of me—Billy. Her body was vibrating in such harmony with mine that each ripple of muscle, the very coursing of blood through her veins was a matter of absolute intimacy . . . body messages of a subtlety and tenderness both exotically strange and deliciously familiar. Deep within, a point of heat in my groin slowly but powerfully and inevitably radiated throughout my body until every cell became a sun emanating its own life-giving fire. My body was an energy field, a set of vibrations with each cell pulsing in phase with every other. And Billy, whose cells now danced the same tune, was no longer a discrete entity but a resonating part of the single set of vibrations. The energy was love.

Exactly twenty-five minutes after administration, the psychologist smiled, sighed, sat up swinging his legs over the side of the couch and said, "It lasted for a million years and for a split-second. But it's over and now it's your turn."

With this reassuring precedent, I took up position on the couch. Margaret sat on the floor holding my hand. The psychologist sat at the foot of the couch, radiating benevolence. The drug was administered.

THE FIRST DMT EXPERIENCE

"My experience with DMT occurred in the most favorable setting. We had just witnessed the ecstatic experience of my colleague and the radiance of his reaction provided a secure and optimistic background. My expectations were extremely positive.

"Five minutes after i.m. injection, lying comfortably on the bed, I felt typical psychedelic onset symptoms—a pleasant somatic looseness, a sensitive tuning-in to physical sensations.

"Eyes closed . . . typical LSD visions, the exquisite beauty of retinal and physical machinery, transcendence of mental activity, serene detachment. Comforting awareness of Margaret's hand and the presence of friends.

"Suddenly I opened my eyes and sat up . . . the room was celestial, glowing with radiant illumination . . . light, light, light . . . the people present were transfigured . . . godlike creatures . . . we were all united as one organism. Beneath the radiant surface I could see the delicate, wondrous body machinery of each person, the network of muscle and vein and bone—exquisitely beautiful and all joined, all part of the same process.

"Our group was sharing a paradisial experience—each one in turn was to be given the key to eternity—now it was my turn, I was experiencing this ecstasy for the group. Later the others would voyage. We were members of a transcendent collectivity.

"Dr. X. coached me tenderly . . . handed me a mirror where I saw my face a stained-glass portrait.

"Margaret's face was that of all women—wise, beautiful, eternal. Her eyes were all female eyes. She murmured exactly the right message. 'It can always be this way.'

"The incredible complex—unity of the evolutionary process—staggering, endless in its variety—why? Where is it going? etc., etc. The old questions and then the laughter of amused, ecstatic acceptance. Too much! Too great! Never mind! It can't be figured out. Love it in gratitude and accept! I would lean forward to search for meaning in Margaret's china-flecked face and fall back on the pillow in reverent, awed laughter.

"Gradually, the brilliant illumination faded back to the three-d[imensional] world and I sat up. Reborn. Renewed. Radiant with affection and reverence.

"This experience took me to the highest point of LSD illumination—a jewel-like satori. It was less internal and more visual and social than my usual LSD experiences. There was never a second of fear or negative emotion. Some moments of benign paranoia—agent of the divine group, etc.

"I am left with the conviction that DMT offers great promise as a transcendental trigger. The brevity of the reaction has many advantages—it provides a security in the knowledge that it will be over in a half hour and should make possible precise explorations of specific transcendental areas."

THE SET AND SETTING FOR THE PROGRAMMED EXPERIENCE

Immediately after my first DMT voyage the drug was administered to the Hindu monk. This dedicated man had spent fourteen years in meditation and renunciation. He was a *sannyasin,* entitled to wear the sacred saffron robe. He has participated in several psychedelic drug sessions with extremely positive results and was convinced that the biochemical road to *samadhi* was not only valid but perhaps the most natural method for people living in a technological civilization.

His reaction to DMT was, however, confusing and unpleasant. Catapulted into a sudden ego-loss, he struggled to rationalize his experience in terms of classic Hindu techniques. He kept looking up at the group in puzzled helplessness. Promptly at twenty-five minutes he sat up, laughed, and said, "What a trip that was. I really got trapped in karmic hallucinations!"

The lesson was clear. DMT, like the other psychedelic keys, could open an infinity of possibilities. Set, setting, suggestibility, temperamental background were always there as filters through which the ecstatic experience could be distorted.

On return to Cambridge, arrangements were made with a drug company and with our medical consultant to run a systematic research on the new substance. During the subsequent months we ran over one hundred sessions—at first training exercises for experienced researchers and then later trials with subjects completely inexperienced in psychedelic matters.

The percentage of successful, ecstatic sessions ran high—over ninety percent. The set-setting hypothesis clearly held for DMT in regard to positive experiences. But there were certain definite characteristics of the DMT experience which were markedly different from the standard psychedelics—LSD, psilocybin, mescaline. First of all, the duration. The eight-hour LSD transformation was reduced to around thirty minutes. The intensity was greater, as well. This is to say, the shattering of learned form perception, the collapse of learned structure was much more pronounced. "Eyes closed" produced a soft, silent, lightning fast, whirling dance of incredible cellular forms—acre upon acre, mile upon mile of softly-spinning organic forms. A swirling, tumbling, soft rocket-ride through the factory of tissue. The variety and irreality of the precise, exquisite, feathery clockwork organic machinery. Many LSD subjects report endless odysseys through the network of circulatory tunnels. Not with DMT, but rather a sub-cellular cloud-ride into a world of ordered, moving beauty which defies external metaphor.

"Eyes open" produced a similar collapse of learned structure—but this time of external objects. Faces and things no longer had form but were seen as a shimmering play of vibrations (which is what they are). Perception of solid structures was seen to be a function of visual nets, mosaics, cobwebs of light-energy.

The transcendence of ego-space-time was most often noticed. Subjects frequently complained that they became so lost in the lovely flow of timeless existences that the experience ended too soon and was so smooth that landmarks were lacking to make memory very detailed. The usual milestones for perception and memory were lacking! There could be no memory of the sequence of visions because there was no time—and no memory of structure because space was converted into flowing process.

To deal with this problem we instituted programmed sessions. The subject would be asked every two minutes to respond, or he would be presented with an agreed-upon stimulus every two minutes. The landmarks would, in this way, be provided by the experimenter—the temporal sequence could be broken up into stages and the flow of visions would be divided into topics.

As an example of a programmed session using DMT, let us consider the following report: The plan for this session involved the experiential typewriter. This device, which is described in a previous article[7] is designed to allow non-verbal communication during psychedelic sessions. There are two keyboards with ten buttons for each hand. The twenty keys are connected to a twenty-pen polygraph which registers an ink mark on a flowing roll of paper each time a key is struck.

The subject must learn the codes for the range of experience before the session and is trained to respond automatically, indicating the area of his consciousness.

In this study it was agreed that I would be questioned every two minutes, to indicate the content of my awareness.

The session took place in a special session room, eight-by-twenty, which was completely covered, ceiling, walls and floor, by warm, colorful India prints. The session followed the "alternating guide" model: another researcher, a psychopharmacologist, was to act as interrogator for my session. The pharmacologist was then to repeat the session with Leary as interrogator.

At 8:10 p.m. I received 60 mgs. of DMT.

THE SECOND DMT EXPERIENCE

Lay back on mattress, arranging cushions . . . relaxed and anticipatory . . . somewhat amused by our attempt to impose time-content mileposts on the flow of process . . . soft humming noise . . . eyes closed . . . suddenly, as if someone touched a button, the static darkness of retina is illuminated . . . enormous toy-jewel-clock factory, Santa Claus workshop . . . not impersonal or engineered, but jolly, comic, light-hearted. The evolutionary dance, humming with energy, billions of varigated forms spinning, clicking through their appointed rounds in the smooth ballet . . .

MINUTE 2. TIM: WHERE ARE YOU NOW? Ralph's voice, stately, kind . . . what? where? You? . . . open eyes . . . there squatting next to me are two magnificent insects . . . skin burnished, glowing metallic, with hammered jewels inlaid . . . richly costumed, they looked at me sweetly . . . dear, radiant Venutian crickets . . . one has a pad in his lap and is holding out a gem-encrusted box with undulating trapezoidal glowing sections . . . questioning look . . . incredible . . . and next to him Mrs. Diamond Cricket softly slides into a lattice-work of vibrations . . . Dr. Ruby-emerald Cricket smiles . . . TIM WHERE ARE YOU NOW . . . moves box towards me . . . oh yes . . . try to tell them . . . where . . .

At two minutes the subject was smiling with eyes closed. When asked to report he opened his eyes, looked at the observers curiously, smiled. When the orientation question was repeated he chuckled, moved his finger searchingly over the typewriter and (with a look of amused tolerance) stabbed at the "cognitive activity" key. He then fell back with a sigh and closed his eyes.

Use mind . . . explain . . . look down at undulating boxes . . . struggle to focus . . . use mind . . . yes COGNITIVE . . . there . . .

Eyes close . . . back to dancing workshop . . . joy . . . incredible beauty . . . the wonder, wonder, wonder . . . thanks . . . thanks for the chance to see the dance . . . all hooked together . . . everything fits into the moist, pulsating pattern . . . a huge grey-white mountain cliff, moving, pocked by little caves and in each cave a band of radar-antennae, elf-like insects merrily working away, each cave the same, the grey-white wall endlessly parading by . . . infinity of life forms . . . merry erotic energy nets . . .

MINUTE 4. TIM, WHERE ARE YOU NOW? Spinning out in the tapestry of space comes the voice from down below . . . : dear kindly earth-voice . . . earth-station calling . . . where are you? . . . what a joke . . . how to answer . . . I am in the bubbling beaker of the cosmic alchemist . . . no, now softly-falling star dust exploding in the branches of the stellar ivory birch tree . . . what? . . . open eyes . . . oh dear lapidary insect friends . . . Ralph and Susan beautiful orange lobsters watching me gently . . . faces shattered into stained-glass mosaic . . . Dr. Tiffany Lobster holds out the casket of trapezoidal sections . . . look at glowing key . . . where is my Venutian ecstasy key? where is key for the stellar explosion of the year 3,000? . . . EXTERNAL PROCESS IMAGES . . . yes . . . hit the key . . . timble back to Persepolic pulse . . .

At four minutes the subject was still smiling with eyes closed. When asked to report, he opened his eyes and laughed. He looked at the observers with twinkling eyes, studied the keyboard of the experiential typewriter and pressed the EXTERNAL PROCESS IMAGE key. He then fell back and closed his eyes.

How nice . . . they are down there . . . waiting . . . no words up here to describe . . . they have words down there . . . see rolling waves of colored forms whirling up, bouncing jolly . . . where do they come from . . . who is architect . . . merciless . . . each undulating dancing factory devouring other . . . devouring me . . . pitless pattern . . . what to do . . . terror . . . ah let it come . . . eat me . . . whirl me up in the ocean of snowflake mouths . . . all right . . . how it all fits together . . . auto-pilot . . . it's all worked out . . . it's all on auto-pilot . . . suddenly my body snaps and begins to disintegrate . . . flow out into the river of energy . . . good-bye . . . gone . . . I that was is now absorbed in electron flash . . . beamed across star space in orgasm pulses of particle motion . . . release . . . flashing light, light, light . . .

MINUTE 6. TIM, WHERE ARE YOU NOW? Earth voice calling . . . you there, meson hurdling in nuclear orbit . . . incorporate . . . trap the streaking energy particle . . . slow down . . . freeze into body structure . . . return . . . with flick of open eye the nuclear dance suddenly skids into static form . . . see two clusters of electrons shimmering . . . the Ralph galaxy calling . . . the Mrs Ralph galaxy smiling . . . the energy dance caught momentarily in friendly robot form . . . hello . . . next to them a candle flame . . . center of million-armed web of light beams . . . the room is caught in a lattice of light-energy . . . shimmering . . . all vision is light . . . there is nothing to see but light waves . . . photons reflected from Ralph's quizzical smile . . . awaits the answer . . . photons bouncing off the quivering keys of the typewriter . . . how easy to beam a radio message down . . . finger taps EXTERNAL PROCESS IMAGES . . .

At six minutes the subject had just finished frowning in what seemed like a passing fear or problem. When contacted to report, he glanced around the room and without hesitation pressed the EXTERNAL PROCESS KEY. He then closed his eyes.

Eyes closed but after-image of candle flame remains . . . eyeballs trapped in orbit around internal light center . . . celestial radiance from the light center . . . light of sun . . . all light is sun . . . light is life . . . live, lux, luce, life . . . all is a dance of light-life . . . all life is the wire . . . carrying light . . . all light is the frail filament of the light . . . solar silent sound . . . beamed out from sun-flare . . . light-life . . .

MINUTE 8. TIM, WHERE ARE YOU NOW? In the heart of the sun's hydrogen explosion . . . our globe is light's globe . . . open eyes drape curtain over sun flare . . . open eyes bring blindness . . . shut off internal radiance . . . see chiaroscuro God holding shadow box . . . where is life? . . . press WHITE LIGHT KEY . . .

At eight minutes the subject, who had been lying motionless against the cushions, opened his eyes. His expression was dazed, surprised. Without expression he pressed key for WHITE LIGHT.

Keep eyes open . . . fixed . . . caught . . . hypnotized . . . whole room, flowered walls, cushions, candle, human forms all vibrating . . . all waves having no form . . . terrible stillness . . . just silent energy flow . . . if you move you will shatter the pattern . . . all remembered forms, meanings, identities meaningless . . . gone . . . all is a pitiless emanation of physical waves . . . phenomena are television impulses crackling across an interstellar program . . . our sun is one point on an astrophysical television screen . . . our galaxy is a tiny cluster of points on one corner of the TV screen . . . each time a supernova explodes it is simply that point on the screen changing . . . the ten billion year cycle of our universe is a millisecond flash of light on the cosmic screen which flows endlessly and swiftly with images . . . sitting motionless . . . not wishing to move, to impose motion on the pattern . . . motionless in speed-of-light motion . . .

MINUTE 10. TIM, WHERE ARE YOU NOW? Ground-tower beaming up navigational query . . . flood of amazed love that we *can* contact each other . . . we do remain in contact . . . where was that cluster then . . . hallucinating . . . science-fiction metaphors . . . where is key . . . there . . . EXTERNAL HALLUCINATIONS . . .

> From eight to ten minutes the subject sat motionless, eyes open in a trance-like state. There was no attempt to communicate. When contacted he moved slowly but surely and pressed the EXTERNAL HALLUCINATION KEY.

Quotes from the Research Questionnaire filled out after the session: loss of space-time . . . merging with energy flux . . . seeing all life forms as physical waves . . . loss of body . . . existence as energy . . . awareness that our bodies are momentary clusters of energy and that we are capable of tuning in on patterns of non-organic patterns . . . certainly that life processes are on "auto-pilot" . . . there is nothing to fear or worry about . . . a feeling of freedom to go back and "freeze" the energy process momentarily in the old ego-robot . . . a reminder of the infinite unfolding complexity and endlessness of the life process . . . sudden understanding of the meaning of terms from Indian philosophy such as "maya," "maha-maya," "lila" . . . insight into the nature and varieties of transcendent states . . . the void-white-light-contentless, meta-life-inorganic ecstasy . . . the Kundalini-life-force-biological-squirming-moist-sexual organic ecstasy . . . the singing-genetic-code-blueprint-temporary-structuring-of-form ecstasy and the . . .

MINUTE 12. TIM, WHERE ARE YOU NOW? Open eyes . . . laugh . . . caught by vigilant ground-tower while orbiting around earthly-mind-figure-it-out area . . . where is key for thinking earth-word thoughts . . . hallucinations . . . no, the thinking game . . . press COGNITIVE KEY. . . .

From the tenth to twelfth minute the subject sat looking blankly and without motion at the wall of the room. When contacted he smiled and pressed the COGNITIVE key.

Above head is light bulb covered with scalloped light blue shade . . . circling up to the glowing shade are ribbons of waves . . . silent . . . beckoning . . . inviting . . . join the dance . . . leave your robot . . . a whole universe of delightful, aerial choreography awaits . . . yes join them . . . suddenly, like smoke rising from a cigarette, consciousness circled up . . . swooping graceful gull-paths up to light source and, soundlessly, through into another dimension . . . from the research questionnaire: a description of the level reached is a prose yoga beyond present attainment . . . there were billions-of-file-cards, helical in shape, which, flicked through, confronted me with an endless library of events, forms, visual perceptions, not abstract but all experiential . . . a billion years of coded experience, classified, preserved in brilliant, pulsating, cool clarity that made ordinary reality seem like an out-of-focus, tattered, jerky, fluttering of peep-show cards, tawdry and worn . . . any thought once thought, instantly came alive and flicked by the shuttered aperture of consciousness . . . but at the same time there was no one to observe . . . I . . . he . . . the one-aware . . . was also computer, computer tape, electronic message . . . all humming in electronic, technicolor sudden SEE! vision for one who has been centuries blind . . .

MINUTE 14. TIM, WHERE ARE YOU NOW? Oh where are we? . . . oh listen, here's where we are . . . once there was a glowing electric dot, a flash reflected from the heart of a cut diamond which, oh there, now, caught the light of sun flame and glittered . . . sudden flash in pre-cambrian mud . . . the dot stirs and quivers with tremble-strain-exultant-singing-throbbing-shuddering twist upwards and a serpent began to writhe up and through the soft, warm silt . . . tiny, the size of a virus . . . growing . . . the enormous length of a microsopic bacillus . . . flowing exultantly, always singing the Hindu flute-song . . . always bursting out, enfoliating . . . now the size of the moss root, churning through fibred-cunt-mattress-moist-spasm churning . . . growing . . . growing . . . ever exfoliating its own vision . . . always blind except for the forward point of light-eye . . . now belts of serpent skin, mosaic-jeweled, rhythmically jerking, snake-wise forward . . . now the size of a tree-trunk, gnarled and horny with the sperm-sap moving within . . . now swelling, tumescent into mississippi flood of tissue writhing . . . pink, silt current of singing fire . . . now circling globe, squeezing green salt oceans and jagged brown-shale mountains with constrictor grasp . . . serpent flowing blindly, now a billion-mile endless electric-cord vertebrated writhing cobra singing Hindu flute-song . . . penis head throbbing . . . plunged into all smells, all color tapestry of tissue . . . blind writhing, circled tumescent serpent blind, blind, blind, except for the one jeweled eye through which, for one frame's flickered second each cell in the advancing parade is permitted that one moment face-to-face, eyeball to solar flame insight into the past future . . . .

TIM, TIM, WHERE ARE YOU NOW? La Guardia tower repeats request for contact with the ship lost out of radar scope . . . where? . . . I am eye of the great snake . . . a fold of serpent skin, radiating trapezoidal inquiry swims into focus . . . register conscious content . . . where are you? . . . here . . . INTERNAL HALLUCINATIONS.

From minute twelve to fourteen the subject sat silent with eyes closed. When contacted he failed to respond and after thirty seconds was contacted again. He then pressed EXTERNAL HALLUCINATION key.

The session continued with two minute interruptions until the twentieth minute in the same pattern: timeless flights into hallucinatory or pure energy vibration fields with sudden contractions to reality in response to the observer's questions.

The session report filled out the next day contained the following comments about this method of session programming.

This session suggested some solutions about the problem of communicating during psychedelic experiences. The person "up there" is being whirled through experiences which spin by so rapidly and contain structural content so different from our familiar macroscopic forms that he cannot possibly describe where he is or what he is experiencing. Consider the analogy to the pilot of a plane who has lost his bearings who is talking by radio to La Guardia tower. The pilot is experiencing many events—he can describe the cloud formations, lightning flashes, the etching of ice on the plane window—but none of this makes any sense to the tower technicians who are attempting to plot his course in the three-dimensional language of navigation. The person "up there" cannot provide the categories. The ground control personnel must radio them "up." "Cessna 64 Bravo, our radar scopes show you are fifteen miles southwest of International Airport. The red glow you see is the reflection of Manhattan. To head on a course for Boston you must change your course to 57 degrees and maintain an altitude of 5500."

But the language of psychology is not sophisticated enough to provide such parameters. Nor are there experiential compasses to determine direction.

What we can do, at this point, is to set up "flight plans." The subject can work out, before the session, the areas of experience he wishes to engage; and he can plan the temporal sequence of his visionary voyage. He will not be able, during the flight to tell "ground control" where he is, but ground control can contact him and tell him where to proceed. Thus, during this session, when Ralph asked, WHERE ARE YOU NOW?, I could not respond. I had to descend, slow up the flow of experience and *then* tell him where I ended up.

When the contact question came I would be hurtling through other galaxies. In order to respond, I had to stop my free rocketing, tumbling flight, return near the earth and say: "I am over New Haven."

This session was a continual, serial "come-down." I repeatedly had to stop the flow in order to respond. My cortex was receiving hundreds of thousands of impulses a second; but in order to respond to ground control's questions I had to grind the ship to a slow stall to say, at that moment. "I am here."

This session suggests that a more efficient way to chart psychedelic experiences would be to: 1) memorize the keyboard of the experiential typewriter so that communication down to ground control could be automatic, and 2) plan the flight in such a way that the ground control would not ask unanswerable questions—"Where am I indeed!" but would tell the subject where to go. Then the communication task of the voyager would be to indicate if he were on course, i.e., that he was or was not following the flight instructions radioed up by ground control.

Ground control should send up stimuli. Suggestivity is wide open. La Guardia tower directs the flight.

DID YOU LEARN ANYTHING OF VALUE FROM THIS SESSION? IF SO, PLEASE SPECIFY: "Session was of great value. I am clearly and strongly motivated to work out methods of ground control and planned flights."

APPROXIMATELY HOW MUCH OF THE SESSION (IN % OF TIME) WAS SPENT IN EACH OF THE FOLLOWING AREAS?
- A) INTERPERSONAL GAMES 10% (fondness for observers)
- B) EXPLORING OR DISCOVERING SELF, OR SELF GAMES 0%
- C) OTHER GAMES (SOCIAL, INTELLECTUAL, RELIGIOUS) 70% (intellectual, struggling with problem of communication)
- D) NON-GAME TRANSCENDENCE 20% (continually interrupted by questions)

REFERENCES

1. Szara, S.: Hallucinogenic effects and metabolism of tryptamine derivatives in man. *Fed. Proc.* **20**: 858–888, 1961.
2. Szara, S.: Correlation between metabolism and behavioral action of psycho-

tropic tryptamine derivatives. *Biochem. Pharmacol.,* **8**: 32, 1961.

3. Szara, S.: Behavioral correlates of 6-hydroxylation and the effect of psychotropic tryptamine derivatives on brain serotonin levels. In: *Comparative Neurochemistry,* ed. D. Richter, pp. 432–452. Pergamon Press, Oxford, 1964.

4. Szara, S. & Axelrod, J.: Hydroxylation and N-demethylation N,N-dimethyltryptamine. *Experientia.* **153**: 216–220, 1959.

5. Szara, S., Hearst E. & Putney F.: Metabolism and behavioral action of psychotropic trypatimine homologues, *International Journal of Neuropharmacol.,* **1**, 111–117, 1962.

6. Schultes, R. E. Botanical Sources of The New World Narcotics. In Weil, G. M., Metzner, R. & Leary, T. (eds). *The Psychedelic Reader.* University Books, New Hyde Park, 1965.

7. Leary, T. The Experiential Typewriter, *Psychedelic Review,* No. 7, 1965.

PART 5

Historical Documents from the Harvard Drug Scandal

When Richard Alpert and Timothy Leary were fired by Harvard in May of 1963, various newspapers and magazines—*The New York Times, The Boston Globe, The Boston Herald, Esquire, Ladies Home Journal, The Reporter, Time, Look,* and *Newsweek*—covered the story with great interest. Numerous follow-up articles about Leary and Alpert appeared during the summer and fall of 1963. However, it is important to realize that the Harvard Drug Scandal did not begin when Leary and Alpert were fired. Like most scandals, there were many smaller episodes that led up to the culminating events of May 1963. The firing of Leary and Alpert was the moment when the scandal started to gain traction in the mainstream press. Before May 1963, the Harvard Drug scandal was only a local story covered by the Boston press and *The Harvard Crimson.*

Historically speaking, the Harvard Drug Scandal is a crucial turning point in the 1960s because it signifies the moment when psychedelic drugs were demonized in the mainstream press. Prior to 1963, psychedelic drugs had actually received favorable coverage in several mainstream publications: *Good Housekeeping, Horizon, Look, The Saturday Evening Post, Time,* and *Life Magazine.** However, after the Harvard Drug Scandal breaks in May of 1963, the media views psychedelic drugs with alarm and suspicion.[†]

Part 5 provides a larger picture of the Harvard Drug Scandal. It includes articles that record the micro-controversies and maneuvers that transpired before Harvard decided to fire Leary and Alpert. "The Statement of Purpose for the International Federation of Internal Freedom" (IFIF) is an early response to the Harvard crackdown on psilocybin research. When Harvard banned further psychedelic research in October of 1962, Leary and many other prominent intellectuals formed IFIF, an autonomous organization independent of Harvard University. Written by Leary and the prominent religions studies scholar Huston Smith, the IFIF "Statement of Purpose . . ." expresses the foundational beliefs of the expansion of consciousness movement and presents an ethical argument for the viability of psychedelic research.

"The Rational for the Mexican Psychedelic Training Center" is an extension of the IFIF manifesto. It outlines the plans for an international research center where IFIF members could experiment with consciousness expansion and where practitioners could be trained as spiritual and

---

*For favorable accounts of psychedelic drugs in the national press, see "Seeking the Magic Mushroom" (*Life Magazine,* May 27, 1957); "Mushroom Madness," in *Time* (June 16, 1958); "Drugs that Shape Men's Minds," *Saturday Evening Post* (October 18, 1958); "The Curious Story Behind the New Cary Grant," *Look* (September 1, 1959); "Psyche in 3-D," *Time* (March 28, 1960); "The Ageless Cary Grant," *Good Housekeeping* (September 1960); "Chemical Mind Changers," *Life* (March 15, 1963); and "Can the Drug Enlarge Man's Mind?" *Horizon* (May, 1963). For an extensive analysis of the media's coverage of LSD and psychedelic drugs, see Stephen Siff's excellent article "Henry Luce's Strange Trip: Coverage of LSD in *Time* and *Life,* 1954–68," *Journalism History* 34, no. 3 (Fall 2008): 126–34.

†The press frequently criticized Leary and Alpert and portrayed psychedelic drugs in an unfavorable light. See Noah Gordon's "The Hallucinogenic Drug Cult," *The Reporter* (August 15, 1963); Martin Mayer's "Getting Alienated with the Right Crowd at Harvard," *Esquire* (September 1963); John Kobler's "The Dangerous Magic of LSD," *Saturday Evening Post* (November 2, 1963); and Andrew Weil's "The Strange Case of the Harvard Drug Scandal," *Look* (November 5, 1963).

therapeutic guides. The last two documents in Part 5—"The Politics of Consciousness Expansion" and Noah Gordon's "The Hallucinogenic Drug Cult"—are directly related to the events of May of 1963. The former article is Leary and Alpert's parting shot to the scandal and controversy; it is directed to the under-thirty generation that is coming of age in the early 1960s. Noah Gordon's "The Hallucinogenic Drug Cult" is an article that appeared in *The Reporter* in August of 1963; it expresses the emerging media backlash against psychedelic drugs. Although it features interviews with the ousted professors, it presents a sensationalist view of psychedelic drugs and the Harvard Drug Scandal.

13

The IFIF Manifesto

*Statement of Purpose of the International
Federation for Internal Freedom (IFIF)*

Timothy Leary and Huston Smith

When Harvard University attempted to severely restrict Leary and Alpert's access to legal drugs (psilocybin and LSD) in the fall of 1962, Leary and other prominent intellectuals opted to form a separate organization, the International Federation for Internal Freedom (IFIF). In theory, IFIF would be entirely independent of Harvard University. Leary intended to leave Harvard after the spring semester of 1963 and work under the aegis of IFIF. The plan was to set up autonomous research groups ("assemblages of six to ten persons who share the general goal of consciousness expansion").

After Leary and Alpert were fired in May of 1963, IFIF was moved to Zihuatanejo, Mexico, for the summer. IFIF had many members who were ready to participate in psychedelic sessions run by Leary, Alpert, and Metzner. However, after only a few weeks in Mexico, the Mexican government grew suspicious of IFIF's plans for a psychedelic summer camp and drug research center and expelled its leading members from the country. Subsequent attempts to relocate to various Caribbean islands—

Antigua and Dominica—in the summer months of 1963 also failed. In each case, various wings of the U.S. government—the ambassador, the CIA, and the Justice Department—lobbied for expulsion.

Although the IFIF Statement of Purpose states that the manifesto was written by the "Chartered Board of Directors of IFIF," the document was actually coauthored by Leary and Huston Smith.* In 1963, Smith was Chair of the Philosophy Department at the Massachusetts Institute of Technology and the author of *The Religions of Man* (1958). Leary and Smith's Statement of Purpose contains a bold utopian message that captures the spirit and idealism of the nascent consciousness-expansion movement of the early 1960s. Many of the IFIF's board members were prominent intellectuals and theologians from the religious community—Smith, Walter Clark, and Alan Watts. The IFIF manifesto posited that hallucinogenic drugs were not simply for kicks and to indulge oneself in hedonism—the view often promoted by the sensationalist newspapers of the early 1960s. Instead, hallucinogenic drugs—psilocybin, mescaline, and LSD—were a legitimate form of philosophic exploration and mystical self-expression.

The IFIF statement is also bold in the sense that it attempts to unite the religious community with the psychological community. The alliance of progressive psychologists and like-minded religious scholars was a unique expression of 1960s idealism. The IFIF statement links the consciousness-expansion movement with the tenets of Emersonian idealism. If Emerson argued in "The Divinity School Address" that one could be a Christian without belonging to a church, IFIF argued that one could conduct ethical drug research without

---

*Proof of Leary and Smith's coauthorship is cited in the bibliography of Leary's 1968 edition of *High Priest* (New York: World Publishers Co.).

belonging to a university. The IFIF statement of purpose recognizes that the right to "internal freedom" is a salient political issue ("the politics of the nervous system"). The IFIF statement of purpose is also proto-counterculture in the sense that it recognizes the need for alternative social institutions ("experimental communities"). Although its language is inclusive and explicitly non-dogmatic, the critics of Leary and Alpert in the mainstream media were apt to insist that IFIF was, in essence, "a drug cult" (see Noah Gordon's "The Hallucinogenic Drug Cult," which comprises the last chapter of this book).

JAMES PENNER

STATEMENT OF PURPOSE OF THE INTERNATIONAL FEDERATION FOR INTERNAL FREEDOM (IFIF)

The Statement of Purpose was prepared and distributed by the Chartered Board of Directors of IFIF; January 24, 1963.

Timothy Leary, Ph.D., and Huston Smith, Ph.D.

I. THE SITUATION

As long as men have reflected about their world—which is to say, for about 3000 years—a basic issue has divided them. There have been those who regard man's normal conceptual models as straightforward mirror reflections of the way things actually are. Over against them have been men who suspect that these models are more like reducing-valves imposed by finite consciousness upon an infinite, evolving reality to reduce it to manageable proportions. The issue is whether the world of normal sense is unqualifiedly real and, indeed, the only reality, or whether reality is far more than mind and sense disclose—not only quantitatively, but qualitatively as well. That things are what they seem, and that they aren't—this has been the great divide that has separated men since they first became philosophers.

What induced those in the second group to fly in the face of sense evidence and assert that things are in truth dramatically different from the way they appear? Reason doubtless played a part, but its speculations must have appeared pale compared with the full-bodied testament of direct experience. For as far back as men have left records, there have been some who reported visions and theophanies in which the veils were lowered, the masks of God removed, and reality disclosed with startling force.

It may be that all these telltale rents in the fabric of normal awareness involved alterations in brain chemistry, however effected. What we know is that experiences strikingly like those reported by mystics, seers, and visionaries of the past can be induced by chemical means. This puts us in the position of being able for the first time to explore experimentally the momentous question of the absoluteness versus the relativity of our sense perceptions and the prevailing conceptual schemes which order our experience.

Another prospect emerges if we approach the mind psychologically rather than epistemologically. Until the last century the West has equated the mind with its conscious manifestations. With Freud, Jung, and their immediate forerunners, there broke upon the West the realization that not only the mind but also much of what within it is most important for our lives, lies below the level of self-awareness. Our ability to change the chemistry of the brain gives us a device for reaching this unexplored material dramatically faster and more fully than was possible before.

The issue arises in a third form, namely socially. Some accept prevailing institutions as God-given and inviolable. Others see them as conventions which can block freedom, stifle creativity, and stunt lives as readily as they can support these and make them possible. One need think only of current patterns of racial discrimination, and prejudice against the mentally ill, for examples. Insofar as our prevailing institutions and attitudes do inhibit the full release of man's potentials, the added awareness that indole substances engender is likely to make this fact more evident. Concern to reform the debilitating institutions should naturally follow, as should attempts to develop new ones.

For the past two and a half years a group of Harvard University research psychologists has been studying these issues. Five research projects on the effects of consciousness-changing drugs have been completed. Their results, supplemented by study of other available data, have led the researchers in question to the following provisional conclusions:

1. Man at present may be using only a fraction (perhaps less than one percent) of his available brain capacity.
2. The politics of the nervous system—psychophysical processes involving censoring, alerting, discriminating, selecting, and evaluating—may be responsible for this restricted use of brain potential.
3. Prevailing patterns of stimulus censorship can be relaxed, thereby admitting to consciousness stimuli otherwise debarred. As a result of this admission, consciousness is expanded—possibly in an absolute sense, but at least in the sense that the mind becomes aware of factors heretofore unknown. Indole substances (LSD, mescaline, psilocybin, etc.) are the most powerful agents yet discovered for opening the mind to new data.
4. *Set* and *setting* control what data are admitted and how they are experienced. *Set* denotes the personality structure of the individual, including his beliefs and mood at the time. *Setting* is physical (weather, feel of the room), social (feelings of persons present toward one another) and cultural (prevailing views as to what is real).
5. Insights gained through the new indole substances appear likely to require innovations in at least the following areas:
   a. *Language.* A new vocabulary is needed to describe experiences which are not only new but different in kind. Beyond this, to experience in areas where vocabulary is lacking and syntax inapposite is to gain new perspective on the role and function of language generally.

b. *Self-understanding.* What does it mean to be a self, a person, a human being?

c. *Metaphysics.* What is real? What unreal?

6. New social institutions are indicated. In particular, it may he important that experimental communities based on new perspectives which indole substances produce be established both to provide support for these perspectives and to test their validity.

7. There is special need to see if indole substances can alter the self- and-reality models of those who are receiving minimum returns from those models they currently possess: criminals, psychotics, delinquents, and the like. Those who see the limitations of their present models—mystics, artists, housewives, the rebellious young—would, for their part, seem to be exceptionally promising candidates for breakthroughs into new outlooks.

8. It is vitally important that responsible research on consciousness-change proceed vigorously; that research institutions not be panicked by unfounded rumors and fears which always seem to spring up around the word "drug"; and that, in view of the importance of *setting* on experience in this area (see point 4 above), research not become the monopoly of a single school of thought on the ultimate significance of the substances in question.

II. ORGANIZATION

To implement the preceding points, there is need for an organization to encourage, support and protect research on psychedelic substances and which will be willing and able to take responsibility for serious studies in the area.

We are fully aware that institutions, however libertarian in their purpose, tend to restrict and inhibit the development of spiritual freedom. They often end in external control of internal freedom. This danger we seek to avoid. This paradoxical tension we recognize and accept. It can be a stimulating and fruitful force.

We have formed a Massachusetts non-profit corporation, the *International Federation for Internal Freedom* (IFIF). Its present Board of Directors consist of:

Richard Alpert, Ph.D.	Ralph Metzner, Ph.D.
Walter Clark, Ph.D.	Huston Smith, Ph.D.
Rolf von Eckartsberg	Gunther Weil
Timothy Leary, Ph.D.	Alan Watts, D.D., S.T.M.
Paul A. Lee	(Honorary Director)
George Litwin	

The basic units of IFIF are small research groups—assemblages of six to ten persons who share the general goal of consciousness exploration and who are involved in a common research project.

The immediate functions of IFIF are:

1. To encourage persons to band together in such research groups for systemic exploration of consciousness.

   The specific research goals are determined by the members of the individual research group. It is understood that the goals of such subgroups would not contradict principles of IFIF. Among those who have already applied for affiliation are groups made up of ministers, educators, psychologists, and persons involved in the field of behavior change and rehabilitation.

2. To act as a local research center, collecting and disseminating the knowledge gained by each research group.

3. To maintain offices to be used as research centers.

4. To offer advice, medical and legal services, and financial and other support to the research groups.

5. To raise funds necessary to support the research, publication and educational programs of the Federation.

6. To obtain drugs and to make them available *(in conformance with existing laws)* to the research groups. This may mean the purchase and development of actual plant facilities to produce

consciousness-expanding drugs and to sponsor needed pharmacological and biochemical research.

7. To establish and support two new journals which will publish scientific and literary articles about consciousness-expansion. A detailed description of this project is available on request. (The first issue of *The Psychedelic Review* appears in June, 1963. Address: P.O. Box 9, Cambridge 40, Mass.)

8. To sponsor the publication of instruction manuals which present a very wide variety of methods and objectives for consciousness-expanding experience.

9. To encourage and assist the development of centers for research in internal freedom in other cities and countries.

The IFIF headquarters office is located at 14 Story Street, Cambridge 38, Massachusetts. (Phone: 617: 547-7244. Cable: IFIFREE—Cambridge.) The Executive Secretary of IFIF is Mr. Frank Ferguson. You are invited to write or visit the IFIF office.

This statement was prepared and distributed by the Chartered Board of Directors of IFIF.

JANUARY 24, 1963

14

The Zihuatanejo Project
of 1962–1963

Rationale of the Mexican Psychedelic Training Center

Timothy Leary, Richard Alpert, and Ralph Metzner

This collaborative article was originally published in Richard Blum's *Utopiates: The Use and Users of LSD 25* (1964), along with a second article on the International Federation for Internal Freedom's "Psychedelic Training Center" in Zihuatanejo, Mexico, in the summer of 1962. Zihuatanejo, a remote fishing village on the Pacific coast, was considered an ideal location for the center because of its tranquil beaches and tropical setting.

"Rationale of the Mexican Psychedelic Training Center" can be read as an extension of IFIF's Statement of Purpose, which had been published in January of that same year. The Statement articulates IFIF's central goal: that of creating an international research center where IFIF members could program psychedelic experiences and train like-minded practitioners to be spiritual and therapeutic guides. In theory, the IFIF training center would operate outside of the jurisdiction of the United States government and the Food and Drug Administration.

A key influence on the so-called "Zihuatanejo Project" was Aldous Huxley's *Island* (1961). In Huxley's novel, the Palanese islanders use psychedelic drugs ("moksha medicine") in coming-of-age ceremonies. The psychedelic initiation experiences, which are conducted with a guide, foster greater self-awareness and a higher level of consciousness in the initiates. "Rationale of the Mexican Psychedelic Training Center" follows Huxley's utopian novel in the sense that it attempts to create psychedelic rituals that produce life-changing transcendental experiences.

Dr. Joseph J. Dowling, a psychiatrist and the director of the San Mateo County Mental Health Department, acted as a professional observer of the Zihuatanejo project during the summer of 1963, and his essay, "Zihuatanejo: An Experiment in Transpersonative Living," is the second article about the center that was published in Blum's *Utopiates*. In his article, Dowling argues that Leary and his IFIF followers attempted to provide an alternative to the "medical-psychotherapeutic" approach to psychedelic drugs. The medical model posits that psychedelic drugs should only be taken with a physician/therapist who provides close supervision for the duration of the drug experience. The medical-psychotherapeutic model also stresses that psychedelic drugs are potentially harmful if used by non-professionals in an unsupervised and non-medical setting.

In contrast to the medical model, Leary, Alpert, and Metzner build on the Harvard model of programming psychedelic experiences in a comfortable and supportive location (i.e., avoiding hospitals and sterile institutional settings). In place of the doctor-patient paradigm, Leary, Metzner, and Alpert advocate the "mentor-disciple model." For the IFIF group, the psychedelic experience is not a medical procedure that requires medical supervision.

"Rationale of the Mexican Psychedelic Training Center" reflects the attempt to blend the scientific ideals of William James and Gustav Fechner with religious concepts derived from *The Tibetian Book of the Dead*. The notion of embracing both science and religious mystical thought was unique to Leary's Harvard period (1960 to 1963). After Leary was fired from Harvard, he was less committed to science and what he terms, "playing the science game."

This article also attempts to legitimize IFIF's practices and ethical approach to psychedelic drugs. The authors attempt to counter the sensationalist articles in the mainstream media that suggest that IFIF was a decadent drug cult: "It has been widely reported in the popular press that IFIF promotes the unrestrained civilian use of drugs. The truth of the matter is exactly the opposite. IFIF was the only psychedelic research group that urged the need for training guides—ecstaticians, if you will—to provide the experience to others. The Mexican center was set up to be such a training center." Thus, the authors attempt to counter the notion that psychedelic drugs should be used casually just for kicks and instead argue for the need for a spiritual context. The use of *The Tibetan Book of the Dead* in Zihuatanejo training sessions eventually led to the publication of a training manual for a wider audience: Leary, Metzner, and Alpert's *The Psychedelic Experience* (1964).

Like many utopian projects, the IFIF training center had a brief history, opening in May of 1963 but only lasting for two weeks. Unfortunately, the Mexican government shut it down and ordered Leary and his followers to leave Mexico within five days. IFIF had unwisely invited the media (*Time, Life, Newsweek, The Saturday Evening Post,* and CBS) to visit the IFIF training center in Zihuatanejo. After the media coverage, the United States ambassador to Mexico lobbied the Mexican government to expel Leary and his followers. Thus, the publicity sought by IFIF was ultimately counterproductive in the sense that it galvanized the anti-drug forces within the governments of the United States and Mexico. If IFIF had chosen to remain quiet and discreet—as they had been in the previous summer of 1962—expulsion might have been avoided.

JAMES PENNER

REFERENCES

Blum, Richard. *Utopiates: The Use and Users of LSD 25.* New York: Atherton Press, 1964.

Dass, Ram, and Ralph Metzner. *The Birth of a Psychedelic Culture: Conversations about Leary, the Harvard Experiments, Millbrook, and the Sixties.* Santa Fe, N. Mex.: Synergetic Press, 2011.

Dowling, Joseph J. "Zihuatanejo: An Experiment in Transpersonative Living." *Utopiates: The Use and Users of LSD 25.* New York: Atherton Press, 1964.

Leary, Timothy, Ralph Metzner, and Richard Alpert. *The Psychedelic Experience: A Manual Based on the Tibetan Book of the Dead.* New Hyde Park, N.Y.: University Books, 1964.

Leary, Timothy. *Flashbacks: A Biography.* New York: Jeremy Tarcher/Pedigree Press, 1990.

Stevens, Jay. *Storming Heaven: LSD and the American Dream.* New York: Harper and Row, 1987.

RATIONALE OF THE MEXICAN PSYCHEDELIC TRAINING CENTER

From *Utopiates: The Use and Users of LSD 25,* by Richard Blum, published in 1964 by Atherton Press: pages 178–86.

Timothy Leary, Richard Alpert, and Ralph Metzner

The Psychedelic Training Center at Zihuatanejo was organized and run by the Harvard-IFIF Research Project. During the three years preceding the Mexican experiment, over thirty-five teaching assistants, research assistants, and faculty members from three Boston area colleges had been engaged in a variety of projects studying the effects of psilocybin and other consciousness-expanding substances. This project, probably the largest organization of scholar-scientists ever assembled to research the psychedelic effect, had sponsored over four thousand drug ingestions. The Mexican center was a logical application of the findings and theories of the project.

From the viewpoint of the history of psychology, the Harvard-IFIF project is seen to be highly orthodox. The research was based directly on the theories of Gustav T. Fechner, the founder of experimental psychology, and William James, the most distinguished American psychologist, and revised in the light of the findings of modern neurology and pharmacology.

The basic theoretical assumptions of the research are neurological. The goals of the research are also neurological—the expansion of consciousness so as to utilize more of the capacities of the brain.

The central metaphor is as follows. The human brain contains over ten billion cells. Any single cell can be in interconnection with up to twenty-five thousand other cells. About one billion impulses flood into the cortical computer each second.[1] The potentialities of consciousness at any one second are thus seen to be of the order of

$$(1{,}000{,}000{,}000) \times (10{,}000{,}000{,}000)^{25{,}000}$$

The educated adult utilizes about five thousand concepts to experience the world within and without. An astonishing filtering and constricting process occurs which reduces the enormous potentials of consciousness to the few cultural modes of experience routinely employed.

Psychedelic drugs are seen as interfering with or counteracting these reductive processes so that the subjects are able to experience immediately, beyond the limits of the learned cultural programs.

The process of going outside, going beyond learned modes of experience (particularly the learned modes of space-time-verbalization identity), is called *ecstasis*. The ecstatic experience. *Ex-stasis*.

The science of ecstatics is the systematic measurement, description, and production of the ecstatic state—that is, the expansion of consciousness.

This process has been studied by every culture in recorded history under many names—*samhadi, satori, numina, nirvana,* mystic or visionary state, transcendence. Those who are concerned with conformity and adjustment like to call the ecstatic state psychotic. Psychoanalysts use terms such as "primary process" or "regression in the service of the ego."

It has been known for centuries that the ecstatic process can be produced by techniques which alter body chemistry—fasting, contemplative focusing of attention, optical alterations, yoga exercises, sensory deprivation, and the ingestion of foods and drugs. The drug-induced *ecstasis* is now called the psychedelic experience.

Philosophers have for several thousand years speculated despairingly about the impossibility of describing the ecstatic experience in words. The fastest verbal communication operates at a slow, sticky-static rate—about ten phonemes, or three words, a second. The neurological potentials of consciousness are several million times faster than verbalization. Then, too, most words in the English language refer to external game artifacts or social game sequences which have little direct relevance to the flashing mosaics of neurological experience.

The energy sciences have found it necessary to develop specialized models and languages capable of expressing the speed and complexity of energy transformations. A new nonverbal language of experience capable of expressing the speed and complexity of our cortical potentials is necessary. The Harvard-IFIF group has worked out some rudimentary steps toward the development of a nonverbal experiential language, and one of the purposes of the Zihuatanejo center was to train people in the use of this language.

THE PRODUCTION OF THE ECSTATIC EXPERIENCE

The goal of the research sessions run by the Harvard-IFIF group was not to produce and study frightening disturbances of consciousness (which was the goal of the most psychiatric investigations of model psychoses), but to produce the ecstatic experience, to expand consciousness, to provide the subject with the most memorable, revelatory, life-changing experience of his life.

The rationale was based on our conception of the almost limitless potential of consciousness, and our actions were guided by the set-setting hypothesis. Most psychologists and behavioral scientists (Jungians excepted) work from a different rationale. This may account for much of the misunderstanding of our activities and aims. Our position is very similar to the post-Einsteinian physicists who labored for decades to release the energy locked in atomic structure. A classic Newtonian physicist would have looked with incredulous dismay at atomic-fission experiments and quantum speculations. Such approaches violating the clockwork symmetry and lacking the control of classic macroscopic experimentation would be denounced as a reckless psychotization of the divinely ordered equilibrium. (See, for example, the controversy between Newton and Whistoh.[2])

Most psychologists have been trained to accept a brain model diagramed like a side of beef, with areas blocked out like fancy cuts—motor, sensory, optical, association, and so on. Our concepts of neurological function supported by psychedelic drug data visualize the brain as an enormous electrochemical network sometimes held in clock-like contracted conceptual game attention but capable of being swept by rapidly changing ecstatic processes.

From the beginning of our research our attention was directed to the engineering of ecstasy, the preparation for, the setting for, the architecture of ecstasy. Like post-Einsteinian physicists we sought to release (harmoniously and peacefully) the neurological energy latent in the cortex. Preparation of the subject. Set and expectancy. Collaboration with the subject in arranging the sort of session he wished. Careful planning of the setting to be supportive, understanding, aesthetic, spiritually meaningful, close to nature, and so on.

After many sessions in urban situations we came to some ironic conclusions about the set and setting of a psychedelic experience. We realized that an ecstatic psychedelic session should be arranged the way a person would arrange his own ideal life situation. He should surround himself with spiritual, relaxed, open, loving, happy people. He should arrange his environment aesthetically. He should approach the occasion with informed trust, intelligent faith, skeptical humor, humility, and, above all, courage. He should direct the experience toward spiritual rather than material goals.

THE IMPORTANCE OF PREPARATION

During the first year of our research, we followed a naturalistic design, scrupulously attempting to avoid imposing our model on the experience. We wanted to see how psychedelic drugs affected a wide range of persons in a wide range of situations with a wide, random range of expectations. We found that, if the setting is supportive, around 70 per cent of volunteer subjects would have pleasant, revelatory experiences.[3] The subsequent interpretation and application of the experience varied. Although over 50 per cent of subjects were reporting changes for the better following their session, follow-up studies suggested that the meaning and value of the experience depended on the subject's over-all situation. There were marked individual differences in the ability of the individual to use his insights. Most people drifted back into the magnetic field of their personal-cultural games. Although it was possible to produce instant *satori,* the illumination tended to be temporary.

We noted that subjects who came to their session after years of intellectual or spiritual preparation tended to get the most from the session. It was obvious that subjects with training in any ecstatic philosophy or discipline could make better use of their experience. Philosophic training (Western or Eastern) was helpful. Professional religious subjects made the best candidates. Subjects with backgrounds in mysticism, Sufi scholars, Hasidic rabbis, monastics, students of Gurdjieff, scientists who had spent time speculating about the metagame aspects of the energy sciences—all these possessed a frame of reference in which to fit the psychedelic voyage.

We gradually came to the conclusion that a psychedelic session should be preceded by a long and thorough training in the nature of the metaverbal, metagame phenomena. Exploration of the speed and breadth of the subject's nervous system should be preceded by as much specialized training as soloing in an airplane or use of a high-speed computer.

It was ironic that, starting with behavioral science assumptions, we came closer and closer to the wisdom of the religious mystics. Rigorous training and a courageous commitment to metapersonal ideals was the best training for an LSD session.

It has been widely reported in the popular press that IFIF promotes the unrestrained civilian use of drugs. The truth of the matter is exactly the opposite. IFIF was the only psychedelic research group that urged the need for training guides—ecstaticians, if you will—to provide the experience to others. The Mexican center was set up to be such a training center. The plan was that carefully selected subjects (who had had one or preferably several psychedelic sessions before coming to Mexico) would learn to run sessions for themselves and others.

THE NEED FOR A CONTINUING PROGRAM

The Harvard-IFIF group does not see the psychedelic session as a medical procedure or as a curative intervention. A new term and a new institutional context are needed, but of existing institutions our concepts were closer to aesthetic-educational-religious.

The psychedelic experience is seen as a tool like a telescope or microscope which brings other space/time dimensions into focus. You have to be trained to use the tool, and you use it not once (for "kicks" or cure), but whenever your situation calls for an examination of other dimensions of reality. You don't go to school once, you don't go to church once in your life, you don't take a plane ride just once in your life. You seek out these experiences when necessary and relevant to your spiritual or secular goals.

The psychedelic session is like sex. Anyone who has not had the experience cannot really grasp the meaning. The first experience is entirely a function of set and setting. A bad first experience does not rule out further trials. And the frequency of its repetition is a highly personal matter. Both the sexual and psychedelic experiences are fiercely attacked and controlled by those who do not like it themselves and do not want others to have it. All of the familiar psychological escapes from and distortions of the sexual impulse are seen to operate in relation to the psychedelic experience—fear, hysteria, rationalizations about protection of the young, repression, rumor, puritanical control.

The Mexican center was the first (and of this date the only) attempt to provide a series of guided psychedelic sessions for prepared volunteer subjects. Like any other form of educational or spiritual experience (including the sexual), the psychedelic experience is most productive if it is built into a systematic and planned sequence. Our training strategy involved a few "free flights" followed by a series of systematic, programmed sessions in the direction of the subject's goals.

Before the Mexican program of 1963, the research group had experimented with programmed sessions. In some of these sessions we employed program charts which allowed the subject to review his set (emotional and cognitive) and plan the sequence of stimuli to which he would be exposed. The chart also had a series of horizontal lines representing the time dimension and making it possible for the subject to plan his session like a symphonic score or like a pilot's flight plan. For example, the subject might plan that at a certain time during the session he would listen to a particular reading (scientific, religious, and so on) or be shown a picture or an object which would be expected to open up a line of associations. After the session the subject would go over his chart and fill in the details, minute by minute, from memory.

The most systematic attempt to program sessions involves the tape recording of eight or ten hours of sound and silence to be played during the session. The tape opens with an introductory statement by the subject about the goals of the session. This is followed by music and silence, occasionally interrupted by the person's own voice giving himself reassurance or instructions. The use of taped programs eliminates almost all need of interruption or action by anyone during the session. The psychedelic state is so sensitive that any action, however innocuous (even changing records), by guides and observers can swirl consciousness off in unplanned-for dimensions.

One of the key training devices planned for the Zihuatanejo program was session programing and session charts. Such techniques can be used only by experienced subjects and are, for the most part, of restricted usefulness in initial sessions.

THE NEED FOR MANUALS

The psychedelic session whirls the subject through eight hours of unimagined experience—to use William James's phrase, the drugs "open a region though they fail to give a map." Although the specific dominant moods and major themes of each session tend to differ, there are certain sequences which occur in many sessions and certain broad types of reaction which reoccur. One of the aims of our research is to obtain more precision in producing, predicting, and describing these reactions. There is no consideration of this problem in the contemporary psychological literature. Consciousness, its expansion, and its control are almost completely ignored by the behavioral sciences and by psychiatry today, though it was, of course, the primary subject of interest for men like Fechner and James.

There is, however, elaborate consideration of states of consciousness in nonpsychological literatures. For instance, the Christian mystics and Eastern philosophers and psychologists have spelled out systems for producing and describing the flow of consciousness from one level to another. Many of our project members and over eighty of our subjects hold theological degrees and contributed to our understanding of nonpsychological attempts to chart the ecstatic process.

It becomes apparent that any system for describing consciousness is metaphorical. To say that the matter is basically neurological is simply to choose the neurological metaphor. It is obvious that manuals—road maps for psychedelic voyages—are badly needed. But which metaphor? Our answer to this question is pluralistic—many maps, many manuals, to fit the linguistic systems of the subjects. Any theoretical system, any cultural or scientific game, provides metaphors which can be applied to the ecstatic process. For every *stasis* there is an *ecstasis*. For every fixed conceptual system there is the metasystem.

Our answer was then translated into the intention of writing manuals which would fit many types of psychedelic experiences. We are writing a manual on the psychotherapeutic psychedelic experience. For the aesthetic. For the interpersonal or group session. We are also "translating" several existing manuals for consciousness-expansion so that they can be applied to psychedelic sessions. The *Divine Comedy* of Dante describes a visionary voyage into three realms of awareness—horrible hellish hallucinations; personal, purgatorial appraisals; celestial lights and radiance. The scenes and details of the *Comedy* are duplicated over and over again in our files of session reports. The *Egyptian Book of the Dead,* the *Tao Te Ching, The Secret of the Golden Flower, Pilgrim's Progress,* the mythic voyages of Aeneas, Odysseus, Gilgamesh, Christ—all these are accounts of voyages beyond our conceptions of space and time, and all come from someone's cortex.

The visionary sequence which seems to be most ideally suited to the psychedelic session is the *Bardo Thödol* (the *Tibetan Book of the Dead*). This manual was reportedly handed down orally from guru to disciple for centuries and appeared in written form only in the eighth century A.D. and in English only in 1927. The metaphor system happens to be Mahayana Buddhist. The book treats of the intermediate state between life and death, but the esoteric aim of the book was to instruct adepts in changing consciousness. It is a book of the living, a manual for recognizing and utilizing ecstatic states of altered consciousness and applying the ecstatic experience in the postsession life. The *Tibetan Book of the Dead* is an uncanny portrayal of states regularly encountered during psychedelic sessions. It is eminently practical, including detailed instructions for the guide and designed to be read by the subject before his experience.

Because of its precise relevance to psychedelic sessions, our project has "translated" the manuscript from the scholarly style of the Evans-Wentz translation into psychedelic English.[4] This manual has been used for over two years by our project in preparing selected subjects for sessions. It must be emphasized that this manual has been revised so that the Buddhist metaphors and the hallucinatory content appropriate to a pastoral people in earlier millenniums have been changed to the visions, ecstasies, and terrors of our times.

THE ZIHUATANEJO TRAINING CENTER

The training center in Zihuatanejo operated for two summers, 1962 and 1963. The first summer program involved only members of the project and was therefore able to reach a higher level of organization and training much more quickly. Starting in May, 1963, the Hotel Catalina was leased for two years as a research-training site.

The interpretations, appraisals, and observations of Joseph J. Downing (Chapter VIII) are his own and differ from those which we would make. It is natural and proper that Dr. Downing choose his own metaphors to describe the events of that time. A more detailed account of the operation based on our records is being prepared and will be published in the near future.

If everyone who was present were to write his own impressions of the Zihuatanejo program, each one would write something different. Dr. Downing's story is neutral, thorough. If every Utopian attempt to set up a transpersonative community had been lucky enough to have a social-psychiatrist-observer of Dr. Downing's caliber, our empirical knowledge of the mechanics of ecstasy would be the richer.

NOTES

1. R. Campbell, "The Circuits of the Senses," *Life,* LIV, No. 27 (1963), 64–76b.
2. L. C. Stecchini, "The Inconstant Heavens," *The American Behavioral Scientist,* VII, No. 1 (1963).
3. Timothy Leary, George Litwin, and Ralph Metzner, "Reactions to Psilocybin Administered in a Supportive Environment," *Journal of Nervous and Mental Diseases,* CXXXVII, No. 6 (1963), 561–573; The Editors, "The Subjective After-effects of Psychedelic Experiences: a Summary of Four Recent Studies," *The Psychedelic Review,* I, No. 1 (1963), 18–26.
4. Timothy Leary, Ralph Metzner, and Richard Alpert, *The Psychedelic Experience: A Manual Based on the Tibetan Book of the Dead* (New Hyde Park, N.Y.: University Books, 1964).

15

Leary and Alpert's Response to the Harvard Drug Scandal

The Politics of Consciousness Expansion

Timothy Leary and Richard Alpert

In 1963, the *Harvard Review* decided to devote an entire issue to the subject of psychedelic drugs. The Harvard Drug Scandal was underway, and when the publication contacted Leary and Alpert for a contribution, both of them knew that their days at Harvard were numbered. In a sense, "The Politics of Consciousness Expansion" can be read as their bombastic parting shot. The essay-cum-diatribe proclaims the citizen's right to alter his/her consciousness; it also demonstrates Leary and Alpert's penchant for LSD evangelism. It juxtaposes quasi-scientific descriptions ("the expanding gaseous cloud whirls into temporary patterned structures") with political slogans ("the politics of consciousness expansion") and catchphrases ("the fifth freedom") that would resonate with the younger generation.

Leary and Alpert's rhetoric is prescient in the sense that

it understands the socio-cultural importance of hallucinogenic drugs in the *zeitgeist* of the 1960s: "[m]ake no mistake about it: the effect of consciousness-expanding drugs will be to transform our concepts of human nature, of human potentialities, of existence. The game is about to be changed, ladies and gentlemen . . . [p]resent social establishments had better be prepared for change." In this passage, Leary and Alpert recognize that consciousness-expanding drugs are not simply a fad; they will in time create a new way of thinking and an alternative society that will demand a break with the values of the previous generation. Leary and Alpert's declamatory essay conveys their understanding of the cultural fissures that characterize American society in the early 1960s, fissures that will lead to the creation of a counterculture. With these divisions in mind, Leary and Alpert attempt to speak directly to the young people who are likely to sympathize with their cause: "Trust your internal machinery. Be entertained by the social games you play. Remember, man's natural state is ecstatic wonder, ecstatic intuition, ecstatic accurate movement. Don't settle for less."

The article's overall effectiveness is certainly debatable. Although Leary and Alpert anticipated the socio-political importance of psychedelic drugs, they also misjudged and underestimated the forces of fear and repression. The footnote at the end of the article reveals their plan to open an autonomous psychedelic research center in Zihuatanejo, Mexico, on May 1, 1963, signifying their desire to thumb their noses at the Harvard establishment. Unfortunately, Leary and Alpert failed to see that discretion might have been a more useful strategy. Their fondness for publicity and "shouting from the rooftops" often backfired. The Zihuatanejo training center was promptly shut down by the Mexican government after being officially open for only two short weeks.

JAMES PENNER

THE POLITICS OF
CONSCIOUSNESS EXPANSION

In the *Harvard Review,* summer 1963, vol. 1, no. 4, pages 33–37.
The article also appeared in abridged form under the title "The Fifth
Freedom: The Right to Get High" in *The Politics of Ecstasy* by
Timothy Leary, published in 1968 by the Putnam Publishing
Group: pages 64–69. Leary's latter article title reflects
the attempt to reach a younger audience.

Timothy Leary and Richard Alpert

Expansion-Contraction. The tension between the flowing process and
the fixed structure.

Inorganic processes: The expanding gaseous cloud whirls into temporary patterned structures. The structures always changing, hurtling
towards eventual entropy.

Organic processes: Watery, electro-biochemical globules cluster into
cells. Cells cluster into temporary hardened forms (vegetative or animal), themselves always changing, eventually returning to the entropic.

Social processes: The free expansive vision is molded into the institutional. Hardly has the institutional mortar set before there is a new
cortical upheaval, an explosive, often ecstatic or prophetic revelation.
The prophet is promptly jailed. A hundred years later his followers are
jailing the next visionary.

One is led naively to exclaim: Will man never learn the lesson of
cyclical process? Must we continue to jail, execute, exile our ecstatic
visionaries, and then enshrine them as tomorrow's heroes?

Naive question, which fails to appreciate the necessary tension of
the expansion-contraction play. Membrane contracts. Life force bursts
membrane. Establishment controls vision. Vision bursts establishment.

The expansion process in physics and biology is described in evolutionary terms.

The expansion process in human affairs is defined in terms of the
word "freedom."

We measure social evolution in terms of increased freedom—external or internal. Freedom to step out of the tribal game and move to construct a new social form. Freedom to move in space. Freedom to experience. Freedom to explore.

Society needs educated priest-scholars to provide structure—the intellectual muscle, bone and skin to keep things together. The university is the Establishment's apparatus for training consciousness-contractors. The intellectual ministry of defense. Defense against vision. This statement is not pejorative but a fact about evolutionary function. We need stability. We need expansion. The far-out visionary. The academic council which sits in learned judgment on Socrates, Galileo, Bacon, Columbus, Thoreau. The protagonists in these dramas are neither good nor evil. No villains, no heroes. They just are. What will be the next step in biological and social evolution? Here are two clues. (1) You are more likely to find the evolutionary agents closer to jail than to the professor's chair. (2) Look to that social freedom most abused, most magically, irrationally feared, by society. Exactly that freedom which *you,* the intellectual, the liberal, would deny to others. Good. Now you are getting close.

The administration always recognizes intuitively the next evolutionary step that will leave it behind. To cast this drama in terms of saints and pharisees is entertaining, but outmoded.

The drama is genetic. Neurophysiological.

So spare us, please, the adolescent heroics of Beethoven—Shakespeare.

Where, then, will the next evolutionary step occur? Within the human cortex. We *know,* yes we *know,* that science has produced methods for dramatically altering and expanding human awareness and potentialities. The uncharted realm lies behind your own forehead. Internal geography. Internal politics. Internal control. Internal freedom.

The nervous system can be changed, integrated, recircuited, expanded in its function. These possibilities naturally threaten every branch of the Establishment. The dangers of external change appear to frighten us less than the peril of internal change. LSD is more frightening than the Bomb!

There are two obvious avenues toward this next stage of human evolution. Biochemical methods of freeing the nervous system, slowed down by heavy learned concepts and starved of tryptamine.*

We are, in a real sense, prisoners of our cognitive concepts and strategies. Passed on from generation to generation. The cognitive continuity of history. And the stuff of it is words. Our current reliance upon substantive and "closing-off" concepts will be the amused wonder of coming generations. We must entertain nonverbal methods of communication if we are to free our nervous system from the tyranny of the stifling simplicity of words.

Biochemical methods of increasing cortical efficiency. "Biochemicals" in the human body, in plants, and in drugs. There exist in nature hundreds of botanical species with psychedelic ("mind-opening") powers. There exists around the indole circle a wide variety of psychedelic compounds. Cortical vitamins.

The existence of these substances has been known for thousands of years, but has been maintained as a well-guarded secret. The scarcity of botanical supply. Now, in 1963, the mind-opening substances (e.g., mescaline, LSD, psilocybin) are available for the first time in limitless, mass-produced quantities. What a threat! What a challenge! What a widespread menace!

The danger, of course, is not physical. A recent editorial in the *Medical Tribune* (March 18, 1963) clearly recognizes the physiological safety of consciousness-expanding drugs. Nor is the danger psychological. In studies reported by Ditman, McGlothlin, Leary, Savage, up to 90 per cent of subjects taking these drugs in supportive environments testify enthusiastically.

The danger is not physical or psychological, but social-political. Make no mistake: the effect of consciousness-expanding drugs will be to transform our concepts of human nature, of human potentialities, of existence. The game is about to be changed, ladies and gentle-

---

*Tryptamine refers to chemicals found naturally in the body, in certain botanical species, and now produced synthetically. Tryptamines alter, probably speed up, synaptic function.

men. Man is about to make use of that fabulous electrical network he carries around in his skull. Present social establishments had better be prepared for the change. Our favorite concepts are standing in the way of a floodtide, two billion years building up. The verbal dam is collapsing. Head for the hills, or prepare your intellectual craft to flow with the current.

Let's try a metaphor. The social situation in respect to consciousness-expanding drugs is very similar to that faced sixty years ago by those crackpot visionaries who were playing around with the horseless carriage. Of course, the automobile is external child's play compared to the unleashing of cortical energy, but the social dilemma is similar.

The claim was made in 1900 that the motor carriage, accelerated to speeds several times that of the horse-drawn vehicle, would revolutionize society. Impossible to conceptualize because in 1900 we possessed no concepts for these possibilities. But we always have the standard objections to the non-conceptual. First of all, we object to the dangers: high speeds will snap nervous minds, gas fumes are fatal, the noise will prevent cows from giving milk, horses will run away, criminals will exploit the automobile.

Then the puritanical objection: people will use cars for pleasure, for kicks.

Then we question the utility: what can we do with speedy carriages? There are no men to repair them. There are no roads, few bridges. There are no skilled operators. The supply of fuel is small. Who will sell you gas?

Then we raise the problem of control: who should be allowed to own and operate these powerful and dangerous instruments? Perhaps they should be restricted to the government elite, to the military, to the medical profession.

But why do we want cars anyway? What is wrong with the good old buggy? What will happen to coachmen, blacksmiths, carriage-makers?

The automotive visionary of 1900 could have pointed out that his skeptical opponent had no concepts, no social structures to implement these possibilities. Remember, if one talks about experiences and prospects for which the listener has no concepts, then he is defined (at best) as a mystic. Our automotive mystic 60 years ago would have asserted the need for a new language, new social forms, and would have predicted that our largest national industry would inevitably develop out of this vision.

Can you imagine a language without such words as convertible, tudor sedan, General Motors, U.A.W., Standard Oil, superhighway, parking ticket, traffic court? These most commonplace terms in our present culture were mystical images three generations ago.

In totalitarian states, the use and control of instruments for external freedom—the automobile, the private airplane—are reserved for the government bureaucracy and the professional elite. Even in democracies, the traditional means for expanding or contracting consciousness (internal freedom) such as the printing press, the radio transmitter, the motion picture, are restricted by law and remain under government control.

Now consider consciousness-expanding drugs in 1963. No language. No trained operators. Lots of blacksmiths whose monopoly is threatened. A few people who do see an inevitable development of a new language, a transfiguration of every one of our social forms. And these few, of course, the ones who have taken the internal voyage.

It is possible that in 20 years our psychological and experiential language (pitifully small in English) will have multiplied to cover realms of experience and forms of thinking now unknown. In 20 years, every social institution will have been transformed by the new insights provided by consciousness-expanding experiences. Many new social institutions will have developed to handle the expressions of the potentiated nervous system.

The political issue involves control: "automobile" means that the free citizen moves *his* own car in external space. Internal automobile. Auto-administration. The freedom and control of one's experiential machinery. Licensing will be necessary. You must be trained to operate.* You must demonstrate your proficiency to handle consciousness-expanding drugs without danger to yourself or the public. The Fifth Freedom—the freedom to expand your own consciousness—cannot be denied without due cause.

A final hint to those who have ears to hear. The open cortex produces an ecstatic state. The nervous system operating free of learned abstraction is a completely adequate, completely efficient, ecstatic organ. To deny this is to rank man's learned tribal concepts above two billion years' endowment. An irreverent act. Trust your inherent machinery. Be entertained by the social game you play. Remember, man's natural state is ecstatic wonder, ecstatic intuition, ecstatic accurate movement. Don't settle for less.

---

*To bring the discussion from the verbal-controversial down to the more practical: a psychedelic "driving school" will open in Mexico on May 1, 1963, in a panoramic Mexican village, Zihuatanejo. There, during the next 22 months, manuals, chemicals, and guides will be available for training those who want proficiency in consciousness expansion.

16

Media Reaction to the Harvard Drug Scandal

The Hallucinogenic Drug Cult

Noah Gordon

When the Harvard Drug Scandal broke in May of 1963, it was covered by a wide range of newspapers and magazines including *The New York Times, The Boston Globe, The Boston Herald, Esquire, Ladies Home Journal, The Reporter, Time, Look,* and *Newsweek.* In many cases, the journalists chose to focus on the sensationalistic aspects of the controversy. Andrew Weil's piece in *Look Magazine,* "The Strange Case of the Harvard Drug Scandal," suggested that psilocybin was used for heterosexual and homosexual seductions, while Noah Gordon of *The Reporter,* also a national publication, focused on sadomasochistic fantasies that were induced by psilocybin: "I have no boundaries—scoop me up off the floor and tie me up in a sack . . ."

Most of the articles that appeared in mainstream publications were critical of Leary and Alpert and the research they conducted at Harvard. The two men were typically depicted as reckless and irresponsible professors who were peddling drugs that produced psychosis. The Socratic sin of "corrupting the youth" was a familiar theme in many of the articles. Noah Gordon even implied that Leary and Alpert had formed a "hallucinogenic drug cult." Gordon reported that many "LSD sects" had emerged and that the leaders of these groups "become quite successful in controlling people in the role of religious leaders or lay therapists."

To truly understand the significance of Leary's research, one has to understand the knee-jerk opposition that he often faced in the early 1960s. His early writings on psychedelic drugs were for written for his psychedelic acolytes in the academy, but they were also written for skeptics; he anticipated the objections of non-users and sought to prove that psychedelic drugs had immense social and therapeutic value. I have chosen to include Noah Gordon's "The Hallucinogenic Drug Cult" in this book because it is a rich historical document and features the cultural prejudices that Leary and Alpert often encountered when they attempted to promote consciousness-expanding drugs in a society that was often fearful and suspicious of psychedelic drugs.

Gordon's article presents a fairly typical example of the anti-LSD stance that prevailed in the aftermath of the Harvard Drug Scandal. Anti-LSD literature typically featured the testimony of an outraged medical authority, and Noah Gordon's article is no exception. "The Hallucinogenic Drug Cult" contains an interview with Dr. Dana Farnsworth, the director of health services at Harvard. Farnsworth opts to make a direct appeal to parents of undergraduates at Harvard: "Parents of college-age individuals should inform them of the genuine peril of experimenting with these drugs . . . [t]his is the most dangerous game I've ever seen."

The efficacy of Farnsworth's alarmist rhetoric is certainly debatable. In many cases, young people are naturally curious and gravitate toward taboo and forbidden cultural activities. While not all anti-drug advocates are as hyperbolic as

Farnsworth, there typically is apt to be a common perspective in anti-drug literature: the tendency to trumpet the "psychotomimetic" interpretation of hallucinogenic drugs. In the early 1950s, medical researchers believed that LSD and psilocybin were psychotomimetic because they were said to mimic psychosis (i.e., temporary schizophrenia). However, by the late 1950s, most medical experts had abandoned the psychotomimetic thesis because it was too reductive.

In 1957, Dr. Humphrey Osmond, while addressing the New York Academy of Sciences, argued that psychedelic drugs ". . . did much more than mimic psychosis, and therefore an appropriate name must include concepts of enriching the mind and enlarging the vision" (*Acid Dreams* 55). Osmond, a British psychiatrist and friend of Aldous Huxley, coined a more neutral term, "psychedelic," that eventually replaced the one-dimensional "psychotomimetic" label. "Psychedelic" implied "mind-manifesting" and suggested that LSD and psilocybin could also be used in a therapeutic capacity.

While the psychotomimetic thesis was considered obsolete in most medical circles by the early 1960s (1960 to 1962), journalists who covered the Harvard Drug Scandal in 1963 often chose to reproduce versions of it in their sensationalist articles. In some cases, the journalists simply had no experience with psychedelic drugs, and, thus they were not particularly well-informed about the latest advances in medical and psychiatric research. In other cases, the psychotomimetic interpretation was recycled simply because it was the easiest theory to understand. To the virginal non-user, it seemed to make the most sense. Lastly—and perhaps most significantly—the psychotomimetic thesis was also popular among journalists because it was the safest interpretation given that journalists and newspaper editors did not want to be accused of endorsing or promoting psychedelic drugs.

The various sensationalist articles on the Harvard Drug Scandal and its aftermath are revealing because they convey the essential paradox of psychedelic drugs: their remarkable ability to arouse fear and suspicion in the non-user.

JAMES PENNER

REFERENCES

Black, Herbert. "Ousted Harvard Researchers Plan 'Retreat' in Mexico." *Boston Globe,* May 29, 1963.

Goldman, Robert. "Instant Happiness." *Ladies Home Journal* 80 (1963): 67–71.

Gordon, Noah. "The Hallucinogenic Drug Cult." *The Reporter* (August 15, 1963): 35–43.

Lee, Martin, and Bruce Shlain. *Acid Dreams: The Complete Social History of LSD: The CIA, the Sixties, and Beyond.* New York: Grove Press, 1985.

Mayer, Martin. "Getting Alienated with the Right Crowd at Harvard." *Esquire* (September, 1963).

"No Illusions." *Newsweek* (June 10, 1963).

Weil, Andrew. "The Strange Case of the Harvard Drug Scandal." *Look* (November 5, 1963).

THE HALLUCINOGENIC DRUG CULT
From *The Reporter,* August 15, 1963: pages 35–43.

Noah Gordon

When the International Federation for Internal Freedom was formed in Cambridge, Massachusetts, during the autumn of 1962, it was unique even in New England, a region not unfamiliar with eccentric social movements. IFIF (pronounced "If-If," as if the speaker is stuttering over some terrifying cosmic question) preaches the gospel that man's salvation lies in the expansion of his own consciousness, a state which, it is asserted, can be achieved through the ingestion of such substances as LSD-25, psilocybin, mescaline, or even the right type of morning-glory seeds.

Although a handful of well-known people—most of them philosophers, mystics, and theologians—have lent IFIF the support of their names, scientific circles have in general been quite critical of many of its expressed beliefs and goals. The support of the theologians and mystics, in combination with the fact that IFIF's cause was unwittingly nurtured within Harvard University, has composed the movement's principal credentials. For many initiates, the credentials have been sufficient. IFIF offers, by its very existence, a certain amount of justification and rationale to those who submit to the dangerous attraction drug-taking holds for college students and young people in general. "Drugs have always attracted college students," I was told recently by Dr. Dana L. Farnsworth, director of the Harvard University Health Services. "But this is the first time in history that an organization has existed to promote their use."

Caught unprepared by the spreading utilization of a variety of hallucinogenic drugs in many areas of the United States, law-enforcement officials and health authorities do not appear at present to possess the means of coping with the problem. They are hampered by a net of vague, ineffectual, and contradictory legal structure. Meanwhile, in IFIF's four-room ground-floor headquarters at 14 Story Street, Cambridge, a varying number of blue-jeaned young people perform the clerical chores of a growing organization, work to spread its chapters and outposts through the country and the world, and push an aggressive promotional drive that has all the earmarks of a proselytizing campaign.

MILLENNIUM IN A MUSHROOM

The moment that engendered all of this activity can be traced back to a day in the summer of 1960 when a thirty-nine-year-old psychologist named Timothy Leary sat by a swimming pool in Cuernavaca, Mexico, and ate a mushroom one of his friends had bought from a mountain crone named Crazy Juana. The mushroom sent him into another world—a world that left him awed, shaken, and determined to explore it again.

When he returned to Harvard, where he was a lecturer in social psychology, Dr. Leary sought out Aldous Huxley, who was then a visiting professor at the Massachusetts Institute of Technology. The English writer had written of his experiences with drugs that induce hallucinations and changes in sense perception. Fascinated by Huxley's experiences, Leary interested half a dozen Harvard graduate students and Dr. Richard Alpert, at that time an assistant professor of Psychology and Education, in a series of experiments.

Leary had arrived at Harvard with some ideas about research that differed sharply from those of most of his colleagues. He believed even then that research should be conducted *with* subjects rather than *on* subjects, and that standard research techniques in which the researcher does not share in the experience of the experiment are essentially undemocratic. Leary's group conducted one formal research program under the official banner of the Harvard Center for Research in Personality, a division of the Laboratory of Social Relations. This was a program of psilocybin administration at Concord Prison in an attempt to see how drug-treated prisoners succeeded upon their return to society. The psilocybin, a derivative of a species of Mexican mushroom, was donated by Sandoz Pharmaceuticals, which had perfected the drug. In addition, on their own time and away from the university, the investigators carried on "naturalistic" research, taking the drugs in the company of a wide variety of individuals and making observations concerning the effect of psilocybin on such things as creativity, somatic feelings, and visual perception and memory. Unlike most other investigators using what are known professionally as "psychotomimetic" drugs, Leary and Alpert did not always insist upon medical and psychiatric examinations and psychological testing to screen out individuals who might be harmed by the substances.

Their reason, according to Dr. Walter M. Presnell, the psychiatrist who participated in the Concord Prison study, was that the more clinical the drug experience became, the more frightening it was to the subject. Leary and Alpert believed that the environment in which the drug is given determines whether the subject enters a drugged hell or a blissful heaven of expanded powers. Therefore, in their "non-prison" studies, they sometimes administered psilocybin to subjects who lolled on deep-pile rugs before flaming fireplaces, with mood music in the background. Since this research was not a formal project of the Harvard Center for Research in Personality, they could not request funds to convert Harvard offices into such places. They held their drug sessions in private apartments, inviting a small group of Harvard graduate students and selected people from the arts. According to their data, during the first year and a half of both the prison program and the parlor drug sessions, ninety-one of their ninety-eight subjects enjoyed pleasurable experiences and sixty-one reported insights and positive changes in their lives because they took psilocybin.

During the fall of 1961, Alpert and Leary were teaching a graduate seminar in introductory psychology. Twelve graduate students had asked for and received the drug. "We began to run more sessions with the drug, and students were involved. The faculty became more and more hostile," Alpert told me recently. Stories of what might be called the nonscientific aspects of the psilocybin sessions began circulating among students at Cambridge.

On October 8, 1961, at a meeting of the staff of the Center for Research in Personality, Dr. David C. McClelland, chairman of the center and the man who had brought both Leary and Alpert to Harvard, passed to each individual present a mimeographed memorandum entitled "Some Social Reactions to the Psilocybin Research Project." In it McClelland revealed in no uncertain terms his growing concern. To judge by the behavior of Mexican *curanderas* and Indian mystics, he said, one would expect the chief effects of psilocybin and similar substances to be to encourage withdrawal from contact with social reality and to increase satisfaction with one's own inner thought life. Research reports from the Harvard project, he said, "are not inconsistent with these expectations."

Certain effects had been noted in those who had taken the drug, he reported. Among these were (1) disassociation and detachment ("Initiates begin to show a certain blandness, or superiority, or feeling of being above and beyond the normal world of social reality"); (2) interpersonal insensitivity (example: "inability to predict in advance what the social reaction of a 'psilocybin party' would be"); (3) omniscience, religious and philosophical naïveté ("Many reports are given of deep mystical experiences, but their chief characteristic is the wonder at one's own profundity rather than a genuine concern to probe deeper into the experience of the human race in these matters"); and (4) impulsivity ("One of the most difficult parts of the research has been to introduce any order into who takes psilocybin under what conditions. Any controls have either been rejected as interfering with the warmth necessary to have a valuable experience or accepted as desirable but then not applied because somehow an occasion arises when it seems 'right' to have a psilocybin session").

The memorandum also contained this grim warning: "It is probably no accident that the society which most consistently encouraged the use of these substances, India, produced one of the sickest social orders ever created by mankind, in which thinking men spent their time lost in the Buddha position under the influence of drugs exploring consciousness, while poverty, disease, social discrimination, and superstition reached their highest and most organized form in all history."

TRANSCENDENTAL TOGETHERNESS

The drug sessions continued and other hallucinogenics were made available. As they increased in number, what at first had been accepted as legitimate scientific research by the colleagues of Dr. Alpert and Dr. Leary now came to be regarded as something else. The more the two psychologists took the drugs, Dr. McClelland told a reporter later, "the less they were interested in science." On March 14, 1962, the staff of the Center for Research in Personality held an open meeting. Dr. Herbert

C. Kelman, lecturer in Social Psychology, reported he had observed that graduate students who had had drug experiences had formed a clannish "insider group." Dr. Kelman expressed doubts as to the appropriateness of the psilocybin project within a graduate training program. "I question whether this project is carried out primarily as an intellectual endeavor or whether it is being pursued as a new kind of experience to offer an answer to man's ills," he said. Opponents of the psilocybin investigation charged it was run nonchalantly and irresponsibly. Dr. McClelland expressed fears of possible permanent effect of the drugs but said he supported the research.

In the face of charges from Dr. Kelman and others that they are a "cult," members of the group readily admit that they feel a special bond for one another. "Taking the drug is such an overwhelming experience that we soon realized that those of us who had done so had something wonderful in common. We wanted to be together constantly, to share time and space," Alpert told me. In order to make this possible, they established two "colonies for transcendental living." Each colony consists of about a dozen people, but the number fluctuates. Members include single persons, married couples, and children. The colonies are contained in two huge traditional houses in separate fine old neighborhoods of Newton Centre, a Boston suburb. Both neighborhoods have treated the colonies and the colonists rather unlovingly.

One woman, who said she had lived for thirty-two years in a house near Dr. Alpert's green ten-bedroom home, said, "Some weekends their house is like a motel. They all wear a beatnik uniform—tight pants and jerseys, no shoes or stockings. One young man in his twenties is letting his blond hair grow down to his shoulders; every time I look at him I want to vomit."

A petition invoking a Newton Centre statute which allows only one-family dwellings in the neighborhood led to a hearing before the planning board in which the colony was represented by Dr. Alpert's father, George Alpert, former president of the New Haven Railroad and a member of the Massachusetts bar. The elder Alpert pointed out that the law does not specify that families must be consanguineous. "They haven't bothered us since," Dr. Alpert said.

"TIE ME UP IN A SACK"

When an account of the open faculty meeting at Harvard was published in the *Harvard Crimson* on March 15, 1962, the story was picked up at once by the *Boston Herald*. As a result of this, an investigation was launched by the Division of Food and Drugs of the Massachusetts Department of Public Health and by the Federal Food and Drug Administration. On April 16, 1962, Dr. George Michaels, head of the state division, acting under state laws that prohibit anyone except a physician, veterinarian, or dentist from administering or giving harmful drugs, announced that Leary and Alpert could continue their research legally only if a medical doctor were present during the administration of the drugs. Moreover, the executive board of Harvard's Laboratory of Social Relations appointed an *ad hoc* faculty group which was asked to form a committee to "advise and oversee" future studies utilizing psilocybin. Dr. Robert F. Bales, director of the Laboratory of Social Relations, proposed "minimum conditions" under which the drug could be used. Included in these was that the laboratory should have "effective control of the drug, to be disbursed only upon written request of the Chairman of the Advisory Committee to the Director of the Laboratory, the drug to be held in custody by the University Health Service." When the Commonwealth of Massachusetts had begun its investigation, at Dr. Bales' request the researchers had turned over a small supply of psilocybin to Dr. Farnsworth and the University Health Services. Dr. Bales felt that this was only a portion of their drug supply, and that their entire supply should be effectively controlled. He asked for agreement to this as well as to other ground rules as conditions to the formation of the committee.

"Leary agreed by letter the next day," Dr. Bales told me later. "Alpert did not agree. He felt that he could not give up control of the drug without infringement of his rights as a citizen."

Remembering this period, Dr. Alpert told me recently: "Tim and I got depressed. This was like the hottest thing we ever were involved in," he said, slipping into the hipster jargon with which he sprinkles his conversation. "And these people kept putting obstacles in our path."

In the summer of 1962, to avoid these obstacles, they went to Zihuatanejo, Mexico, during the vacation period and rented a hotel, using money provided by several small foundations.

"We brought all kinds of people to Mexico—religionists, scientists, artists, writers, housewives," Dr. Alpert told me.

The drug users have reported progressing through various levels—"psychic elevator stops," as Dr. Alpert calls them—beginning with an "unbelievable intensification of colors and sounds" and culminating in "a pervading sensation of white light and a religious ecstasy that fills your consciousness." Other versions of the experience have been less alluring. Dr. Gerald D. Klee of Baltimore, writing in the May, 1963, issue of *Archives of General Psychiatry*, published by the American Medical Association, puts it this way: "Changes in somesthetic perception are striking and profound. Feelings of numbness and paresthesias of the entire body are experienced. Feelings of depersonalization and derealization may be marked. Subjects report: 'My body is no longer my own.' . . . One psychiatrically unsophisticated subject reported: 'I feel as though my body is melting away; I have no boundaries—scoop me up off the floor and tie me up in a sack to give me some limits.' . . . Subjects may also have difficulty in differentiating themselves from other persons or even from inanimate objects . . ."

THE MIRACLE OF MARSH CHAPEL

Can some of history's religious revelations be explained by chemical phenomena similar to those which take place when the human body is exposed to psilocybin? Some theologians have demonstrated an intense interest in this hypothesis. In a paper written with Dr. Leary and published in the May-June, 1963, issue of *Religious Education,* Walter Houston Clark, professor of the Psychology of Religion at Andover Newton Theological Seminary, revealed that when psilocybin was administered to more than four hundred volunteers, "less than ten percent of our original sample were orthodox believers or churchgoers, yet such terms as 'God,' 'divine,' 'deep religious experience,' 'meeting the infinite,' occurred in over half of [their] reports."

Clark and Leary noted that psilocybin and its companion chemical, mescaline, a peyote derivative, have been used in esoteric religious rituals, both ancient and modern, "presumably as a stimulus to religious experience." During any profound emotional experience, they said, religious or otherwise, chemical or hormonal bodily changes occur.

"Furthermore, we know that the natural chemistry of the body includes biochemical substances, known as the *indoles,* which are similar in structure to the consciousness-expanding chemicals and seem to be associated with some of the same psychological states as those produced by psilocybin. The question then immediately arises whether a naturally-occurring excess of the indoles might not predispose some people to certain kinds of mystical experience or whether a mystical state of mind might not, on the other hand, stimulate chemical changes in the body."

Last year interest in this area gave rise to an unusual and unpublicized experiment. Dr. Walter Pahnke, a physician who is a candidate for the Ph.D. in the Philosophy of Religion at Harvard, had analyzed Christian literature and had established nine categories which he felt described a genuine religious mystical experience. If a group of extremely religious individuals were to take the drug, how many of these qualities would manifest themselves?

Harvard University officials, Dr. Alpert said, refused to sponsor the experiment. According to Dr. Bales, the *ad hoc* faculty group refused to release to the experimenters the supply of psilocybin held by Dr. Farnsworth. "Our committee had not been formed," Dr. Bales said. "We were asked to release the drug only a day or two before the experiment was to be held. We didn't think we had the right to release it."

Nevertheless, the experiment was conducted on Good Friday in Marsh Chapel at Boston University, a long-established Methodist-affiliated institution, after representatives had been dispatched, according to Alpert, to round up a sufficient quantity of "non-Harvard" psilocybin. The experiment was carried on in two small rooms off the main chapel, with the reverent sound of the Good Friday service piped in by loudspeaker.

It was a double-blind experiment. The subjects were twenty divinity students from the Andover Newton Theological Seminary. Ten of them were given psilocybin. The other ten were given nicotinic acid, a vitamin which causes the taker to experience a mild sense of facial flushing but which has no mental effect. Nobody knew whether he had been given the drug or not. Dr. Pahnke, whose doctoral dissertation is now being considered by Harvard, refused to comment upon the experiment until the publication of his thesis. But for "purposes of comparison" Alpert has revealed that of the ten men who did not receive psilocybin, only one reported a single descriptive quality that met the criteria for religious mysticism. Of the ten who took psilocybin, nine reported experiencing four or more of the nine qualities of religious mystical experience.

While most religious leaders would probably be unenthusiastic over the idea of the drugged approach to religion, *Archives of General Psychiatry* reports that recently one lawsuit brought attention to a pastor who told his congregation that LSD could bring them all closer to God.

It should not be believed that hallucinogenic drugs are in themselves religious, Professor Clark of the Andover Newton Theological Seminary told me. But like organ music, he said, they may be the means to religious experience for some people. In the paper he wrote with Dr. Leary, Professor Clark reported that "about one-half of the 'hardened cynics' who were given the drug behind the walls of Concord Prison experienced 'classic mystic conversion reactions.'"

❖ ❖ ❖

The prison project has been shelved for lack of physician participation. Dr. Walter M. Presnell, the psychiatrist who participated in the study, has left the service of the Commonwealth of Massachusetts for private practice and has resigned from IFIF. I asked him why he had broken with the IFIF group. This was his reply:

"I felt that subjects should be screened for psychiatric trouble and such physical ailments as previous liver disease or hepatitis. Also, I'm interested in medical research into mental illness; Alpert and Leary are more interested in how the drug affects artistic work."

In an effort to gauge the effects of hallucinogenic drugs on creativity, Alpert and Leary have given sessions for artists, writers, composers, musicians, and poets. During one such session held in his Newton Centre home, Alpert said, the poet Allen Ginsberg ripped off all his clothing in his exultation and then raced for the telephone, determined to call Kennedy and Khrushchev and urge them both to take the drug in the interest of world peace.

A PARTING OF WAYS

Dr. Leary, who reportedly has ingested more hallucinogenic substances than anyone else in his group, stopped being a Harvard faculty member in April of this year simply by discontinuing the practice of showing up in his classroom. After a period of initial puzzlement, the university authorities removed his name from the payroll. Instead of teaching, Dr. Leary traveled to the West Coast and to Mexico in the interests of IFIF, which had been formed six months before. According to the IFIF "Statement of Purpose," in addition to Leary and Alpert, the organization's board of directors included Dr. Huston Smith, professor of Philosophy, M.I.T.; Dr. Clark of the Andover Newton Theological Seminary; Dr. Ralph Metzner, a psychopharmacologist; Dr. Gunther Weil, who has served as director of the psilocybin rehabilitation program, Concord prison; George Litwin, assistant professor of Group Relations, Harvard Business School; and Alan Watts, a specialist in Far Eastern philosophy.

In November, 1962, shortly after the announcement of IFIF'S creation, Dr. Farnsworth and John U. Monro, dean of Harvard College, had written a letter to the editor of the *Crimson,* warning of "the effect of LSD, psilocybin, mescaline and other mind-distorting drugs. Our concern for this development is such," they wrote, "that for more than a year we have had an agreement that Harvard University experimenters studying the effects of such drugs should not employ undergraduates as subjects in their research work.

"It is important to warn undergraduates that the ingestion of these drugs may result in serious hazard to the mental health and stability even of apparently normal persons. The drugs have been known to intensify seriously a tendency toward depression and to produce other dangerous psychotic effects." There were several other semi-official warnings during the next six months.

Then, on May 27, 1963, President Nathan M. Pusey of Harvard publicly fired Dr. Alpert. It was the first time such a thing had happened at Harvard in the twentieth century. Pusey said the action had been taken because Dr. Alpert had violated an agreement that he would not involve undergraduates in his work with drugs, and recalled that last November Alpert had assured the administration that he had not given drugs to any undergraduate.

Two weeks later I visited Alpert and Leary at IFIF headquarters. The mood was one of carefully controlled gloom, despite the cheery presence of rows of young morning-glory plants that stretched their green necks out of the earth in a tray on the kitchen table. Neither Alpert nor Leary seemed saddened that they had been dropped from the Harvard faculty; the reason for the gloom was the closing down of the Zihuatanejo research center, on the grounds that its staff had entered the country as tourists and were engaged in unauthorized activity.

I asked Dr. Alpert to give me his version of why he had been fired. Dressed in slacks and a T shirt, he lay on his back on a divan that was covered by an Indian blanket. He was shoeless, and the bare sole of one foot patted the wall from time to time.

"I did break a contract," he said finally.

"A year and a half ago I had a very close friend who was a junior at Harvard. I want to keep his name out of this.

"He had been having black-market-type experiences with the drugs and they had been pretty lousy.

"I was spending my weekends with him. When you have something and it means something to someone you care about, but you can't give it to him, it bugs you.

"I gave him a very light dose.

"I had been so good. I turned down over two hundred guys. But my friend had a buddy [Andrew Weil] who got very irate and went to the authorities.

"Some day it will be quite humorous that a professor was fired for supplying a student with 'the most profound educational experience in my life.' That's what he told the Dean it was."

The philosophy of "noble drug-taking" is being promoted on a wide front. According to IFIF's *Newsletter* of last month, "Offices now exist in Los Angeles, New York City, Mexico City, as well as the headquarters office in Cambridge." Leary and Alpert hope for a world in which huge masses of people will seek God, love, and expanded mental powers through the ingestion of potions of hallucinogenic drugs. There are good medical reasons why an attempt to achieve this must he regarded with some trepidation. Suicidal attempts have been reported following drug sessions, and deleterious mental effects have "echoed," recurring as late as two years after a drug has been taken. "Playing with these drugs is psychic Russian roulette," said Dean Monro, who has repeatedly warned his Harvard undergraduates about them. "We must counteract the notion that every red-blooded young American must do this, by emphasizing the sad truth that a certain number of them will land in mental institutions." This fate has already befallen several young people in the Cambridge area, and, according to Dr. Farnsworth, a number of students have become patients of the Harvard University Health Services as a result of the drugs.

Some of them have tried to tell their doctors what their experiences were like.

"On some of the drugs, especially on mescaline, I had a strong urge for a sexual experience," one of the students said. "This is a well-known effect. It's understood you will have intercourse. We take it in groups and people go off into a room two at a time."

Another student kept a journal while on drugs. "Later I read it and it was horrible. People were tearing each other apart. Also, I felt I was reading the worst pornography I ever read."

Other individuals have reported to psychiatrists that they experienced homosexual episodes while under the influence of the drug.

"It is unpredictable even in one individual as to what will happen from one ingestion of the drug to the next," Dr. Farnsworth said. "Two roommates who took one of these drugs reacted quite differently, although both seemed to be quite normal. One didn't mind it. The other sobbed uncontrollably for six hours. Another individual who took one of these drugs felt for two whole days that he was only six inches tall. During this period he had to be cared for by his friends because he was entirely helpless."

NOISE AND SLOW TIME

I spoke to an intense twenty-two-year-old brunette Radcliffe graduate who had had two experiences with the morning-glory seeds. "The first was good. The second was half-good and half-bad."

The good part, she said, allows "you to get into a state of mind when you realize that the whole world is all right, the whole world is beautiful." This is how her first experience turned out, she said. To obtain her second experience, which she "shared with two friends in a private home," she ground the flower seeds, soaked the mash in warm water, and then ate the paste. She had four "good" hours and then her friends took her home and left her. "A little while later the bad part began."

First there was vomiting, but this didn't cause her concern. "That's trivial. It's well known that you often get sick to your stomach with the synthetic things, too." After she had gone to bed she became aware of a loud noise that grew louder, so loud it prevented her from sleeping. It was the dripping of the faucet on the other side of the apartment. Then the ticking of her clock grew loud. "Pretty soon there was so much noise in the room I became frightened and got out of bed, because I was certain that someone had entered."

From that time on, her experience was "very bad. What was coming in was too intense. I tried to get out of the experience, but you shouldn't do that, it only makes things worse." After a long time she looked at the clock. The hands stood only a little after 1 A.M. "I thought that it had stopped, but I could hear it ticking. I thought to myself, 'My God, if time moves this slowly, how long am I going to be like this?' I called my friends and they came over to be with me and lend support. I had to stay in bed for eight or nine hours before the bad part of the experience was over."

Her experience was not unique. "I had a horror show after taking the morning-glory seeds," one patient told a Harvard University doctor. "I felt my brain would blow up. I felt I was losing my mind. I felt I was going to die but I couldn't communicate it to anyone. I tried to tell my brother but couldn't make him understand."

Dr. Alpert and Dr. Leary display signs of impatience when asked about bad experiences with the drug.

"If you got airsick during your first trip in an airplane, does that mean you wouldn't give it a second try?" Alpert asked.

The subject of hallucinogenic drugs was recently discussed in the *Archives of General Psychiatry* by Dr. Sidney Cohen of the Los Angeles Veterans Administration Hospital and Dr. Keith S. Ditman of the University of California Medical Center. Regarding the "transcendental" aspects of the LSD experience, they reported that "Commonly the chemical ego dissolution results in intense feelings of unity, death and rebirth, salvation, and redemption." Even after the effects of the drug have worn off, the report went on, the "belief that the individual has been chosen to convert others to the new faith may be retained. Small LSD sects have been established on this basis. The leaders gain considerable gratification out of their position of omnipotence, which includes granting their disciples the LSD experience." Drs. Cohen and Ditman said that while it is not difficult to recognize those who openly express their feelings, there are others "who are sufficiently aware of the reality of the situation to keep the knowledge of their own omnipotence hidden. They can become quite successful in controlling people in the role of religious leaders or lay therapists."

THE QUESTION OF CONTROLS

According to Alpert, his group's use of hallucinogenic drugs has recently attracted the attention of the Ethics Committee of the American Psychological Association. In the Washington, D.C., offices of the association, Dr. Joseph B. Margolin, secretary of the Committee on Scientific Ethics and Conduct, emphasized that he could not discuss any member of the association. Dr. Margolin could talk of problems, however. "From a professional point of view, there is strong feeling against a psychologist utilizing drugs," he said.

Explaining the function of his committee, Dr, Margolin said that on several occasions in the past it has caused psychologists to be removed from membership in the APA for practicing in an unfitting manner.

How restricting is such an action?

"It is a social control," Dr. Margolin said. "But at the present time forty-one states have either legal or non-statutory forms of certification for psychologists. Within the next two years, nearly all the states will have certification. If the same person who presses charges with the APA should do so with the state, and if the charges should be upheld and certification should be withdrawn, the man who has been judged guilty cannot be referred to as a psychologist within state borders."

Dr. Alpert has told me that he expects to be censured by the APA. "Not because we're dirty boys doing dirty things," he said, "but on the grounds that we have failed to concern ourself with behavioral toxicity and emotional side effects of the drugs.

"This is not true. We are watching these things very closely. We don't deny that personality changes are occurring. But we think they are changes for the better."

Intraprofessional attempts at social control obviously are inadequate to solve the problems raised by hallucinogenics. The geographical spread of the new craze was demonstrated recently when, at about the time that the Breck's Garden Centers in downtown Boston and Newton sold out their entire supply of morning-glory seeds, the Ferry-Morse Seed Company, one of the largest seed dealers in San Francisco, became alarmed at the run on morning-glory seeds and announced that for the time being it would sell the seeds only to legitimate seed houses and stores. But seeds are not the only sources of supply open to misguided thrill seekers. Black markets in hallucinogenic drugs exist in large cities and on university campuses. Although Sandoz Pharmaceuticals now gives experimental psychiatric drugs only to recipients of National Institute of Mental Health grants and to researchers of state and Veterans Administration hospitals, drugs continue to be distributed by underworld suppliers. On April 3, FDA agents in San Francisco made two seizures of smuggled black-market LSD-25 totaling about 3,300,000 micrograms, the equivalent of about 66,000 doses. Sugar cubes containing a single drop of LSD have sold for one dollar apiece in marketplaces like Harvard Square.

"Psilocybin is not very much around," an undergraduate told me. "But mescaline sells for from five or six dollars to fifteen dollars or more, for a dose of 500 milligrams."

Two years ago, the same boy told me, while he was still in his first year at the Cambridge campus, he and nine other undergraduates decided they would like to have a drug experience. They wrote to drug suppliers asking for mescaline and describing themselves as "a small group of intelligent young men at Harvard University" who wished to carry on a program of experimentation. "I checked with Dr. Leary and he said it was O.K. to use his name and to say that the Center for Research in Personality was available for consultation, so we did," the student said.

They received four replies. "One company asked no questions and would supply the drug at three times the ordinary price. Three other companies sent catalogues and Food and Drug Administration forms. We chose one of the companies and filled out the form quite honestly. It should have been obvious that we were students. We got the drug, and we took it." Since that time at least one firm of drug suppliers has been enjoined by the FDA against distributing harmful drugs through the mails. But the legal position in drugs is confused.

WHAT OF THE LAW?

The Federal laws that supposedly control those who traffic in these drugs are loose and ambiguous. Federal agencies apparently are limited or totally without policing power. Even in the case of admittedly dangerous narcotics, the law does not state that addiction or narcotic using is an offense—only illegal possession of the narcotic. The U.S. Narcotics Bureau states that it is not empowered to act in the area of hallucinogenics since these drugs are not listed in Federal narcotics statutes as addictive substances. The Food and Drug Administration can act, but only when a drug has crossed state lines illegally. The Federal Food, Drug and Cosmetic Act classified peyote as "habit-forming," but the FDA has declared mescaline (a peyote derivative), psilocybin, and LSD "new" drugs or substances that have not been proved safe or clinically beneficial. In the new Washington office of the chief of the FDA's Investigational Drug Branch, a unit formed after her celebrated achievement in the thalidomide case, Dr. Frances O. Kelsey told me of the legal obstacles facing any organization wishing to sponsor a new drug for distribution to investigators. Before the drug may be legally distributed, I was told, under the Kefauver-Harris Drug Amendments of 1962 the sponsoring group must submit to Dr. Kelsey's office a "Notice of Claimed Exemption for a New Drug"—Form FD 1571.

Among other things, Dr. Kelsey said, the notice must include details concerning the composition of the product "and such animal studies as have been done with the drug, together with the qualifications of the persons who evaluate the pharmacologic studies. The notice must also include a description of the planned clinical studies, as well as a description of the facilities and the qualifications of the investigators undertaking such studies."

A few weeks following the interview at which I received this information, it became evident that this procedure was not a fixed one. The FDA announced that the National Institutes of Health is being allowed on a trial basis, to avoid submission of the detailed Form FD 1571 by investigators proposing to use drugs for nontherapeutic purposes. Instead, approval by the Clinical Research Committee of the NIH Medical Board will be the screening procedure used. In lieu of the form, the NIH will be permitted to file memoranda containing the required information.

Does this mean that in the future private organizations like IFIF may be able to avoid the necessity of using the protective form in applying for permission to distribute new drugs such as psychotomimetics? "We would be glad to consider an outside organization's in-house method of control," I was told by Franklin D. Clark, assistant to FDA Deputy Commissioner John L. Harvey. "We are not wedded to Form FD 1571."

On the state level, the legal status of hallucinogenic drugs is no clearer than in Federal statutes. In Massachusetts, for example, under Section 197 of Chapter 94 of the General Laws, "peyote or any preparation thereof or any salt, compound or derivative of the same" is declared a narcotic drug. State authorities have interpreted the so-called "Harmful Drug Law" as prohibiting the use of other psychotomimetic drugs by persons who are not physicians. In some states, similar statutes exist. In others they do not.

Those who take on the formidable task of drafting legislation to provide legal uniformity cutting across state lines will be caught between the dangers of the uncontrolled use of drugs and the hazard of over-controlling scientific research. While legal protection must be provided for the public, responsible scientists surely must not be deprived of their freedom to investigate fully any possibility offered mankind by hallucinogens. They have been used in several fields of serious scientific research—in studies of schizophrenia (whose characteristics they were at first thought to reproduce), as an adjunct to psychotherapy techniques, and in experimental work on alcoholism.

One answer to this dilemma might be to assign priority to investigations that fully delineate and fully explore areas of hazard in the use of the drugs. Recently Dr. Norman E. Zinberg, assistant director of psychiatry at Beth Israel Hospital, Boston, offered a bit of medical history that can serve as a precedent and a warning. "Morphine, cocaine, heroin: each in turn was seen by its enthusiastic discoverers as too marvelous, too important for all mankind to be withheld long enough for careful experimentation. The results in every instance were disastrous." (Heroin in particular was at first hailed for its "miraculous" cures of people addicted to morphine and opium.)

BACK TO SCHOOL!

New laws will not be drafted and passed overnight. Yet, before many more nights have passed, students will be flocking back to campuses all over the United States. Obviously, many of them already have discovered the availability of hallucinogenic substances, and promotional activities of those who wish to spread the drug practice undoubtedly will bring seductive information regarding such drugs to even greater numbers of individuals in the future. Guidance on the home level can help protect young people from this type of recruitment, according to Dr. Farnsworth of Harvard, who has spent years safeguarding the health of his university community. "Parents of college-age individuals should inform them of the genuine peril of experimenting with these drugs, not in a manner which will dare them to do so, but in a way that will make them aware of the very possible consequences," he said. "This is the most dangerous game I've ever seen."

AFTERWORD

Leary and Psychedelic Research in the Twenty-first Century

James Penner

As I write, a revival of psychedelic medicine is underway. Just this week the *New York Times* published an article about researchers in Switzerland who conducted the first controlled trial of LSD on human beings in more than forty years.* The Swiss study explores how patient-centered LSD psychotherapy can be used to mitigate anxiety associated with life-threatening diseases. Although the study was very small (12 patients), the results are promising for future research trials. In the last ten years, several important medical research programs (Johns Hopkins, Harvard, New York University [NYU], the University of California at Los Angeles [UCLA], and the University of Arizona) have conducted

---

*See Benedict Carey's "LSD, Reconsidered for Therapy." *New York Times*, March 3, 2014. A full-length article on the Swiss study, to be published in the *Journal of Mental and Nervous Disease*, was posted online on March 4, 2014: Peter Gasser, Dominique Holstein, Yvonee Michel, Rick Doblin, Berra Yazar-Klosinski, Torsten Passie, and Rudolf Brenneisen, "Safety and Efficacy of Lysergic Acid Diethylamide-assisted Psychotherapy for Anxiety Associated with Life-threatening Diseases," http://journals.lww.com/jonmd/Documents/90000000.0-00001.pdf (accessed March 14, 2014).

FDA-approved studies that used psilocybin to treat cluster headaches (Harvard), Obsessive Compulsive Disorder (University of Arizona), and to alleviate anxiety and depression in people with terminal cancer (UCLA and NYU). Future studies are planned for psilocybin to treat alcoholism, nicotine addiction, and end-of-life anxiety. As scientific research moves forward at home and abroad, it will be harder for medical authorities and politicians to ignore the efficacy of psychedelic substances and patient-centered treatment methods.

As we enter the new era—hopefully an era of greater tolerance for psychedelic medicine and therapy—there is much to learn from Leary's early work and the period when psychedelic drugs were still legal. Although contemporary medical researchers often attempt to distance their research from Leary's advocacy of LSD in the late 1960s, it is important that Leary's utopian writings on LSD and psilocybin be read and understood today. Any serious appraisal of Leary's legacy needs to consider his seminal writings from the early 1960s and not just his hyperbolic writings from the late 1960s and his self-consciously whacky writings from the 1970s and 1980s. The Leary of the early and mid-1960s was a pragmatist with regard to drug regulation. When LSD was still legal, Leary did not favor unrestricted recreational access to LSD. Instead, he favored licensing LSD to medical professionals, psychologists, counselors, and spiritual guides who would use LSD in a spiritual and therapeutic capacity. When LSD was declared illegal in 1966, Leary moved away from the licensing model of regulation.

In the present moment, it is useful for some researchers to separate themselves from the Leary of the late 1960s. In some cases, Leary is cited as the researcher "who went 'AWOL and promote[d] unrestricted recreational use . . . [of LSD].'"* I believe that if Leary were alive today he would not object to being characterized as "irresponsible" by the proponents of psychedelic medicine who need to acquire approval from

---

*From Alexander Zaitchik, "Flashback! Psychedelic Research Returns." Salon.com., September 28, 2011, www.salon.com/2011/09/28/the_new_lsd_cure (accessed March 11, 2014).

medical authorities and state regulators. Leary would be more than happy to do his part in the ideological struggle to move research forward and to liberate psychedelic substances from the enduring grip of prejudice and fear.

MANATI, PUERTO RICO

MARCH 2014

Index